D1190450

THE HISTORY OF THE CZECH REPUBLIC AND SLOVAKIA

THE HISTORY OF THE CZECH REPUBLIC AND SLOVAKIA

William M. Mahoney

The Greenwood Histories of the Modern Nations
Frank W. Thackeray and John E. Findling, Series Editors

 GREENWOOD

AN IMPRINT OF ABC-CLIO, LLC
Santa Barbara, California • Denver, Colorado • Oxford, England

Library of Congress Cataloging-in-Publication Data

Mahoney, William M.
    The history of the Czech Republic and Slovakia / William M. Mahoney.
       p. cm. — (The Greenwood histories of the modern nations)
    Includes bibliographical references and index.
    ISBN 978–0–313–36305–4 (hardcopy : acid-free paper) — ISBN 978–0–313–36306–1 (ebook) 1. Czech Republic—History. 2. Slovakia—History. 3. Czechoslovakia—History. I. Title.
DB2063.M34   2011
943.7—dc22   2010051686

ISBN: 978–0–313–36305–4
EISBN: 978–0–313–36306–1

15 14 13 12 11   1 2 3 4 5

This book is also available on the World Wide Web as an eBook.
Visit www.abc-clio.com for details.

Greenwood
An Imprint of ABC-CLIO, LLC

ABC-CLIO, LLC
130 Cremona Drive, P.O. Box 1911
Santa Barbara, California 93116-1911

This book is printed on acid-free paper ∞

Manufactured in the United States of America

Contents

Series Foreword   vii

Acknowledgments   xi

Timeline of Historical Events   xiii

1   The Czech Republic and Slovakia Today   1

2   Origins and Medieval Legacies   19

3   The Late Middle Ages   41

4   Religious Controversies and Military Conflicts (1400s–1700s)   63

5   Into the Modern Era: Reform, Revolution, and National Awakening (1740–1914)   93

6   World War I and the First Czechoslovak Republic (1914–1938)   129

7   The Munich Agreement and World War II
        (1938–1945)   163

8   The Postwar Era and the Communist Regime
        (1945–1989)   193

9   The Velvet Revolution, the "Velvet Divorce," and
        the Two Republics (1989–2009)   231

Notable People in the History of the Czech Republic
and Slovakia   265

Bibliography   273

Index   279

Series Foreword

The *Greenwood Histories of the Modern Nations* series is intended to provide students and interested laypeople with up-to-date, concise, and
analytical histories of many of the nations of the contemporary world.
Not since the 1960s has there been a systematic attempt to publish a
series of national histories, and as series advisors, we believe that this
series will prove to be a valuable contribution to our understanding
of other countries in our increasingly interdependent world.

Some 40 years ago, at the end of the 1960s, the Cold War was an
accepted reality of global politics. The process of decolonization was
still in progress, the idea of a unified Europe with a single currency
was unheard of, the United States was mired in a war in Vietnam,
and the economic boom in Asia was still years in the future. Richard
Nixon was president of the United States, Mao Tse-tung (not yet Mao
Zedong) ruled China, Leonid Brezhnev guided the Soviet Union, and
Harold Wilson was prime minister of the United Kingdom. Authoritarian dictators still controlled most of Latin America, the Middle East
was reeling in the wake of the Six-Day War, and Shah Mohammad
Reza Pahlavi was at the height of his power in Iran.

Since then, the Cold War has ended, the Soviet Union has vanished,
leaving 16 independent republics in its wake, the advent of the

computer age has radically transformed global communications, the rising demand for oil makes the Middle East still a dangerous flashpoint, and the rise of new economic powers such as the People's Republic of China and India threatens to bring about a new world order. All of these developments have had a dramatic impact on the recent history of every nation of the world.

For this series, which was launched in 1998, we first selected nations whose political, economic, and sociocultural affairs marked them as among the most important of our time. For each nation, we found an author who was recognized as a specialist in the history of that nation. These authors worked cooperatively with us and with Greenwood Press to produce volumes that reflected current research on their nations and that are interesting and informative to their readers. In the first decade of the series, more than 40 volumes were published, and as of 2008, some are moving into second editions.

The success of the series has encouraged us to broaden our scope to include additional nations, whose histories have had significant effects on their regions, if not on the entire world. In addition, geopolitical changes have elevated other nations into positions of greater importance in world affairs, and so we have chosen to include them in this series as well. The importance of a series such as this cannot be underestimated. As a superpower whose influence is felt all over the world, the United States can claim a "special" relationship with almost every other nation. Yet many Americans know very little about the histories of nations with which the United States relates. How did they get to be the way they are? What kind of political systems have evolved there? What kind of influence do they have on their own regions? What are the dominant political, religious, and cultural forces that move their leaders? These and many other questions are answered in the volumes of this series.

The authors who contribute to this series write comprehensive histories of their nations, dating back, in some instances, to prehistoric times. Each of them, however, has devoted a significant portion of their book to events of the past 40 years because the modern era has contributed the most to contemporary issues that have an impact on U.S. policy. Authors make every effort to be as up to date as possible so that readers can benefit from discussion and analysis of recent events.

In addition to the historical narrative, each volume contains an introductory chapter giving an overview of that country's geography, political institutions, economic structure, and cultural attributes. This is meant to give readers a snapshot of the nation as it exists in the contemporary world. Each history also includes supplementary information following the narrative, which may include a timeline that represents a succinct chronology of the nation's historical evolution, biographical sketches of the nation's most important historical figures, and a glossary of important terms or concepts that are usually expressed in a foreign language. Finally, each author prepares a comprehensive bibliography for readers who wish to pursue the subject further.

Readers of these volumes will find them fascinating and well written. More importantly, they will come away with a better understanding of the contemporary world and the nations that comprise it. As series advisors, we hope that this series will contribute to a heightened sense of global understanding as we move through the early years of the 21st century.

Frank W. Thackeray and John E. Findling
Indiana University Southeast

Acknowledgments

I would like to thank Kaitlin Ciarmiello, my editor at Greenwood Press, for her guidance, good cheer, and ability to keep me on track in a very positive manner. I would also like to thank the editors of the *Greenwood Histories of the Modern Nations* series, Frank W. Thackeray and John E. Findling, for the opportunity to undertake this challenging and rewarding project. For all concerned, patience was indeed a virtue.

I extend my gratitude to my colleagues in the Department of History and International Studies at West Virginia Wesleyan College for their support of my research and their collegiality and cooperation during my year or so as a sometimes distracted chair. My thanks, as well, to our departmental majors and to other students at the college who showed genuine interest in and enthusiasm for the project, provided much-needed comic relief, and tolerated occasional delays in the grading process. It is a pleasure to acknowledge the contributions of the genial and always helpful staff of the college's Annie Merner Pfeiffer Library, who render excellent assistance and offer a fine mug of coffee to wandering scholars. Finally, my appreciation to the administration of the college for their support and for the sabbatical semester that allowed for concentrated work on the manuscript.

My thanks, as well, for the Fulbright-Hays Summer Seminars Abroad Program in Poland and Czechoslovakia in 1992 and to the National Endowment for the Humanities for the research seminar "Democracy and Ethnicity in Eastern Europe," hosted by the University of Maryland during the summer of 1994. Travelling with students affords an occasion to view a nation's history and culture in new and sometimes unique ways, so I value my participation in a five-college student travel project in East Central Europe under the auspices of the Appalachian College Association in 2005. That trip inspired a similar project, developed by myself and my literature-oriented colleague Devon McNamara, that allowed 20 students from West Virginia Wesleyan College to explore Prague, Bratislava, Vienna, and Budapest during May Term 2009. The personal and professional experience gained on these trips and in the seminar has proven invaluable.

Finally, I would like to thank my mother, Doris Mahoney, my siblings, and all the members of my family for their love, support, and patience during my period of reduced visibility and occasional inability to cross the hills and cover the distance to attend gatherings of the clan.

Timeline of Historical Events

ca. 450 BCE	The Boii, Volcae-Tectosages, Cottini, and other Celtic tribes settle in the area of today's Czech Republic and Slovakia.
9 BCE	Defeated by Roman legions, the Marcomanni move eastward and join the Quadi and other Germanic tribes in bringing Celtic civilization to a close in the region.
170s CE	Emperor Marcus Aurelius writes sections of his *Meditations* along the Hron River in Slovakia while leading Roman forces against the Quadi in the Marcomannic Wars.
500s–600s	Slavic tribes cross the Carpathian Mountains from the northeast and settle in the future Bohemia, Moravia, and Slovakia.
568	The Avars, a nomadic people from Central Asia, invade the Middle Danube region and begin subjugating the Slavic peoples of the area.
623–658	Rebellion against Avar rule led by the Frankish merchant Samo leads to the establishment of a Slavic tribal federation, the kingdom of Samo.

796	Defeated by Charlemagne's sons Charles and Pepin, the Avars depart Slovak territory.
833	Empire of Great Moravia established by Mojmír I after he unites the principalities of Moravia and Nitra.
863	Arrival of Cyril and Methodius, brothers and missionaries of the Orthodox Church, who bring Christianity and a written alphabet to the Slavs of Great Moravia.
870	Bořivoj I becomes duke of Bohemia and founds the Přemyslid dynasty.
874	Peace of Forchheim signed between Great Moravia and the Frankish kingdom.
896	Arrival of the Magyars under the leadership of Árpád.
907	Empire of Great Moravia collapses after attacks by the Magyars.
935	Murder of Václav I (St. Wenceslas), Duke of Bohemia.
955	German forces under Otto I defeat the Magyars at Lechfeld.
1000	Magyar prince Stephen of the Árpád dynasty crowned first king of Hungary as Stephen I (St. Stephen).
1035	Czech crown lands established with the union of the crown lands of Bohemia with the margravate of Moravia.
1085	Vratislav II of the Přemyslids crowned the first king of Bohemia.
1212	Frederick II issues the Golden Bull of Sicily, affirming the independence of the Kingdom of Bohemia.
1278	Přemysl Otakar II defeated by the forces of Rudolf of Habsburg at Dürnkrut on the Marchfield.
1301–1321	Matúš Čák (Matthew Cak) of Trenčín and his allies rebel against the Hungarian monarchy and take control of most of Slovakia, gaining Čák the nickname, "Lord of the Váh and Tatras."
1306	Přemyslid dynasty comes to an end with the murder of Václav III.
1346–1378	Rule of Karel IV (Charles IV) as king of Bohemia and from 1355 to 1378 as Holy Roman Emperor.

1381	Louis I issues a decree, "Privileges for the Slovaks," granting Slovaks rights equal to those of Germans in Žilina and opening the way to bilingualism in certain cities and towns.
1415	Bohemian religious reformer Jan Hus burned at the stake as a heretic by order of the Council of Constance.
1420–1434	The Hussite Wars take place.
1434	Battle of Lipany ends the Hussite Revolution as radical Hussites are defeated by Utraquist and Czech Catholic forces.
1458	Utraquist nobleman Jiři z Poděbrad (George of Podebrady) elected "Hussite King" of Bohemia. Matthias Corvinus chosen as king of Hungary.
1526	Ferdinand of Habsburg elected king of Bohemia as Ferdinand I, the first Habsburg ruler of the Czech lands. A decisive defeat for Hungarian forces under Louis II at Mohács allows the Ottoman Turks to occupy much of the Hungarian kingdom.
1576–1612	Reign of Rudolf II as king of Bohemia and Holy Roman Emperor.
1618	Defenestration of Prague and the beginning of the Thirty Years' War.
1620	Bohemian forces led by Protestant nobles are defeated by a Habsburg-Catholic coalition at the Battle of White Mountain (Bíla hora).
1683	Ottoman armies are defeated at Vienna, leading to a peace treaty in 1699 allowing for the reunification of the Hungarian kingdom.
1713	Charles VI's Pragmatic Sanction provides for female succession in the Habsburg monarchy.
1740–1780	Reign of Maria Theresa.
1764–1790	Reign of Joseph II.
1781	Patent of Tolerance permits religions other than Roman Catholicism to be practiced in the lands of the Austrian Empire.
1780s	Slovak national revival begins with Anton Bernolák's initial efforts at codification of a Slovak literary language.

1791	Hungarian Diet begins process of Magyarization by issuing first legislation supporting dominance of Hungarian language in the legal system.
Late 18th c.	Beginning of the Czech National Revival.
1805	Napoleon and his Grand Army defeat a coalition of Austrian and Russian forces at the Battle of Austerlitz (Slavkov u Brna) in Moravia.
1809	Napoleon's army lays siege to Pressburg (Bratislava), leading to the burning of the castle and the destruction of nearby Devín Castle.
1840s	Ľudovit Štúr and a group of Slovak scholars codify the Slovak written language and publish the first dictionary of the Slovak language.
1844	Hungarian Diet institutes Magyar as the sole language of administration and education as Magyarization challenges Slovak culture and language.
1848	Bohemian revolt led by František Palacký and Czech liberals. Czechs convene a Slav Congress to discuss cooperation among the Slavic people of the Austrian Empire.
1848–1849	Slovak nationalists draw up "The Demands of the Slovak Nation" for presentation to Hungarian authorities. Slovaks later undertake an armed uprising in support of national independence from Magyar rule.
1848–1916	Reign of Francis Joseph I.
1861	Slovak nationalists meet in Turčianský Sväty Martin and adopt a "Memorandum of the Slovak Nation," calling for the creation of an autonomous Slovak district in North Hungary.
1862	Founding of *Sokol* as a patriotic Czech organization.
1863	Opening of *Matica Slovenská*, an institute dedicated to Slovak culture.
1867	As a result of the *Ausgleich* (Compromise), the Austrian Empire becomes the Austro-Hungarian Empire with the Czech lands ruled by Austria and Slovakia by Hungary.
1871	Founding of the Slovak National Party (SNS) in Turčiansky Sväty Martin.

1875	Hungarian authorities order the closing of *Matica Slovenská* and three Slovak gymnasia.
1907	The "Černová massacre" claims 15 lives as Hungarian police fire on crowds in this Slovak town.
1913	Founding of Slovak People's Party (SĽS) by Andrej Hlinka and others.
1914	Archduke Franz Ferdinand, heir to the Habsburg throne, is assassinated by Bosnian Serb nationalist Gavrilo Princip, setting off a chain of events leading to World War I.
1915	Cleveland Agreement signed by the Slovak League of America and Czech National Council agreeing to the establishment of a federal state comprising Bohemia, Moravia, Czech Silesia, and Slovakia, with a separate Diet and administration for the Slovaks.
1916	Creation of Czech National Council in Paris, shortly to be renamed the Czecho-Slovak National Council.
1918	The Martin Declaration and the Pittsburgh Pact endorse the creation of a common state of Czechs and Slovaks.
1918	First Czechoslovak Republic founded with Tomáš Garrigue Masaryk as president.
1919	Paris Peace Conference takes place.
1919–1920	The Czechoslovak Legion returns home from Russia by crossing Siberia and then sailing from Vladivostok.
1921	Founding of the Czechoslovak Communist Party under Bohumíl Šmeral.
1925	The Slovak People's Party is renamed the Hlinka Slovak People's Party (HSĽS).
1935	Masaryk resigns as president due to ill health and Edvard Beneš is elected in his place.
1938	The Munich Agreement in late September transfers the Sudetenland to German control and the subsequent Vienna Arbitration cedes areas of Slovakia to Hungary.
1939	An invasion by Nazi Germany in March results in a dismembered Czechoslovakia with the Czech lands a "Reich Protectorate of Bohemia and Moravia," and Slovakia

allowed "independence" under the one-party HSĽS administration of Jozef Tiso.

1939   The German invasion of Poland begins World War II.

1941   Slovakia joins Nazi Germany in the Operation Barbarossa invasion of the Soviet Union. The Allies recognize Beneš as president of a Czechoslovak government-in-exile.

1942   The acting Reich Protector, Reinhard Heydrich, is assassinated in Prague, after which the Germans exterminate the villages of Lidice, near Prague, and Lezáky in East Bohemia.

1944   The Slovak National Uprising begins in August.

1945   The Prague Uprising occurs in early May, prior to the city's liberation by the Soviet Red Army and the surrender of Germany. Edvard Beneš and the National Front government arrive from Kosice as the "wild transfer" of ethnic Germans begins.

1947   Former Slovak president Jozef Tiso is sentenced to death and executed.

1948   The Czechoslovak Communist Party (KSČ) seizes power in the February Coup and Beneš resigns as president.

1948–1949   The First Five-Year Plan and the collectivization of agriculture transform the economy as Czechoslovakia enters the Soviet-led Comecon.

1952   During the political purges and show trials, 14 high-ranking KSČ officials, including KSČ chief Rudolf Slánský, are found guilty of treasonous activities, and 11 are executed.

1954   Gustáv Husák and other top leaders of the Slovak Communist Party (KSS) are placed on trial as Slovak "bourgeois nationalists" and granted prison sentences.

1960   Czechoslovakia adopts a new constitution declaring the successful creation of a socialist state under the leadership of the Communist Party. The constitution eliminates Slovak autonomy.

1968   Alexander Dubček replaces Antonín Novotný as first secretary of the KSČ. Dubček's support for reforms and "socialism with a human face" helps inspire the Prague Spring before the experiment is cut short by a Soviet-led Warsaw Pact invasion in August.

1969   Gustáv Husák replaces Dubček as first secretary of the
              KSČ and ushers in the period of "normalization."

1970s and 1980s   "Normalization" dominates social, economic, and politi-
              cal life in Czechoslovakia as stagnation and apathy
              become chronic problems.

1975   Husák elected president of Czechoslovakia during a year
              in which the country becomes a signatory of the Helsinki
              Accords guaranteeing protection of human rights.

1976   Members of the rock bands The Plastic People of the Uni-
              verse and DG 307 are put on trial for performing music
              without official approval.

1977   Charter 77 founded by Václav Havel and other leading
              dissidents in defense of human and civil rights.

1985   Mikhail Gorbachev becomes general secretary of the
              Communist Party in the Soviet Union and introduces the
              reforms of *glasnost* and *perestroika*.

1987   Miloš Jakeš replaces Gustáv Husák as general secretary of
              the KSČ.

1989   The Velvet Revolution begins in the wake of an attack on
              student demonstrators on November 17. Civic Forum
              and Public against Violence are founded as demonstra-
              tions and strikes lead to the collapse of the Communist
              regime. Václav Havel is elected president.

1990   The Czech and Slovak Federative Republic is established
              as economic reforms and mass privatization begins. Free
              and democratic elections are held in June.

1991   The end of the Warsaw Pact and the withdrawal of Soviet
              troops from Czechoslovakia.

1992   After the June elections, Václav Klaus and Vladimír
              Mečiar are chosen as prime ministers of the Czech and
              Slovak republics, respectively. The negotiated "Velvet
              Divorce" leads to the dissolution of Czechoslovakia and
              the creation of two independent republics, the Czech
              Republic and Slovakia, at the end of the year.

1993   Václav Havel is elected president of the Czech Republic
              and Michal Kováč president of Slovakia. The Slovak
              Republic enters the United Nations after the Czech
              Republic inherits Czechoslovakia's membership.

1998   Mikulaš Dzurinda replaces Vladimír Mečiar as prime
            minister of Slovakia.

1999   The Czech Republic enters NATO. Rudolf Schuster is
            elected president of Slovakia by direct vote.

2004   The Czech Republic enters the European Union. The Slo-
            vak Republic enters NATO and the EU.

Map of the Czech Republic. (Cartography by Bookcomp, Inc.)

Map of Slovakia. (Cartography by Bookcomp, Inc.)

1

The Czech Republic and Slovakia Today

Two nations with different paths of historical development, two neighbors with a common history in Czechoslovakia for much of the 20th century before the "Velvet Divorce" led to the creation of two independent countries in 1993. Today's Czech Republic and Slovakia lie in Central Europe, a region that has traditionally been home to Germans, Austrians, Hungarians, and the West Slavic peoples, Poles, Czechs, and Slovaks. Distinct from Western, Eastern, and Southeastern Europe, the broad center of the continent has been influenced throughout history by events and social, cultural, political, and religious trends occurring beyond the region's borders. Although Prague has been known as the city at the heart of Europe, the region of Moravian Slovakia is considered by many to be the frontier between the cultural zones of Eastern and Western Europe, with the origins of the Slavic peoples and their languages in the East and the formative civilization of Latin Christianity to the West.

THE CZECH REPUBLIC

Geography

The Czech Republic (*Česko republika*), or Czechia (*Česko*), is a land-locked nation of moderate size located in the European heartland and sharing borders with Poland, Germany, Austria, and Slovakia. The country has total land boundaries of 1,169 miles and, contrary to William Shakespeare's geographical references to Bohemia in his play *The Winter's Tale*, the Czech Republic possesses no desert or seacoast.

The Czech lands of today are similar in composition to the crown lands of the historical Bohemian kingdom, with the inclusion of Bohemia, Moravia, and parts of Silesia. Bohemia, the largest of the regions, forms the western two-thirds of the Czech Republic and accounts for 20,367 square miles of the nation's total land area of 30,450 square miles. The Czech Republic is comparable in size to Ireland and Austria in Europe and only slightly smaller than South Carolina in the United States.

Located in central Bohemia, Prague (Praha) serves as the nation's capital city with a population of approximately 1.2 million. Brno, long the administrative center of Moravia, is the second-largest city in the Czech Republic with 370,592 inhabitants. Other major cities include Plzeň (169,273), Liberec (100,914), Ústí nad Labem (95,289), České Budějovice (94,936), and Hradec Králové (94,497) in Bohemia, and Ostrava (307,767) and Olomouc (100,373) in Moravia.

The Czech Republic is a moderately mountainous land with over 93 percent of the country situated at an average altitude of between 656 and 3,280 feet above sea level. The nation lies on the divide between the Bohemian massif and the Western Carpathians, which leaves the Bohemian basin surrounded by a mountainous belt separated in the east toward the Bohemian-Moravian plateau. Mountains have long served as a natural frontier between the Czechs and the neighboring Germans and Poles, with the Krkonoše (Giant Mountains) and Orlické Hory (Eagle Mountains) in the northeast and the Šumava blending into the Česky Les, or Bohemian Forest, in the south and west. To the east, the Bílé Karpaty, or White Carpathians, separate Moravia from Slovakia.

Encircled by low mountains, Bohemia is a land of plains, plateaus, and hilly terrain, while Moravia features hills, highlands, and the basin of the Morava River, which flows into the Danube on the southern border. The Krkonoše include the highest mountain in the land, Sněžka (derived from the Czech word for snow), which is 5,260 feet above sea level.

The Czech lands have been called the "roof of Europe" in reference to the passage through the region of the main European watersheds separating the river basins of the two seas (North Sea and Baltic Sea) that lie to the north and the Black Sea to the southeast. From the Králický Sněžník (4,668 feet) peak and the Sněžník massif on the Polish border, water flows toward the three seas according to the patterns of precipitation on the various slopes.

Although the number of lakes in the Czech lands is quite small, Bohemia and Moravia are home to numerous mineral springs and spas, as well as to catchment areas for the Elbe, Morava, and Oder rivers. The source of the Elbe can be found in the Krkonoše mountain range, and the river connects with nearly all the other rivers in the Czech Republic, including the most important of its tributaries, the Vltava, which flows through the capital city of Prague and drains the entire southern region of the country. Because of its importance to the greatest of Czech cities, the Vltava is considered the Czech national river. After its confluence with the Vltava, the Elbe flows to the northwest, passes through the valley of Porta Bohemica, the Bohemian Gate in the volcanic massif of the Bohemian Uplands, and then continues for hundreds of miles across Germany before emptying into the North Sea. The Elbe also includes the point of lowest elevation in the Czech Republic at 378 feet above sea level.

The most important river in Moravia is the Morava, which has its source in Králický Sněžník and then flows south through the lowlands to join with the Dyje before draining the southwestern area of Moravia, crossing the Austrian border, and flowing into the Danube on its path to the Black Sea. The third major river, the Oder (Odra), has its headwaters in northern Moravia but only a small presence in the Czech Republic as it flows through Silesia and then crosses Poland to empty into the Baltic Sea at the port city of Szczecin.

The Czech Republic maintains a number of national parks and protected areas, including those in the highland and mountainous regions of Bílé Karpaty, Krkonoše, Jizerské Hory, and Šumava.

Population and Demography

In 2009, estimates placed the population of the Czech Republic at just over 10.2 million, which would rank the nation 82nd among the world's 193 nations. Based on 2005 estimates, the population density of the Czech Republic is 337 per square mile, with the highest density in central Bohemia and Moravia. Approximately 74 percent of the population resides in urban areas. The median age is 40.1 years (2009 estimate), with 13.6 percent of the population aged 0–14, 71 percent aged 15–64, and 15.5 percent aged 65 and above. The Czech Republic has a reported literacy rate of 99.8 percent.

The ethnic composition of the Czech Republic is 94 percent Czech (Moravians and Bohemian Czechs) and includes Slovaks (3 percent), Poles (0.6 percent), Germans (0.5 percent), Ukrainians (0.4 percent), Hungarians (0.2 percent), and others, including Silesians and a growing Vietnamese community. Official estimates place the Roma, or Gypsies, at 0.3 percent, although the number may actually be as high as 2.5 percent of the total population. The once-thriving German population of Czechoslovakia was reduced by 95 percent during the half-decade following World War II due to expulsions and emigration at the conclusion of Nazi Germany's occupation of Bohemia and Moravia. The Jewish population of the Czech lands is likely no larger than a few thousand, since the Jewish community has never recovered from the losses suffered in the concentration camps of Nazi-occupied Europe.

Although religious rebellion and warfare played a pivotal role in Czech history, the Czech Republic today is considered one of the least religious nations in Europe, with some 40 percent of the citizens declaring themselves to be atheists, agnostics, or nonreligious. Of those with a declared faith, 39.2 percent profess to be Roman Catholic, 4.6 percent Protestant, and the remainder members of other faiths, which include the small remaining Jewish community.

The official language of the Czech Republic is Czech (*čeština*), which is a member of the West Slavic sub-branch of the Slavic language group and therefore related to Polish and Slovak, the latter of which is mutually intelligible with Czech. Spoken Czech includes several regional dialects, and it is an Indo-European language in common with nearly all the languages of Europe.[1]

Economy

Since the momentous events of 1989 and the collapse of communist regimes in Central and Eastern Europe, the Czechs have maintained one of the most developed and industrialized economies in the region. This economic tradition arose during the 19th century, when Bohemia and Moravia emerged as the industrial center of a heavily agrarian Austro-Hungarian Empire. As the Czechs made the transition from a communist, centrally planned economy to capitalism and a market economy, the government made strong efforts to create a healthy climate for investment, which in recent years has established the

Czech Republic as an attractive target for foreign investors. In order to create a framework for privatization and to generate conditions for healthy consumer production and a more efficient industrial base, the government of what was then Czechoslovakia initiated a program in the early 1990s by which most state-owned industries were privatized through a voucher system. Citizens received the opportunity to purchase vouchers that could be redeemed for shares in state-owned enterprises, which accounted for approximately 97 percent of all companies and businesses during the communist era. Enterprises outside the private sphere account for less than 20 percent of the total today. Overall, the transformation of the Czech Republic's economy remained a work in progress 20 years after the collapse of the communist system.

The Czech Republic's central location, infrastructure, well-educated population, and skilled labor force have contributed to an investment climate that received a further boost from the nation's entry into the European Union on May 1, 2004. Integration into the European system required the harmonization of Czech laws and regulations with those of the EU and led to the elimination of most barriers to trade in industrial products, as well as free trade in the service and agricultural sectors. Greater regulation and increasing labor costs make competition difficult for Czech producers, but EU membership also produces benefits in the form of structural funding and agricultural supports.

Overall, these positive factors allowed an economy with a heavy emphasis on exports to undergo annual growth of over 6 percent from 2005 to 2007, although the growth rate fell to 3.2 percent in the midst of the global economic crisis in 2008. With a gross domestic product (GDP) of approximately $217 billion in 2008, the Czech Republic was ranked 40th in the world by the International Monetary Fund (IMF) and 37th by the World Bank. During the first decade of the new century, the Czech Republic moved toward entry into the euro currency zone contingent upon fulfillment of required criteria by 2012. In the meantime, the Czech Republic would continue to use the *koruna česká*, or Czech crown, as the nation's official currency.

Official employment estimates in 2008 included 5.37 million in the work force, with 56 percent employed in government and other services; 40 percent engaged in the industrial, construction, and commercial sectors; and 4 percent involved in agriculture. In connection with the global economic downturn, unemployment rose from 5 percent in May 2008 to 8.6 percent in October 2009 with a higher jobless rate among less-skilled and older workers in areas of northern Bohemia and northern Moravia dependent upon the production of coal and steel.

Environmental Issues

Air and water pollution remains a problem in industrial areas of northwest Bohemia and northern Moravia around Ostrava and there are continuing health risks caused by the long-term use of low-grade brown coal in the production of energy. The coal is a major source of pollution, as are industrial concerns contributing to the ongoing problem of acid rain and the damage inflicted on forested areas. However, programs designed to bring Czech industry in line with EU codes are predicted to have a positive effect on pollution overall.

According to the Czech Statistical Office, coal-driven, combined, and combustion power plants accounted for 67.3 percent of the electricity produced in the Czech Republic in 2007, with 29.7 percent generated by nuclear power plants, and just over 3 percent from hydropower and other renewable resources. However, construction of a nuclear power plant at Temelín, located near the Austrian border in southern Bohemia, has generated conflict from its inception. In 1986, the same year that the catastrophe at the nuclear power plant in Chernobyl, Ukraine, took the lives of 31 persons and led to the evacuation of 100,000 people, the communist government of Czechoslovakia announced plans to construct a Soviet-style nuclear power plant on a hilltop near Temelín. In neighboring Austria, polls taken in 1986 showed that 90 percent of the respondents rejected any development of nuclear energy. This general rejection of nuclear power plants, combined with safety concerns in regard to the design of the Temelín project, inspired organized demonstrations and occasional blockades at border crossings in opposition to a Soviet-style plant near the Czech-Austrian border.

After the fall of the communist regime in 1989, many local Czech residents and political leaders began to protest against the plant, and it became a national issue after the establishment of the Czech Republic in 1993. However, and despite numerous construction-related delays and problems, the first reactor at Temelín came online in 2000 and the second two years later. Government sources claimed that a strong emphasis on safety standards has contributed to an increasingly more positive public view of nuclear energy and that 60 percent of the Czech population would come to support the development of nuclear energy.

The Government of the Czech Republic

The Czech Republic is a parliamentary democracy established on January 1, 1993, in the wake of the "Velvet Divorce" dissolution of Czechoslovakia into the Czech Republic and Slovak Republic at the end of 1992. The constitution was signed on December 16, 1992.

In the executive branch, the president of the Czech Republic serves as formal head of state and is indirectly elected through a joint session of the bicameral parliament for a five-year term, with the right to seek reelection for one additional term. The president possesses the responsibility for convening the parliament and may dissolve the parliament under certain constitutional conditions. In addition, the president signs parliamentary legislation and has the right to veto legislation and return it to the parliament, although the president may not amend that legislation. The president serves as commander-in-chief of the armed forces and, as representative of the state in its relations with other nations, may negotiate and ratify international treaties and agreements. The constitution does not provide the president with strong executive authority, and the office is therefore largely ceremonial.

The first president of the Czech Republic was Václav Havel, who had been elected by the Czechoslovak Federal Assembly on December 29, 1989, in the midst of the transition from the communist regime to a democratic Czech and Slovak Federative Republic. Havel's successor as president of the Czech Republic was the former prime minister and founder of the Civic Democratic Party, Václav Klaus. Klaus was elected by the parliament on February 28, 2003, and then voted a second term on February 15, 2008, after earlier electoral rounds on February 8 and 9 proved inconclusive.

One of the primary duties of the president of the Czech Republic is to appoint the prime minister on the basis of national election results, and with the head of the party receiving the plurality of the votes usually receiving the invitation to form a government. Upon recommendation of the prime minister, the president then appoints the other ministers of the government to serve as deputy prime ministers and the Cabinet. When warranted, the prime minister and other ministers submit their resignations to the president, who may then set in motion the formation of a new government.

The bicameral legislature of the Czech Republic includes a Chamber of Deputies (200 seats) and a Senate (81 seats). Members of the Chamber of Deputies are elected from 14 administrative districts (*kraje*) in Bohemia and Moravia, including the capital city (*hlavní město*) of Prague. Suffrage is universal, equal, and direct at age 18, and deputies are elected by secret ballot for four-year terms and on the basis of proportional representation. The Senate, modeled on the U.S. Senate and first elected in 1996, includes members elected for six-year terms with one-third elected every two years. All Czech citizens 40 years of age and older are eligible for election to the Senate as nominated by political parties or as independent candidates in 81 constituencies.

Candidates earning more than 50 percent of the votes cast earn a seat in the Senate. If none of the candidates receives a majority of the votes, a runoff election takes place between the two candidates who received the highest numbers of votes.

The judicial system of the Czech Republic is founded upon the civil law system of the former Austro-Hungarian Empire, modified to eliminate the Marxist-Leninist legal theory of the communist era and to meet the obligations of the Organization on Security and Cooperation in Europe. The system of civil law includes a hierarchy of courts, from the district, regional, and high (or superior) courts to the Supreme Court as the nation's highest court of appeal. The Czech Republic also maintains as a separate body a Constitutional Court which rules on constitutional issues and whose members are appointed by the president for 10-year terms.

Parliamentary political parties in the Czech Republic include, in order of electoral performance in the June 2006 national elections, the Civic Democratic Party (ODS), the Czech Social Democratic Party (ČSSD), the Communist Party of Bohemia and Moravia (KSCM), the Christian Democratic Union–Czechoslovak People's Party (KDU-ČSL), and the Green Party. The Civic Democratic Party is a right-center party that was founded in April 1991 after a division of Civic Forum, while the center-left Czech Social Democrats are similar to other European social democrats in their support of a socially conscious state with a market economy. The KDU-ČSL carries the banner of conservative Christian democracy and is part of a long tradition in Czech political affairs, while the far-left Communist Party of Bohemia and Moravia is the heir to another tradition, that of the Communist Party of Czechoslovakia, which governed that nation from 1948 to 1989. As a result, the Communists tend to be an "anti-system" party and have not participated in any government since the founding of the Czech Republic. The Green Party is dedicated to ecological issues and generally supports liberal measures in a manner akin to other "green" parties in Europe.[2]

In 2004, the Czech Republic became a member of the European Union and held the presidency of the Council of the European Union from January 1 to June 30, 2009. The Czech Republic also maintains membership in the United Nations (UN), North Atlantic Treaty Organization (NATO), International Monetary Fund (IMF), and Organization for Co-operation and Security in Europe (OSCE).

The flag of the Czech Republic consists of two horizontal bands of white and red with a blue isosceles triangle on the hoist side. A separate presidential flag bears the slogan, "Truth Prevails" (*Pravda vítězí*). The national anthem, "Where Is My Home?" (*Kde domov můj?*), is taken from the incidental music written for the comic play, *Fidlovačka*, or *No Anger and No Brawl*, first performed in 1834, Written by the composer František Škroup and the playwright Josef Kajetán Tyl, the song was later adopted as an unofficial anthem by Czech nationalists living under Austrian Habsburg rule.

SLOVAKIA

Geography

Slovakia (*Slovensko*), or the Slovak Republic (*Slovenská republika*), is a landlocked nation with a varied topography shaped by mountains and rivers that divide the country into different geographical regions. Rugged mountains lie in the central and northern parts of Slovakia and lowlands in the south. At 18,932 square miles, Slovakia is roughly twice the size of the state of New Hampshire and stretches for 266.5 miles between its easternmost and westernmost points.

Slovakia shares boundaries with Poland, the Czech Republic, Ukraine, Austria, and Hungary. The Danube River serves as the border for 109 miles of the common frontier with Hungary, and Slovakia's capital city, Bratislava, is situated on both banks of this critical European waterway.

Historically, Slovakia has been divided into three regional cultural areas—western, central, and eastern—marked by a common culture, but with distinct regional dialects of the Slovak language and local cultural characteristics. Geography has played a role in this diversity through the variations in physical environments, from the mountains to the lowlands in the south and southeast. These lowlands include the Eastern Slovak Lowland, Záhorská Lowland, and Danubian Lowland, offering fertile soil and a very different environment from the valleys, hills, highlands, and mountains elsewhere. Part of the Greater Danubian Plain, the lowlands feature prairies and pine meadows, as well as forests, moors, and brine swamps.

In a country where mountainous terrain accounts for 30 percent of the land, the Carpathian Mountains dominate Slovak topography through their associated mountain chains in the northern part of the Great Carpathian Bow. These chains include the Slovak Ore Mountains, Low Tatras, Štiavnica Mountains, Greater Fatras, and Lesser Fatras. The High Tatras, the highest mountains in Slovakia and the only range in the country with Alpine characteristics, form part of the border with Poland in the north and include the highest point in Slovakia, Gerlach Peak, at 8,710 feet. The Little, or White Carpathians, divide Slovakia from the Czech Republic and then continue south into Austria, where they join the Alpine system. The Slovak Ore Mountains stretch from Zvolen in central Slovakia to Kosice in the east, a distance of approximately 90 miles. The mountain environment is also rich in mineral and thermal springs, which feed spas at Bardejov, Piestany, Smrdaky, Lucky, Novy Smokovec, and other locations.

Rivers also play an important role in Slovakia, with one of Europe's most important waterways, the Danube (*Dunaj*), linking Slovakia with territories from Germany to the Black Sea. Bratislava and Komarno serve as Slovakia's two key ports on the Danube, with daily ferries linking the Slovak capital to the Austrian capital city of Vienna close by to the north. In the west, the Morava River forms the boundary with Moravia in the Czech Republic, and in the east, the Uh River separates Slovakia from Sub-Carpathian Ruthenia in western Ukraine.

Other important rivers include the Tisa, which forms part of the border with Hungary. At 286 miles, the Váh originates in the central region and flows to the west and then south to the Danube as the longest river located entirely in Slovakia. The lowest point of Slovakia lies at 308 feet above sea level near the village of Klin nad Bodrogom, close to where the Bodrog River crosses the border into Hungary.

Population and Demography

Slovakia's population of 5,412,254 ranked 113rd in the world at the end of 2008, making the Slovak Republic a small nation in a strategically important region of Europe. Population distribution in Slovakia is irregular, with the greatest population density found in the large cities and the Danubian Lowland. Even with the development of a modern European economy and society, approximately 45 percent of the Slovakia's inhabitants live in villages of fewer than 5,000 people, and 14 percent in villages of fewer than 1,000. The East Slovak Basin and Záhorská Lowland are less populated areas, and low population density is characteristic of the northern mountainous regions and the east of the country due to the scarcity of fertile soil.

Slovakia's major urban areas include the capital, Bratislava, with a population of 428,791 (late 2008 estimate) and Košíce in the eastern part of the country with 233,659 inhabitants. Other large Slovak cities include Nitra (84,070), Trnava (67,726), Trenčín (56,826), and Prievidza (50,664) in the west; Žilina (85,327), Banská Bystrica (80,106), and Martin (58,433) in central Slovakia; and Prešov (91,273) and Poprad (54,621) in the east.

With a population density of 110 persons per square kilometer, Slovakia's growth rate, inclusive of natural increase and net migration, varied from 4.2 percent in 1993 to 0.0 in 2001 and 2.1 in 2008. The mean age of the population was 38.3 in 2008, with 15.45 percent in the 0–14 age range, 72.46 percent between the ages of 15 and 64, and 12.09 percent 65 and older. Females comprised 51.41 percent of the population, and males 48.59 percent. The nation has a literacy rate of 99.6 percent.

The ethnic composition of the Slovak Republic includes a Slovak majority of 86 percent in addition to a number of ethnic minorities. The word "Slovak" is considered a derviation of "*Slovan*," the Slovakian term for "Slav." Hungarians, or Magyars, living largely in the southern lowlands near the Hungarian border, are the largest of the minorities at approximately 10 percent of the nation's inhabitants. Official estimates place the Roma, or Gypsy, population at approximately 1.7 percent of the total, but unofficial estimates offer numbers possibly as high as 6–10 percent. This is due in part to many Roma self-identifying as Hungarians or as members of other ethnic groups. Czechs account for a further 1.4 percent of the population, and the remainder includes Ukrainians (0.1 percent), Germans (0.1 percent), Moravians (0.07 percent), and Poles (0.1 percent). Rusyns, an east Slavic people also known as Ruthenians or Carpatho-Ruthenians, the latter in reference to their mountain villages in the Carpathians, comprise 0.3 percent of the population.

Slovakia remains a solidly Roman Catholic nation, with 69 percent of Slovak citizens professing an adherence to that faith. Protestants are the second-largest group at approximately 10 percent, followed by Greek Catholics (4 percent), Orthodox Christians (0.9 percent), and a Jewish population of fewer than 4,000 with a Holocaust-surviving group of fewer than 1,500, the smallest in Europe.[3]

The official language of the Slovak Republic is Slovak (*slovenčina*) a west Slavic and Indo-European language related to Polish and more closely to Czech, especially in regard to Czech dialects spoken in neighboring Moravia. Hungarian is commonly spoken in the southern part of the country. Ruthenian, Romany, and Ukrainian exist as the languages of the smaller ethnic groups. In 1995, the Slovak government passed a state language law designed to preserve the state language by designating punishments for failure to use Slovak in official communication without regard for the percentage of the minority in that area. When the offending conditions were later determined to be in violation of the Slovak constitution by the Constitutional Court, they were abolished. As a condition of membership in the European Union,

Slovakia was required in 1999 to accept a law on minority languages that provided for the public use of minority languages in areas of at least 20 percent majority. Ten years later in 2009, however, an amendment to the law of 1995 sought to establish the primacy of the Slovak language as a reflection of the sovereignty of the Slovak Republic. The revised law provided a small number of exemptions in the public and official spheres, but otherwise sanctioned the use of Slovak in written and spoken form by describing penalties of 100 to 5,000 euros for failure to use Slovak as set out in the law and in the wake of written warnings. The 2009 amendment drew strong criticism not only from Slovakia's Hungarian minority, but also from the government of neighboring Hungary.

Economy

Entry into the new era of an independent Slovak Republic in January 1993 brought with it the commitment to completing the economic transformation from the centralized planning of the communist era to a market-oriented system in which state-owned enterprises would be transferred to private ownership. This difficult and complex process required extensive reforms and a successful process of privatization, but the transition slowed considerably during the 1994–1998 period due to corruption and questionable fiscal policies under the government of Prime Minister Vladimir Mečiar. Those years were marked by economic growth and the overall improvement of some sectors of the economy, although some of the perceived growth could be attributed to high government spending and overborrowing. Often-reckless government policies led to the rapid growth of trade deficits, as well as high levels of public and private debt. Cronyism, insider deals, and questionable decision making brought slow and erratic progress in privatization during the 1990s, as reflected in the decline of real annual GDP growth from a peak of 6.5 percent in 995 to 1.3 percent in 1999.

Under the government of Prime Minister Mikuláš Dzurinda, economic reforms received new impetus through revisions of the taxation system, large increases in the privatization process, and progress with the labor code and pension systems. This was especially true of Dzurinda's second term (2002–2006), during which the Slovak Republic experienced economic progress leading to a growth rate of 8.3 percent in 2006, representing the highest rate of economic growth among members of the Organization of Economic Co-operation and Development (OECD). In 2007, the rate of economic growth reached 10.4 percent as the Slovak economy continued to exceed expectations. Consumer price inflation fell from 26 percent in 1993 to 4.5 percent in 2006, then dropped below 2.4 percent early in 2007 as favorable global energy prices and an improvement in the exchange rate supported economic growth. In 2008, Slovakia's gross domestic product (GDP) of approximately $95 billion was ranked 56th in the world by the World Bank and 57th by the International Monetary Fund (IMF).

Having fulfilled the Maastricht Criteria, Slovakia entered the Euro Zone on January 1, 2009, as the euro replaced the *Slovenska koruna*, or Slovak crown, as the national currency. The Slovak Republic has also experienced sharp increases in foreign investment as a result of moderate labor costs, a skilled work force, liberalized labor policies, strategic location, and favorable system of taxation that included a 19 percent flat tax on individuals and corporations. By 2009, major privatization neared completion, foreign investment in the automotive and electronic concerns continued to grow, and the nation's banking sector was almost entirely foreign-owned. The positive economic growth suffered a setback, however, as the impact of the European recession on Slovak exports led to a contraction of 5.4 percent during the first quarter of 2009.

In 2008, Slovakia's labor force included an estimated at 2.254 million workers, with 39 percent engaged in industry, construction, and commerce; 56.9 percent in government and other services; and 4 percent in agriculture. The national unemployment rate, which had risen to 18 percent in 2003–2004, stood at 9 percent in September 2008 after rising from the 7.6 percent rate recorded in June of the previous year. By March 2009, the rate reached 10.5 percent due to the continent-wide economic downturn, and Slovakia had one of the highest rates of joblessness in the European Union.

Environmental Issues

Air pollution caused by metallurgical plants and other industrial concerns remains a health issue, while acid rain and the consequences of deforestation continue to threaten the nation's extensive forests. Environmental concerns have also played a key role in the much-publicized and long-running dispute over construction of the Gabčíkovo-Nagymaros dams on the Danube. In 1977, the socialist governments of Czechoslovakia and Hungary signed a bilateral treaty to cooperate in the construction of a system of dams between Gabčíkovo in Slovak territory and Nagymaros in Hungary. The project called for the diversion of the Danube into an artificial canal on Czechoslovak territory by means of a dam and relief sluice, in connection with construction of a hydroelectric power station near Gabčíkovo, southeast of Bratislava. A second, smaller power station would be erected near Nagymaros in Hungary. The goals of the project were to create a better mechanism for flood control and to produce cleaner energy in the heavily polluted regions of northern Hungary and Czechoslovakia.

Facing difficult economic conditions in 1981, the government of Hungary proposed abandoning the project and then in 1983 negotiated an agreement with Czechoslovakia to slow work on construction of the dams. In the face of growing public protests against the power plant at Nagymaros, Hungarian leaders suspended construction in 1989 and then announced in 1992 that it was terminating the 1977 treaty. Hungarian opposition to the project evolved into a major international conflict when the Slovaks initiated the diversion of the Danube at Gabčíkovo, resulting in a two-meter drop in the water level of the river. Widespread concern had already arisen over the environmental consequences of diverting the Danube and damming the river for the production of hydroelectric power, especially in light of the long stretch of the Danube affected by the original plan.

Intervention by the European Community (EC) convinced both nations to submit the case to the International Court of Justice (ICJ) in The Hague. In September 1997, the court ruled that Hungary's suspension of the 1977 treaty represented an illegal action in light of the treaty's definition of the collaborative project as "single and indivisible." However, the court also ruled that the diversion of the river at Gabčíkovo, the so-called "Variant C" plan, also violated the treaty in ignoring the "single and indivisible" nature of the hydroelectric dam project. Furthermore, the court ruled that the 1977 treaty remained in effect and that Hungary and Slovakia must continue negotiations on fulfillment of the treaty, even though each nation would continue to interpret the terms of the treaty differently. These negotiations would continue over the next decade, with Hungary objecting to the construction of the lower dam at Nagymaros and Slovakia demanding that the dam be built as planned.

The Government of the Slovak Republic

The Slovak Republic is a parliamentary democracy formally established as a direct consequence of the division of Czechoslovakia into two sovereign and independent republics. Ratification of the constitution of the Slovak Republic occurred on September 1, 1992, and the document became effective on January 1, 1993. The constitution was later amended in September 1998 to allow direct election of the president, and again in February 2001 to allow for NATO and EU membership.

Slovakia is divided into 8 administrative regions (*kraje*) and 79 districts, with Bratislava as the capital and seat of government. The flag of the Slovak Republic features equal horizontal bands of white (top), blue, and red superimposed with the coat of arms of Slovakia slightly to the hoist side of center. The coat of arms is in the form of a red shield bordered in white and dominated by a white Cross of Lorraine atop three blue hills. The Slovak national anthem, *Nad Tatrou Sa Blýska* (Lightning over the Tatras), written in 1884, celebrates the revolutionary spirit of the 1840s through Janko Matúška's addition of new lyrics to the melody of a traditional folk song, *Kopala studienku* (She Dug A Well). The lyrics urge Slovaks to arise and defend themselves against the threat represented by lightning and thunderstorms over the mountains of their homeland.

In the Slovak political system, the executive branch includes the president as head of state and the government consisting of the prime minister, the deputy prime ministers, and the other ministers of the Cabinet. The president of the Slovak Republic is directly elected by eligible voters for a five-year term, with the possibility of reelection for a second term. Suffrage is universal, direct, and equal at age 18 and voting is by secret ballot. If a candidate fails to achieve an absolute majority of votes, a second ballot may be scheduled as a runoff between the two candidates receiving the highest vote totals. The victorious candidate in the second round would then be named president.

The president serves as commander-in-chief of the armed forces and as representative of the Slovak Republic in international relations with the power to negotiate or ratify international agreements. In addition to appointing the prime minister and accepting the head of government's recommendations for other ministerial positions, the president may sign legislation proposed by the parliament, or National Council, or return the legislation to that body with his own recommendations. The president may also dissolve the National Council according to certain constitutional conditions.

On April 4, 2009, Ivan Gašparovic, supported by the Direction–Social Democracy (Smer-SD), and Slovak National Party (SNS) alliance, became the first Slovak president to gain reelection by popular vote after defeating Iveta Radičová of the Slovak Democratic and Christian Union (SDKU-DS) 55.5 percent to 45.5 percent in the second round of the presidential race. Gašparovic, aligned at the time with the Movement for Democracy and SMER (HDZ-Smer) earned his first term on April 3, 2004, as a result of a second-round electoral victory over Vladimír Mečiar of the Movement for a Democratic Slovakia–People's Party (HZDS-LS). A central figure in the "Velvet Divorce" that led to the establishment of an independent Slovak republic, Mečiar had served as prime minister of Slovakia three times during the 1990s and briefly as acting president in 1998 when the National Council was unable to agree on a successor to Michal Kováč, whose term had expired.

As head of the government, the prime minister is usually appointed by the president from the majority party or a minority coalition after elections for the National Council. The prime minister may then request acceptance by the president of a new government comprising deputy prime ministers and ministers of the Cabinet. Led by the prime minister, the government is responsible for enacting programs as chief formulator of the nation's public policy and within the adopted national budget.

The legislature of Slovakia is the unicameral National Council of the Slovak Republic, whose 150 members are elected by popular vote for four-year terms and on the basis of proportional representation. Convened by the president, the National Council has the power to pass and implement laws, propose the holding of a referendum, approve the national budget, establish government departments and bodies, ratify international treaties and agreements, declare war against another nation, and approve the deployment of troops outside the Slovak Republic. The National Council may also override a presidential veto with a simple majority and schedule a vote of no-confidence in a government or an individual minister with an absolute majority necessary for passage.

Parliamentary elections held on June 17, 2006, led to the appointment of Robert Fico as prime minister of the Slovak Republic after Fico's party, Direction–Social Democracy (Smer-SD, 50 seats) established a coalition with the Slovak National Party (SNS, 20 seats) and the People's Party–Movement for a Democratic Slovakia (LS-HZDS, 15 seats). Other parliamentary parties include the Slovak Democratic and Christian Union (SDKU-DS, 31 seats); Hungarian Coalition Party (SMK-MKP, 20 seats), and Christian Democratic Movement (KDH, 14 seats). Parties participating in the election but failing to gain seats in parliament include the Communist Party of Slovakia (KSS), Free Forum (SF), Alliance of the New Citizen (ANO) and some smaller parties.

As in the neighboring Czech Republic, the legal system of the Slovak Republic has its roots in the civil law system of the former Austro-Hungarian Empire, modified to reflect the elimination of Marxist-Leninist legal theory and to comply with of the Organization of

Security and Cooperation in Europe. The judicial branch of the Slovak government includes the Supreme Court, or highest appellate court, whose judges are elected by the National Council and sit on panels that rule on civil and criminal matters, confer on decisions made by regional, district, and military courts, and review the legal basis of decisions made by governmental bodies. A special Constitutional Court serves as an independent judicial body with the authority to rule on constitutional issues. The Constitutional Court consists of 13 judges appointed for 12-year terms from a group of nominees nominated by the National Council and approved by the president.

The Slovak Republic maintains membership in a number of leading international organizations, including the European Union and NATO, which Slovakia joined in the spring of 2004. Slovakia is also a member of the United Nations, Organization for Co-operation and Security in Europe (OSCE), Organization for Economic Cooperation and Development (OECD), International Monetary Fund (IMF), and various other regional, European, and global organizations dedicated to economic, scientific, and security concerns.[4]

NOTES

1. For information on the population of the Czech Republic, as well as on topics such as geography and economics, see the following online resources: Czech Republic—the Official Website (Ministry of Foreign Affairs of the Czech Republic, http://www.czech.cz/en/discover-cz/facts-about-the-czech-republic); *CIA: The World Factbook* (https://www.cia.gov/library/publications/the-world-factbook/geos/ez.html); U.S. Department of State, "Background Note: Czech Republic" (http://www.state.gov/r/pa/ei/bgn/3237.htm); and United Kingdom Foreign and Commonwealth Office, "Country Profile: Czech Republic" (http://www.fco.gov.uk/en/travel-and-living-abroad/travel-advice-by-country/country-profile/europe/czech-republic?profile=politics&pg=7). The United Nations Statistics Division also offers information on demographics at UNdata (http://data.un.org/CountryProfile.aspx?crName=CZECHREPUBLIC).

2. Official online government resources of the Czech Republic include the presidential Web site Prague Castle (http://www.hrad.cz/en); Government of the Czech Republic (http://www.vlada.cz/en/default.htm); and Parliament of the Czech Republic, Senate (http://www.senat.cz/index-eng.php?ke_dni=11.05.2010&O=7), and Chamber of Deputies (http://www.psp.cz/cgi-bin/eng/sqw/hp.sqw). Results of recent presidential and parliamentary elections can be found at the Election Guide of the International Foundation for Electoral Systems (IFES) (http://www.electionguide.org).

3. For information on the population, economy, and geographical features of Slovakia, consult the following online resources: *CIA: The World Factbook* (https://www.cia.gov/library/publications/the-world-factbook/geos/lo.html); U.S. Department of State, "Background Note: Slovakia (http://www.state.gov/r/pa/

ei/bgn/3430.htm); United Kingdom Foreign and Commonwealth Office, "Country Profile: Slovakia" (http://www.fco.gov.uk/en/travel-and-living-abroad/travel-advice-by-country/country-profile/europe/slovakia). UNdata of the United Nations Statistics Division (http://data.un.org/CountryProfile.aspx?cr Name=SLOVAKIA) provides demographic data for the Slovak Republic.

4. Official Web sites of the government of the Slovak Republic include: President of the Slovak Republic (http://www.prezident.sk/?introduction); Government Office of the Slovak Republic (http://www.government.gov.sk/9711/government-of-the-slovak-republic.php?menu=1290); and National Council of the Slovak Republic (http://www.nrsr.sk/Default.aspx?Lang=en). The Election Guide of the International Foundation for Electoral Systems (IFES) (http://www.electionguide.org) offers information on recent elections in Slovakia.

2

Origins and Medieval Legacies

PREHISTORY AND EARLY SETTLEMENT

The first Indo-European peoples arrived in East Central Europe as early as the end of the third millennium BCE by following a route that took them from the Caucasus through the lands north of Black Sea. Their arrival coincided with the emergence of Europe's earliest civilization in the Aegean region, and they were responsible for developing the Únětice culture, named after a location near Prague, as the first regional culture of the early Bronze Age. Archaeological evidence shows that they worked metal to produce weapons and ornaments, which were often placed alongside the deceased in flat graves or the less common stone cairns. Copper daggers, flint arrowheads, clay cups, and similar objects served as burial possessions for males, while arm-rings, bracelets, and pins of copper or bone accompanied females in death. The Únětice culture influenced other cultures in central Europe, spreading across southern and central Germany as well as western Poland.

The Indo-European Celts arrived in Bohemia in the mid-fourth century BCE as part of their gradual occupation of territories stretching from the shores of the Atlantic to the Balkans and Asia Minor. One Celtic tribe, the Boii, settled in Bohemia and took control of the territory as the first recorded inhabitants of a land populated to that time by peoples who left no written evidence. The Celts, however, were familiar to the Greeks and especially to the Romans, who referred to the land of the Boii as *Boiohaemum*. During the Middle Ages, scholars writing in Latin borrowed from the work of Roman geographers in naming the tribe *Boemii* (or *Bohemani*) and their land, *Bohemia*. In the German lands, the region became known as *Böhmen*.

Other Celtic tribes, the Volcae-Tectosages and the Cottini, settled in the lands of present-day Moravia and Slovakia, respectively. Over time, the population of Celts in East Central Europe benefited from a flow of fellow Celts from the territories of the West, primarily the lands that would become France and Switzerland.

Associated with the Hallstatt culture (750–450 BCE) of the late Bronze and early Iron ages, the Celts later established contact with the Etruscans and Greeks and introduced the La Tène culture (500–50 BCE) into the Danube region and elsewhere. The Celtic phase of history was characterized by technological advances in ironwork and crafts as the iron ploughshare, potter's wheel, and stone wheels for grinding corn contributed to the development of specialized production. The Celts were effective at producing simple, everyday goods, which was especially true of a La Tène culture based on the extensive use of iron for the production of tools and weapons. Blacksmiths, potters, and jewelers inspired the growth of exchange and trade, and by the end of the second century BCE, the Celts were minting coins of gold and silver. Celtic art of the La Tène culture featured abstract geometrical patterns and simplified animal forms.

The Celts established settlements in large, well-fortified sites that Roman leader Julius Caesar referred to as *oppida*. With Roman expansion reaching the Rhine and Danube rivers, incursions by the Germanic tribes to the north left the Celts of Central Europe in a precarious position and may have precipitated construction of these sites from the end of the second century BCE. Bohemia suffered such incursions during the final century BCE as Germanic authority came to dominate local Celts and undermine their institutions and culture. When Gaul fell to Julius Caesar in 58–51 BCE, the resulting decrease in contact with the West precipitated the decline of the Bohemian and Moravian Celts, who all but disappeared by the end of the La Tène period and the beginning of the Christian era, thus ending five centuries of Celtic culture that represented the highest stage of prehistorical development in the region.

In 9 BCE, a defeat at the hands of Roman legions led the Marcomanni, a Germanic tribe, to move eastward into territory inhabited by the remnants of the Boii in eastern Bavaria and Bohemia. The imposition of strong Germanic rule under King Marobuduus and the disruption of the Celtic economy represented a reversal of historical development as the potential creation of a rudimentary Celtic state was thwarted and agriculture returned to a pre-Celtic level of technology.

The Marcomanni and the Quadi, a neighboring Germanic tribe under King Vannius in southwest Slovakia and Moravia, maintained diplomatic relations with the Romans, who occasionally intervened in local political affairs or took military action when deemed necessary. The potential military threat on the borders persuaded the Romans to establish a *Limes Romanus*, or network of fortified towns linked by roads along the Danube frontier. Roman settlements at Vindobona (Vienna) and nearby Carnuntum, where the Amber Road crossed the Danube, served as the two main military bases in what is today Austrian territory. Incursions by the Marcomanni and their Quadi allies into the Roman province of Pannonia led to the outbreak of the Marcomannic Wars (166–172 and 177–180 CE) during the reign of Emperor Marcus Aurelius (161–180 CE), who wrote sections of his *Meditations* in Carnuntum and along the Hron River in Slovakia in the midst of the military campaign. However, the Romans never established any permanent presence beyond the Danube, and an inscription carved on a rock below the castle in the Slovak city of Trenčín offers one of the few lasting reminders of their presence.

THE ARRIVAL OF THE SLAVS

By the midpoint of the sixth century, critical new historical forces were at work in the eastern reaches of Central Europe. The collapse of the Western Roman Empire in the late fifth century and the decline of the Germanic population in the region coincided with the rise of a Byzantine Empire in Greece and the emergence of the Catholic (Roman) and Orthodox (Greek) forms of Christianity. It was during the sixth and seventh centuries that the Slavic transmigration brought new peoples into the region stretching from Central and Eastern Europe to the Balkans. Originating beyond the Dnieper, Slavic tribes migrated into the Carpathian region and the Danube basin, occupying Slovakia, Moravia, and Bohemia. An abundance of arable land, the presence of extensive forests, and the benefits of established trade routes, roads, and navigable rivers proved attractive to the Slavs, who settled in formerly occupied towns and built villages of simple huts in a colonizing process that relied more on peaceful agricultural pursuits than on military action.

These new arrivals called themselves *Sloveňi*, after *Slovo* (the word). Initially composed of indistinct tribes and speaking dialects of a common tongue, these settlers gradually mixed with or absorbed older peoples and developed larger tribes, which over time developed into the West Slavic peoples—Czechs (Bohemians and Moravians) and Slovaks, along with the Poles who established their own lands to the north.

The Slavs lived in fortified settlements, farming communal land and breeding cattle that were property of the tribe. Tribal chieftains exercised their authority in villages that remained scattered and fairly autonomous in the absence of any centralized authority. Slaves were introduced as a source of labor in the seventh century, and the communal nature of society began to change as free members of the tribes no longer performed the hardest work. The tribal system evolved into a clan system, and chieftains acquired land as the property of their own clans rather than as the communal property of a larger tribe.

In his twelfth-century *Chronica Boemorum* (Chronicle of the Czechs), the Czech cleric Cosmas of Prague (1054–1125) wrote of a mythical Slavic leader called Bohemus, who led his people in search of a land of prosperity that they could claim as their own. Upon reaching Mount Řip, between the Ohre and Vltava rivers, Bohemus declared that they had arrived at the land of their destiny, "a land subject to no one, filled with wild animals and fowl, wet with nectar, honey and milk, and, as you yourselves see, air delightful for living."[1] Thus the people of Bohemus took possession of the land that would bear his name as Bohemia. This myth evolved as a central element of the Czech historical imagination over the centuries, altered somewhat in the early 14th century when another chronicler related tales of the equally mythical Čech as founder of the land that bore his name as Čech (Czechia).

By the mid-sixth century, a new force arose to dominate the Pannonian basin as the Avars arrived from Central Asia and created a large khanate with its center located between the Danube and Tisa rivers. Nomadic warriors and herders, the Avars established supremacy over the Slavs and the remaining Germanic peoples, the Gepids and Lombards. Although the Slavs possessed a warrior culture, disunity among the tribes prevented the formation of a common language or central authority, which, in turn, left the Slavs initially vulnerable to the military power of the Avars. However, attacks by the Avars eventually drove the Slavs to unite the tribes and rebel in defense of their lands in 623–624.

According to the Frankish Chronicle of Fredegar, the semi-mythical leader of the rebellion against the harsh rule of the Avars was a merchant named Samo from the Germanic kingdom of the Franks, who created an alliance of Slavic chieftains to protect traders and to defend the Slavic lands in the northwestern reaches of the khanate. Under the personal leadership of Samo (ruled 623–658), this federation developed into an independent territory likely to have included lands in southwestern Slovakia, parts of Moravia and Lower Austria, and possibly Bohemia. When the Merovingian king Dagobert I ordered a Frankish military incursion into Samo's territory in 631, Samo's warriors defeated the Frankish force in a three-day battle at Wogastisburg. Samo continued to rule the empire until his death in 658, but this early attempt at a unified Slavic state did not survive his passing. The Slavs abandoned organization and returned to tribal affiliations as the eighth century witnessed both the decline of Avar ruling power and the emergence of Slavic princely families founded upon kinship, marriage, and intermarriage.

With the collapse of Avar power, hastened by military defeats at the hands of the Franks during the decade of the 790s, the Slavs faced a new challenge in the form of a powerful empire arising on their western borders. On Christmas Day in the year 800, Pope Leo III placed a crown upon the head of the German ruler of the Frankish kingdom and declared him "Emperor of the Romans," thereby hoping to reconstitute the Roman Empire in the West and establish a strong connection between the Church and German rulers. Charles (r. 768–814), known to history as Charlemagne, had already expanded his empire by undertaking numerous military campaigns in Italy, northern Spain, and Germany, and in the latter case he added the lands of the Saxons and Bavarians to his growing empire. At its peak, the Carolingian kingdom included most of Western and Central Europe and, with the devastation of the Avars to the east, a new border from the Adriatic to the Baltic. In 805, Charlemagne's troops invaded the Czech lands, and the Czechs suffered a significant loss when an important leader, Lech, fell during the fighting. One year later, a new Frankish incursion drove the Czechs to accept a form of vassalage and to agree to provide tributes to the empire as part of the network of dependent Slavic territories along the imperial frontier. Threatened by a superior force, the Moravians were forced to submit as well.

THE GREAT MORAVIAN EMPIRE

The proximity of the Slavs to the Germanic empire encouraged mercantile activity as well as Christianizing missions by Frankish and Irish missionaries who spread the Roman Catholic faith among the Slavs.

Since the Frankish church was closely linked to Charlemagne through its bishops and abbots, the missionary activity also enhanced imperial influence in the region and drew the Slavs closer to Latin Christian traditions.

Efforts to subjugate the neighboring Slavs led Charlemagne's successors to launch repeated military campaigns into Bohemia and Moravia during the ninth century. However, the vast empire that Charlemagne had created failed to survive him by more than a generation. In 843, Charlemagne's three grandsons brought an end to nearly constant fighting by signing the Treaty of Verdun, which divided the empire and provided the basis for the historical evolution of nations and states across Europe. Louis the German (r. 843–876) gained the eastern lands of the future Germany and attempted to reestablish control of the Slavic tribes through military power and the expansion of Frankish religious influence under the leadership of eastern German bishoprics. In order to ensure control over religious affairs to the east, Bohemia was placed under the authority of the Bishop of Regensburg and Moravia under the Archbishop of Salzburg and the Bishop of Passau. By the ninth century, contemporary documents began to reflect the more direct associations that Slavic tribes had developed with the lands they inhabited, from the Bohemian Slavs in the west and the Moravian Slavs to their east to the *Slověni* living along the Nitra, Hron, and Vah rivers of today's Slovakia.

With the defeat of the Avars, reunification of the western and southern Slavs became a distinct possibility with the potential for a large Slavic state on the borders of Charlemagne's empire. The long-standing tradition among the Slavic tribes allowed the free males to meet as an assembly and select the leader (*kniže* in Czech; prince or duke) from among the families of the warrior elite. During the 9th and 10th centuries, the elite families began to blur the boundaries between tribes in a process that led to the unification of formerly independent, autonomous tribes under a single leader, or prince. In this manner, the Slavic principalities of Morava and Nitra emerged under Moravian princes who gained authority over the tribes and ruled as lords with command over military affairs.

Contact with the Frankish empire led the princes to develop a rudimentary state and to solidify the growing influence of Christianity by constructing churches of stone and bringing in priests and monks from northern Italy, Bavaria, and the Byzantine coast of the Adriatic. The oldest known church in Moravia, built around 800, is in Modra, near Velehrad. Center of a principality located in western and central Slovakia, the town of Nitra was the site of the first Christian church on

Slovak soil, consecrated by Archbishop Adalran of Salzburg in 828. Although still a pagan, Pribina, the prince of Nitra, supported the spread of churches and monasteries across the lands under his authority.

Chief among the princes was Mojmír I (r. c. 830–846), leader of the Principality of Moravia, who successfully strengthened his own position by weakening tribal associations and accepting baptism by the Bishop of Passau in 831. Mojmír then worked to spread Christianity among the Moravians, who established churches in their fortified settlements. Under Mojmír's leadership, the Moravians expanded into southwest Slovakia and north toward Nitra, uniting both Slavic principalities into an Empire of Great Moravia in 833.

Pribina fled Nitra with his retainers and eventually made his way to the court of Louis the German in Regensburg. Embracing Christianity along with his followers, Pribina became a Frankish vassal and was rewarded with grants of land in Pannonia, where he settled in 839 and ruled the principality from his castle at Blatnohrad-Mosaburg.

Mojmír's Great Moravia also became a vassal state of the East Frankish ruler and was required to pay annual tribute accordingly. The payments, however, became a source of internal discord as some members of the nobility in Nitra opposed the requirement and created tension between the principalities of Nitra and Morava. In 846, the ongoing conflict convinced Louis the German to intervene in the affairs of Great Moravia by siding with Mojmír's nephew, Prince Rastislav of Nitra, who ordered Mojmír arrested and expelled from the empire.

Rastislav (r. 846–861) assumed the title of king with the support of Louis the German, who believed that the new ruler would continue in the cooperative manner of his predecessor. Once in power, however, Rastislav worked to limit Frankish political and religious influence in Great Moravia in concert with his policies of expansion and consolidation. Rastislav expanded the empire's holdings in the east and established a border with the Bulgarian kingdom to the south. In 853–854, Rastislav became involved in internal struggles within the East Frankish kingdom, supporting Ratbrod, the margrave of the Ostmark, against Louis the German. Louis responded by invading Great Moravia in 855 with the intention of overthrowing Rastislav, a goal he failed to achieve as fighting continued until 859.

After agreeing to a peace treaty with the Franks, Rastislav sought to gain religious autonomy for Great Moravia by hindering Frankish missionary activity, developing a Slavic liturgy, and convincing the Holy See in Rome to establish an ecclesiastical province in Great Moravia that was beyond the influence of the German dioceses. In 861–862, Rastislav requested assistance from Rome, petitioning Pope Nicholas I to send teachers who could communicate with the people of Great Moravia in the Slavonic language. When written correspondence and the arrival of a delegation in Rome failed to generate the desired results, Rastislav dispatched a delegation to the court of the Byzantine emperor Michael III in Constantinople, seeking the ruler's assistance in helping the people of Great Moravia to embrace Christianity in their own tongue. In 862, Emperor Michael dispatched teachers and a bishop to Rastislav's empire, thereby introducing Byzantine influence into a region where the Western civilization of the Germanic Franks and the Roman Catholic Church had already made inroads. Pope Nicholas I gave his support to the Byzantine connection, likely due to concerns over the emergence of a more independent East Frankish, or German-dominated, church in Central Europe.

THE ARRIVAL OF CHRISTIANITY IN GREAT MORAVIA

In 863, the Greek monks Constantine (later called Cyril) and Methodius arrived in Great Moravia with their followers to spread Christianity through teaching, missionary activity, and the translation of religious works into the Slavonic language. Of noble birth and sons of a Greek military commander in Thessaloniki, the brothers Constantine and Methodius would be revered as the "Apostles of the Slavs" for their work among the Moravians.

Collaborating with Constantine in his missionary activities and serving as co-translator for many works was his brother Methodius, a specialist in canon and civil law. Methodius authored the legal code of Great Moravia, the first such code among the Slavic peoples, by combining the local customary law with the advanced system of Byzantine law. The writings and translations of Cyril and Methodius represent the earliest literature to appear in the Slavonic languages.

In order to facilitate the translation of scriptural and liturgical works into Slavonic, Constantine had earlier developed a "Glagolitic" script that utilized Greek ciphers and Christian symbols adapted to the spoken sounds of the Slavonic tongue. This became the basis for the language known as Old Church Slavonic. The later "Cyrillic" alphabet, based upon Byzantine Greek letters, was likely the work of scholars and students of Cyril and Methodius living in the Old Bulgarian kingdom during the early 10th century.

Because the introduction of the vernacular to the liturgy seemed to offer the Orthodox Church and Byzantium a distinct religious, and therefore political, advantage over the Franks and the Roman Catholic faith, Frankish clergy opposed the work of Constantine and Methodius in Great Moravia and sought intervention by the Holy See in Rome in the internal affairs of their eastern neighbor. In 864, Louis the German convinced his Bulgarian allies to wage war on their Great Moravian rival, but when the Byzantine Empire responded by attacking the Bulgarians, the result was not a Frankish victory over Great Moravia, but rather a peace agreement in which Rastislav renewed feudal links to the Franks by accepting the terms of suzerainty from the Frankish ruler.

Rastislav, however, refused to abandon plans to create a separate and independent ecclesiastical province in the Great Moravian kingdom. In 867, Constantine and Methodius, having received an invitation from Pope Nicholas I to defend their work, departed for Rome with the intention of having students from their seminaries consecrated as priests for Great Moravia. The following year, Pope Hadrian II, successor to Nicholas I, welcomed the brothers to Rome and consecrated Methodius as bishop, appointing him to serve as archbishop of a new, independent Slavic diocese in Great Moravia and Pannonia. Two of the pope's bishops ordained the seminarians, who received permission to officiate at church services in their own language. Aware that Constantine and Methodius had already been called upon to offer public defense of the use of vernacular in liturgy, the pope examined and sanctioned the translated versions of the Holy Scriptures and religious texts, allegedly blessing the works on the altar of the Basilica of Santa Maria Maggiore. While in Rome, Constantine took the vows at a Greek monastery and adopted the monastic name Cyril, but died there three months later.

Angered by papal support for Great Moravia, the Franks invaded Rastislav's kingdom in 869, led by Carloman of Bavaria, margrave of the Ostmark and eldest son of Louis the German. When Great Moravia proved unable to mount an effective defense against the Frankish attack, Rastislav's nephew, Svätopluk, Prince of Nitra, formed an alliance with Carloman and assisted in the arrest of his uncle, who was transported to Bavaria in chains. Tortured and blinded under orders from Louis the German, Rastislav was confined in a Bavarian monastery and died shortly thereafter.

Returning from Rome after Rastislav's deposition, Methodius was arrested under order of the Frankish clergy and taken to a synod in Regensberg, where in the presence of Louis the German, he was charged with exercising ecclesiastical authority in a diocese not his own. Methodius suffered two and a half years of imprisonment before papal intervention by Pope John VIII delivered both his freedom and a restoration of his ecclesiastical authority in Great Moravia and Pannonia. Although the use of the vernacular in liturgical affairs remained prohibited beyond its use in preaching sermons, Methodius likely ignored the ban.

Following their victory over Rastislav, Carloman and the Franks attempted to take control of the Moravian lands and place them under Frankish authority. Contrary to this, Svätopluk hoped instead to eliminate the Frankish influence in Great Moravia and create a stronger and more unified empire. Carloman's appointment in 871 of two Frankish noblemen, Engelschalk and Wilhelm, to administer Great Moravia led to Svätopluk's resistance, arrest, and removal to Bavaria to face a charge of violating his oath of loyalty. When Slavomír of Morava led a revolt in response to the brutal policies of the Frankish lords, Svätopluk was released from imprisonment in order to assist Carloman's forces in suppressing the revolt. In the midst of battle, however, Svätopluk changed his allegiance and allied himself with Slavomír in turning back the Franks. With Engelschalk and Wilhelm casualties of the fighting, Svätopluk I (r. 871–894), emerged as the new ruler of Great Moravia in 871.

The following year, the Franks responded to Svätopluk's rise to power by launching an attack led by Saxon and Thuringian troops, who were dispatched by Louis the German. Svätopluk's forces successfully thwarted the Frankish invasion using tactics that, according to chronicle, involved Slavic women ambushing fleeing horsemen. In 874, Svätopluk concluded the Peace of Forchheim which required the Slavic ruler to pay tribute to Louis the German and Franks on an annual basis, although in return for a Frankish promise to abstain from aggressive policies toward Great Moravia.

During the eight years of peace that followed, Svätopluk expanded his territories by moving north into Polish lands, west into the Czech lands and Lusatian Serbia, and south to a common border with Bulgaria. Svätopluk's acquisitions represent the furthest extension of Great Moravia's territory and authority in the region.

In 879, Svätopluk requested papal protection in an effort to counter Frankish interests through better relations between Great Moravia and the Holy See. A year later, and in the wake of accusations of heresy by the Frankish clergy over the use of the Slavonic liturgy, Methodius set off for Rome with a delegation from Great Moravia. While in Rome, Methodius received a promise of papal protection from Pope John VII, who granted Great Moravia and its ruler status equal to all the other states and rulers of Europe. The pope also presented Methodius with the papal bull, *Industriae tuae* (Your Work), which supported the earlier creation of an independent ecclesiastical province in Great Moravia with Methodius serving as archbishop and holding authority over all the priests in Great Moravia. Although the Gospel would still be read in Latin, the pope otherwise approved the use of Old Church Slavonic, which received recognition as a liturgical language alongside Latin, Greek, and Hebrew. Finally, the pope agreed to the creation of a new see in Nitra and consecrated Svätopluk's candidate, the Swabian monk Wiching, as bishop of Nitra.

Svätopluk's support for Wiching and his collaboration with Louis the German contributed to the growing friction between the bishop of Nitra and Methodius. However, and in spite of Methodius's threats to excommunicate Wiching, conditions did not escalate into serious conflict until after the death of Methodius in April 885. Svätopluk had written to the Holy See against Gorazd as Methodius's chosen successor and in support of Wiching, who was appointed administrator of the church in Great Moravia. The pope refused to recognize Gorazd, and when Wiching was certain of papal support, he took the offensive against the disciples of Methodius, exiling them from Great Moravia in 885. Pope Stephen V also banned the use of the vernacular in liturgical matters, thereby delivering a victory to the Frankish and Latin clergy in their efforts to eliminate the Slavonic liturgy in Great Moravia. It was after taking up residence in the Bulgarian empire that the disciples of the Greek brothers founded religious schools and eventually developed the Cyrillic alphabet from Constantine's Glagolitic script. As a result of their work among the Slavs, Cyril and Methodius were venerated as saints as early as the beginning of the 10th century.

THE RISE OF BOHEMIA

In the lands of the Bohemian Slavs, authority over political and military affairs passed to a new elite group, the dukes, who accumulated influence with the assistance of a military retinue, or body of warriors dependent solely upon the duke they served. The assembly of free men chose the duke or prince from among the prominent families emerging in Bohemia. These dukes were generally independent in outlook and actions, although they were also capable of uniting in common cause at significant moments, such as in January 845, when 14 Czech dukes arrived at the court of Louis the German in Regensburg prepared to embrace Christianity through baptism. The term "Duke of the Land" also appeared in early documents in relation to the primary, nonhereditary ruler of the Bohemian lands.

History recognizes Prince Bořivoj (r. 872–889) of the Přemyslid family as the first duke of Bohemia, although little evidence exists regarding the origins of the Přemyslid dynasty. The chronicler Cosmas of Prague provided mythical origins for the the Přemyslids in the tale of Princess Libuše, daughter of Krok and granddaughter of the founding father, Bohemus. According to the tale, Libuše, a prophetess and beloved ruler and lawgiver, came to believe that her people would be happier guided by the stronger hand of a male prince. She thereby prophesized that a delegation would find her future husband, a peasant named Přemysl, plowing his fields by the banks of the Bílina River. Libuše also predicted that the descendents of Přemysl would rule the lands forever and later related her vision of a man building the doorway of his house in the middle of a forest near a mountain called Petřin and close to the river Vltava. At that spot, she told her people, they would build a settlement to be known as Praha (Prague), which would become the "mistress of all Bohemia." Cosmas's tale of Libuše and Přemysl thereby endowed Prague Castle, the seat of power for future dukes and kings, with origins rooted in legend and prophecy. However, it was from a castle on the plateau of Vyšehrad that the Přemyslid line would frequently rule the Bohemian lands until 1306.

When Frankish forces moved into Bohemia in 872 after Svätopluk's accession, Bořivoj and five other Bohemian dukes cooperated in impeding the Frankish advance toward the area of the lower Vltava. Bohemian support for Great Moravia in the conflict with the East Frankish kingdom soon turned to subservience, however, after Svätopluk seized possession of the Bohemian lands in 883 and installed Bořivoj as the dependent ruler of central Bohemia. It is likely that Bořivoj and the other Czech dukes were required to offer formal recognition of obligations to their overlord, Svätopluk, who had granted authority to Bořivoj primarily because Great Moravia could not spare the warriors to rule Bohemia directly. Svätopluk also encouraged Methodius to undertake evangelizing efforts in Bohemia, and it was Methodius who performed the baptisms of Prince Bořivoj and his wife, Ludmila, allegedly at the court of Svätopluk. Bořivoj sponsored the construction of the first church in Bohemia at Levý Hradec, just northwest of Prague, and later had a smaller church consecrated to the Virgin Mary near the Vltava River. In spite of their rúler's enthusiasm for his new faith, however, Bořivoj's subjects failed to turn away from paganism and to accept Christianity in great numbers.

From his fortified hilltop bastion at Levý Hradec, Bořivoj I worked to consolidate Přemyslid power in central Bohemia by weakening paganism and tribal ties, undermining the traditional authority of the assembly, and establishing a hereditary basis for ducal power that would remain in the hands of the Přemyslid dynasty. Creation of a social and economic foundation for the extension of the prince's authority entailed the intensification of serfdom among the peasantry and the collection of compulsory dues from villages. Territories beyond central Bohemia remained in the hands of dukes dependent upon the Přemyslids until 935.

Bořivoj's son Spytihněv I (r. 894–915) contributed to the founding of Prague by erecting a castle of wood and clay along with churches of stone on the fringe of the site known today as Hradčany. From the early 900s, Czech martyrs would be buried on this spot in what eventually became the residence of the ruling member of the Přemyslid dynasty and the focal point of an emerging Czech state in Bohemia. Defended by walled fortifications along a narrow section of hilltop, the castle lay across the Vltava River from Prague's main town situated on the right bank. Settlements developed outside the castle and below the hill in what would later become known as Malá Strana, the "Lesser Quarter" or "Little Side."

In defense of their base of power in Prague, the Přemyslids constructed a circular defensive line of frontier fortifications raised at distances of roughly 20 miles from Prague. These castles served as outposts of Přemyslid administration as well as ecclesiastical centers in imitation of the system employed in Great Moravia. Ultimately, however, Přemyslid efforts at establishing a nascent Czech state would not have been possible without the existence of the first Slavic state in Great Moravia.

In 892 and 893, the East Frankish king Arnulf attacked Great Moravia and convinced the recently arrived Magyar tribes, the Bulgarians, and other southern Slavs to join the military campaign. As a result, Arnulf likely acquired Moravian territory that included the Balaton Principality in what is today western Hungary, although he failed to achieve total conquest of Great Moravia during the struggles of the mid-890s. Arnulf's efforts to divide Bohemia and Moravia proved successful in 895, when Bohemia rejected the overlordship of Great Moravia in favor of closer ties to Arnulf, who accepted Bohemia as his vassal and reached an agreement that rescued Bohemia from potential invasion. In June 895, Czech princes, led by Spytihněv, offered their feudal submission to King Arnulf and swore their allegiance to the Frankish ruler.

THE END OF GREAT MORAVIA

By the time of Svätopluk I's death in 894, the Great Moravian state had already begun to weaken. According to the chronicle of Byzantine emperor Constantine Porphyregenet, Svätopluk had warned his three sons upon his deathbed that their continued unity would be essential to the preservation of Great Moravian territory and power. Failure to heed that advice contributed to the rapid demise of Svätopluk's fragile kingdom as fraternal disputes in the face of external threats and weak internal organization left Great Moravia in a vulnerable state. A product of conquests and composed of fairly autonomous Slavic tribes and principalities, Svätopluk's state lacked the centralized authority or administrative structure needed to hold its disparate pieces together without his personal leadership.

After Svätopluk's eldest son succeeded him as Mojmír II (r. 894–907), a power struggle began between the new king and his younger brother Svätopluk II, ruler of the appanage principality of Nitra. With the support of the East Frankish king Arnulf, Svätopluk II precipitated rebellions against Mojmír II in 895 and then again in 897, when Arnulf sent Frankish troops to help defend Svätopluk II against his brother's attacks.

A new threat then emerged in the form of the Magyar tribes, which moved into the Carpathian Basin after attacks by the nomadic Pechenegs forced the Magyars to move westward from their lands near the Black Sea in 895. According to legend, the chieftains of the seven Magyar tribes elected Árpád as the first prince and bestowed upon him the mission of securing a new homeland for his people. Finding northern Transylvania and the plains between the Danube and the Tisa (*Tisza* to the Magyars) free of the control of the Moravians and Germans, the Magyars crossed the Carpathians in 896 and settled in the region as nomadic warriors, whose skills as mounted cavalry proved formidable in fighting new neighbors unfamiliar with Magyar battlefield tactics. Having already raided the Balaton Principality and other territories, the Magyars settled in Great Moravian territory along the Tisa river in the mid-890s before occupying the poorly defended Pannonian territory and invading Frankish-controlled Transdanubia, a former possession of Great Moravia, in 900–901.

After renewed fighting at the end of the century's final decade, the East Frankish kingdom negotiated a peace settlement with Great Moravia in 901, bringing reconciliation between Mojmír and Svätopluk, cooperation between Bavaria and Great Moravia against the Magyars, and an end to the ongoing conflict between Great Moravia and Bohemia that had begun six years earlier. The Magyar threat, however, remained undiminished for the East Frankish kingdom and Great Moravia, since the treaty of 901 convinced the Magyars to turn against Mojmír II and his empire. Mojmír was forced to confront Magyar encroachments in 902 and 904, receiving support from the Bavarians during the latter conflict.

In 906, Magyar forces attacked Great Moravia, and in a major confrontation possibly along the Slovak section of the Danube, Mojmír II's army suffered a critical defeat that left a number of leading Moravian lords dead on the battlefield. It is possible that Mojmír himself perished during the battle. The Bavarians then moved against the Magyars the following year, but suffered a crushing loss near the future site of Bratislava on August 4, 907. The Bavarian prince fell during the fighting, and his successor negotiated a peace agreement that would secure the border between Bavaria and an emerging Hungarian kingdom for a hundred years.

The defeat at the hands of the Magyars marked the end of Great Moravia as "the first sustained political organization in Central Europe and the first state among the Slavs with its own indigenous dynasty."[2] In the end, the confluence of political and religious conflicts undermined the developing Great Moravian state, which had brought the Slavic peoples of Central Europe into the sphere of Greco-Roman civilization and Roman Catholicism. Frankish expansion and the concurrent spread of religious authority in the hands of the Frankish high clergy proved a very formidable obstacle for the Moravian rulers to overcome, even with the support of a papacy determined to limit the influence and independence of the East Frankish clergy in the region. The arrival of the Magyars helped to hasten the fall. According to historian Francis Dvornik, "The new state succumbed to the German swords and was stamped into the ground by the hoofs of Magyar horses."[3]

Elements of the Great Moravian state would likely have endured in limited form for a short time during the 10th century, although the component territories and conquered lands had already begun to drift away. Moravia eventually came under the influence of a rising Bohemia, and the Slovaks became subjects of the Magyar kingdom of Hungary. The Magyar victory and the fall of Great Moravia led not only to the separation of Slovakia from the Czech lands for a thousand years, but also to the permanent division of the Slavs in Central Europe from those to the south as a result of the Germans, Magyars, and Romanians. Any opportunity for a unified Slavic state or the emergence of strong Slavic political and cultural influence in Central Europe had been lost.

SLOVAKS AND MAGYARS (955–1038)

For the Magyars, a major defeat at Lechfeld in 955 brought an end to westward raids that ranged as far as the borders of modern-day France. Instead, the Magyars built permanent settlements in lands they had already taken along the Danube and west of the Carpathians, including lands inhabited by the Slovaks. With the decline of Great Moravia, the Magyars established their own principalities in formerly Slavic lands as clan chieftains occupied existing fortresses and exercised local authority through their retainers. The central lands of the former Moravian empire, especially the Principality of Nitra, were granted to Árpád as leader with other territories distributed to the various clans. Slav notables who cooperated with the Magyars are assumed to have retained control of their lands, and Slavs engaged in agriculture were allowed to continue under the supervision of the Magyar chieftains.

Along with permanent settlement came a transition from the clan system to a social and administrative organization based on territory and the relative autonomy of the principalities. The Slavic lands provided taxes and dues to Magyar authorities and the emerging Hungarian state, but were otherwise allowed a measure of control over their own affairs. In the territories north of the Danube and in the Tatra valleys, Slovaks developed their own language and culture, although it later became a point of contention among linguists whether Slovak had actually emerged as a unique and separate Slavonic language as early as the 10th and 11th centuries.

The terms "Slovakia" and "Slovak" are problematic in relation to the medieval period, because they are essentially the product of modern nationalism as it emerged after the 18th century. During the ninth century, the Slovak lands were generally known as "Lower Moravia" and, with the imposition of Magyar rule, as "Upper Hungary" or "Upper Land." Because it was considered an appanage principality, "Upper Hungary" traditionally fell under the administration of the heir to the Hungarian throne or to the brother of the king who would manage the territory from the capital city known as Posonium in Latin and Pozsony in Hungarian. The city would later be known as Prešporok (Slovak), Pressburg (German), and, after 1919, Bratislava. Many Hungarian rulers would receive their coronation at the hands of the Slovak archbishop of Nitra.

The consolidation of Magyar lands began under Gejza (r. 945?–977), great grandson of Árpád, who convinced most of the clan chieftains to accept his unified authority as grand prince of the Magyars. Those who opposed Gejza's efforts at a centralization of power were defeated and had their land seized. Gejza also sought to make peace with the Germans by abandoning the Vienna basin and dispatching representatives to the Imperial Diet of the Holy Roman Empire in 973 to petition for bishops who could organize missionary activities in the Magyar lands. Although Gejza was allegedly baptized, he continued to worship pagan gods and viewed the Christianization of his people as a means of gaining foreign support and eliminating the ancestor worship that perpetuated tribal identity through the shamans. Gezja's plans for unifying Hungary under a feudal monarchy in the European style would not come to fruition until the reign of his son, Vajk, the first king of Hungary.

Vajk received a Christian baptism as Istvan, or Stephen, in 985, and according to legend, St. Adalbert of Bohemia performed the baptism. Stephen received the principality of Nitra and established blood ties with the Germans through his marriage to Gisela, sister of Henry, duke of Bavaria. This made Stephen the brother-in-law of the future Holy Roman Emperor, Henry II. Upon the death of his father, Stephen I (r. 997–1038) requested that the pope offer him formal recognition as king of Hungary, and so in 1001, Hungary gained a royal crown and joined the lands of Western Christendom with the full support of Pope Sylvester II and Emperor Otto III.

During Stephen's reign, Christianity made extensive inroads into the Hungarian heartland. Parishes and churches were established and an archbishopric created in Esztergom, a city north of Budapest, where Gejza had spent a great deal of time and from whose castle Stephen chose to rule his kingdom. The Church canonized the first king of Hungary as St. Stephen in 1083.

Stephen sought to create a centralized state in a medieval sense by dividing the lands of the Hungarian kingdom into royal counties (*comitats*) and placing each under the authority of a count (*comes*, or *ispán* in Hungarian) chosen by the king. All residents of the *comitat* owed direct allegiance to the *ispán*, who dispensed justice, managed local fairs, and collected taxes, tolls, and customs fees, of which he would retain one-third of the revenue with the remainder bound for the royal treasury. In Upper Hungary, where some 85 percent of Slovak land was held by the king, the *comitat* of Nitra included the lands of western and central Slovakia. By the early 14th century, the lands of modern-day Slovakia played host to 12 provincial governments that kept the inhabitants under Hungarian authority.

BOHEMIA UNDER THE PŘEMYSLIDS (921–999)

With the disappearance of Great Moravia, the Czechs were relatively free to pursue their own course with an eye on developments in the German lands to the west. When the last Carolingian ruler of the East Frankish kingdom died in 911, the dukes of the individual territories—Bavaria, Saxony, Thuringia, Franconia, and Swabia—engaged in a struggle for power in which the Czechs, ruled by Vrastislav I (r. 915–921) and dependent upon the Bavarians, chose to support Bavaria's Duke Arnulf against the Saxons. In 919, a victor emerged when the duke of Saxony, Henry I, known as Henry the Fowler, was recognized as king by the other dukes and then gained the support of Arnulf two years later.

When Vrastislav died in 921, his son Václav (Latinized as Wenceslas, r. 921–935) was 13 and therefore not of age to rule as duke of Bohemia. This led to the establishment of a regency, with Václav's mother Drahomíra governing in his name. When Drahomíra repudiated Arnulf's declaration of support for Henry I, friction arose between Drahomíra and Václav's grandmother, Ludmila, the wife of Bořivoj I, who had assumed responsibility for raising Václav as a Christian. Drahomíra's efforts to maintain influence over her son led to an open dispute with Ludmila, who sought refuge in Tetín Castle, where Drahomíra convinced two noblemen to arrange her murder. According to legend, Ludmila was strangled to death with her own veil. When Václav reached the age of 18 and began exercising his own authority over the government, he had the remains of his beloved grandmother transferred to Prague, where the clergy with whom she had worked venerated her as St. Ludmila.

Although Václav sought constructive rapport with the lands of Western Christendom, his overly guarded relations with Henry I and Saxony led the East Frankish king to launch a joint invasion of Bohemia alongside Arnulf of Bavaria in 929. Henry's forces defeated the Přemyslid defenders and advanced on Prague, where Václav conceded defeat and agreed to swear an oath of loyalty to Henry I in order to prevent Bohemia from falling under German control. Václav also agreed to provide 500 silver pieces and 120 oxen as tribute to the king. In return, Václav was granted the status of other dukes in Henry the Fowler's realm and received the relics of St. Vitus from Saxony. Václav placed the third-century saint's relics in a rotunda, later St. Vitus Cathedral, that he established in Prague Castle.

As ruler, Václav sought to create a more unified and organized state by reasserting his authority over the dependent dukes who had exploited the circumstances of the regency to their own ends. In the early 10th century, Bohemia remained a collection of sometimes discordant principalities, with varying degrees of allegiance to the Přemyslids and not all of them sharing a conversion to Christianity. Václav's mother Drahomíra had been born into a pagan family and later underwent her conversion to Christianity upon her marriage to Vrastislav. Having been raised in a strong Christian manner by

Ludmila, Václav viewed the faith as an ally in the creation of a more ordered administration of the Bohemian lands.

In opposition to Václav's more cautious strategy, his younger brother Boleslav proposed that the extension of Přemyslid power over the principalities required the use of military force against the dukes and the centralization of authority under a common administration. A more unified and efficient administration would, in turn, possess the resources to raise an army capable of defending Bohemia against attacks from neighboring lands. Václav's disagreement with Boleslav over the proposed strategy intensified their fraternal rivalry, which culminated in Václav's murder at the hands of three of Boleslav's associates in Stará Boleslav during the Feast of Saints Cosmas and Damian on September 28, 935 (or possibly 929).

What had been the politically motivated murder of a ruling duke quickly took on religious overtones as clerics proclaimed the young defender of the faith a martyr who had sacrificed his life for his Christian beliefs and who was the source of reported miracles in the wake of his demise. Tenth-century accounts of his life likened Václav's betrayal at the hands of Boleslav and his accomplices to the treatment of Christ by Judas and the Jews. Václav's remains were interred in the rotunda of St. Vitus, and he received canonization shortly after his death, thereby taking his place alongside St. Ludmila as a patron saint of the Czech lands. The achievements of Václav and Ludmila and their resulting sainthood "gave charisma to the Přemyslids and Christian legitimacy to the Czech state."[4]

The death of Vacláv and the rise of Duke Boleslav I (Boleslav the Cruel, r. 935–972) marked the end of the initial stage of the development of the Czech state under the Přemyslids and the opening of a new era of radical change. It had become apparent by Boleslav's time that the reliance of a hereditary Přemyslid dynasty upon small groups of armed retainers and dukes protective of their semi-independent status had reached its limits as an effective means of exercising authority and collecting taxes and dues. However, Boleslav's goal of creating a "great guard" of several thousand warriors under the control of the Přemyslid ruler required economic resources that could not be produced in central Bohemia alone. Only the mobilization of resources across all of Bohemia would allow for the development of both a "great guard" and a state administration; but this, in turn, necessitated the elimination of semi-independent principalities in favor of an extension of Přemyslid control over the Bohemian lands in their entirety.

To facilitate the creation of a unified state, Boleslav defeated the Bohemian princes, many of whom had cast their lots with Otto I (Otto the Great), successor to Henry the Fowler. Boleslav established a new network of castles with churches, presided over by members of the Duke's retinue, who administered local resources and managed the collection of taxes and dues. The castles, along with the resident clergy and magistrates, allowed for the extension of the Přemyslid ruler's control, the spread of Christianity, and the institution of a more expansive state administration. The introduction of a peace tax, required of all freemen, brought financial support for the princely administration of Bohemian affairs on a more extended and local basis. In return for payment of this first state tax, the freemen received the protection of their prince.

During the first half of the 10th century, there was a shift northward of the major east-west trade route from the Cordoban Caliphate in Western Europe to the eastern commercial center of Kiev and onward to the Khazars on the lower Volga, the Middle East, and China. This lucrative route had been redirected from along the Danube north to Prague so that it passed through Central Europe via Regensburg, Bohemia, Silesia, Moravia, and Cracow. Since the merchants involved in this dynamic commercial network were required to contribute a protection fee of 10 percent of the value of their merchandise, Boleslav sought to increase his access to this lucrative source of revenue by supporting Bohemian exports such as slaves, tin, and furs. Boleslav also introduced the minting of the first denarii in imitation of the Bavarian style of coinage and encouraged local commercial activities by foreign merchants, who included Germans, Italians, and Jews.

With a steady source of revenue from trade and through the collection of taxes, Boleslav was able to fulfill his goal of creating a "great guard," of several thousand armed warriors to protect Přemyslid interests and to assist in the acquisition of new territories needed as a source of further revenue and resources. In 950, 14 years of conflict with Otto I came to an end with Boleslav's renewal of feudal bonds through a sworn oath of fealty to the Saxon ruler. In great part, Boleslav's acceptance of his role as Otto's vassal rested upon a strategy of reserving his military forces for expansionist campaigns against neighboring Silesia, Moravia, and Little Poland. The tribute and spoils of war extracted from new territories were essential to the upkeep of the new military retinue, which could not otherwise draw enough resources from within the existing borders of Bohemia.

On August 10, 955, Boleslav I and his "great guard" joined the German king Otto I in turning back a Magyar invasion at the decisive Battle of Lechfeld, south of Augsburg. Czech horsemen, a thousand strong, participated in the struggle along the Lech River. After their defeat at Lechfeld, the remnants of the Magyar forces moved against Bohemia, where they were defeated by Boleslav's warriors. In 962, Pope John XII presented Otto with the imperial crown in an event that marked the beginning of the medieval Holy Roman Empire. Bohemia became one of the lands of the empire, although the emperor never held land there or exercised direct authority over the Czech lands.

Having protected Moravia against further Magyar incursions, Boleslav then launched campaigns leading to the acquisition of Upper Silesia and Małopolska (Little Poland). Wary of growing Polish power to the north, Boleslav negotiated the marriage of his daughter Dubrawka to Mieszko I, the Piast duke of Poland. Mieszko then converted to Christianity the year after his marriage, thus linking Poland to the Christian West. By the end of Boleslav's reign, Přemyslid conquests had incorporated into the Bohemian kingdom new territories from northern Moravia and regions of Slovakia to Cracow and further east to the Bug River and the border with Kievan Russia.

After Boleslav's death in 972, his son succeeded him as Boleslav II (Boleslav the Pious, r. 972–999). Shortly after his accession as duke of Bohemia, Boleslav II successfully separated Bohemia from the direct authority of the German clergy in Regensburg by convincing the pope to establish the first Bohemian bishopric in Prague. With the support of the Holy Roman Emperor Otto II, the diocese of Prague was placed under the authority of the archbishop of Mainz. Boleslav and his sister Mladá also persuaded the Holy See in Rome to establish the Convent of St. George, the first convent in Bohemia, near the royal palace in 973. Mladá later became the first abbess of the Benedictine convent and St. George's Basilica became the center of the cult of St. Ludmila.

Although the authority of the clergy in Regensburg had been curtailed in regard to Prague, the influence of foreign clerics had not completely disappeared, as evidenced by the appointment of a Saxon, Thietmar (Dětmar), as bishop in Prague. Even in the lesser ranks, the Bohemian clergy would include foreigners for a long period of time, with Germans and other non-Czechs dominating the higher church offices until the middle of the 11th century. This foreign influence, along with the education of Czech clerics abroad, contributed to the further spread of Western Christian civilization into the Czech lands, as well as the development of an indigenous intelligentsia.

In 982, a native Bohemian received consecration as the second bishop of Prague. A member of the Slavník clan of eastern Bohemia, Vojtěch, who took the name Adalbert upon consecration, later completed the conversion of Bohemia to Christianity and supported the appointment of clerics to positions of secular administration, similar to the system that evolved in the German lands. History records that Adalbert (Vojtěch) converted Prince Vajk (later St. Stephen) of the Magyars to the Christian faith, thus contributing to a critical moment in the development of the Hungarian kingdom.

Because of his Benedictine reformism and his frustration over the lingering influence of paganism in his diocese, Vojtěch spent a good deal of time outside of Bohemia, departing for Rome in 988 and then returning four years later when summoned by Boleslav II, who registered frequent complaints regarding the absence of his bishop. While abroad, Vojtěch resided in Rome or in the company of the Otto III, the young Holy Roman Emperor. However, Vojtěch's blood ties to the Slavník clan, the chief rivals of the Přemyslids, left him in a precarious position in Prague. The bishop's departure from Bohemia in 994 likely saved his life, because one year later, Boleslav commanded his retinue to massacre all of Vojtěch's closest family members at the Slavník castle at Libice. Vojtěch remained abroad until his death, undertaking missionary activities to extend Christianity to the Poles and Magyars.

Having converted Hungary and previously expressed the desire to bring Christianity to the Baltic Prussians, Vojtěch embarked upon a mission on behalf of the pope to convert the Prussians in 997. Accompanied by troops dispatched by Poland's Bolesław the Brave, Vojtěch reached the shores of the Baltic, where he suffered a martyr's death at the hands of the Prussians. In 999, he received support for canonization by the Holy Roman Emperor, Otto III, with whom he had become close in earlier times. A year later, Otto undertook a pilgrimage to Vojtěch's tomb in the Polish capital of Gniezno, where Bolesław had brought the relics and erected a cathedral after purchasing the bishop's remains for their weight in gold. With Bolesław's support, Otto was successful in having Vojtěch canonized as St. Adalbert, later the patron saint of Poland. Not until 1039 and Břetislav I's invasion of Poland would Vojtěch's remains be returned to Prague and reburied in Hradčany.

NOTES

1. Cosmas of Prague, *The Chronicle of the Czechs*, trans. and ed. Lisa Wolverton (Washington, DC: Catholic University of America Press, 2009), 35–36.

2. Vladimir Bubrin, "Great Moravia: Slovak History in its Formative Stages" in *Reflections on Slovak History*, ed. Stanislav J. Kirschbaum and Anne R. C. Roman (Toronto: World Slovak Congress, 1982), 5.

3. Francis Dvornik, *The Slavs in European History and Civilization* (New Brunswick, NJ: Rutgers University Press, 1962), 4.

4. Hugh Agnew, *The Czechs and the Lands of the Bohemian Crown* (Stanford, CA: Hoover Institution Press, 2004), 13.

3

The Late Middle Ages

BOHEMIA IN THE 11TH AND 12TH CENTURIES

In the years after Duke Boleslav II of Bohemia's death in 999, a struggle for power ensued as his sons quarreled over the right to rule. This dynastic dispute ushered in a period of chaos and uncertainty marked by Bohemian involvement in a long conflict between the Holy Roman Emperor Henry II and Poland's Bolesław I (Bolesław the Brave). The eldest son of Boleslav II succeeded him as Boleslav III (Boleslav the Red, r. 999–1002) until a revolt by the powerful Vršovci clan drove him to flee to Germany in 1002. Bolesław the Brave replaced Boleslav III with his alcohol-plagued cousin Vladivoj (r. 1002–1003), a Pole who ruled as duke of Bohemia until his death a year later.

In February 1003, Boleslav the Red regained control of Bohemia with the support of Poland's Bolesław I, and as a consequence, Boleslav's brothers and rivals, the Přemyslid princes Jaromír and Oldřich, were expelled from the kingdom. Boleslav III then quickly eroded his own position by ordering the Lenten massacre of the leading Vršovci nobles at Vyšehrad. When the surviving nobles appealed to the Polish ruler for assistance, Bolesław I invited Boleslav the Red to his castle, where he was blinded and then imprisoned for the next three decades until his death in 1037. The Polish ruler, son of the Přemyslid Dubrawka, marched on Prague and installed himself as the duke of Bohemia, ruling as Boleslav IV (r. 1003–1004) for just over a year and taking possession of Moravian and Slovak territories in the process. Bolesław's goal of uniting the territories of Bohemia and Poland under a common ruler met with strong resistance from the German ruler Henry III, who chose instead to support Jaromír and Oldřich, who succeeded Boleslav IV and alternately ruled Bohemia from 1004 to 1034.

Oldřich's son, Břetislav I (r. 1035–1055) attempted to stabilize Bohemia as a regional power by consolidating Bohemian control over Moravia and combining the lands of Poland and Bohemia into a unified state. To this end, Břetislav had invaded Hungary during his father's reign in order to regain the eastern Moravian territories and to prevent expansion of the Magyar kingdom under Stephen I. Ultimately, failure to incorporate the eastern lands into Bohemia would leave the lands of the future Slovak nation separated from the Czech lands and under Hungarian control for centuries

Eight years later, in 1039, Břetislav moved against Little and Great Poland in order to regain territories that had been lost to the Poles. Břetislav took Poznan and launched a successful assault on Gniezno, gaining possession of Adalbert's relics so that the saint's body could be returned to Prague. On his return journey, Duke Břetislav seized parts of Silesia that included the city of Wrocław.

In 1041, however, the German forces of Henry III successfully attacked Bohemia and laid siege to Prague, forcing Břetislav to accept Bohemia's status as a fief of the Holy Roman Empire and to abandon all of his territorial claims save for Moravia, which would remain important to the Czech crown because of its value as a reward granted to members of the ruler's family or members of his retinue. Since the ducal succession still rested upon the election of a new ruler by the Bohemian magnates, Břetislav wanted to circumvent the law of primogeniture and the electoral rights of the nobility by having the senior prince in the Přemyslid lineage possessing sovereignty over the consolidated territories of Bohemia and Moravia while the younger Přemyslids ruled over individual territories in Moravia.

Under Vratislav II (r. 1061–1092), Bohemia gained status and influence with the coronation of Vratislav as the first king of the Czech lands. In recognition of Vratislav's assistance in suppressing a rebellion among the Saxons and in a military campaign against the Italians, Holy Roman Emperor Henry IV granted the Přemyslid duke the title "King of Bohemia and Poland," although only for the duration of his lifetime.

Upon his death, Vratislav was succeeded by his sons Břetislav II (r. 1092–1100) and Vladislav I (r. 1110–1118, 1120–1225), although the reign of Břetislav ended tragically. Břetislav II hoped to institute Břetislav I's plan to eliminate the magnate's role in electing the ruler, but the leading families defended their rights and authority by exploiting conflicts among the Přemyslids. On December 22, 1100, Břetislav II was murdered by his enemies while visiting the hunting lodge of Zbečno outside of Prague.

The reign of Vladislav's younger brother Soběslav I (r. 1125–1140) brought a measure of internal stability and relief from the ongoing dynastic struggles among the Přemyslids, although Soběslav possessed no legitimate claim to the throne. The German king Lothar attempted to impose his own candidate by invading Bohemia in 1126, but Soběslav defeated the Germans on the battlefield at Chlumec. According to a Czech chronicle, one of Soběslav's warriors claimed to have experienced a vision of St. Václav clad in white robes and astride his white horse, joining the Czechs in battle against their old enemy from the west. As a consequence of his defeat by the Czechs, Lothar granted Bohemia to Soběslav as a fief, thus providing imperial support for his position and legitimizing his authority against the Bohemian magnates.[1]

TOWARD A CZECH NATIONAL IDENTITY

It has been proposed that the first stirring of a Czech national identity could be observed in reports of the victory at Chlumec, as well as in contemporary chronicles. The emergence of a feudal nobility out of the duke's retinue and the notable families coincided at the time with the appearance of the Czech language and the veneration of indigenous saints in a manner that linked the defense of the homeland with Christianity and developments in the cultural sphere, both oral and written. The cult of St. Václav succeeded in making the martyred duke a national symbol to be embraced as God's chosen leader of the Czechs and his representative in earthly affairs. As a result, the tale of St. Václav's appearance on the battlefield at Chlumec would have evoked a strong sense of pride in Czech knights fighting alongside their patron saint in defense of the home soil against a centuries-old enemy.

During the middle decades of the 10th century, the first legend of St. Václav (Wenceslas) appeared in Old Slavonic, to be followed during Boleslav II's reign by new legends of St. Václav, initially in Old Slavonic and then in Latin. One traditional legend that endured over the centuries claimed that in a time of great crisis, Václav would return to command a large army of knights who lay sleeping under the mountain of Blaník. The veneration of native patron saints contributed to the national feeling emerging at a time that also witnessed the emergence of Old Czech as a language distinct from Old Church Slavonic. The Slavonic tradition was reflected in the Czech hymn, *"Hospidine, pomiluj ny"* ("Lord, Have Mercy on Us"), written at the turn of the 11th century, but the hymn itself represented the earliest literary work written in the Czech language.

TOWARD A BOHEMIAN KINGDOM (1140–1310)

As successor to Soběslav I, his nephew Vladislav II (r. 1140–1172), benefited from the electoral support of the rising nobility, who viewed him as an instrument of their own interests. However, the new duke faced an early challenge to his authority from fellow Přemyslids and the local dukes of Znojmo, Olomouc, and Brno in Moravia. The Moravians defeated Vladislav at Vysoká and then laid siege to Prague, but with the assistance of the bishop of Olomouc, Vladislav gained an ally in Conrad III, the first Hohenstauffen king of Germany. The hostilities came to a close when Conrad moved into Bohemia in Vladislav's defense, which later allowed Vladislav to regain control of key regions of Moravia.

In 1147, Vladislav accompanied Conrad on the Second Crusade to the Holy Lands, but only traveled as far as Constantinople before returning to his homeland. His alliance with Conrad's nephew and successor, Frederick I Barbarossa, however, produced significant rewards for the Czechs. Crowned king of Germany in 1152 and then Holy Roman Emperor three years later, Frederick Barbarossa became embroiled in an investiture controversy with the pope as well as a struggle for control over the wealthy cities of northern Italy. Vladislav took Frederick's side in the investiture controversy and also led Bohemian troops to Italy, where their military efforts as allies of Frederick were very successful, especially during the siege of Milan. With Frederick's support, Vladislav thus became the second crowned king of Bohemia in 1158, although, as before, the crown could not be passed on to a successor.

With the goal of establishing a hereditary crown, Vladislav voluntarily abdicated in 1172 in order to ensure that his son Bedřich (Frederick) would not be a victim of the elective process of succession. However, Bedřich ruled for only a short period before being deposed in 1173 due to opposition from Frederick Barbarossa and the Bohemian magnates, who rejected the new ruler on the basis of his not having been elected. Seeking greater influence over Bohemian affairs, Frederick Barbarossa proclaimed Moravia an independent margravate and granted the territory as a fief to Conrad Otto of a rival branch of the Přemyslids.

For the Czechs, the next quarter-century would be marked by political instability caused by brief ducal reigns and dynastic struggles that frequently bore traces of imperial interference.

During Conrad Otto I's abbreviated reign as duke of Bohemia (r. 1189–1191), the Czechs received their first written legal code by means of a ducal statute in 1189. However, Conrad Otto failed to achieve his goal of unifying the lands of Bohemia and Moravia, and by 1193, power shifted once again to the main branch of the Přemyslids with the rise of Přemysl Otakar I (1197–1273). Přemysl Otakar succeeded in reestablishing the royal crown in 1198 with his coronation in Mainz, thereby advancing the development of the medieval Czech state to a new level of power and influence. Henceforth, Bohemia would be ruled by kings in place of the traditional dukes.

In 1204, Pope Innocent III offered formal recognition of Přemysl Otakar's monarchy, and the Church introduced another Czech saint with the canonization of St. Procopius, once the abbot of the Slavic monastery at Sázava who, it was claimed, had forcibly expelled German monks in the 11th century. With ongoing friction between popes and emperors coinciding with dynastic struggles within the Holy Roman Empire, Přemysl Otakar might have exploited the weakening of the Holy Roman Emperor to press for the establishment of an independent Bohemian kingdom free of imperial authority. However, the Bohemian king chose instead to remain within the orbit of the empire and to pursue a strategy of offering support to either side in return for concessions.

Otakar's policies succeeded in increasing Bohemia's standing within the Holy Roman Empire when in 1212, the young Hohenstauffen king and future emperor, Frederick II, issued the *Golden Bull of Sicily*, granting hereditary status to the Bohemian crown and declaring that only a king elected or accepted by the Bohemians themselves would receive recognition by the emperor. The bull defined the responsibilities of the Bohemian king within the empire as the ruler of an independent kingdom, but also freed the king from imperial appointment and weakened the electoral power of the magnates by applying the principle of primogeniture to the succession process, as was the case in England and France. The increased prestige of the Bohemian monarch within the empire is reflected in the appointment of the Bohemian king as one of the seven electors of the Holy Roman Empire, possessing shared responsibility for electing the king of the Romans.

Přemysl Otakar I's son and successor, Václav I (r. 1230–1253), pursued constructive relations with the empire through ties to Frederick II and by marrying Kunhuta Štaufská (Kunegunde Hohenstauffen), daughter of Duke Philip of Swabia. However, Václav's designs on Austria became a source of friction as the death of the last Babenberg duke of Austria opened competition for the Austrian territories. In the latter decades of the 10th century, the Babenbergs had been granted a margravate, raised to a duchy in 1156, on the eastern frontier of the German empire. The Babenbergs ruled this duchy known as *Ostarrichi*, or the "eastern realm," from their residence in Vienna on the Danube, and their territory would come to be known as Austria, or in German as *Österreich*.

Early in Václav's reign, Bohemia faced the threat of an Austrian invasion under the Babenberg duke Frederick II (Frederick the Quarrelsome), who planned to expand his holdings at the expense of neighboring Bohemia, Bavaria, and Hungary. When Frederick II died in battle during a border conflict with the Hungarians in 1246, the absence of a male heir ended the Babenberg line and left the ducal succession open to dispute.

In 1248, Václav faced a rebellion led by his own son, Otakar, who held the royal crown briefly from July 1248 to November 1249 before being imprisoned by his father. Having quelled the rebellion, Václav then turned his attention to Austria and invaded the duchy in 1251. Václav released his son Otakar and initially proclaimed him margrave of Moravia before having him elected duke of Austria with the support of the nobility. In order to establish rights of succession, and in spite of a 20-year difference in age between them, Václav arranged Otakar's marriage in 1252 to Margaret of Austria, a female member of the Babenberg line and sister of Duke Frederick II.

Václav's death in September 1253 allowed Otakar to assume the Bohemian throne as Přemysl Otakar II (r. 1253–1278), and from 1253 to 1334, Přemysl Otakar and his successors held the dual titles of king of Bohemia and margrave of Moravia. As ruler of Bohemia, Přemysl Otakar, known as the "King of Gold and Iron," followed an expansionist policy with the goal of creating a kingdom that stretched from the Baltic in the north to the Adriatic in the south. In the mid-1250s, Přemysl Otakar joined German and Polish knights in a crusade against the pagan Prussians and Baltic peoples before attempting to move south into the Alpine territories of Styria, Carinthia, and Carniola. His strategy in acquiring all of the Babenberg lands involved gaining the support of the regional nobles and high clergy, and offering the promise of stable leadership after years of uncertainty and the cession of Styria to the Hungarian king Béla IV. When the Bohemians defeated the Hungarians at Kressenbrunn in 1260, Přemysl Otakar took possession of Styria and then strengthened the peace by ending his union with Margaret and wedding Béla's granddaughter, Kunigunde. In 1269, Přemysl Otakar inherited the territories of Carinthia and Carniola, thereby expanding the borders of his kingdom from Silesia to the Adriatic.

In the wake of another victory over the Hungarians, and with the influence of the emperor at an ebb, Přemysl Otakar stood as the most powerful ruler in the empire and staked a claim to the imperial crown. However, the Bohemian king failed to gain the crown when in 1273 the German princes instead chose Rudolf of Habsburg, who had designs on the territories lost to the Czechs. Přemysl Otakar also faced growing opposition from Austrian nobles whose rebellion in 1276 was matched the following year by a rebellion of Czech nobles, driven to action by their king's efforts to use royal towns and monasteries as a means of extending his power over their lands. After ending the rebellion at home, Přemysl Otakar hoped for a decisive battle against Rudolf and his allies that would allow him to regain the lands recently lost in Austria as a result of Rudolf's support for the rebellion there.

On August 26, 1278, Přemysl Otakar met defeat at Dürnkrut on the Marchfield after undertaking an advance on Vienna. Přemysl Otakar's troops fought well against the forces of Rudolf and his Hungarian allies, but as the Czech knights faced exhaustion after three hours of fighting in cumbersome armor, a surprise attack on their flank by Austrian and Hungarian cavalry routed the Bohemians and forced a retreat. Although successful in turning the battle, the surprise attack violated the chivalric code of warfare, which promoted frontal attacks by opposing knights. Přemysl Otakar, true to his chivalric values, refused to yield and was slain.

With his defeat of the Czechs, Rudolf gained possession of Austria and Styria, opening the way for the ascendance of the Habsburgs in the Danube region. Taking a measured approach in handling Bohemia, Rudolf negotiated with the widowed Kunigunde to allow her child Václav to succeed his father as king of Bohemia, with the stipulation that Otto of Brandenburg would serve as regent and the young heir would be betrothed to one of Rudolf's daughters. Along with the loss of territories gained under Přemysl Otakar II and the appointment of Rudolf's representative to administer Moravia, the Czech monarchy was undermined by a seizure of royal lands at the hands of both the regent and members of the Bohemian nobility.

In 1283, Václav II (r. 1278–1305) returned to Bohemia at age 12 after being confined by Otto in various locations. Members of the highest ranks of the nobility and clergy had pressured Otto to return their ruler and were also successful in convincing Rudolf to pull out of

Moravia. Václav's marriage to Judith of Habsburg influenced his decision to avoid direct confrontation with the Habsburgs and led him to look north to Poland, where Polish nobles in Upper Silesia ceded him Cracow in advance of his being crowned king of Poland in Gniezno in 1300.

By Václav's time, economic changes in Bohemia made it possible to provide the ruler with independent sources of revenue that freed royal power from some of the old restrictions. Royal revenues derived from customs, royal estates, and royal towns and monasteries established by the kings combined with the profits gained from mining and minting, especially after the discovery of silver ore at Jihlava in the 1230s and 1240s and at Kutná Hora in the 1280s. The latter experienced rapid expansion and became home to a royal mint.

In 1298, Václav II arranged his son Václav's engagement to Elizabeth, the daughter of the Hungarian ruler Andrew III. When the Árpád dynasty ended with the death of Andrew in 1301, Václav used his family connection to claim the Hungarian throne, accepting the crown from Hungarian supporters and granting it to his son, who was crowned Ladislas V (László) in August of that same year. For a brief period, the crowns of Bohemia, Poland, and Hungary were united for the first time until opposition from the pope and the emperor, as well as from leading Hungarians, caused Václav II to remove his son from Hungary in 1304.

Václav III (r. 1305–1306) abandoned his claim to the Hungarian crown and ruled briefly as king of Bohemia before being assassinated at Olomouc in advance of a planned expedition to secure the Polish throne. Since Václav's marriage produced no children, the male line of the Přemyslid dynasty ended with Václav's murder.

Subsequent Habsburg efforts to control the Bohemian throne led to the brief reign of Rudolf I (r. 1306–1307), son of Albrecht von Habsburg, who had arranged Rudolf's marriage to Václav's widow, Eliška Rejčka (Elizabeth Richeza) of Poland. In order to outmaneuver a rival claimant in Henry of Carinthia, Albrecht occupied Prague and installed his son on the Bohemian throne, although Rudolf perished from dysentery in 1307 and left no heir, while Albrecht was murdered by his nephew a year later. Henry of Carinthia, brother-in-law of Václav III, was elected to rule as king and held the crown until 1310, when the nobles and high clergy of Bohemia moved against Henry with the cooperation of the new German monarch, Henry IV of Luxemburg. Henry arranged the marriage of his son John to Eliška (Elizabeth) Přemyslovna, sister of Václav III, and negotiated with the Bohemian elites to have John granted the crown. In 1310, John led a campaign against Henry and succeeded in deposing him, taking the crown for himself and establishing a new Bohemian ruling dynasty in the Luxemburgs, who would rule the Czech lands until 1437.

BOHEMIA UNDER THE HOUSE OF LUXEMBURG

Born in Paris and educated in France, John of Luxemburg (Jan Lucemburský, r. 1310–1346) also served as count of Luxemburg and titular king of Poland. John could not speak the language of his Czech subjects, and he spent much of his reign residing in France and Luxemburg or traveling across Europe. He was well versed in French and German affairs, but resented as a foreigner by a Czech nobility gaining confidence in its growing ability to influence political affairs. John affirmed the rights and status of the nobility upon receiving the crown, but his dedication to promoting the House of Luxemburg in continental affairs and his support for the burghers of Prague in their efforts to acquire political influence eventually turned the nobility against him.

As codified in the "imperial diplomas" issued at the beginning of his reign, John's negotiations with the nobles of Bohemia and Moravia secured a compromise that allowed John to reside in Luxemburg and institute special taxes in return for the right of the nobility to manage the Czech lands with little royal interference. John confirmed the traditional rights and privileges of the aristocracy, reaffirmed the elective nature of the monarchy in the case of a dynasty lacking a male heir, and preserved the freedom of the nobility to choose whether or not to take military action on behalf of the king in foreign wars, although the obligation remained to take up arms in defense of the Czech lands in the event of a threat from beyond the borders. The compromise placed some restrictions on royal power, including the demand of the nobility that foreigners not be appointed to high office in place of Czechs. John violated the agreement regarding foreign officials due his insecurities regarding Czech affairs, but resentful members of the Czech nobility forced the king to expel his German courtiers from the realm in 1315.

During his reign, John further weakened his authority as king by granting members of the high nobility possession of royal lands in return for cash payments, a policy that removed numerous royal estates and castles from the king's possession. Further financial resources to support his international activities came from the towns, which received commercial and administrative privileges from the king in return for supplying the royal treasury with a regular source of funds.

In 1316, John's son Charles was born in Prague and given the name Václav, although he would later be confirmed as Charles, the name of his uncle, Charles IV of France, and of the great Charlemagne. Seven years later, he was sent to the royal court of his uncle in France, where he was married to Blanche of Valois. While in Italy in 1333, Charles received a request to return to Bohemia on behalf of Czech nobles seeking to prevent further degradation of royal power. John invested his son as margrave of Moravia, the traditional title for the heir to the throne, in order to establish Charles's legitimacy as administrator of Czech affairs. However, Charles was despondent when he arrived in Bohemia without the companionship of parents or siblings and discovered the sorry physical condition of royal properties. Upon his return to Bohemia, Charles worked to regain lost royal estates and to seek the support of the leading nobles and high clergy. Fluent in French, German, Latin, and Italian, Charles had lost his ability to communicate in Czech, but soon relearned the language.

While on a crusade in Lithuania in 1336, John lost his eyesight due to a medical condition and was henceforth known as John the Blind. In the following year, the outbreak of the Hundred Years' War between France and England caused John to ally himself with France's Philip VI against the English. Charles joined his father in France, but John was slain and Charles wounded in the Battle of Crécy on August 26, 1346.

With the help of Pope Clement VI, his former tutor at the royal court of France, Charles outmaneuvered the emperor Louis IV and was elected king of the Romans by five of the seven electors in July 1346. The possibility of conflict was averted when Louis died in 1347 and Charles married the emperor's daughter Anna after the passing of his wife, Blanche of Valois. Having succeeded his father after his death at Crécy, Charles received the Bohemian crown in September 1347 and, through his actions and policies, opened the way to a golden age of Czech history.

THE GOLDEN AGE OF CHARLES IV (1347–1378)

As king of Bohemia, Charles IV (Karel IV, r. 1347–1378) proved to be a dedicated, intelligent, and pragmatic ruler. Charles actively embraced the Slavic heritage of the Czech lands and proclaimed that through maternal descent, he belonged to the ancient line of Přemyslid rulers. On occasion, Charles also referred to himself as the heir to Great Moravia.

Charles planned his coronation ceremonies to reinforce links between the Luxemburg royal line and the traditions preserved by the Přemyslid dynasty, including a coronation-eve procession on foot from Prague Castle to Vyšehrad, which had not been the seat of royal power since the reign of Soběslav I in the 12th century. Held in September 1347, the coronation included the singing of *"Hospodine, pomiluj ny"* and the presentation of a modified crown, altered according to Charles's wishes to reflect the influences of the Přemyslid and French royal crowns and dedicated to St. Václav, patron saint of Bohemia.

In 1349, Charles received the crown as king of the Romans a second time, but with all seven electors now in attendance. Six years later, in 1355, Charles traveled to Rome to receive the imperial crown as Holy Roman Emperor Charles IV, or Karl IV in German. The Italian scholar and humanist Francesco Petrarca implored that Charles create a new Roman Empire out of his territories, but Charles chose instead to focus on German and Bohemian affairs north of the Alps. Upon his coronation, Charles set out to achieve two immediate goals: consolidating support by issuing privileges to his allies, and defining the role of Bohemia in the Holy Roman Empire, of which Prague was now the imperial capital. Charles issued his *Golden Bull* in Nuremburg the following year, creating a legal basis for an independent and self-governing kingdom of Bohemia within the empire, instituting a majority vote for imperial election, and confirming the permanent and preeminent status of the king of Bohemia as one of the seven princes and bishops serving as electors. The dukes and kings of Bohemia had already held the title of imperial cupbearer since the early 12th century.

Inspired by Charles's own multilingualism, the 1356 charter required that the sons of the prince electors be instructed in German, Italian, and Czech from the age of seven. Under Charles IV, Latin was used extensively at the royal court, German was fairly common, and Czech entered the administrative and legal realm with the first extent official document in Czech dating to 1370. The cosmopolitan nature of the court is reflected in the presence of French and Italian as languages of culture and, in the latter case, of emerging humanism. Leading Italian humanists such as Petrarca and Cola di Rienzo made their way to Prague as acquaintances of Charles IV.

Charles IV promoted the use of the Czech language, in part because of his strong interest in his Slavic heritage. However, Charles also understood the significance of the Czech tongue in defining the relationship between the nobility and the monarch and in the association of the nobles with the kingdom's political and administrative institutions. By encouraging the use of Czech among the languages employed at the royal court, Charles sought to strengthen his dynastic authority with the support of nobles who previously viewed the Czech language within the context of their opposition to increases in monarchical power at the expense of the native aristocracy.

The institution of primogeniture under the last rulers had eliminated the role of the nobility in electing the king, but John of Luxemburg had guaranteed the presence, and therefore influence, of nobles in high office and in the execution of judicial matters. In the 1350s, Charles proposed the codification of laws designed to strengthen the powers of the monarchy, but opposition from the nobility led to the rescinding of the *Maiestas Carolina* in 1355. Political relations remained much as they had been, with nobles retaining high offices in the royal court, although Charles IV's policy was to counterbalance their role in state and royal affairs by selecting educated clergymen as administrators and members of the prosperous burgher class as chamberlains and masters of the mint.

During the reign of Charles IV, the medieval kingdom of Bohemia achieved its highest level of international influence and prosperity. As imperial capital, Prague emerged as a center of European culture, with approximately 40,000 inhabitants benefiting from the emperor's strong interest in commerce and diplomacy. Bohemia had escaped the worst ravages of the Black Death from 1347 to 1350, and factors such as the relative absence of warfare would lead to an increase in population by the end of the century. However, the spread of plague caused outbreaks along trade routes and disruptions in commerce with the rest of Europe. When times were stable and prosperous, however, Bohemia's international trade relied upon exports of raw materials, silver, and coins in return for wine, spices, salt, fruit, fish, and luxury goods for the social and clerical elites.

Prague's status as site of the imperial residence made the city the beneficiary of Charles's interests in architecture, urban development, and cultural affairs. Shortly after Charles convinced Pope Clement VI to raise the Prague bishopric to an archbishopric in 1344, construction began on a new cathedral dedicated to St. Vitus and located on the grounds of Prague Castle. The area around Prague Castle underwent further development as the castle town of Hradčany.

In order to renovate the castle and the cathedral in the prevailing Gothic style, Charles employed eminent foreign masters such as the French architect Matthias of Arras, brought to Prague from Avignon, and the German master mason Peter Parler of Gmund. Charles wanted to honor the kingdom's patron saint with one of the finest chapels in the world, and the result was the highly ornate Chapel of St. Václav, built over the saint's resting place in St. Vitus Cathedral and decorated with wall paintings and gemstones.

Peter Parler assumed responsibility for completing the cathedral after the death of Matthias of Arras in 1352 and later served as builder of the Church of Our Lady Before Týn in the Old Town (Staré Město) and a long stone bridge with Gothic towers that spanned the Vltava. Later named the Charles Bridge (Karlův Most), the latter structure linked the Old Town with Malá Strana, the "Lesser Quarter" at the base of Prague Castle. Parler was also the primary designer of the New Town (Nové Město), founded in 1348 as a result of creative urban planning that produced a quarter of broad streets and squares in an area outside the city walls and to the south and east of the central Old Town. Attractive to merchants and artisans alike, the New Town became a prosperous part of Prague and developed its own powerful urban patriciate.

Other major building projects included the renovation of Vyšehrad and the enclosure of all the Prague towns by defensive walls with seven gates and the bridge across the Vltava to link the town's quarters. Charles commissioned the construction of Karlštejn Castle on a hilltop some 22 miles outside of Prague and became personally involved in overseeing construction and the decoration of interior spaces. Completed with the consecration of the Chapel of the Holy Cross in 1365, Karlštejn served as repository for holy relics and the Czech and imperial coronation jewels.

As a proponent of education and culture, Charles IV realized a dream in 1348 with the opening of a university in Prague, which in modern times would be known as Charles University in honor of its royal patron. Influenced by leading universities such as Bologna in Italy and the Sorbonne in Paris, the university in Prague drew students from across Europe and became a highly influential center for intellectual affairs in Central Europe. Supported financially by the Bohemian state and presided over by the archbishop of Prague as chancellor, the university featured the image of St. Václav on its seal and hosted faculties similar to those of the leading European institutions of higher learning. The Prague university became instrumental in overseeing those schools in many of the royal towns that were not monastic or administered by the church.

In the cultural sphere, Charles encouraged Czechs to look to Italy and to France for inspiration as students departed Bohemia to study at Bologna, Paris, and the English universities at Oxford and Cambridge. Establishing direct connections to the Italian humanists and to France also meant that cultural and intellectual affairs were no longer filtered through the German lands before reaching Prague. The court culture of the last Přemyslid had rivaled those of England,

France, and Naples and the tradition continued under Charles IV. Members of the court supported the arts by commissioning works from painters, illuminators, and sculptors, with portraits holding a special appeal for the wealthy and powerful. Italian artists and scholars at the university in Prague introduced courtiers to the humanist tradition emerging in the wealthy city-states of Italy during the early stages of the Renaissance and helped to make Prague the locus of early humanism in Central Europe.

As ruler of Bohemia, Charles IV's diplomatic maneuverings were dedicated to creating a kingdom that possessed territory commensurate with the realm's status within the empire. Additionally, Charles hoped to extend his kingdom across Central Europe to the Rhine, Luxemburg, and the borders of France. Charles chose to wield Bohemian influence in European affairs less through conflict and warfare than through diplomacy and opportunities created through marriage. To this end, Charles opened negotiations with the Habsburgs and the Polish and Hungarian kings to secure the borders of his territories and eliminate potential sources of friction.

After the death of Blanche of Valois in 1348, Charles entered into marriage three additional times, with each marital connection bringing territorial gains. Through the family connections of his third wife, Anna of Świdnica, the heir to Duke Henry II, Charles gained access to the last remaining independent duchy in Silesia. This marriage also produced a child, Václav, which allowed Charles to alter plans that would have raised his brother Jan Jindřich (John Henry), Margrave of Moravia, to the throne. After Anna's passing, Charles married Elizabeth of Pomerania, granddaughter of the Polish king Casimir and potentially heir to the throne of Poland. Upon Casimir's death, however, the Polish throne passed to the king of Hungary, Louis the Great, who at that time possessed no heirs of his own.

Recognizing that the rise of the House of Luxemburg was altering European relations in ways that could generate opposition and conflict, Charles IV sought an alliance with the papacy that would require the pope to accept Charles's diplomatic policies. The crisis over the Avignon papacy offered the Bohemian ruler an opportunity to gain papal support by promoting the return of the papal court to Rome, where the pope would be free of direct French influence and obliged to accept protection from Charles IV. This period, known as the "Babylonian Captivity," had begun in 1305 with the election of a French pope, Clement V, and his decision to reside in Avignon rather than travel to Rome.

In 1370, Charles purchased the imperial territory of Lower Lusatia from the Wittelsbach Elector, Margrave Otto V of Brandenburg, incorporating the region into the Bohemian crown lands alongside Upper Lusatia, which had been acquired by his father. By 1373, Otto appeared to be retreating from a negotiated agreement that would have established Charles IV's sons as heirs to the margravate of Brandenburg. However, Charles rejected a military solution in favor of purchasing Brandenburg for his sons, Zikmund (Sigismund) and Jan (John), and granting the territory special status as a possession of the Bohemian kingdom. The acquisition of Brandenburg gained Charles the city of Berlin, as well as the vote of a second imperial elector, the Margrave of Brandenburg.

In order to clarify the Bohemian and imperial successions and to organize the distribution of royal possessions among his sons, Charles had his eldest son crowned king of Bohemia in 1363 while Václav was only two years of age. Fourteen years later, Charles arranged Václav's election as king of Rome with Bohemia and territories in Germany, Silesia, and the Lusatias as his inheritance and with royal authority over the Bohemian crown lands. Sigismund, the second son, received the majority of territory in Brandenburg, and the third son, Jan, received Upper Lusatia and a section of Brandenburg. Jošt and Prokop, the sons of Jan Jindřich, would rule over Moravia as holders of fiefs under the Bohemian crown.

Charles IV died in Prague in November 1378 and was interred there as the "Father of the Homeland," a title he received upon his passing. As a result of his policies and territorial expansion, the House of Luxemburg stood as the most powerful dynasty in Europe at the end of the 14th century, with dynastic holdings that stretched from the Baltic to the Adriatic and from Hungary to the borders of France. Following the death of Charles IV, however, the reign of his son Václav IV (r. 1378–1419) as king of Bohemia and Holy Roman Emperor was far different from the golden age over which his father had presided.

WOMEN AND CULTURE IN BOHEMIA

Due in great part to the predominance of religious writing produced in monasteries and by educated clerics, the medieval centuries were not a fertile era for women who desired to write. There were certainly exceptions, such as Agnes of Prague (St. Agnes), who as abbess of the Franciscan convent of the Poor Clares corresponded in Latin with popes and with Clare of Assisi in the 13th century. However, literature for women most likely entailed lay and clerical patronage of male writers producing works for female readers.

The tradition of artistic and literary patronage by women produced several notable and influential contributors by the 15th century. Perhaps the most significant female patron of the medieval period was Kunigunde of Bohemia (1265–1321). Daughter of Přemysl Otakar II and Queen Kunigunde, she became abbess of the Convent of St. George at Prague, offering patronage to writers and illustrators while establishing an extensive collection of books in her library.

Eliška (Elizabeth) Rejčka (1288–1335), widow of the penultimate Přemyslid ruler Václav II, established her own court at Brno in Moravia during the reign of John of Luxemburg. In addition to creating a court superior to that of the Luxemburgs in Prague, Eliška opened a scriptorium and commissioned magnificent illuminated manuscripts prepared for the convent of Cistercian nuns, which she sponsored.

The Bohemia of Charles IV was characterized by a dynamic and cosmopolitan society in which literature, architecture, and the arts flourished due to the open support of the royal court and the nobility. In this milieu, women of the upper strata gained recognition and respect through their sponsorship of the arts. However, the religious struggles of the 15th and 16th centuries would eliminate the favorable social and cultural environment and replace it with one in which women were expected to return to traditional roles in regard to faith and family.[2]

THE LUXEMBURGS AFTER CHARLES IV

Ascending the throne at age 17, Václav displayed little of his father's political acumen and chose not to continue the policy of using the clergy to counterbalance the political influence of the nobility. As a result, royal power declined as the king became less successful in fending off challenges and preserving order. In 1393, Václav's disputes with the archbishop of Prague over the king's plans for a new bishopric in western Bohemia led to the martyrdom of the archbishop's general vicar, Jan of Pomuk, who was thrown from a stone bridge into the Vltava under orders from the king. In 1792, the Church canonized the murdered vicar as St. John of Nepomuk.

The arrival of plague in 1380 reduced Bohemia's population by 15 percent and caused major disruptions in silver mining and trade, as well as lost income for landowners who were forced to negotiate new contractual obligations that were more beneficial to the remaining peasants. Declining conditions inspired widespread criticism of social and political institutions, as well as dissatisfaction with a Church divided by charges of corruption, the Babylonian Captivity, and a Great Schism that led to the election of first two, and later three, rival popes.

In the late 14th century, Europe witnessed a growing antagonism toward Jews as a result of religious intolerance, resentment over prosperity, and accusations of ritual murders and Jewish responsibility for the outbreak of the Black Death. Bohemian pogroms sometimes offered opportunities for burghers and nobles to eliminate evidence of debt or other financial obligations. In Prague, Charles IV tolerated attacks on the Jewish community in order to placate members of the nobility who were angry over his efforts to increase royal power through the *Maiestas Carolina*. During the reign of Václav IV, members of the Prague clergy enflamed anti-Semitic sentiments by spreading accusations of Jewish blasphemy and desecration of the host. On April 18, 1389, anger and discontent erupted into an open pogrom against the Jewish community in Prague as buildings in the ghetto were set ablaze, hundreds murdered, and many women and children forcibly baptized into the Christian faith.

By the close of Václav IV's reign, Bohemia had become a densely populated country with nearly two million inhabitants and over a hundred large towns complementing several times more urban communities on a smaller scale. Little remained of the forests that had covered the earliest areas of settlement as population growth and colonization created greater demand for usable land. Some 30–40 percent of that land belonged to the Church, which had created its own kingdom-wide system of over 2,084 parishes in addition to numerous monasteries and convents.

At the highest level, however, mounting problems and accusations of incompetence caused Václav IV to be taken prisoner by nobles in 1394 and then by his brother Sigismund in 1402, although negotiations brought an end to conflict within the Luxemburg family. Václav fared little better in his role as king of the Romans as he was deposed in 1400 and confronted with the election of an antiking. In 1410, Václav abandoned his claims to the Roman crown and passed it to his cousin Jošt of Moravia, whose short reign ended with his death in 1411. The crown then passed to Václav's brother Sigismund, who had already ascended to the throne of Hungary in 1387. Upon Václav's death in 1419, Sigismund became the titular king of Bohemia, but 17 years of civil strife and religious warfare would pass before the Czechs accepted him as king, thereby uniting the crowns of Bohemia and Hungary in 1436.

HUNGARY AND THE SLOVAKS AFTER STEPHEN I (1038–1437)

Hungarian affairs had grown more complicated after the death of St. Stephen in 1038 because the Árpád dynasty had not defined set rules for royal succession. Dynastic struggles arose immediately, and German attempts to influence the Hungarian succession led to military engagements during the decades after Stephen's demise. The potential for ongoing internal disputes and foreign intervention inspired the institution of a system in which the Royal Council approved the new ruler. In 1077, the nobles exercised this right and selected Ladislas I (László, r. 1077–1095), bypassing the primary claimant to the throne in the process.

Ladislas continued the consolidation of the Hungarian state begun under his predecessors and advanced the development of the legal system by sponsoring the codification of criminal law and the introduction of specific and severe penalties for criminal behavior. A new bishopric in Nitra became the first located entirely in Slovak territory, while a second in Jager (Eger) served the eastern region of Slovakia. Subjugation of the Croatian kingdom gained Ladislas the crown of Croatia and allowed him to expand Hungarian territory by uniting Croatia and Hungary in a personal union. In recognition of his achievements and strong faith, the Roman Catholic Church canonized Ladislas as a saint in 1192.

By the reign of Béla III (r. 1173–1196), the medieval monarchy in Hungary had reached a level of development that allowed the king to generate revenues that were the equal of the kings of France and England. The strong influence of the nobility remained, however, and in 1222, Andrew II (r. 1205–1235) was forced to issue the *Golden Bull*, a document similar in spirit and content to England's Magna Carta of 1215. Angered by the king's transference of crown lands to the great magnates who supported him, the lesser nobles forced the king to make peace by accepting a charter of feudal rights. The *Golden Bull* required the Hungarian monarch to free the nobility and clergy from all forms of taxation, make royal ministers responsible to the diet, and accept the right of the nobles and clerics to resist royal violations of the law and constitution without facing the charge of high treason. The charter placed limits on royal power and established equality of rights and privileges for all of the nobility.

During the reign of Andrew II's son, Béla IV (r. 1235–1270), disaster struck the Árpád kingdom with the arrival of the Mongols in early 1241. When Béla failed to defend the eastern borders of his kingdom, these nomadic warriors struck at towns and villages across Hungary, defeating Béla's forces in a battle at Muhi in April 1241. Mongol cavalry attacks occurred in the southwest region of Slovakia and in areas of the eastern lowlands, although after the death of Ögedei Khan in the spring of 1242, the Mongols withdrew homeward, ending the invasion. In connection with plague and food shortages, the Mongol incursions cost Hungary 20–40 percent of its population and left many population centers devastated.

In spite of ongoing economic progress, the power of the Hungarian monarchy had been seriously weakened due to Béla IV's failure to defend the kingdom. Dynastic crises ensued, and in 1272, the throne passed to Ladislas IV, who gained the crown at age 10 and was assassinated in 1290. The prime beneficiaries of the decline in monarchical power were the members of the feudal elites, who began to exercise their own influence in a kingdom where the great nobles and high clergy continued to possess great authority and the lesser nobility held sway in regional affairs through their administration of the *comitats*. As a result, this period witnessed the rise of half a dozen great noble families, including the Caks of Trenčín, who exploited uncertain political conditions for their own gain.

When Andrew III (r. 1290–1301) died in 1301, the male line of the Árpád dynasty died with him and royal power had already fallen victim to great magnates such as Matthew Cak (Mátyás Csák in Hungarian, Matúš Čák in Slovak), who controlled large areas of the kingdom. Upon Andrew's death, some nobles chose to offer the throne to the Přemyslids of Bohemia, although the French Angevin family claimed the Hungarian crown through the earlier marriage of Stephen V's daughter Maria to Charles II of Anjou. Matthew Cak chose to support the Bohemian Václav, who ruled in Hungary as Ladislas V from 1301 to 1305, but then decided to abdicate the Hungarian throne and rule Bohemia as Václav III upon his father's death.

When Otto of Bavaria made a claim to rule Hungary, Cak, who had acquired land and influence under Ladislas, supported the Angevin claimant Charles Robert instead. In an effort to restore order, the magnates agreed to offer Charles Robert the throne, although some of the most powerful nobles had long opposed the Angevin's candidacy. Shortly after Charles Robert received the crown as Charles I (r. 1308–1342), Cak was appointed one of three palatines in the kingdom with authority over Upper Hungary, or a territory equivalent to modern-day Slovakia.

By the summer of 1311, Matthew Cak turned against the king and opened a siege of his capital at Buda. Charles successfully defended his capital and, one year later, defeated the combined forces of Cak and his new allies, the powerful Amadei family of eastern Slovakia, in a battle at Rozhanovce (Rozgony). Cak ceased military operations against the king, although he gained an ally in Frederick III of Austria and mounted attacks on Moravia in 1314. Matthew Cak continued to rule Slovakia as self-proclaimed "Lord of the Váh and the Tatras" from his castle in Trenčín; but with no successor upon Cak's death in 1321, his lands became the possession of the king, Charles Robert.

Because of Matthew Cak's authority over Upper Hungary and his employment of many Slovak troops and administrators, some Slovak historians have promoted Cak as a Slovak national hero, pointing to the celebration of "Matias Trenciansky," or Matthew of Trenčín, in Slovak oral culture. For others, however, Cak was simply a Magyar nobleman who utilized available resources and alliances with leading Slovak families in support of his own feudal authority and political agenda.

During the 14th and 15th centuries, the absence of major wars and major epidemics allowed the Kingdom of Hungary to enjoy an age of peace and economic growth accompanied by an increase in population and the growth of towns. This was true of the new mining settlements in Slovakia, which provided the realm with silver, copper, iron, and gold from some of the most productive mines in Europe. The importance of the mines and the need for skilled workers led the king to invite German colonists to settle in the mining towns in return for special legal and economic privileges within the feudal system.

The period of economic progress inspired commerce in Upper Hungary and made the Slovak lands one of the wealthiest regions of Hungary. Trade links extended from Bratislava to other parts of Europe, while Košice, Levoča, Trnava, Žilina, Bardejov, and Prešov also served as hubs of international commerce that brought in salt, crafts, and luxury goods in return for exports such as wine, horses, livestock, and raw materials.

Ethnic Slovaks began to develop a sense of identity as they lived alongside Germans and Magyars, but in the towns, the disproportional representation of Germans on town councils led to friction with Slovak burghers demanding a fair and equal voice in urban affairs. During the reign of Louis I (r. 1342–1382), efforts to ease growing ethnic tensions led the king to issue the royal document, *Privilegium pro Slavis* (Privileges for the Slovaks, 1381), which granted equal status to Slovaks and Germans on the city council of Žilina and declared that the position of mayor would alternate between the two ethnic groups. Bilingualism would also become the official policy in a number of Slovak towns and cities.

After the relative calm of Louis I's reign, however, political instability arose as three rulers occupied the Hungarian throne in only five years. The last of these was Sigismund of Luxemburg (r. 1387–1437), son of the Bohemian king Charles IV and husband of Louis I's daughter, Mary of Anjou, whom he had married after she succeeded her father as Hungary's ruler. Sigismund conspired to gain the throne for himself in 1387, but he faced strong opposition from the Hungarian nobility, from the Jagiellon dynasty of Poland, and from Louis I's nephew, Charles of Durazzo and Naples. Years of struggle ensued before Sigismund could assume full control of the kingdom.

NOTES

1. For a comprehensive analysis of Czech society and the nature of political life in Bohemia during the Late Middle Ages, see Lisa Wolverton, *Hastening toward Prague: Power and Society in the Medieval Czech Lands* (Philadelphia: University of Pennsylvania Press, 2001).

2. See John Klassen, *Warring Maidens, Captive Wives, and Hussite Queens: Women and Men at War and at Peace in Fifteenth Century Bohemia* (New York: Columbia University Press, 1999), and Alfred Thomas, *Anne's Bohemia: Czech Literature and Society, 1310–1420* (Minneapolis: University of Minnesota Press, 1998).

4

Religious Controversies and Military Conflicts (1400s–1700s)

By the end of the 12th century, religious reform began to spread in Bohemia as elsewhere in Europe. The appearance of heresy in the Czech lands may have coincided with the arrival of Waldensians among the German colonists who settled in Bohemia at the time. The Waldensians were followers of Peter Valdes, a merchant and wandering preacher from Lyons who aroused the ire of Church officials by preaching voluntary poverty and the translation of the Bible into the languages of the people.

Due to the ongoing problems associated with the "Babylonian Captivity," as well as the perception of corruption at all levels of the Church, support for religious reform intensified in Bohemia. During the reign of Charles IV, members of the Bohemian clergy joined mendicant preachers and religious writers in calling for reform, a call that received the tacit support of the emperor as he invited radical preachers to visit Prague and offered encouragement to Arnošt of Pardubice, the reformist archbishop of Prague. Charles, however, engaged as many rulers did in the practice of simony, or purchase of Church offices, which became a target of the reformers due to the neglect and abuses engendered by royal or noble interference in ecclesiastical administration. Other issues of importance to Charles and the reformers included the sale of indulgences and the growing financial burden imposed by popes during the Babylonian Captivity and in the wake of the schism of 1378, which ushered in an era of two and occasionally three rival popes at a time.

In an effort to save the Church through reform, Charles IV sought to eradicate corrupt practices by encouraging evangelical preaching in urban and rural communities. Among the most influential of the reformist preachers invited to the imperial capital was Konrad Waldhauser of Austria, an Augustinian whose powerful sermons in German resonated in the Týn Cathedral on Prague's Old Town Square. Waldhauser denounced the immorality of many clerics and railed against the practices of simony and fraud in regard to the treatment of holy relics.

A second commanding figure among the preachers supported by the emperor was the former Dominican, Jan Milíč of Kroměříž. The incendiary Moravian embraced poverty and preached the Gospel as successor to Waldhauser, in addition to warning his congregation of the imminent arrival of the Apocalypse and, in 1369, accusing Charles IV of being analogous to the Antichrist. Milíč also challenged the social hierarchy by preaching a message of egalitarianism that granted everyone from the monarch to the peasant equal status in the eyes of God.

The translation of the Bible into the Czech language proved a boon to reformers during the 1370s and 1380s, as did the founding in 1391 of the Bethlehem Chapel in Prague by Czech reform preachers. The Bethlehem Chapel offered a large space that could accommodate an audience of 3,000 clergy and laypersons listening to sermons delivered in Czech rather than Latin.

At the end of the 14th century, the writings of the English reformer and Oxford professor John Wyclif arrived in Bohemia and helped transform the nature of religious debates. Before his death in 1384, Wyclif had been declared a heretic by Church authorities for challenging the authority of Church officials and the clergy, criticizing the wealth of the Church, and declaring the Bible to be the true source of divine law, as opposed to having God's word interpreted by the pope and high Church officials. Wyclif promoted the use of the vernacular in religious services and the translation of the Bible into the language spoken by the common people. To that end, Wyclif completed a translation of the Bible into English in 1382. Wyclif's followers, calling themselves Lollards, demanded the use of religious texts in English and challenged what they believed to be social and political injustices.

When Wyclif's works appeared in Prague, they inspired divisive discussion and debate at a Prague university separated into four student nations: Bohemian, Polish, Bavarian, and Saxon. Whereas the masters of the Bohemian nation were primarily Czech, the masters of the other nations were generally German. In 1403, the university proposed a vote on whether the institution should issue a condemnation of Wyclif's writings for containing serious theological errors. When the three foreign nations voted in favor of condemnation and in opposition to the Czechs, religious and national passions within the university began to intensify.

The growing conflict at the university in Prague coincided with Václav IV's efforts to have the Roman Catholic Church convene a special conference at Pisa to discuss the issue of rival popes. Václav hoped to gain support for his bid to be crowned king of Rome, but the three foreign nations at university voted against the proposal for a council at Pisa. In 1409, Václav responded by issuing the Decree of Kutná Hora, which reduced the three foreign nations to a single collective vote while awarding three votes to the Czech nation. Although one consequence of this decree was the departure of foreign masters and students to other universities in Erfurt, Leipzig, and elsewhere, another was the conversion of Prague university into a critical center of religious reform in Bohemia.

JAN HUS

In the wake of the changes instituted by the Decree of Kutná Hora, a leading spokesman for the Czech student nation at the university in Prague, Jan Hus (c. 1370–1415), accepted the position of rector to oversee the institution's academic affairs. Born into the peasantry of South Bohemia, Hus had studied at the university before assuming teaching duties and becoming a popular lecturer there. He was ordained a priest, but the influence of 14th-century theologians turned him in the direction of reform and an association with Bethlehem Chapel, where he began preaching alongside other reformers in 1402. Hus became confessor to Queen Sophia, who visited the chapel to hear him preach.

As a reformer, Hus was attracted to the writings of Wyclif, especially in his rejection of the Church hierarchy and his belief that a priesthood

was unnecessary if individuals maintained direct spiritual connections with Christ as the true head of the Church. Salvation would be
achieved not through rituals and ecclesiastical decrees, but through
strict adherence to the Bible and the teachings of Christ. This would,
in turn, necessitate the availability of the Bible and sacred texts in
Czech, the language of the Bohemian faithful.

Although Hus counted King Václav and Queen Sophia among his
supporters, his criticism of the Church brought him into conflict with
Archbishop Zbyněk Zajíc of Prague, who issued a ban on preaching
in unapproved locations and gained the support of Pope Gregory XII
against Hus and the king. In 1410, the archbishop ordered Wyclif's
writings burned in public and then had Hus excommunicated for
his defense of Wyclif's ideas and his refusal to cease his activities at
Bethlehem Chapel. Hus defiantly organized a protest at the university
against the archbishop's actions and issued an appeal to the Vatican,
but the Papal Curia declared Hus a heretic and reinforced the decree
of excommunication.

Since Václav IV received financial benefits from the sale of indulgences in Bohemia, he had allowed representatives of Pope John XXIII to
engage in the practice as a means of collecting money for the pope's
military activities. Hus's criticism of the sale of indulgences therefore
worked against the king's interests, especially after crowds of students
demonstrated in Prague against indulgences and in support of Hus
in July 1412. The students were led by Master Jeroným (Jerome) of
Prague, a friend of Jan Hus and the man who is alleged to have
brought Wyclif's writings to the Czech lands after visiting the England
of Richard II and Anne of Bohemia.

When the king ordered the execution of three journeymen in retaliation for their speaking out in church against the royal policy on indulgences, Hus's movement gained its first martyrs. The Schism-era
antipope John XXIII threatened Prague with interdiction, which would
have denied sacraments to the faithful and condemned their eternal
souls. In October 1412, Hus departed the capital for the safety of South
Bohemia, where he could continue to preach and to write under the
protection of the local nobility. During this period, Hus made important
contributions to the development of the modern Czech language by
standardizing spelling and introducing diacritical marks to create
clearer links between letters and spoken sounds.

South Bohemia soon became the heartland of a Hussite movement,
which spread to royal towns across the kingdom as the followers of
Hus established key centers in Plzeň, Hradec Králové, and Žatec. Hus's
supporters gained control of the town halls in roughly one-third of the

towns, allowing Hussite reformers to wield administrative influence in support of religious reform in various urban areas.

In 1414, Václav IV's brother, Sigismund of Luxemburg, used his influence as Holy Roman Emperor to convene the Council of Constance in order to end the divisive era of rival popes. Churchmen arrived in the Swiss city of Constance from across Europe and, by 1418, ended the schism with the election of Martin V. However, Sigismund also viewed the great gathering of notable clergy as an opportunity to address the issue of the Hussite "heresy" by inviting Jan Hus to address the council in Constance and confront the charges brought against him.

Upon receiving the summons and a promise of safe conduct from the emperor, Hus set out for Constance. When he arrived there in October 1414, he was arrested in violation of the promise of immunity and then spent the winter locked away in a castle, in shackles and exposed to the cold. When finally granted a public trial and confronted with demands that he abandon his heretical stance, Hus refused to recant his beliefs or admit that his writings contained religious errors. He declared instead that to betray his conscience even before a council of the Church would be a mortal sin that would condemn his soul for eternity. Accounts of his last words record Hus as declaring that he was innocent of many of the charges regarding the content of his preaching and proclaiming that he was happy to die for his beliefs. On July 6, 1415, Jan Hus was burned at the stake and had his ashes cast into the Rhine River so that they would never be returned to his Bohemian homeland. Five centuries later, on July 6, 1915, the city of Prague commemorated the death of a national hero by erecting a large statue of Jan Hus in the Old Town Square.

During the several years after Hus's execution, his Hussite supporters ousted papal loyalists from churches in Prague and elsewhere in the kingdom, seizing church lands and property in the process. At the Prague university, the leading master Jakoubek of Štribro instituted the practice of requiring Holy Communion in both kinds, bread and wine, and although Hus had not promoted this reform of the sacrament, he granted his approval prior to his death. Because of the significance of allowing the laity to receive the wine, the chalice became the symbol of the Hussite movement and the distribution of communion *sub utraque specie* ("in both kinds") gave rise to the "Utraquist" label for the moderate Hussite faction.

Before completing its work in 1418, the Council of Constance turned its attention once again to the issue of heresy in Bohemia and condemned the practice of offering the laity communion in two kinds. The following year, Sigismund demanded that his brother Václav suppress the Hussite radicals or face the threat of a crusade against Bohemia for harboring a heretical movement. Although sympathetic to the Hussite cause, Václav appointed opponents of the Hussites to the town council of Prague's New Town and returned priests loyal to Rome to the churches of Prague and to many churches in rural areas. The Hussites responded to the loss of their churches by holding services on open ground, often on the tops of hills upon which they bestowed biblical names. In July 1419, one such hilltop at Tábor played host to radical reformers from all across Bohemia and Moravia as the Hussite movement began to gain in both unity and momentum.

THE HUSSITE REVOLUTION

On July 30, 1419, a radical preacher named Jan Želivský led an attack on the New Town Hall in Prague to free Hussite prisoners being held there. Želivský's supporters threw 11 opposition councilors out the window (the first Defenestration of Prague), murdered them, and then installed Hussites in their place. Over the next three days, crowds in Prague assaulted churches and monasteries and destroyed the residences of German-speaking burghers, forcing many of them to depart Prague to ensure their own safety.

The election of Sigismund of Luxemburg (r. 1419–1437) to the Bohemian throne in 1419 provided the spark for a revolution that would only allow him direct control over the kingdom from 1436 to 1437. Due to his instrumental role in the trial and execution of Jan Hus, Bohemian nobles opposed Sigismund's coronation as their king and initiated 17 years of conflict over religious freedom and national rights.

For many at the time, "Hussitism appeared as a holy war between the Cross and the Chalice."[1] However, the situation was complicated by splits within the ranks of the Hussites and by the participation of German nobles in what was often viewed as a Czech national movement. The Hussites had become divided along geographical and doctrinal lines right from the early days as the moderate factions embraced Hus's teachings as they stood and eventually proved willing to seek compromise rather than to sustain a prolonged conflict that made Bohemia a pariah kingdom in Europe. The moderates tended to include nearly all the highest Hussite nobles, their allies among the lesser nobility, and many of the burghers from the Old Town in Prague. In contrast, the radicals sought to push reforms much further than originally intended and to incorporate elements of social justice into their goals and demands. Because of the appeal of their religious and social agenda to the common people, the radicals were most active in the countryside and in some of the towns of eastern and northern Bohemia. In Prague, ongoing friction existed between the more radical burghers of the New Town and the predominantly moderate Hussites of the Old Town under the leadership of Jakoubek of Štribro and Jan Rokycana.

In the South Bohemian town of Tábor, the radical Táborites established a fortified encampment that was initially home to an egalitarian community of peasants and artisans living as Hussite brothers and sisters. The Táborites rejected the authority of the Church and emulated early Christians by embracing the Bible as the source of their faith and instituting the communalization of property. Tábor quickly became the leading member of a regional military league willing to collaborate with the radical cities of North Bohemia in defense of their faith.

The emperor Sigismund's response to developments in Bohemia was to cooperate with the papacy in launching a crusade against Hussite heretics in March 1420. In consequence, the Czech nobility denounced Sigismund as an enemy of the peoples of the Bohemian crown lands and moved to prevent the emperor from receiving the Bohemian crown in Prague. The nobles then met in Prague Cathedral in May to approve a common Hussite program known as the Four Articles of Prague. The Articles called for the freedom to preach, the right of the clergy and laity to receive communion in both kinds, the expropriation of Church property and elimination of the secular power of the Church, and to satisfy the Táborites and other radicals, the punishment of sinners by secular authorities.

When Sigismund's crusading force of German, Austrian, Italian, Hungarian, and French soldiers arrived at Prague in May 1420, the Hussites of the Prague towns called for military assistance from the Táborites and their allies as Sigismund's forces besieged the town and attacked the Hussite defenders atop Vítka (today's Žižkov) hill. Led by Jan Žižka z Trocnova, a member of South Bohemia's lesser nobility, over 3,000 Táborite brothers and sisters arrived as reinforcements and helped lift the siege. Sigismund's failure to take the city led to a retreat and the abandonment of the unsuccessful First Hussite Crusade. However, before he departed Prague, Sigismund arranged a hasty coronation in St. Vitus Cathedral in Prague Castle to ensure that he departed Bohemia as king.

Over the next 14 years, the Hussites faced four more crusades aimed at returning Bohemia to the fold of Catholic Europe. The Hussite military forces were led by Žižka, a half-blind former mercenary soldier who had proven his ability to lead an army of peasants into battle with weapons often adapted from farm tools. In order to defend against attacks by feudal cavalry, Žižka relied on a highly disciplined peasant infantry driven by religious zeal and the belief that religious freedom would also bring greater social equality and a betterment of their condition. The Hussites marched into battle singing the war hymn "*Ktož sú boži bojovníci*" (All ye warriors of God), which frequently undermined the morale of their enemies as fighting commenced. Hussite forces also relied upon military innovations such as Czech howitzers using gunpowder and heavy war wagons that could be used to form defensive barricades.

During this period, administration of the kingdom's affairs fell to local nobles as Hussites seized Church lands and property, attacked monasteries, and took action against enemies, real and perceived. Violence was unleashed upon towns and villages deemed to be in opposition to the Hussites and German-speaking inhabitants were killed or chased from their homes. Jewish inhabitants of the kingdom also became victims of the religious conflict as many were declared heretics or allies of the Hussites. In 1426 the margrave of Moravia proposed that all Jews be expelled from the royal town of Jihlava in a campaign that eventually led to similar expulsions from Brno and three other Moravian royal cities in 1454. The sixth royal town, Uherské Hradiště, completed the process in 1514.

Internal conflicts turned violent in February 1422 when moderate Utraquist burghers in Prague's Old Town murdered the radical Jan Želivský and nine of his comrades at Old Town Hall as a consequence of a growing dispute over the policies and activities of radical artisans. After Želivský's beheading, his followers engaged in a frenzy of destruction targeting the houses of town officials and masters, as well as the city's Jewish ghetto. When the violence died down, the Utraquist nobles began to consider closer ties to their Catholic peers.

Žižka's death from the plague on October 11, 1424, provided a setback for his followers, who henceforth identified themselves as Orphans and continued to fight under the command of Žižka's successor, Prokop Holý (Prokop the Bald). In 1431, the emperor launched a fourth crusade against the Hussites, with two armies driving into Bohemia from the north and west. After two days of forced march, the Hussites arrived at Domažlice on August 14, and routed the enemy after many foreign soldiers were said to have fled upon hearing the Hussite war hymn.

After the humiliating defeat at Domažlice, the pope abandoned a military solution in favor of opening negotiations with the Hussites, whose growing disunity was underscored by an Utraquist acceptance of negotiations and a radical rejection of a diplomatic option. A Czech delegation arrived in Basel in 1433 with the goal of taking the first steps toward a negotiated settlement at the Ecumenical Council meeting in the Swiss city. Sigismund supported the diplomatic efforts in large part because he still wished to secure the Bohemian crown.

During the summer of 1433, military operations by radical Hussites against the town of Plzeň led to cooperation between Utraquist and Catholic nobles in confronting the radicals. On May 30, 1434, a joint force of Utraquists and Czech Catholics inflicted a decisive defeat on the radicals in a pivotal battle at Lipany. With Prokop Holý a casualty of the battle and the armies of the radicals reaching an end, the Battle of Lipany brought the Hussite Revolution to a close.

In 1435, the Utraquist Jan Rokycana was elected Hussite archbishop of Prague and formally recognized by Sigismund. A year later, in 1436, negotiations at Basel produced the *Compactata*, or Compacts of Basel, which reconnected the Hussites with the Roman Catholic Church and addressed the demands set out in the Articles of Prague. By agreement, the laity could receive communion in both kinds in Bohemia and Moravia, but not in the other crown lands. This represented a unique privilege in Catholic Europe, although the remainder of the four articles were either eliminated or weakened. An additional concession allowed nobles who had taken possession of Church lands to retain those lands. With the cessation of hostilities, Sigismund traveled to Jihlava in Moravia and received the Crown of St. Václav in a ceremony on a town square on August 14, 1436.

As a consequence of the Hussite wars, Bohemia emerged a kingdom transformed by social and political changes, some of which were the consequence of long-term trends that arose at the end of the Middle Ages and predated the Hussite Revolution. The conflict seriously undermined the Bohemian economy, but it also led to changes in the rural order as large amounts of Church land and other properties came into the possession of the nobility. For the lesser nobility and the burghers, the revolution meant a stronger sense of identity and greater participation in the political life of the country. These new social and political currents would affect the relationship between the king and the estates during the reigns of Sigismund's successors

JIŘI Z PODĚBRAD

After Sigismund's passing, the Estates of Bohemia, Austria, and Hungary elected Albrecht (Albert) of Habsburg, Sigismund's son-in-law, to serve as their common ruler. In opposing Albrecht's selection, radical Hussites of eastern Bohemia and their Táborite allies gained the support of Rokycana, the Utraquist archbishop, in promoting the candidacy of Poland's Prince Casimir of the Jagiellon dynasty. In the ensuing military struggle, Albrecht's Austrian forces earned a military victory over the Poles and their Bohemian allies at Tábor in August 1438, but his supporters forfeited their cause when Albrecht died in October 1439. Albrecht held the Bohemian crown from 1437 to 1439, but never gained control of the kingdom. With his death, the union of Bohemia, Austria, and Hungary dissolved, and the nobility refused to recognize Albrecht's son as king. As a result, the Czech lands entered a period of interregnum until 1453, and during that time, maintaining order became the responsibility of authorities at the provincial and local levels.

The Utraquist nobleman Jiři z Poděbrad (George of Poděbrady) was chosen to serve as regent for Albrecht's 13-year old son, Ladislav Pohrobek (Ladislav Posthumous, r. 1453–1457) when he assumed the Bohemian throne in 1453. Called "Posthumous" because Albrecht had died before he was born, Ladislav ruled for four years before being taken by disease. Upon his death, the Czech estates held an election in March 1458 and made the extraordinary decision to offer the throne to Jiři z Poděbrad (r. 1458–1471), a member of the Czech nobility without connections to previous dynasties. The first Czech ruler since the end of the Přemyslid dynasty, Jiři z Poděbrad was also known as the "Hussite" king because of religious beliefs and his relationships with Jan Hus and Jan Žižka.

The election of Jiři z Poděbrad provided a source of controversy from the start as only Bohemia among the Czech crown lands initially chose to accept his royal authority. He was recognized by the emperor, but not by representatives of the pope. In 1462, Pope Pius II withdrew his support for the *Compactata*, or Compacts of Basel, and four years later, he excommunicated the Bohemian king as a heretic, opening a new crusade against Hussitism in the Czech lands.

With his own designs on the Bohemian crown, Hungary's Mathias Corvinus, son-in-law of Jiři z Poděbrad, launched a military offensive against the Czech Hussites in 1468. The following year, the Hussites addressed their allies in Bohemia and Moravia with a "Call to Arms in Defense of the Truth" that sought to rally Czech patriotism in defense of language, culture, and soil. However, when Lusatia and Silesia joined many Moravian nobles in accepting Matthias Corvinus's claim to the Bohemian crown, Jiři z Poděbrad was left with only the territory of Bohemia under his direct control. The conflict continued until the death of Jiři z Poděbrad in March 1471, whereupon the first

Czech king in 150 years became the final Czech ever to wear the Crown of St. Václav.

When the reign of Jiři z Poděbrad ended without provisions for a direct heir, the Bohemians lost a critical opportunity to establish a native Czech dynasty in possession of the Crown of St. Václav. Where the Kingdom of Bohemia might have followed the path of Western European countries such as England and France in developing a centralized monarchy under a native ruling family, Bohemia instead passed into the hands of foreign rulers, Polish and Habsburg, who had little sense of identification with the peoples of the Czech lands.

BOHEMIA UNDER THE JAGIELLONS

Before his death, Jiři z Poděbrad had accepted the recommendation of Poland's Casimir IV that he support the candidacy of the Jagiellons for the crown of Bohemia rather than attempting to initiate his own dynastic succession. Out of respect for Jiři's wishes, the Diet met at Kutná Hora at the end of May 1471 and elected Vladislav Jagellonský (Władysław Jagiellon), Casimir's son, to rule as Vladislav II (r. 1471–1516).

With its contingents of burghers and artisans among the knights and nobles, the Diet of 1471 reflected the political changes that had in great part been caused by the Hussite Revolution. Traditionally, each of the lands under the Bohemian crown possessed its own political community in a Land Diet that included the nobles, knights, and clergy as individual estates. The general Bohemian Land Diet long claimed the right to elect kings, but each of the Land Diets had the right to legislate, approval royal requests for taxes, grant citizenship, determine local participation in foreign military campaigns, and protect the greater good of the local population. On occasion, a ruler could summon at Prague the general diet of representatives from all five of the lands under the Crown of St. Václav to discuss matters of importance to the entire kingdom.

The second half of the 15th century saw the rise of the estates as a political force, but with the exception of Moravia and Lower Lusatia, the Hussite Revolution had weakened the role of the Church in secular matters and allowed for the emergence of a new estate in the diets, one representing the free towns. The burghers would eventually gain that political status in Moravia, but not to the extent of their peers in Bohemia. By 1471, however, the lesser nobility and the burghers clearly played a more significant political role in the workings of the diets, which gained in influence during a long period of uncertainty.

When Vladislav II was offered the crown, he was required to swear an oath to accept the conditions of the Basel *Compactata* as ruler of a

Bohemian kingdom of Hussites and Roman Catholics. Matthias Corvinus rejected this arrangement, having declared himself king of Bohemia in 1469, and with his armies occupying Moravia, Silesia, and Lusatia, Matthias Corvinus became the uncrowned "antiking," fighting for the right to rule. In 1479, Vladislav II and Matthias Corvinus agreed to the Peace of Olomouc, which established Vladislav as ruler of Bohemia and Matthias as sovereign of the other Czech lands.

When Vladislav II died in 1516, he had already outlived his rival, Matthias Corvinus, who departed in 1490. The crown of the Czech lands passed to Vladislav's son, Ludvík I (Louis, r. 1516–1526) whose separate election as king of Hungary established a personal union of Bohemia and Hungary. Like his father, Ludvík had little direct contact with Bohemia, visiting Prague only once in comparison with Vladislav's three appearances in the capital after 1490.

THE HABSBURGS IN BOHEMIA

The election of the Habsburg Ferdinand I (r. 1526–1564) in 1526 brought significant changes to the administration of the Bohemian kingdom due to Ferdinand's efforts to create a system of absolutist royal administration similar to that of Spain, the Habsburg kingdom in which he was born. In Bohemia, an expansion of royal power required that Ferdinand weaken the authority of the towns and district diets in favor of governance by royal officials. To this end, Ferdinand eliminated the district diets and worked to bring Prague and other towns to heel. When Czech nobles joined many of the royal cities in a revolt against the crown in 1547–1548, Ferdinand successfully ended the uprising and used the opportunity to place royal officials in charge of civic administrations and to introduce a new Court of Appeals that took precedence over town and district courts.

Ferdinand's goal of establishing a hereditary Habsburg succession in Bohemia and Hungary led him to introduce greater royal control over the diets in the Bohemian kingdom, stripping the Czech Diet of its right to elect kings and requiring recognition of the Habsburgs as the rightful hereditary dynasty. The Diet could no longer elect the ruler, but it retained the right of acceptance. Ferdinand reorganized the administration of the Czech lands by creating a Privy Council to manage foreign and domestic policies and a Court Chamber in Vienna to manage the finances of his lands. The organized and regular collection of taxes provided the financial resources for the Habsburg administration, which would gradually erode the independence of the Bohemian kingdom in favor of integration with the Austrian empire.

THE REFORMATION

On October 31, 1517, the German monk Martin Luther (1483–1546) nailed his "Ninety-five Theses" to the door of the Castle Church in Wittenberg, Saxony, and thereby set in motion the religious struggles of the Reformation in Europe. Luther's criticisms of the sale of indulgences and other Church practices were well received in a Bohemia that had already undergone its own Czech Reformation at the hands of the Hussites in the 15th century. Luther openly expressed his admiration for Jan Hus as a pioneer of religious reform and recognized that his own opposition to the sale of indulgences was in line with Hus's criticism of the practice in the early 1400s.

The Lutheran Church established by Luther and his followers found ready support in the Czech lands, especially in the German communities of Bohemia and Moravia. The Hussite Church, long isolated from the rest of Europe, now existed alongside a denomination that had broken away from the Roman Catholic Church when Lutherans realized that they would not be able to profess their beliefs within the existing Church.

The religious conflicts of the Reformation era brought to the fore a uniquely Czech church, the *Jednota bratrská*, or Union of Brethren. Arising out of the radical factions of Hussitism in the mid-1400s, the Brethren chose to disassociate themselves from the Catholic Church, unlike the Hussites who believed that they were still a part of a broader Church community in spite of their differences with Rome. The Brethren initially embraced the vision of the radical Christian writer Petr Chelčický, who criticized both the Catholics and the Hussites and rejected violence and warfare in favor of practicing nonresistance. Chelčický also preached that the faithful should refuse to hold public office, engage in commerce, or enter the army.

The Brethren separated themselves from the other faiths by relying on an elected priesthood of preachers and members of the laity. In the early years, the Brethren primarily attracted commoners to their faith, but their numbers and social diversity increased when they moved away from Chelčický's bans on service and occupation. With the arrival of Lutheranism and then Calvinism in Bohemia, the Brethren gravitated from the former to the latter over the course of the 1500s, although their emphasis had always been more on the everyday practice of Christianity rather than Christian theology.

Because of their radical approach to Christianity, the Brethren had already suffered persecution before Vladislav II conceded to papal demands and instituted a ban on Brethren churches and writings in 1502.

The Brethren continued to exist in Bohemia and Moravia, however, often relying on the financial resources of nobles and burghers as well as the active participation of peasants and artisans. Although many of the Brethren left Bohemia during the reign of Ferdinand I, Moravia remained a center of Brethren activities, including the printing of the *Bible kralická* (Kralice Bible), a vernacular translation of the sacred text by Moravian members of the church.

As a consequence of the Reformation, the large majority of Bohemians likely belonged to Protestant denominations by the beginning of the 1600s. Many nobles and burghers adhered to these faiths, although over time, the highest offices in the Habsburg administration were occupied by Roman Catholics. The initial successors to Ferdinand I, including his son Maximilian II (r. 1564–1576), tended toward religious tolerance or even sympathy toward the Protestant faiths, but that too would change by the end of the second decade of the 17th century.

For the Jewish communities of Bohemia, the age of religious fervor provided uncertain conditions as frictions between Catholics and Protestants occasionally turned violent and royal policies changed with the ruler. By the 1520s, population growth and the occupation of limited space by new buildings led some members of the community to leave the Jewish quarter and establish new Jewish communities elsewhere in Prague, a city that is said to have undergone a doubling of the Jewish population between 1522 and 1541.

Pressure from the burghers caused Ferdinand I to consider expelling Jews from all the royal cities in Bohemia in 1557, but the decree was never put into effect before being canceled by Maximilian II at the beginning of his reign. Conditions improved under Maximilian to the point that the Jewish Town hosted an unprecedented ceremonial visit by the king and his court in 1571. In his Charter of 1577, Rudolf II decreed new rights and privileges for Jews that allowed for participation in crafts and professions previously denied to Jews, who had traditionally supported themselves as money lenders and peddlers. Guilds were no longer restricted to Christians, so Jews were therefore able to become artisans or to open shops and to engage in commerce outside the Jewish quarter and in the markets of the Old Town.

THE RUDOLFINE ERA

In 1576, Rudolf II (r. 1576–1612) gained the throne held by his father and grandfather. Born in Vienna, Rudolf spent eight years in Spain before he reached the age of 19 and returned to Vienna. Like his Habsburg predecessors, Rudolf had to decide between Vienna and

Prague as a seat of power. Rudolf chose Prague, which again became the imperial capital and an important cultural center as Rudolf reigned as king of Bohemia and Holy Roman Emperor.

Rudolf exhibited little warmth toward the Czechs and became more distant as a sickly disposition led him to rely on a small group of Catholic officials to govern the kingdom. Throughout his life and reign, Rudolf indulged his interests in the arts and sciences, especially in the then-accepted scientific fields of astrology and alchemy. Rudolf gathered an impressive art collection at the castle and recruited artists and intellectuals from across Europe to his court. Notable scientists included the botanist Charles de l'Ecluse and the astronomers Tycho Brahe and Johannes Kepler, who developed the Rudolfine tables for charting the movements of stars. The alchemists Edward Kelley and John Dee were present to assist Rudolf in his mission to find the Philosopher's Stone, the legendary chemical capable of converting lead and other base metals into gold. Rudolf's other interests were on display in his botanical gardens, exhibition of exotic animals, and enormous *Kunstkammer*, or collection of curiosities

For all of Rudolf's successes as a patron of the arts and sciences, however, his abilities as a statesman were not strong enough to allow him to avoid major setbacks as ruler. By the beginning of the new century, Rudolf suffered a gradual worsening of a psychological condition that moved from occasional bouts of manic depression to chronic paranoia and schizophrenia. The emperor's declining psychological health affected the royal court, as intrigues undermined administrative affairs and disreputable individuals exploited the uncertain conditions at court for their own ends.

Rudolf's efforts to unite all of Christian Europe against incursions by the Ottoman Turks from their empire to the southeast led to a major outbreak of hostilities that continued until 1606. When an anti-Habsburg rebellion broke out in Hungary in 1605, Rudolf placed Hungarian affairs in the hands of his brother, the Archduke Matthias, who successfully negotiated an end to the rebellion and the war with the Turks. After Rudolf complained that Matthias had forfeited too much in the treaties, Matthias exploited growing anger toward Rudolf to demand that Rudolf surrender to him the Hungarian Crown of St. Stephen as well as the crown of Austria

When Bohemian Protestants demanded guarantees of religious freedoms in 1609, Rudolf was able to maintain possession of the Bohemian crown only by defining religious liberties in a Letter of Majesty that confirmed the rights of Lutherans, Calvinists, and other Protestant denominations. Further demands by the Protestants forced Rudolf to request that his cousin Leopold, the Bishop of Passau, send an army that he could use to suppress the Protestants before moving against his brother Matthias. However, Protestant appeals to Matthias brought his assistance in removing Rudolf from the throne, whereupon Rudolf was kept prisoner until he relinquished the crown to Matthias in 1611, a year before his death. An aging Matthias held the Bohemian crown until the election of Ferdinand II (r. 1617–1637) in 1617.

THE BOHEMIAN REBELLION

On May 23, 1618, a group of Protestant Czech nobles arrived at the offices of two of Ferdinand II's governors in Prague Castle and threw the two officials and their secretary out one of the windows in what has become known as the Defenestration of Prague, or more precisely, the Second Defenestration of Prague. The victims of this forced ouster survived a plunge of 60 feet by landing in a pile of manure in the moat below. This action of the nobles on behalf of the Bohemian Estates was inspired by opposition to Ferdinand's election, as well as by the belief that the closing of Protestant churches on land claimed by the Catholic Church represented a violation of rights set out in the Letter of Majesty in 1609. The consequences of the defenestration contributed to the outbreak of the Thirty Years' War that dominated European affairs from 1618 to 1648.

In August 1619, the Czech Diet rejected the Habsburg right of succession and elected Frederick of the Palatinate (r. 1619–1620), a member of the Wittelsbach family, to serve as king. Frederick resided in Prague Castle as antiking to Ferdinand and sought assistance from the princes of the Protestant Union and from England's James I, father of his wife, Elizabeth Stuart. The "Winter King," as he was deemed, wore the crown for just over a year before Ferdinand II ended the rebellion and removed Frederick from the throne.

On November 8, 1620, some 20,000–21,000 Bohemian soldiers and mercenaries skirmished with a larger Habsburg-Catholic coalition force at White Mountain (Bíla hora) outside of Prague. Led by Duke Maximilian and Count Johann von Tilly, the Habsburg forces and their allies in the Catholic League defeated the Czechs in a battle that would set the course of Czech history until the early 20th century. The battle itself was not a national one in the sense of Czechs fighting Germans; rather, it was a struggle between Bohemian Protestant nobles, Czech and German, and the Catholic Habsburgs and their allies. The defeat, however, would have ramifications for the Czech nation, from aristocrat to peasant.

Ferdinand II decided to punish the Czechs for the rebellion in a manner that would break resistance to Habsburg rule, restore Catholicism, and undermine the Czech national identity, declaring, "Better a desert than a country full of heretics."[2] On the morning of June 21, 1621, 27 nobles and burghers were executed in Prague's Old Town Square, their heads later placed on public display on one of the towers of Charles Bridge. The heads remained there over the next decade until the victims could be given formal burial in Týn Cathedral. Twenty-seven white crosses are now embedded in the pavement outside the Old Town Hall on the square.

Following the executions, Frederick moved against the Czech nobility and burghers by seizing lands belonging to Protestant nobles and selling or granting them to Habsburg loyalists. Mercenary officers who had led Habsburg forces were compensated with land, thereby adding new Spanish, Flemish, Irish, Italian, and German nobles to the ranks of the landowning elites. The Catholic clergy regained their lost status as an estate and remained a powerful ally of the Habsburgs.

In 1624, Frederick followed his earlier expulsion of non-Catholic priests and ban on laypersons receiving communion in both kinds with an imperial decree that defined Catholicism as the only denomination permitted in the Bohemian kingdom. Three years later, in July 1627, the Re-Catholicization Patent forced Protestant nobles to choose between Catholicism or expulsion, with the eventual result being the departure of approximately 20 percent of the nobility from Bohemia and Moravia.

In an administrative context, Bohemia was pulled further into the orbit of Vienna as capital of the Austrian empire, particularly with the relocation of the Czech Chancellery to Vienna in 1624. Under Ferdinand III (r. 1627–1657), Land ordinances in Bohemia (1627) and Moravia (1628) eliminated the authority of the Estates in legislative and judicial affairs, while also declaring the lands of the Crown of St. Václav to be hereditary possessions of the Habsburgs.

Habsburg policies in Bohemia directly targeted Czech culture and the indigenous intelligentsia, as some intellectuals faced execution, others emigrated, and those who remained found it extremely difficult to pursue their work. Among the Protestant intellectuals who left their homeland was Jan Ámos Komensky (Comenius), a humanist and educator whose 1623 satirical work, *The Labyrinth of the World and the Paradise of the Heart*, remained unavailable in Bohemia until the end of the 18th century. Comenius had been a leader of the Brethren in Moravia and became a Brethren bishop after joining others of his faith in escaping the policies of the Counter-Reformation in Bohemia.

Comenius eventually settled in Amsterdam, where he died in 1670, leaving behind a legacy in the field of education celebrated by various institutions that bear his name, including Comenius University in the Slovak capital of Bratislava.

The university in Prague, long the intellectual center of religious reform, was placed under the authority of the Jesuits, who merged it with their Klementinum in 1653. Rectors of the resulting Karl-Ferdinand University held responsibility for administering all the schools in the kingdom and upheld the restrictions imposed by heavy censorship. As an instrument of that censorship, the Jesuit Antonin Koniáš's "Index of Prohibited or Dangerous and Suspicious Books" included nearly all literature in Czech and especially works of Hussite, Lutheran, and Calvinist writers. Since even the language itself became suspect, instruction in Czech would be allowed only at the early levels of schooling. As German acquired the status of official language, Czech became the language of the lower strata and German the language of nobles and burghers.

THE THIRTY YEARS' WAR (1618–1648)

While Habsburg policies and the Counter-Reformation altered the religious, political, and cultural landscape in Bohemia, the Thirty Years' War spread across much of Europe, including the Bohemian crown lands. As the last major religious war in Europe, the Thirty Years' War developed out of the Bohemian rebellion in 1618 and raged across the continent until 1648, expanding from a defenestration in Prague to a conflict between German Protestant rulers and a coalition of the Habsburg Holy Roman Emperor and his Catholic allies. From there, it unfolded across its four stages as a power struggle involving the great dynasties of Europe.

Ferdinand II gained an experienced military commander when the Bohemian nobleman Albrecht von Wallenstein (Valdštejn) offered to supply the emperor with 20,000 troops in support of the Catholic cause. Wallenstein, a lesser noble educated in schools run by the Brethren, had converted to Catholicism in 1609. Hoping to expand his landholdings by aiding the emperor and his Catholic allies, Wallenstein soon emerged as a leading commander of imperial forces and was rewarded accordingly. Military successes and the acquisition of territory in northern Bohemia earned Wallenstein the title of duke of Friedland in the mid-1620s. His military role and prestige then increased as Denmark entered the conflict on the side of the Protestant princes and Wallenstein assisted in the defeat of Christian IV's Danish armies, for which Wallenstein was awarded the Duchy of Mecklenberg.

In 1629, Ferdinand II reignited religious controversy by issuing the Edict of Restitution, which ordered the restitution of all Catholic lands seized since 1552 and threatened the Protestant denominations by banning Calvinists from worship. The following year, Catholic and Protestant princes, fearing Wallenstein's motives and concerned over the size of his mercenary army, convinced the emperor to remove Wallenstein as military commander. However, Swedish victories over the imperial general Count Tilly, killed at Lech in 1632, and the Saxon invasion of Bohemia convinced the emperor to reinstate Wallenstein to his command. The Saxons, who had occupied Prague, were driven from Bohemia before Wallenstein moved to engage Swedish forces under Gustavus Adolphus II. Wallenstein met the Swedes in a major battle at Lützen in November 1632, and although a stalemate forced Wallenstein to withdraw to Bohemia, the Protestant cause suffered a severe setback when Gustavus Adolphus perished during the fighting.

In following his own interests, Wallenstein opened secret negotiations with Saxony as well as with France, Sweden, and some of the Czech exiles, likely in hopes of gaining his own independent land to rule and possibly in pursuit of the Bohemian crown. When imperial authorities grew suspicious of Wallenstein's ambition and his motives, the emperor once again removed him as commander as charges of treason began to circulate. On February 25, 1634, at the fortress of Cheb, Wallenstein was murdered by one of his own captains who was furious at his commander's treachery.

For the Bohemian kingdom, the final phase of the Thirty Years' War was marked by Swedish military actions in Bohemia from 1639 to 1624 and in Moravia in 1642. When the Habsburgs negotiated a peace with Transylvania, the Swedes departed from Moravia. In 1648, Swedish troops returned to Prague to lay siege to the city, looting Prague Castle and Rudolf II's art collection in the process. Student volunteers held the stone bridge across the Vltava against the Swedes, and the Jewish community defended parts of the city walls and contributed financially to the resistance efforts. Frederick III rewarded the Jews of Prague with a temporary easing of the tax burden and by delivering delayed payments for military supplies, but these benefits were tempered by the *Judenpatent* of 1648, which placed restrictions on Jewish rights and privileges.

The signing of the Peace of Westphalia officially ended the Thirty Years' War in 1648, and within the Holy Roman Empire, the conditions of the Treaty of Augsburg (1555) were restored and expanded to include the Calvinist denominations. Guided by the principle of *curius regio, eius religio* (whose the rule, his the religion), the religious peace allowed the individual ruler to determine the religion of the entire population. Although the subject peasantry lacked the right to choose, other subjects could either convert to the official faith or depart. For the Czech exiles, the selection of 1634 as the base year meant that they would not be returning to their homeland. A Catholic victory in Bohemia contributed to the success of the Counter-Reformation in the kingdom, although by agreement with Saxony, the Lutherans in Silesia retained the right to worship.

For Bohemia, three decades of warfare brought economic chaos and a drastic reduction in population as a result of conflict, famine, disease, and emigration or exile. Due to the division of Hungary during the Turkish wars, Bohemia stood as the largest of the Habsburg territories in spite of having lost Upper and Lower Silesia in 1635. In the towns, many burghers faced poverty or financial distress due to the war's physical toll on urban areas and their economic activities. For rural Bohemia, the transfer of lands to the Church or to the high nobility reduced the lesser nobles to ownership of 10 percent of the land, when only a century earlier, they had surpassed the great nobles in combined land ownership. Some 90 percent of the population lived as subject peasants on land owned by the Catholic Church and nobility, while the continuation of the "second serfdom" in Central Europe meant the preservation of feudal practices that had disappeared or were soon to be discarded in the West. As a result of the failed Peasant Revolt of 1680, Leopold I (r. 1657–1705) reaffirmed the long-standing labor (*robota*) requirement that committed peasants to the traditional three days of service to the lord per week or as many as seven days during times such as the harvest.

In a cultural context, the reconnection of Bohemia with the Catholic countries of Europe allowed for the penetration of the Baroque style and other influences into the Czech lands. In the spirit of the Counter-Reformation, a revitalized Catholic Church promoted the Baroque style of the late 17th century as a means of inspiring religious passion through a bold and dynamic approach that could reach even the illiterate masses, even if the first Baroque church in the Bohemian kingdom was the work of Lutherans. Baroque architecture in Bohemia displayed the touch of Italian and Austrian masters, but also the inspiration of resident architects such as Christoph Dientzenhofer and his son Kilian Ignaz Dientzenhofer, whose Church of St. Nicholas in Prague's Malá Strana district stands as a masterpiece of Bohemian Baroque. The Baroque era proved artistically fertile under Habsburg rulers Leopold I and Josef I (r. 1705–1711), but the primary contributions were in the areas of art and architecture, rather than in literature.

RELIGIOUS REFORM IN SLOVAKIA

The Hussite reform movement first appeared on Slovak soil during the reign of Sigismund of Luxemburg as king of both Hungary and Bohemia. Táborite forces moved into the region, and Hussite armies established themselves in towns such as Trnava, Skalica, and Žilina. Hussite refugees escaping the fighting in Bohemia, Moravia, and Silesia also arrived in Upper Hungary. However, Hussitism never followed the same path of expansion that it had in the Bohemian kingdom, in part because the Slovak lands lacked a center of intellectual and cultural activity that could play a role similar to Prague. Support for the Hussite cause in Slovakia came primarily from the lower nobility, and the faith was strongest in areas where the Hussites maintained a military presence. However, as was the case with Bohemia, the Hussite push for religious reform would establish a foundation for the later reformers of the Reformation.

When a succession struggle ensued after death of Albrecht of Habsburg (r. 1437–1439), Albrecht's widow Elizabeth promoted the candidacy of her infant son Ladislas V (László; Ladislav Posthumous) for the Crown of St. Stephen. The crown, however, went to the Polish king Władisław Jagiello I (Ulászló; r. 1440–1444), the choice of leading Hungarian nobles and the king of Hungary until he fell in battle against the Turks at Varna in 1444. The throne then passed to Ladislas V (r. 1444–1457) with János Hunyadi serving as regent for the young king from 1446 until 1453.

When the military threat of Turkish expansion led the Hungarian Diet to appoint seven captains for different parts of the kingdom, the captaincy of Upper Hungary went to Jan Jiskra z Brandýsa, an ally of Albrecht's widow Elizabeth during the succession crisis. Jan Jiskra was a Moravian Hussite who arrived in Slovakia with the Hussite armies in the 1420s. Jiskra was also a mercenary soldier who joined other Hussites in offered Sigismund his services against the Turks after the radical Hussites were defeated at the Battle of Lipany in 1434. From 1438 to 1453, Jiskra controlled most of southern Slovakia from bases in Zvolen and Kosice.

János Hunyadi received the captaincy of Lower Hungary and was frequently at odds with Jan Jiskra, who left Slovakia in frustration in 1453 only to return a year later in fulfillment of a request to defeat the Czech Brethren. However, the Brethren did not finally succumb until they were defeated in 1467 by king Matthias Corvinus, the son of János Hunyadi. Corvinus then invaded Moravia at the behest of Hussite nobles in 1468 and declared himself king of Bohemia a year later.

MATTHIAS CORVINUS

Matthias Corvinus (Mátyás Corvin, r. 1458–1490) was 15 years old when the Diet elected him king in January 1458. Like Jiři z Poděbrad in Bohemia, Matthias was elected by fellow nobles and lacked any dynastic connections to support his selection as king. Also like Jiři z Poděbrad, Matthias claimed the crown of Bohemia, although he ruled that kingdom only as the antiking from 1469 to 1490.

Possessing a strong interest in the Italian Renaissance, Matthias became a patron of the arts in Hungary and amassed the largest collection of secular works in Europe in a library second only to the Vatican's in size. Humanists and scholars resided at a court that was well known for its splendor and for the taxes that made it possible.

In 1465, Matthias Corvinus made an important contribution to education and intellectual affairs in the Slovak lands by establishing a university, the *Academia Istropolitana* (*Istros* was the Greek name for the Danube), in Bratislava. The university opened two years later with faculties in law, medicine, theology, and the liberal arts, but weak financial support by the king and ineffective administration led to the closing of the institution in 1490.

When Matthias died in 1490, he left only an illegitimate son, János, as a potential successor. However, the nobility rejected János as a candidate for the throne and thereby allowed Matthias Corvinus to share with Jiři z Poděbrad the fate of being the last indigenous ruler of his kingdom. He would be remembered in popular culture as "Matthias the Just."

THE TURKISH WARS

Matthias Corvinus was succeeded by the two Polish Jagiellon kings of Bohemia, Vladislas II (Vladislav or Ulászló r. 1490–1516) and Louis II (Ludvík or Lajos, r. 1516–1526). Vladislas acquired the title "Ladislas the Good" due to his habit of nodding his head and offering a "Good" or "Okay" when asked to respond to a request and for almost always acquiescing to the nobility. Overall, the Jagiellon rulers offered little in the way of constructive leadership and, as a result, left Hungary in a weakened position in regard to Turkish expansion after the fall of the Serbian city of Belgradein in 1521 eliminated a crucial defensive position for the Hungarians.

Led by the Sultan Suleiman I (Suleiman the Magnificent), a massive Turkish army moved up the Danube in 1526 and met a Hungarian force of some 24,000 or more knights and mercenaries near the southern Hungarian village of Mohács on August 29 of that year. Under the command of Louis II, the Hungarians, along with Czech, German, and Polish mercenaries, chose to fight on a plain bordered by marshy terrain, following a strategy that, although chivalrous in a feudal sense, resulted in a direct charge that was "somewhere between stupid and suicidal."[3] The Turks opened the field to their artillery and then routed the badly outnumbered and decimated knights, finishing off the ones who remained and leaving few in the defending force alive. Louis II fled the battlefield and died three days later, a victim of either an accidental drowning during a river crossing or a vengeful noble in his entourage.

After the decisive defeat at Mohács and the death of Louis II, Archduke Ferdinand of Austria claimed the Crown of St. Stephen, although many Hungarian nobles supported Transylvanian prince János Zapolya in opposition to Habsburg efforts to link the crowns of Hungary and Bohemia. Armed conflict, much of it on Slovak soil, eventually led to the Peace of Nagyvárad in 1538, in which Zapolya and Ferdinand agreed to split Hungary, with Transylvania gaining relative autonomy under Turkish suzerainty. When the Turks entered Buda in 1541, Ferdinand was forced to accept peace terms granting the Turks control of the great central plains and recognizing Ferdinand I (r. 1526–1564) as king of a rump "Royal Hungary," stretching from the Slovak lands of Upper Hungary to the Adriatic. Under the authority of the Habsburgs, the Hungarian Diet moved to Pressburg (Bratislava), which became the new center of Hungarian administration and therefore the coronation city of Hungarian kings. The division of Hungary into three regions did not receive full recognition until 1568 and after Maximilian II (Miksa; r. 1564–1576) succeeded Ferdinand I as king of Hungary. The defense of Europe against Turkish expansion now became a critical mission for the Habsburg rulers in Central Europe.

In 1529, Turkish troops had moved through Hungary on the way to Vienna, the last obstacle to Turkish incursions into the heart of Europe, but their siege of the Habsburg capital ended in failure. The following year, Turkish attacks in Upper Hungary caused great destruction in the Nitra, Váh, and Hron valleys as a lack of warning led to many casualties and caused large numbers to flee into the less accessible forests and hills.

The proximity of the Turks and the threat of conflict on the central plains drove nearly two-thirds of the Magyar nobles to settle in the seemingly safer towns and lands of Slovakia. The nobles built residences in the towns, while the towns constructed new Renaissance-era defensive fortifications and housed military compounds. For the Slovaks, the Turkish wars brought changes to the ethnic composition and languages of the towns as the arrival of the Magyar nobles introduced a greater Hungarian element into the region and established Hungarian as the third language of the growing urban areas alongside Slovak and German.

During the Fifteen Years' War (1591–1606), Turkish efforts to push further into Central Europe made the Slovak territories vulnerable to attacks with areas coming under Turkish administration subject to heavy taxation and restrictive administrative regulations. Evasion of such taxes had been one of the precipitating causes of the war, so the Turks responded to resistance to taxation with raids on offending towns and regions. The war ended in 1606 without a clear victor, and with both sides drained of finances and resources, human and otherwise.

REFORMATION, REBELLIONS, AND COUNTER-REFORMATION

The early decades of the Turkish wars also witnessed the arrival of the Reformation in Slovakia, although religious reform appeared a century earlier in the form of Hussitism. The influx of Hussites from Bohemia and Moravia created stronger cultural and religious links between the Slovaks and their Slavic neighbors to the west. In the 16th century, the theological criticisms and teachings of Martin Luther reached Upper Hungary and were embraced by Germans living in the mining towns of eastern Slovakia. From the towns, Lutheranism spread to the rural gentry and among the peasantry.

The presence of Slovak students at the University of Wittenberg, where Luther served as a professor of theology, allowed for the training of Lutheran pastors to serve congregations in Slovakia and elsewhere in Hungary. When the Czech Brethren arrived in Slovakia, they introduced the Czech Bible, *Biblia Kralická* (Kralice Bible), which was published in the late 1500s and became essential to the liturgy of the Slovak Lutherans. As a result, the Czech language began to exercise a strong influence over the development of Slovak as it appeared in Protestant sermons and writings. In 1581, the Slovak edition of the *Catechism of Martin Luther* was published in Czech, and after the Battle of White Mountain in 1620, Czech émigrés helped inspire the use of Czech as the literary language of Protestant scholars and writers in Slovakia until the 19th century.

In January 1604, Catholics seized a Lutheran church in the eastern Slovak town of Košice. Protestants in the Diet at Pressburg (Bratislava) spoke out against the seizure, but the Habsburg ruler Rudolf II (r. 1576–1608) responded by reinforcing laws against Protestants and banning discussion of religious issues in the Diet. A Protestant revolt against the Habsburgs ensued under the leadership of a Calvinist noble-man, Štefan (István) Bocskay, who was elected prince of Transylvania in 1605. Bocskay moved his forces through the mountain passes of the Carpathians and into Upper Hungary, quickly gaining control over most of Slovakia, with the exception of Pressburg. The first of the magnate rebellions ended in June 1606 with the signing of an agreement in Vienna that granted religious freedom to all and guaranteed that high offices in the Hungarian kingdom would be held by Hungarians regardless of religious denomination. The treaty also promised amnesty for Bocskay's supporters in the rebellion. Bocskay then played a key role in bringing the Habsburgs and the Turks together to sign the Peace of Zsitvatorok in 1606, ending the Fifteen Years' War and defining relations between the Habsburg and Ottoman empires for decades.

By 1614, the granting of religious freedoms allowed Lutheran synods to bring organization to the new church by establishing admin-istrative regions in the Slovak lands. Lutherans opened over 100 schools by the end of the 1600s, although all but 10 would be closed under pressure within decades. At one point, most Slovaks had turned to the Lutheran church from their traditional adherence to the Roman Catholic faith. However, small groups of more radical Calvinists appeared in Slovakia, primarily in the south and east, while denomi-nations such as the Czech Brethren, Zwinglians, Anabaptists, and others developed their own small congregations.

When the Fifteen Years' War drew to a close in 1606, Rudolf II was able to redirect his attention from the Turks to the Protestant inhabitants of his empire. The appointment of the former Calvinist Peter Pazmary as bishop of Ostrihon in 1616 reflected a shift in Church policy in Upper Hungary away from forced conversions in favor of utilizing education in defense of the faith. The Counter-Reformation as guided by Pazmary resulted in the restoration of the seminary in Trnava and the founding of the University of Trnava in 1635, making that city the center of Jesuit activities in Royal Hungary. In 1655, the printing press at the Trnava university produced the Jesuit Benedikt Szölösi's *Cantus Catholici*, a Catholic hymnal in the Slovak language that reaffirmed links to the earlier works of Cyril and Methodius.

During the reign of Ferdinand II (r. 1619–1637), a second magnate rebellion occurred just before the Bohemian revolt opened the way to the Thirty Years' War. The revolt began in August 1619 when the Transylvanian prince Gabor Bethlen occupied the Slovak city of Košice and then drove onwards to the outskirts of Vienna, plundering towns and villages on the way. The rebellion was primarily aimed at allowing Protestant nobles to seize property that the Catholic Church had recently taken or regained, but the murder of three Jesuits at the hands of Bethlen's supporters in Košice created martyrs later to be canonized by the Church. In September 1620, Bethlen agreed to end the hostilities by signing an agreement with Ferdinand II, but fighting broke out again after the Battle of White Mountain (1620) and lasted until peace was restored in January 1622. When Ferdinand II agreed to abide by the Viennese settlement of 1606, Bethlen withdrew from Slovakia and returned home

The third magnate rebellion commenced in 1644 during the final phase of the Thirty Years' War as Transylvania's Gyorgy Rákóczi opened negotiations with the enemies of the Habsburgs, Sweden and France. Rákóczi occupied areas of central and southeastern Slovakia until the inability of either side to gain an advantage led to the Peace of Linz between Rákóczi and Ferdinand III (r. 1637–1657) during the summer of 1645. The agreement reaffirmed the treaty of 1606 and stipulated that the Catholic Church would restore to Protestant hands land and churches that had been turned over to the Church.

In 1663, Turkish armies under Grand Vizier Mohammed Koprülü moved into Hungary and penetrated into the central regions of Slovakia with costly and destructive consequences for the Slovaks. The Habsburg ruler Leopold I (Lipót, r. 1657–1705) recruited allies in France, Italy, Spain, and German lands of the Holy Roman Empire, meeting the Turks on the Austrian border and defeating Ottoman forces near St. Gotthard on August 1, 1664. Rather than press an advantage, Leopold negotiated a peace settlement that generated strong anti-Habsburg sentiment among many nobles, Catholic and Protestant alike. Protestant ire increased during the 1670s as many of their churches were seized and accusations of anti-Habsburg conspiracies placed numerous Protestant pastors and educators in the position of having to choose between abandoning their faith or facing incarceration.

Sporadic revolts began in Slovakia as a prelude to the fourth magnate rebellion under Imre Thököly, whose *kurucz* (crusader) bands left a path of destruction across Upper Hungary from 1678 to 1681. When Leopold I's settlement failed to prevent Protestants from taking further action, Thököly appealed to the Turks, who recognized him as ruler of Upper Hungary. Thököly then assisted the Ottomans in their advance up the Danube to Vienna in late March 1683.

The Turks lay siege to Vienna with a large force under the command of Kara Mustafa Pasha, but suffered a critical defeat on September 12 when Charles of Lorraine appeared with reinforcements for the Habsburg forces inside the city. The arriving force of Saxons, Bavarians, Franconians, and other Germans joined the Polish cavalry under King Jan III Sobieski in assaulting the entrenched Turkish invaders. A cavalry charge by Sobieski's Polish lancers penetrated Ottoman lines and, with the coordinated advance of Austro-German forces, drove the Ottomans from Vienna after the 15-hour battle. An allied Lithuanian army then defeated the Hungarian rebels at Orava before engaging in a destructive march down the valley of the Váh in Slovakia. The Thököly revolt collapsed, and the Ottomans withdrew from the lands of Upper Hungary. By the end of the century, a Habsburg offensive forced the Turks to abandon the rest of Hungary, as well as Transylvania. In 1699 the Turkish sultan agreed to the terms of the Peace of Karlowitz, which required Ottoman withdrawal from all Hungarian lands with the exception of some territories along the border.

In 1687, the Habsburgs exploited their military successes against the Ottomans to pressure the Diet in Bratislava into accepting the hereditary succession of the male line of Habsburgs to the crown of Royal Hungary. The Habsburgs also convinced the Diet to accept the primacy of the Roman Catholic Church and to eliminate the right of the nobility to resist the monarchy, as granted by the *Golden Bull* of 1222. Protestants received reaffirmation of property rights gained in the settlement of 1681, but obstacles to the exercise of those rights contributed to anti-Habsburg sentiment and eventually to the final magnate rebellion.

Led by Ferenc Rákóczi, the count of Sáros in the northeastern region of Upper Hungary, the *kurucz* rising took advantage of the withdrawal of Austrian troops during the War of the Spanish Succession to target the absolutist practices of the Habsburgs in 1703. Rákóczi's revolt has been termed a "people's war," or war of national liberation, because supporters of the rebellion included Magyars and Slavs, as well as different strata of society and religious denominations. Rákóczi's efforts to depose Joseph I (r. 1705–1711) and end Habsburg rule led to splits in the ranks of the nobility in 1707, especially when Joseph promised to maintain their exemptions from taxation. Defeat near Trenčín in 1708 and the surrender of Košice three years later caused Rákóczi to accept a negotiated peace that brought the final magnate rebellion to a close in 1711.

In 1711, Juro Janošík, a former soldier in the Habsburg army, gained notoriety as the "Slovak Robin Hood" for his exploits as leader of a group of brigands in Upper Hungary. Janošík's group harassed local authorities and aided the oppressed as they ranged through the valleys and highlands of the Slovak lands before Janošík's arrest and execution in 1713. Celebrated in oral culture, Janošík later appeared in poetry of the Romantic era and in the 20th century as the subject of an opera and several films.

CHARLES VI AS RULER OF BOHEMIA AND HUNGARY

The Habsburg Holy Roman Emperor Charles VI (r. 1711–1740) succeeded to the Crowns of St. Václav and St. Stephen after the death of his brother Joseph I from smallpox in 1711. With only his daughters Maria Theresa and later Maria Anna surviving to adulthood, Charles instituted the Pragmatic Sanction of 1713, which declared his land indivisible and provided for female succession in the Habsburg dynasty, the beneficiary of which was to be Maria Theresa. The Diets of Austria, Bohemia, Moravia, and Silesia accepted the Pragmatic Sanction in 1720, and were joined by the Hungarian Diet three years later.

Looking to gain the support of the Church hierarchy, Charles instituted repressive measures against the Protestants in the Kingdom of Bohemia. Book burnings and the persecution of suspected heretics reinforced Catholic authority in the Czech lands, and the *Resolutio Carolina* of 1731 reaffirmed the religious policies of Leopold I. Restrictions limited the right to worship, as conversions were banned and acceptance of public office required the swearing of a Catholic oath. Additionally, Lutheran education could not progress beyond the level of the grammar schools.

In order to end the Rákóczi revolt and gain the support of the rebellious Hungarian nobles, Charles had signed the Peace of Szatmár on April 30, 1711. By the terms of the treaty, Charles recognized the estates of Transylvania and Hungary and accepted the status of the two lands as separate territories. Charles also agreed to rule Hungary not as Holy Roman Emperor, but as a Hungarian king within the context of Hungary's constitution and laws. As a result of the compromise, 12,000 former supporters of Rákóczi's revolt swore allegiance to the Habsburg dynasty at Szatmár. The Peace of Szatmár allowed Charles VI to gain the support of the Hungarian Diet for the Pragmatic Sanction, which guaranteed the existence of a hereditary monarchy under a Habsburg for as long as the dynasty could produce a legitimate heir.

As ruler of the restored Kingdom of Hungary, Charles reorganized the administration of the country in a manner that would produce

Hungary's first modern, centralized system of authority. He established a permanent army based in Hungary and composed primarily of non-noble Hungarian and foreign soldiers, with the former representing only one-third of the military force. The Imperial War Council in Vienna maintained authority over the army, and the government collected taxes from Hungarian subjects to provide the army with financial support. Religious policies in Hungary under Charles VI were similar to those instituted in Bohemia, with a ban on conversion to the Protestant faiths and the requirement that public officials be Catholic.

When Charles VI died in 1740, his daughter Maria Theresa (r. 1740–1780) received the Habsburg crown and succeeded Charles as ruler of the Bohemian and Hungarian kingdoms. Her reign during the century of the Enlightenment would be characterized by a mixture of absolutist policies and reform as the Habsburg lands moved toward the modern era and the Czechs and Slovaks entered the age of nationalism.

NOTES

1. František Šmahel, "The Hussite Movement: An Anomaly of European History?" in *Bohemia in History*, ed. Mikulaš Teich (Cambridge: Cambridge University Press, 1998), 81.

2. Cited by Henry Wickham Steed in the Introduction to Thomas Garrigue Masaryk, *The Making of a State: Memoirs and Observations 1914–1918* (London: George Allen & Unwin Ltd., 1927).

3. Lonnie R. Johnson, *Central Europe: Enemies, Neighbors, Friends* (Oxford: Oxford University Press, 2002), 76.

5

Into the Modern Era: Reform, Revolution, and National Awakening (1740–1914)

During the early decades of the 18th century, Europe entered the period of the Enlightenment and witnessed the spread of a critical, questioning spirit inspired by a faith in reason born of the popularization of science and intellectual breakthroughs of the previous century. By midcentury, the Enlightenment reached a mature stage as the spirit of criticism inspired new ideas regarding the rational reorganization of social and political life. In place of intolerance, irrationalism, and repression, the philosophers of the Enlightenment promoted reason, happiness, liberty, secularism, and humanity. It was generally agreed that progress toward personal and civic liberties required that the state govern as a function of the social contract and according to the rational laws of nature, although leading philosophers remained divided over the form that the state should take.

In the Habsburg lands, the Catholicism of the Counter-Reformation contributed to an intellectual environment that proved inhospitable to similar critics of the status quo, as was the case in Prussia and Russia, albeit for different reasons. This left the process of progress and reform in the hands of absolutist rulers, who although inspired by the writings of the French, tended to equate the welfare of the people with the creation of a rational, ordered, and professionally administered state under the guidance of the benevolent ruler. This theory, reflected in the reforms of Joseph II, resulted in "enlightened absolutism," or a managed "Enlightenment from above," as opposed to the liberal and democratic "revolution from below" that would occur in France.

THE REIGN OF MARIA THERESA

Maria Theresa (r. 1740–1780) was 23 years old when, in October 1740, she succeeded her father Charles VI, whose Pragmatic Sanction of 1713 made it possible for a female member of the dynasty to rule over the Habsburg dominions. Raised in a Baroque court marked by devout adherence to the Roman Catholic faith, Maria Theresa possessed no natural affinity for the philosophical writings of the Enlightenment. However, the realities of war and statecraft would encourage her to undertake reforms in the spirit of "enlightened despotism" and designed to create a more rationally organized state and economy as a means of confronting external threats and internal problems.

Maria Theresa faced an immediate challenge from Charles Albert, the elector of Bavaria, and son-in-law of the Holy Roman Emperor and king of Bohemia, Joseph I. Charles Albert refused to accept the Pragmatic Sanction and claimed the Austrian and Czech lands for himself, forging an alliance with France to this end in 1741. A second crisis arose when Frederick II (Frederick the Great), only recently crowned king of Prussia, attempted to seize the prosperous territory of Austrian Silesia and parts of northwestern Bohemia. The ensuing War of the Austrian Succession (1740–1748) involved struggles over territories in Austria, the Czech lands, Italy, and the Austrian Netherlands, as well as hostilities between the British and French in North America and other overseas territories. Combined with Saxon demands for Moravia and Upper Silesia, the Bavarian and Prussian claims nearly succeeded in dividing the lands of the Czech crown.

Charles Albert invaded Bohemia and marched into Prague in May 1741, whereupon the majority of the Bohemian Estates chose to recognize him as king of Bohemia. Maria Theresa gained the Crown of St. Stephen in Hungary and appealed to the Hungarians for assistance, which she received and for which she would later reward the

Hungarians. Charles Albert departed the Bohemian capital in 1742 in order to attend his coronation as Holy Roman Emperor, but a successful offensive by Maria Theresa's forces drove the Bavarians and their French allies out of Bohemia the following year. Maria Theresa received the Bohemian crown in St. Vitus Cathedral in May 1743 and, after the death of Charles Albert in September 1745, negotiated the election of her husband to the imperial throne as Holy Roman Emperor Francis I, since as a female, she could not gain election to the imperial throne for herself.

The War of the Austrian Succession drew to a close with the Peace of Aix-la-Chapelle in 1748, with the Habsburgs having lost most of their most economically advanced province, Silesia, and its resources in textiles and metallurgy. For Maria Theresa and her ministers, the war had clearly displayed the military advantage that Prussia held over the Austrians. Her response was to begin a process of reorganization and centralization in the Austrian and Czech territories that would modernize and strengthen the administrative and military institutions of the Habsburg realm. The Hungarians received many benefits in the wake of the assistance granted Maria Theresa during the war, and although they were encouraged to increase productivity in agriculture, the Hungarians were spared the centralization process that occurred elsewhere. This proved to be a key factor in setting out the different paths of development that marked the eastern and western Habsburg possessions prior to the creation of the Dual Monarchy in 1867.

The forfeiture of Silesia drove Maria Theresa and her ministers to adopt measures to improve the state's financial status and to encourage industrialization in Bohemia in order to offset the loss of Silesian industrial production. By 1754, the continuous growth of population in the Czech crown lands brought the number of inhabitants of Bohemia to 2.1 million and of Moravia to 900,000. The integration of Bohemia and other lands of the multinational Habsburg domain into a centralized and well-managed state became a primary goal of Maria Theresa's policies in addition to the promotion of economic progress and the creation of a more stable and productive system of state finances.

In 1749, Maria Theresa's government eliminated the separate Court Chancelleries for Bohemia and Austria, later introducing the joint United Bohemian and Austrian Court Chancellery and a new Supreme Court to assume responsibility for judicial affairs. Furthermore, in 1753, district affairs came under more direct control from Vienna as officials became salaried civil servants of the district bureaucracy in place of the traditional practice of administration by members of the estates. Ten years later, authority over the separate territories of Bohemia and Moravia shifted away from the Czech Estates and into the hands of royal officials called *gubernia*, appointed from Vienna and granted authority over taxation and military affairs. The establishment of a customs union between Austrian and Czech lands in 1775 drew the economies of these two territories closer together and contributed to the further loss of independence for the Kingdom of Bohemia.

Unresolved tensions and territorial disputes caused the outbreak of the Seven Years' War (1756–1763) in 1756. The Prussian invasion of Saxony, an Austrian ally, initiated the conflict, which continued with a Prussian advance into northern Bohemia and the siege of Prague in 1757 before an Austrian counterattack drove the Prussians away from the city and into defeat at the Battle of Kolín. The coalition of Habsburg, French, and Russian forces defeated Frederick II in several battles in 1759 and 1760, but overseas setbacks at the hands of the British diminished French support for Austria, and dynastic struggles after the death of the Empress Elizabeth caused the Russians to withdraw from the fighting in 1762. As a consequence, Maria Theresa was made to reaffirm Prussia's possession of Silesia in 1763, thereby reducing the Czech lands to the territories of the former Přemsylid dynasty: Bohemia, Moravia, and several duchies in Silesia.

After the death of her husband in 1765, Maria Theresa's son was elected to succeed him as Holy Roman Emperor Joseph II. Maria Theresa appointed Joseph to serve as co-regent of the Habsburg lands, but she was careful not to allow her son to usurp her own authority. Unlike Maria Theresa, Joseph (coruler, 1765–1780; r. 1780–1790) distrusted the Catholic Church and embraced the scientific and philosophical aspects of the Enlightenment, which he absorbed as he traveled the continent, reading the works of noted scholars and writers such as Voltaire and meeting with leading Enlightenment figures during two sojourns in France.

Joseph held the enlightened belief that the state must be organized along rational lines in order to allow all elements of government and society to function in harmony for the good of a population that was educated, healthy, and able to live productive lives. The creation of an organized, centralized, prosperous, and powerful state would come through a process of bureaucratic modernization, which reorganized the major components of state and public life through practical reforms and in the spirit of Enlightenment rationalism.

As a consequence of the Seven Years' War, an increase in state debt made the implementation of new social and financial measures essential to the financial health of the Habsburg dominion. In the Bohemian lands, the peasantry continued to bear the burden of *robota* obligations as well as committing 70 percent of limited income to the landlords, church, and state. Widespread famine contributed to the misery in 1771 as half a million people died in Bohemia, reducing the population by some 12 percent. After personally inspecting the situation in Bohemia in 1771–1772, Joseph was deeply disturbed by the conditions he observed, and a commission was set up to undertake a fairer distribution of government requirements for peasant and lord. A peasant uprising in northeast Bohemia in 1775 underscored the need for rural reforms that would alleviate some of the distress in rural areas and prevent social upheavals in the future.

THE REFORMS OF JOSEPH II

After Maria Theresa's death in 1780, Joseph II distanced himself from the conservatism of his mother by instituting reforms that would regulate many areas of life in the empire. The Toleration Patent of 1781 granted religious freedom to Protestants, Orthodox Christians, and Jews and thereby eliminated the restrictions on Protestantism that had existed in Bohemia since White Mountain in 1620. Lutherans, Calvinists, and others were now free to own landed property, hold office in the government and military, open schools, and enter formerly proscribed professions. However, Catholicism remained the only faith allowed to operate openly in the public sphere as other houses of worship were prohibited from possessing entrances, spires, or other architectural or design elements that marked their religious purposes. In 1784, Joseph ordered the closing of numerous churches, monasteries, and convents in order to use the properties as financial resources in support of education and relief for the poor.

Although full legal emancipation would not come until the late 1800s, Joseph II's Edict of Toleration expanded economic and professional opportunities for Jews as a means of increasing their value to the state and making them loyal subjects of the Habsburgs, although ownership of landed property remained an elusive right. Educational opportunities increased as universities admitted Jewish students and Jewish communities in Bohemia and Moravia received government support for opening state-administered schools or for sending children to Germany-Jewish elementary schools in areas where funding education proved difficult. However, government policies on the use of language prevented Jews from maintaining the records of businesses and synagogues in Hebrew or Yiddish. Modernization brought greater integration into civil society in the Habsburg lands as Jewish citizens gained individual freedoms, but it also eroded the traditional autonomy of Jewish communities in various areas of local governance and culture.

Joseph II's most radical reform was embodied in the Serfdom Patent of 1781, which abolished personal serfdom and granted peasants the freedom to marry, travel, pursue an education, enter trades, or resettle without requiring the permission of the landlord. Peasants also received the right to file complaints or lawsuits against the lord, although the patent did not eliminate *robota* subject labor or financial responsibilities to the lord and state. Peasants could now compensate landlords with cash for land received and benefitted from a restructuring of taxation in the late 1780s, which created a more equitable and state-regulated distribution of taxes. The reforms did not eliminate financial problems for the peasant or grant them ownership of land, but they offered emancipation and an opportunity for education and the betterment of the peasant's life. After Joseph II's death, however, determined opposition by the nobility led to the repeal of the Serfdom Patent and a reversal of the new policies.

Further Josephine reforms eased restrictions on publishing and the press, eliminating church supervision of censorship and the "Index" of banned books. Institution of a unified code of criminal law placed all citizens on an equal legal footing and eliminated long-established means of execution and manners of punishment, as well as the use of torture as a tool of legal examination. Language became an instrument of uniformity in administration and education as German became the official language of governance and higher education in the multinational lands of the Habsburgs. In 1784, the Prague university formally replaced Latin with German as the language of instruction.

By 1789, Joseph II was in extremely poor health and suffering great despair over foreign policy setbacks and resistance to his reforms and centralizing policies, especially among the rebellious nobility, peasants, and intelligentsia of Hungary. After his death in February 1790, Joseph was followed by his brother Leopold II (r. 1790–1792), who successfully resolved some of the lingering diplomatic crises and worked to restore stability in the Habsburg lands. Positive relations with the Czechs allowed Leopold to receive the Crown of St. Václav in Prague on September 6, 1791, after he had returned the crown from Vienna. However, Leopold's brief reign turned back the clock on Joseph II's reforms as Leopold eliminated many of his brother's policies in negotiating concessions to the estates.

SLOVAKIA IN THE 1700S

The Slovak lands in the age of enlightened absolutism supported a population of 2 million, with a majority of the inhabitants ethnic Slovaks. Towns and cities in Slovakia remained small in size, with Pressburg (Bratislava) the largest urban area with a population of 10,000. As part of Hungary, Slovakia remained relatively unaffected by Maria Theresa's reform of taxation and the military in the Habsburg lands and was not a party to the customs union established between Austria and Bohemia in 1775, although Slovakia remained a region of great importance to the Hungarian economy.

Centralizing policies and the reorganization of the state proved more difficult to implement successfully in Hungary because of the strong resistance of the Hungarian nobility. Joseph II responded to Hungarian resistance by refusing to accept the Crown of St. Stephen and by never summoning the Diet to meet during the decade after 1780. Reacting to continued opposition in the Hungarian counties and the ineffective implementation of his policies by nobles in charge, Joseph abolished the long-standing system of administration in Hungary in 1785, replacing the nobles who had traditionally administered the counties with civil servants appointed by the state. Hungary now comprised 10 districts with four or five counties in each and with three of them—Košice, Banská Bystrica, and Nitra—located in Slovakia. As in Bohemia and other regions under Habsburg rule, German had already become the official language of administration in Hungary the previous year.

Other reforms of Maria Theresa and Joseph II affected Hungary and the Slovaks as well. Reforms in education were designed to create better citizens by extending literacy and schooling to all, regardless of background. The University of Vienna served as the model for reforms in higher education at the University of Trnava before that institution was moved to Buda in 1777, thus depriving Slovakia of an important and influential intellectual and cultural center. Maria Theresa's *Ratio Educationis* of 1777 reorganized the system of Catholic education from the elementary schools to the universities and allowed non-Catholics access to all levels of schooling. In 1786 German became the language of instruction for classes above the elementary-school level in Hungary.

Joseph II's most radical reforms addressed social and religious issues in Hungary as elsewhere. The Edict of Toleration of 1781 granted equality to non-Catholics and allowed Protestants and Jews to worship within the same restrictions on public professions that applied to Austria and Bohemia. In 1785, the Peasant Patent abolished serfdom and redefined relationships between peasant and landlord.

By 1789, most of the counties of Hungary were registering complaints over obligations to provide soldiers and supplies to the army in Joseph II's ongoing struggle with the Ottoman Turks. County assemblies refused to cooperate to the point that armed uprising seemed imminent in Hungary. Joseph's advisors recommended concessions as the only viable solution to the growing resistance in a year that witnessed the storming of the Bastille in Paris on July 14, 1789. On January 28, 1790, Joseph II announced that he was revoking all of his reforms save those such as the Edict of Toleration and the abolition of serfdom. He also restored all Hungarian administrative and judicial institutions to the status they held at the start of his reign, and he promised to summon the Hungarian Diet in 1791. However, with his Hungarian policies in tatters, Joseph II died shortly thereafter.

By virtue of Joseph's actions in 1790, Hungary regained its independence as a kingdom, possessing unique national rights, subject to Hungarian law, and ruled by a monarch in legal possession of the Crown of St. Stephen. Encouraged by this recognition of national rights, the Hungarian elites embraced a new Magyar nationalism founded upon the concept of a true Magyar nation in which the non-Magyar majority of the population would be assimilated through a process of "Magyarization." The Old Hungary and its multicultural conception of patriotism had reached an end, and Hungary now faced two possible paths of development: as a state with a dominant and unifying Magyar culture, or as a country composed of multiple nations—Magyar, Croat, Serb, Ruthene, and Slovak.

THE EMERGENCE OF SLOVAK NATIONALISM

Over the centuries since the Great Moravian Empire faded away, the Slovaks had not been in a position to develop an independent history of their own. Living in northern Hungary, Slovaks were aware that language and ethnicity differentiated them from Magyars, Germans, and even their fellow Slavs—the Czechs, Poles, and Ruthenians. As an early stage of development, the Great Moravian period offered heroic individuals such as Cyril and Methodius, but these historical figures were shared with other Slavs. Slovaks lacked the mythological origins that the Czechs had created in the tales of Čech, Libuše, and other characters from the chronicles. As a result, national identity tended to be linked to language and literature, leading to debates over when the Slovak language first emerged as a clear and distinct Slavonic vernacular.

During the Reformation, the popularity of the Kralice Bible allowed Biblical Czech (*biblíčtina*) to gain a linguistic foothold in Slovakia because it offered a written language that could be "slovakized," or adapted to spoken Slovak. Protestants in Slovakia wrote in *bibličtina* and used it in their liturgy, which in turn helped preserve the works of Czech Protestants after the defeat at White Mountain in 1620.

When the Counter-Reformation began the process of re-catholicizing Slovakia, the Jesuits in Trnava used their printing press to circulate works in what was known as "Jesuit Slovak," an alternative to the *bibličtina* of the Protestants and a means of reaching the Slovak people through a literary language based on the dialect of educated inhabitants of western Slovakia. Protestants intellectuals, largely Lutheran, preferred to write in *bibličtina* as the Slovak high nobility adapted the language and culture of their Magyar peers and the lesser nobility and peasants communicated in regional dialects of Slovak.

In 1787, the Catholic priest Anton Bernolák published a work on philology in which he attempted to establish the foundation for a Slovak literary language. While attending the seminary in Bratislava, Bernolák had worked with other seminarians to produce a Slovak translation of the Bible. In 1790 Bernolák began his codification of the Slovak literary language by publishing a book on Slavic grammar, *Grammatica slavica*, which borrowed from an earlier book on Czech grammar.

In 1792, Bernolák formed the Slovak Learned Society in Trnava to promote the use of his literary language, *bernoláčina*, or Bernolák Slovak. The new literary language combined elements of the central and western dialects with aspects of Jesuit Slovak and folk speech. *Bernoláčina* closely resembled the Czech literary language in form and structure (morphology), but the patterns of sounds (phonology) were quite different. The first work in *bernoláčina* appeared in 1789, and although Bernolák began work on a Slovak Czech-Latin-German-Hungarian dictionary in the late 1780s, his death in 1813 preceded the publication of the six volumes in 1825–1827. Critically, Bernolák's work and the related contributions of Catholic intellectuals separated the Slovak language from Czech, but *bernoláčina* never gained the support of Slovak Protestants who continued to write in literary Czech, or of Slovaks with a preference for their local dialects.

By the 1830s, two sons of Lutheran pastors, Ján Kollár and Pavel Jozef Šafárik, began promoting a common "Czecho-Slovak" literary language as a means of uniting the neighboring Slavic peoples through a common culture. While studying in Germany, Kollár embraced the concept of "nation" as defined by Romantic-era philosophers and writers such as Johann Gottfried Herder and Johann Gottlieb Fichte. Herder, Fichte, and the prophets of Romantic nationalism viewed a nation as organic in nature and defined by language, traditions, geography, and blood. In Kollár's Pan-Slavic version, there existed a broad Slavonic nation represented by four languages: Czecho-Slovak, Russian, Polish, and South-Slav. Whereas Bernolák had viewed the Slovaks within the context of the *natio hungarica* and Magyar rule, Kollár and his colleague Šafárik defined the Slovaks as a nation within the broader framework of ancient Slavic culture and traditions according to evidence Šafárik discovered in his study of Slavic antiquities, languages, and literature. As a result, it was imperative for Slovaks to resist the assimilationist policies of Magyarization and turn instead to the Czechs and a Slavic cultural unity founded not upon the old Biblical Czech, but rather upon a new Czecho-Slovak language.

Although the Pan-Slavic theories of Kollár and Šafárik resonated with many Protestant and Catholic intellectuals, others rejected the idea of a national awakening that linked the Slovaks to the Czechs, a people with whom they seemed to have little common history. Because Šafárik wrote in Czech and moved to Prague in 1833, he became with Kollár a key figure in the Czech national awakening, which was occurring over the same decades.

Herder's warning that the Magyar language and culture would soon be overwhelmed by the Slavic peoples seemed to justify for many the cultural assimilation policies of Magyarization, which would subsume Slovak culture and language under a dominant Magyar culture in the Hungarian lands. The direct threat of Magyarization to Slovak culture and language brought Catholics and Protestants together in the belief that the creation of a common Slovak literary language was essential to the preservation of the Slovak identity.

A Lutheran scholar, Ľudovit Štúr, argued in opposition to Pan-Slavism that although the Germans represented a distinct nation based upon their common language, the diversity of the Slavic peoples and their languages prevented them from forming a unified Slavic nation. Instead, the Slovaks represented a unique national community within Slavdom and with the natural right both to their own language and to some manner of control over their own political affairs.

In 1846, Štúr published a work rejecting the call of Kollár and Šafárik for a Czecho-Slovak language and proposing instead that agreement be reached on a Slovak literary language. Štúr had already completed his own Protestant codification of the Slovak language several years earlier and therefore his *štúrovčina*, or Štúr Slovak, became a focal point of linguistic deliberations. *Štúrovčina* borrowed elements of Bernolák Slovak but utilized the Tatrin dialect of Central Slovak because of its accessibility to those living in the east and west of the

Slovak lands. Catholics generally refused to use *štúrovčina* until a compromise in 1851 led to the gradual drift away from *bernoláčina* among Catholics and *bibličtina* among Protestants.[1]

THE FRENCH REVOLUTION AND NAPOLEONIC WARS

In 1789, the evolving political crisis in France moved into a revolutionary phase when the Parisian crowds stormed the royal fortress of the Bastille on July 14. French commoners took to the streets in the name of "Liberty, Equality, and Fraternity," seeking natural rights and participation in a political system marked by absolutist rule and domination by the elites. The Habsburg ruler Leopold II had earlier shown some sympathy for enlightened reforms, but the opening events of the French Revolution drove him to consider policies directed at preventing upheaval in his own lands. However, when Louis XVI accepted the new constitution in 1791, Leopold assumed that revolutionary threat would subside as France progressed into a new era of constitutional monarchy.

Upon Leopold's death in March 1792, Francis II (r. 1792–1835) succeeded his father as ruler of the Habsburg lands and was elected Holy Roman Emperor in July. Unlike his father, however, Francis refused to accept the need for even moderate reforms. Instead, the new emperor altered the course of recent Habsburg rulers by openly espousing conservative values and promoting the defense of Europe against the spread of revolution. On April 20, 1792, the Legislative Assembly of France issued a declaration of war on Francis as ruler of the Habsburg lands, with Prussia soon joining Austria in the first of several coalitions against France. The reign of Francis II ended any hope of progress as the revolution and subsequent rise of Napoleon Bonaparte dominated Habsburg affairs into the early 19th century.

The Habsburg dominion increased in size as Austria, Russia, and Prussia completed the partition of Poland during the mid-1790s, but the Austrian military did not fare well against the French during the campaigns of 1796–1797 in northern Italy. Habsburg forces fell to the French under Napoleon Bonaparte at Marengo and Hohenlinden before the subsequent Peace of Campo Formio ended the war of the First Coalition in 1797. During the winter of 1798–1799, Russian troops moved through Bohemia in their advance on Italy and then returned while on the way home during the war of the Second Coalition. This direct exposure to soldiers of the greatest of the Slavic lands came at a time of national renewal for the Czechs and reminded them of the culture and military power of the Russian empire that lay to the east.

In 1804, Francis used his authority as Holy Roman Emperor to declare himself emperor of Austria, which as an empire consisted of all of the Habsburg lands including Bohemia and its Crown of St. Václav. From 1804 to 1835, he would rule Austria as Francis I, the first Austrian emperor and the only ruler to hold those two imperial crowns before the dissolution of the Holy Roman Empire in 1806.

After his own coronation as Emperor Napoleon I, Napoleon Bonaparte once again moved against the Austrians as a consequence of their refusal to declare neutrality in France's conflict with Great Britain. Napoleon advanced on Vienna in November 1805 and then earned his greatest victory against the combined Austrian and Russian armies at Austerlitz (Slavkov) outside Brno in Moravia on December 2. Austrian acceptance of the Peace of Pressburg temporarily ended the fighting, and in August 1806, Francis abdicated as Holy Roman Emperor after Napoleon's creation of a 16-member Confederation of the Rhine rendered the Holy Roman Empire irrelevant. The end of the Holy Roman Empire further eroded the status of the Kingdom of Bohemia, which had long held the right to elect the emperor and to seat delegates in the Imperial Diet and other imperial bodies. Slovak nationalists initially hoped to find an ally in Napoleon after his troops occupied Vienna, Bratislava, Trnava, and sections of western Slovakia in 1805 and again in 1809. However, the siege of Bratislava in the latter year caused great physical destruction to the city in addition to the burning of Bratislava Castle and the destruction of nearby Devín Castle on a promontory above the Danube and Morava rivers.

In 1812, Austrian forces joined Napoleon's Grand Army in the invasion of Russia, but as the campaign unraveled, the Austrians agreed to a truce with Russia and then in 1813 joined the Quadruple Alliance as an ally of Russia, Prussia, and Great Britain. After Napoleon's defeat at Leipzig in October 1813 and his abdication in April of the following year, Francis I and his chief of diplomacy, Prince Klemens von Metternich, hosted the Congress of Vienna, which completed its work shortly after Napoleon's "Hundred Days" return ended with his final defeat at Waterloo in June 1815.

By virtue of the Vienna settlement, Austria forfeited claims to the Austrian Netherlands in return for some lost territories and the addition of Lombardy and Venetia in northern Italy. The Austrians also gained the presidency of the 39-member German Confederation established in place of the defunct Holy Roman Empire and inclusive of Bohemia, Moravia, and the Silesian territories of Austria and Prussia. The great powers—Austria, Russia, Prussia, and Great Britain—agreed to cooperate in the restoration of legitimate rulers, the creation of a stable state system, and the suppression of revolution in Europe. Austria's Metternich became a champion of this new conservative order and, after being named chancellor in 1821, utilized the centralized bureaucracy, police, and censors to suppress liberalism and the threat of revolution in the Austrian Empire.

THE CZECH NATIONAL RENASCENCE

The emergence of a Slovak national identity during the late 18th and early 19th centuries found a Czech equivalent in the Czech national renascence that began during the latter decades of the Enlightenment and led to the development of the modern Czech nation. While the centralization reforms of Maria Theresa and Joseph II affected the Kingdom of Bohemia directly and resulted in the loss of much of the kingdom's independence, the Czechs had not completely forfeited the historical rights of statehood under the Habsburg monarchy. In the age of nationalism, efforts to preserve historical rights differentiated the Czechs from the Slovaks, who in lacking a historical state turned instead to the concept of natural rights in defining their status under the Magyars.

At the beginning of the 18th century, Bohemia remained a kingdom of large landed estates and small-scale peasant cultivation. After mid-century, economic expansion began in areas such as textiles, iron, and glass as Habsburg policies encouraged industrialization. The abolition of serfdom in 1781 liberated the peasants from feudal restrictions, and as the population increased, large numbers departed the countryside for the cities. The shift in population not only expanded the size of the towns and cities, but also increased the percentage of Czech-speaking inhabitants in urban areas.

After the defeat at White Mountain in 1620, Czech declined as a written language in Bohemia even as it was being preserved by Slovak Protestants using Biblical Czech, or *bibličtina*, in their liturgy and writings. German had replaced Czech as the language of the nobility and high clergy, but Czech remained the spoken language of the commoners—of the peasants and the parish priests whose activities required familiarity with the vernacular. Under Maria Theresa and Joseph II, the new professional bureaucracy employed German as the language of administration, but civil servants were required to communicate with the population in the local vernacular.

The requirements for education in the Czech language, combined with the emergence of a Czech intelligentsia, led to the establishment of chairs of Czech language and literature in Vienna and later in Bohemia with Leopold II's creation of a similar chair at the Prague university in 1791. Czech scholars and writers studied the Czech language and the literary works of the past, in addition to translating foreign works into Czech. Theatres performed Czech plays or foreign plays translated into Czech, and the national culture as a whole blossomed during the Enlightenment, even before Joseph II's easing of censorship restrictions in 1781. The proliferation of books in German, Latin, and Czech during the 1700s increased dramatically at the end of the century.

The first phase of the Czech National Revival belonged to the Bohemian nobility and to scholars such as Josef Dobrovský and his contemporaries, who revived interest in the history of Bohemia, real and imagined. In their Bohemian *Landespatriotismus* (land patriotism), the Bohemian nobility defined "nation" in the traditional sense as the group in society that guided the political life of the kingdom, meaning the nobles themselves. With the reforms of the Habsburgs threatening the traditional role and rights of the nobility, the Bohemian nobles looked to the past and to the independent status of a unique Kingdom of Bohemia in defense of those rights. What the Enlightenment added to the evolution of Bohemian patriotism was the element of identification with the territory in which one lived, in the sense of Czech loyalty to the Bohemian crown lands and the self-identification of German-speaking nobles as Bohemian Germans.

Because of this identification with the land, patriotic nobles tended to emphasize collections of historical materials, historical mythology, and national heroes such as St. Jan Nepomuký (St. John of Nepomuk), canonized in 1729 and memorialized in a statue on Charles Bridge. The patronage of the nobles led to the creation of patriotic societies and provided financial support for the opening of the National Museum in Prague in April 1818.

Along with his colleague Gelasius Dobner, the philiologist and historian Josef Dobrovský engaged in the study of Czech history in order to refute the mythology surrounding St. Jan Nepomuký, who was reputed to have been thrown into the Vltava from the stone bridge (now the Charles Bridge) under orders from Václav IV in 1393. The alleged justification for the clergyman's punishment was his refusal to violate the sanctity of the confessional in regard to the queen's confession. An examination of historical records, however, supported the theory that the saint was actually based upon two different individuals who had been combined by the Jesuits in order to counter the popularity of the Protestant hero Jan Hus with a Catholic hero of their own.

Dobrovský's historical studies celebrated the unique character of the Czech language and culture, which pleased the Czech nobles in their efforts to distance themselves from Habsburg reforms. In 1783, Dobrovský collaborated with František Martin Pelcl in publishing a first volume of Czech writings, which included the historical chronicle of Cosmas of Prague. Dobrovský's codification of the Czech language and his publication of a *History of Czech Language and Literature* and a *Czech-German Dictionary* made him a leading figure of the Czech national revival. At the core of Dobrovský's work lay his belief, as expressed in a 1791 address, that the battle at White Mountain in 1620 represented a critical turning point in the history of the Czechs, who emerged from the defeat a broken people yet to recover from the national tragedy.

The search for a heroic past and the scholarly efforts to define the unique character of the Czech people seemingly gained an important body of evidence with the alleged discovery of *Rukopis královédvorský* (Dvůr kralové, or Kingscourt, manuscript) in 1817 and *Rukopis zelenahorský* (Zelená Hora manuscript) a year later. The writer Václav Hanka made public the Dvůr kralové manuscript after claiming to have discovered it in the tower of a church. Containing lyrics and text describing the Czech defeat of foreign invaders, the 13th-century manuscript was purported be the oldest document in the Czech language. A year later, a second manuscript was discovered at Zelená Hora and appeared to have been written in the 10th century, meaning that it predated the medieval German epic, the *Niebelungenlied* (The Song of the Nibelungs). The RMZ manuscripts, as they were known, became a great source of pride for Czech patriots because they offered proof that the Czech language and culture were as old and worthy of respect as those of the Germans and other major European peoples. However, although the manuscripts would influence scholars, artists, and writers for decades, they would be exposed as fakes by the end of the 19th century.

At the beginning of the 19th century, the concept of the Czech nation generally incorporated all the Czech-speaking inhabitants of Bohemia, Moravia, Silesia, and, for many, the Slovak lands due to the close linguistic relationship that existed. But the creation of a Slovak literary language and the early stirrings of a Slovak national identity undermined efforts to create a common "Czechoslovak," or "Czecho-Slovak," language and culture. The Czechs also moved further away from the Slovaks in terms of economic development as industrialization continued at a rapid pace in Bohemia. As modernization continued to alter old social and economic relationships, a Czech middle class grew in size and influence, demanding political rights and playing an active role in the second stage of the Czech national renascence.

During the first half of the 19th century, the population of Bohemia grew from 4.8 million in 1815 to 6.7 million in 1847, in spite of a major outbreak of cholera at the beginning of the 1830s and two smaller reoccurrences in 1836–1837 and 1843. During that period, the percentage of Czech speakers in Bohemia stood at approximately 60 percent and in Moravia, with a slightly different dialect, at 70 percent. In Austrian Silesia, Czech speakers accounted for only about 20 percent of the population due to the majority presence of ethnic Germans and Poles.

Romantic nationalism and 19th-century liberalism provided impetus for the next stage of the national awakening after 1815, although censorship remained a major obstacle as a function of the police and the administrative *gubernia* of Bohemia and Moravia-Silesia. Borrowing from Herder, Fichte, and other philosophers of Romantic nationalism, Czech patriots viewed their evolution as a "historical nation" in terms of the centuries-old struggle for freedom against foreign oppression, especially in regard to the Germans. In the view of many nationalists, the Slavs were characterized historically as a democratic and peace-loving people in contrast to the hegemonic Germans, whose aggression toward the Czechs fostered a sense of national and cultural inferiority in the latter. This theme could be found in *Slávy dcera* (Sláva's Daughter, 1824) a highly influential work of poetry by the Slovak Protestant writer Ján Kollár, who contributed to the Czech national revival with collections of folk songs and writings in Czech.

However, whereas Herder and others equated "nation" with language, culture, and blood, the French Revolution had defined the "nation" as the people, or citizens possessing natural rights and the desire to participate in the political process. For many Czech patriots, the reawakening of culture and identity coincided with the liberal goals of rightful freedoms, political representation, and the restoration of the historic rights of the Bohemian kingdom. National consciousness became directly linked to national rights as the Czechs sought to alter their status as a nation without a state.

One of the leading proponents of romantic nationalism in Bohemia was the philologist and pedagogue Josef Jungmann, who became rector of Prague university in 1840. Jungmann's interest in the Czech language stemmed from his patriotism and his desire to create a Czech language that was more than just the vernacular of the shops and countryside. He believed that an individual was genuinely Czech only if he or she spoke the Czech language as a primary form of communication. Jungmann therefore set out to develop Czech into a language appropriate for artists, writers, and scientists, initially by translating foreign writers and scholars like Goethe, Schiller, and Milton (*Paradise Lost*) into Czech.

During the first half of the 1820s, Jungmann published the Czech reader *Slovesnost* (*Poetics: A Collection of Examples, with a Short Treatise on Style*) and the first modern history of Czech literature, before completing work on a five-volume Czech-German dictionary by the end of the 1830s. Along with the Protestant Moravian historian František Palacký and others, Jungmann founded scientific and scholarly societies, one of which sponsored the creation in 1831 of the literary organization *Matice cĕská* (Czech Mother), which published Jungmann's dictionary.

The early decades of the 19th century witnessed a revival of interest in Jan Hus and the Hussites as Czech national heroes and in works like Comenius's *Labyrinth of the World* which had been banned after White Mountain. In his multivolume *History of the Czech Nation*, Palacký explained the history of Bohemia and Moravia in terms of the romanticized vision of Slavs in constant conflict with the laws and culture of expansionist Germandom. In Palacký's interpretation of Czech history, the democratic-minded Slavs, as represented by the Hussites and others, have either engaged in armed struggle against German feudalism or chosen the path of cooperation as a means retaining their Slavic cultural identity. The first three volumes of the work were published in German by *Matice cĕská* in 1836–1842, and the first volume in Czech appeared in March 1848.

By the 1820s, organizations linked to the national movement began to appear in towns across Bohemia and Moravia. Women, whose participation had been limited due to restrictions on education, now joined groups that celebrated Czech nationalism with cultural events, patriotic songs, and other public displays of national pride. During the 1830s and 1840s, the number of social and political groups continued to grow as they promoted Czech literature and music and led members on organized visits to sites of historical significance. The writer Božena Němcová is considered a founding mother of the National Revival for her collections of folklore and for her much-loved novel *Babička* (The Grandmother, 1855), as well as for her work with other leading Czech patriots.[2]

In February 1840, the lyricist Josef Kajetán Tyl organized a ball to commemorate the opening of the first Czech theater in Prague, and the event gained great notoriety when the tickets, menu, and other documents were printed in Czech. Tyl had already gained personal acclaim for his opera *Fidlovačka*, which premiered at the end of 1834 and included the song "*Kde domov můj?*" (Where Is My Home?), later adopted as the Czech national anthem.

At the end of the 1830s, the Bohemian Estates received Vienna's permission to appoint Palacký as their official historian, and in 1843, they invited the scholar to present a program of lectures on the Estates constitution since White Mountain. Palacký was openly critical of the recent Habsburg rulers, and his enthusiastic promotion of the Hussites as Czech national heroes did little to endear him to the Austrian authorities. Palacký's lectures on the constitutional rights of the Estates served as a reminder of the political ground that had been lost since the centralization measures of the Habsburgs had virtually eliminated the political power of the Land Diets. In February 1847, the Estates produced a formal assertion of their rights, which was then rejected by the imperial government in Vienna. With Palacký serving as advisor, the Bohemian Diet responded in May with the "Deduction of the Legal Continuity of the Constitutional Rights of the Czech Estates" and submitted the document to Ferdinand I (r. 1835–1848). In their August session, the Estates took their challenge a step further by refusing to accept the government's tax proposals, although their actions could not prevent the collection of the required taxes.

From the opening years of the century to the beginning of the revolutionary year of 1848, the Czechs had come a long way in developing a national consciousness distinct from the Bohemian *Landespatriotismus* of the nobility and German Bohemia ideology of the German liberals in the arenas of culture and politics. Historians and other scholars defined the Czech nation in relation to other Slavs, which in turn led many to embrace Pan-Slavism or to promote Austroslavism, the latter a belief that cooperation among the Slavic peoples of the Austrian Empire would allow all the Slavs to achieve their goals. For the Czechs, this meant greater autonomy and historic rights within the empire and parity between ethnic Germans and Czechs within the borders of the Bohemian crown lands.[3]

THE SLOVAKS AFTER 1815

The period after the fall of Napoleon began badly for the Slovaks with declining grain prices and a famine in Eastern Slovakia in 1817–1818. During the 1820s and 1830s, the persistence of feudalism in rural society and economic affairs prevented industrial progress and inspired peasant uprisings in 1820 and 1831.

In the belief that there were individuals in the imperial court sympathetic to the Slavic peoples of Hungary, Slovak leaders submitted a petition of grievances to the Chancellor Metternich in 1842 requesting the creation of a chair of Slavonic languages at the University of Pest, the protection of churches and schools from further Magyarization, and the continued instruction of the Slovak language in schools. The imperial authorities expressed little interest in the petition when it was delivered by a delegation, and Hungarian liberals such as Lajos Kossuth denounced the Slovak actions as treason. In 1844, the Hungarian Diet imposed Magyar as the language of administration and education in Hungary, ending the traditional use of Latin in those contexts.

As a leading liberal nationalist, Kossuth promoted reforms and national unity, but his nationalism was solidly Magyar in nature. Kossuth believed that the non-Magyar peoples of Hungary should be assimilated into the Hungarian nation, and that since the Slovaks possessed no claim of historic state rights, they did not deserve consideration in terms of separate territorial identification or administration. In 1847, Kossuth entered the Hungarian Diet, where he joined the Slovak national revivalist Ľudovit Štúr, whose *Grievances and Complaints of the Slavs in Hungary Concerning the Abuse of Power by the Magyars, Collected by a Hungarian Slav* (1843) had been published in Leipzig after Hungarian publishers refused to accept the work. In his capacity as a politician, Štúr argued on behalf of social and economic reforms, including the abolition of serfdom, but his promotion of Slovak national interests failed to generate support among fellow members of the Diet.

THE CZECHS AND THE REVOLUTIONS OF 1848–1849

In late February 1848, barricades appeared in the streets of Paris as riots forced the abdication of the French king, Louis Philippe I. This outbreak of revolutionary violence triggered uprisings across Europe into March, as crowds took to the streets in hopes of altering the social and political status quo. With social upheaval occurring simultaneously in many European capitals, the revolutionary year of 1848 seemed to offer the promise of a "Springtime of Nations" that would fulfill the transformational goals of liberals and nationalists from Paris to Vienna.

On March 11, radical members of the national organization Bohemian Appeal planned to hold a large gathering at St. Václav's Bath in Prague's New Town. Bohemian Repeal had been founded by predominately middle-class Czechs and Germans with the goal of liberating the Bohemian lands from the centralized authority of the imperial government, although a small faction of the group professed more radical and democratic ideals. Under the leadership of Palacký and the young journalist Karel Havlíček Borovský, the St. Václav Committee drew up a petition in March that reaffirmed the unity of the Bohemian territories and called for greater self-government through the Bohemian Land Diet and a common diet representing Bohemia, Moravia, and Austrian Silesia. The petitioners demanded the abolition of all remaining *robota* requirements, the civil equality of Czechs and Germans, and the granting of fundamental liberties. A delegation departed for Vienna to present the petition to the imperial government, but student-led street demonstrations on March 13–15 had already changed the political environment in the capital as Metternich's resignation accompanied the emperor's promise of a constitution, elected assembly, and cessation of censorship.

On March 3, Lajos Kossuth had addressed the Hungarian Diet in Bratislava and put forth demands that would shortly become the core of the "March Laws" as presented to the emperor Ferdinand. Kossuth called for liberal social reforms such as the elimination of the *robota*, but the primary focus of his speech concerned the creation of an autonomous Hungary connected to the Austrian Empire solely through the person of the ruler as king of Hungary and emperor of Austria. As set down in the March Laws, Kossuth and other liberals in the Diet demanded a Diet elected by male property holders and a Cabinet whose ministers reported directly to the elected body. Hungary would conduct its own foreign relations and manage its own army. The imperial court, beset by revolution in Vienna, had little choice but to have the emperor visit the Diet in Pressburg in April and approve the March Laws. The new Hungarian government immediately acted to abolish *robota* obligations for peasant landholders and to institute a range of civil liberties. The problem for the Slovaks, however, was that Kossuth and the other Hungarian leaders had little interest in granting similar rights to non-Magyars in Hungary.

In comparison with the Hungarian demands, the petition delivered by the Czechs appeared far more moderate than initially assumed. The delegation returned to Prague on March 27 with little to show for its efforts, and two days later, it produced a new petition calling for an elected government for the unified lands of the Bohemian crown with independent ministers based in Prague. When a delegation delivered the revised petition to Vienna, the imperial government delayed discussion of unified crown lands until the next session of the imperial Reichstag in July, but otherwise acceded to Czech demands for a common diet, a separate administration for Bohemia, and the equality of Czechs and Germans. For many German Bohemians, however, the goal was not the political unification of Bohemia, but rather the inclusion of Bohemia and Austria in a unified German nation.

By mid-May, demonstrations had once again broken out in the streets of Vienna as the government deliberated on the constitution. In consequence, the government announced that a popularly elected Reichstag would assume responsibility for drafting the document and that the imperial court would be departing Vienna for Innsbruck on May 17.

In Bohemia negotiations over elections and a provisional government, the National Committee, led to a split between the moderate middle-class liberals led by Palacký and the radical students and artisans who sympathized with their fellow radicals in the streets of Vienna. Middle-class Germans in the National Committee and other organizations supported demands for reform, but grew angry over the narrowly Czech nature of the calls for Bohemian autonomy, while many in the Moravian Diet opposed the proposal to merge the Bohemian crown lands. In spite of the less-than-ideal conditions for voting in all areas, 284 delegates were elected to the body, with 178 of them Czechs and the remainder Germans. Palacký, Pavel Jozef Šafárik, František Ladislav Rieger, and others represented the liberal cause in the new Bohemian Diet.

As German liberals moved forward with negotiations on a unified Germany, Palacký received an invitation to represent Bohemia in a preparatory committee for the Frankfurt Parliament, the elected body tasked with unifying the lands of the German Confederation. On April 11, Palacký turned down the invitation in a long statement in which he proclaimed loyalty to the Habsburg empire and declared that as a Bohemian and therefore a Slav, he could not accept the connection between Bohemia and the German lands as anything other than the consequence of personal links between rulers. Palacký recognized Bohemia's role in the former Holy Roman Empire, but argued that as a nation separate from the Germans, the Czechs should not be a part of German unification and that Austria and Bohemia must not be dissolved in the name of a unified Germany. When the Czechs then attempted to prevent elections to the Frankfurt Parliament in Bohemia, Germans left the National Committee and held elections in predominately German-speaking areas.

Palacký and other Czech leaders decided to counter German interests and the Frankfurt Parliament by sponsoring a Slav Congress in Prague in hopes of encouraging cooperation among the Slavic peoples of the Austrian Empire. When the congress opened in June, Šafárik delivered the keynote speech to the assembled Czechs, Slovaks, South Slavs, Poles, and Ruthenes. Primarily the work of Palacký, the manifesto drawn up at the congress was addressed to the nations of Europe in calling for the reorganization of the empire into a federation where the rights and freedoms of all the nations were respected. The document condemned the oppression of the Slavs by the Germans and ended with the French call for liberty, equality, and brotherhood in regard to the individual nations. An address to the Austrian emperor proposed autonomy for the Slavic nations of the empire, but the congress proved that the Slavs were far from unified in their goals and too often unwilling to overcome their own differences or their suspicion of Czech leadership and demands. Before the Slav Congress completed work on specific proposals, however, events in Prague led to the dissolution of the body in June 1848.

On June 12, revolution erupted in the streets of Prague as university students, workers, and artisans erected barricades and clashed with the army after the celebration of a special mass in Wenceslas Square. Stirred up by the Slav Congress and by radical speakers and pamphlets, the students and their allies demanded revolution in the name of an independent Czech republic. However, the military governor of Bohemia, Prince Alfred von Windischgrätz, had already prepared for such an eventuality by moving troops and artillery into position around Prague in an action that had driven the radicals to hold mass meetings and demonstrations prior to June 12. Some 1,200 Prague citizens and 500 members of the national militia stood against the 10,000 troops under the command of Windischgrätz. After several days of skirmishes in the streets of the Old Town and New Town, Windischgrätz withdrew the army from the city and began shelling the Old Town from the heights of Hradčany. Meanwhile, Palacký and the moderates failed in their efforts to curtail the violence, and the radicals proved unable to stir the peasants into a national rising. On June 17, the city surrendered after days of bombardment and Windischgrätz instituted a martial law crackdown, ordering the arrest of the uprising's leaders. With the capitulation of Prague, the revolution in Bohemia drew to a close and the National Committee and Slav Congress ceased to exist.

In August 1848, Ferdinand I and the imperial court returned to Vienna by invitation of the Reichstag, which had assembled on July 22, and because victories by Windischgrätz in Bohemia and Radetzky in northern Italy had turned the tide in favor of the counter-revolutionaries. The following month, the Austrians invaded Hungary in cooperation with Croatian forces under Baron Josip Jelačić in an effort to suppress the "Lawful Revolution" of Kossuth and the Hungarians. When the Hungarians attempted to bring their case to the Reichstag, the Czechs led the majority in rejecting the request for a hearing. However, Viennese radicals supported the cause of Hungarian autonomy or even independence and organized protests on October 6 as authorities attempted to send a Viennese military garrison to fight the Hungarians. With the city in turmoil, the emperor and his court fled

Vienna while Windischgrätz and the army fought the radicals in the streets, regaining control of the imperial capital at the end of the month.

Due to the uncertain situation in Vienna, Ferdinand relocated the Reichstag to Kroměříž in Moravia, where deliberations on the constitution continued in November. Ultimately, however, both the Reichstag and the constitution became victims of a failed revolution as a new administration attempted to roll back reforms granted during the months of revolution. On November 27, 1848, Prince Felix zu Schwarzenberg, the brother-in-law of Windischgrätz, assumed the responsibilities of prime minister, with Rudolf Stadion as minister of the interior and Alexander Bach as minister of justice. The empire then underwent a transfer of monarchical power on December 2 as Ferdinand I abdicated the imperial throne in favor of his nephew, Francis Joseph I (r. 1848–1916).

For the Czechs, the "Springtime of Nations" in 1848–1849 ended with the arrest and trials of radicals and the understanding that a policy of cooperation with imperial authorities had failed to produce any significant results for Czech nationalists. With the exception of figures such as Karel Havliček, who kept up the struggle for civil liberties and liberal reforms, Palacky, Rieger, and key leaders of the national movement retired for the moment into scholarly and other activities. Havliček continued to publish *Národní noviny* (National News) until the government officially suspended the newspaper in January 1850. After his arrest in December 1851 and exile to the Austrian Tyrol for several years, Havliček returned to Prague in 1855 to find that his former colleagues had little interest in reestablishing contact with him. Miserable and sick with tuberculosis, Havlíček died on July 29, 1856, and became revered as a martyr to the cause by many Czech nationalists.

HUNGARY AND THE SLOVAKS IN 1848–1849

For the Slovaks, unrest spread rapidly after the institution of the March Laws and leaders of the Slovak national movement like Štúr, Hodža, and Hurban attempted to mobilize support for petitions for presentation to the Hungarian administration. On March 28, 1848, a meeting of Slovak nationalists produced a moderate petition requesting permission for instruction of the Slovak language in elementary schools located in areas containing a Slovak-speaking majority.

After the Hungarians refused to grant the desired permission, Slovak leaders convened a larger session on May 10–11 at Liptovský Sväty Mikuláš in northern Slovakia. With more time to prepare, Hurban, Štefan Marko Daxner, and other Slovak nationalists drew up a list of

14 demands, "The Demands of the Slovak Nation," which called for the abolition of serfdom, the right of landownership, and the institution of civil liberties such as freedom of the press. The petition also included a proposal for the reorganization of the Kingdom of Hungary into a federation based on the equality of nations, each of which would possess a regional parliament elected through universal manhood suffrage and voting equality. A unified Hungarian parliament would link all of the nationalities, and the autonomous Slovak nation would receive the right to use Slovak as the language of education and administration, to maintain a national militia with a Slovak officer corps, and to raise the red and white colors of the Slovak nation beside the flag of Hungary.

The response of the Hungarian ministers to the Slovak petition was to order the arrests of Štúr, Hodža, and Hurban, who left northern Hungary in an effort to negotiate with other Slavs and, in the case of Štúr, to serve as an unofficial delegate of the Slovak nation to the Slav Congress in Prague. What Štúr discovered at the Congress, though, was that the Slovak desire for equality within Hungary ran counter to the Austroslavism of Palacký and other Czech leaders who viewed the merger of Czechs and Slovaks as a desirable option for advancing their own agenda.

As the Slovaks looked to the South Slavs for assistance in promoting their national goals, the potential for an armed struggle increased as the Habsburg-appointed governor of Croatia, Jelačić, moved against the Hungarians in September 1848. In mid-July, however, Kossuth and the Hungarian Diet had appropriated funding for a new Hungarian army, the Honvéd, which was initially successful in turning back Jelačić's forces. As the conflict continued, Štúr, Hodža, Hurban, and others established a Slovak National Council and set about creating a fighting force of some 600 volunteers, the majority of them students under the command of two Czech officers.

On September 19, the Slovak National Council declared the independence of Slovakia from Hungary and called for a national rising in support of the volunteer force, which was engaging the Hungarians in battle at the time. Although poorly equipped and lacking organized support and supplies, the Slovak volunteers and their foreign comrades defeated the Hungarians at Brezová on September 22 and then prepared to cooperate with the forces of the imperial government upon their arrival. Hungarian authorities branded the Slovak leaders as traitors and deprived them of their citizenship as they instituted a retaliatory policy of mass arrests and executions.

In the wake of these new developments and with the arrival of armies under Jelačić and Windischgrätz, Slovak leaders met with the emperor in Olomouc on March 20 and requested the creation of an autonomous Slovakia with a parliament and administration directly connected to the imperial government in Vienna. The interior minister Stadion saw some merit in the plan as a means of undermining the Hungarians, but on April 4, Kossuth and the Diet declared an end to Habsburg rule in Hungary, and Kossuth became governor-president of an independent Hungarian nation. The Slovak profession of loyalty to the emperor now brought Austrian assistance in creating a Slovak National Army to combat the Honvéd and Hungarian guerillas operating on Slovak soil. In early June, the reactionary czar Nicholas I ordered 100,000 Russian troops into Hungary and a smaller force into Transylvania, thereby rendering the conflict unwinnable for the Hungarians.

The Hungarian surrender to the Russians at Vilagos on August 11 ended the period of revolution and warfare and led to both the elimination of the Hungarian constitution and the institution of a limited Stadion Constitution, which lasted until the end of December 1851. For the Slovaks, the constitution brought some gains, although they were far short of demands set out in the national program of 1848–1849. Slovaks were granted the right to hold administrative offices and to use the Slovak language in primary schools and administrative affairs, but the dream of an autonomous Slovakia failed to materialize in spite of the willingness on the part of many to fight for that goal. As Slovak leaders came to understand, neither the conservative, Magyarized nobility nor the peasants had supported the national struggle in 1848–1849. Disillusioned with the Hungarians and the Czechs, Slovak leaders also now had little reason to trust the imperial administration in pursuing a Slovak national program.

THE CZECH LANDS, 1849–1880

The failure of the revolutions in 1848–1849 allowed the counterrevolutionaries to institute a system of neoabsolutism in the Austrian Empire over the next decade. Felix zu Schwarzenberg continued to head the government until his death in 1852, but the administration of the empire bore the stamp of the minister of the interior, Alexander Bach. A product of postrevolutionary conservatism, the "Bach system" combined a highly centralized bureaucracy with extensive use of the army, police, and informers against regional interests and opponents of the regime. German became the official language of the government and the Catholic Church an ally of the administration through the 1855 Concordat, which granted the Church broad influence over censorship and education as well as protected Church property and sanctioned church courts. The Sylvester Patent of December 31, 1851, eliminated any rights gained during the revolution beyond the abolition of serfdom, religious freedom, and civic equality.

By the end of the 1850s, setbacks in foreign policy undermined the neoabsolutist policies of the imperial government. Austria's neutrality during the Crimean War (1854–1856) left the Habsburg empire isolated among the major powers as the period of diplomatic equilibrium in Europe reached an end. French intervention on behalf of the Piedmontese and other Italians in the Italian war of 1859 resulted in Austria's forfeiture of Lombardy in northern Italy and an economic crisis back home. Bach resigned his ministerial duties after the defeats at Magenta and Solferino, thereby bringing the Bach era to a close and opening the way to Emperor Francis Joseph's halting efforts at altering the administration's neoabsolutist course.

The Imperial Diploma of October 20, 1860, established a central parliament, the Reichrat, which would cooperate with restored provincial diets and could meet without the participation of the Hungarians. This October Diploma introduced elements of federalism into the administration of the empire, especially in regard to the Hungarians, who received recognition of their special historical status as a basis for restoring an autonomous legislature, county administrations, and pre-1848 government offices. In the February Patent of 1861, however, revisions to the diploma established a House of Lords and House of Deputies in the now-bicameral Reichrat, weakened the Hungarian Diet, and transformed the district diets from legislative bodies into instruments of centralized administration. The Hungarian response was to boycott the Reichsrat and claim that the March Laws of 1848 represented their rightful constitution. Czech liberals sided with the nobility in demanding recognition of the historic state rights of Bohemia, but initially decided against a boycott as Palacký received appointment to the Reichrat's upper house and Rieger served as leader of the Czech representatives in the lower house. From 1863 to 1879, however, Rieger and the Czechs refrained from participating in the Reichrat after failing to gain ground on behalf of the federalist cause.

In 1866, the Austrians suffered another critical military setback as the rivalry with Prussia in the German Confederation contributed to the outbreak of the Austro-Prussian War in June of that year. Under William I and his chancellor Otto von Bismarck, the Prussians invaded Bohemia after defeating Austria's primary allies among the German states. After suffering a decisive defeat at Sadowá (Königgrätz) near Hradec Králové on July 3, Francis Joseph and his government found themselves divorced from the process of German unification and vulnerable to Hungarian demands for greater autonomy.

Defeat in 1866 generated major financial deficits and exposed the internal weaknesses of the empire, leading to the creation of a dualist system for Austria and Hungary through the *Ausgleich*, or Compromise, of 1867. The December Constitution of 1867, as passed by the Reichrat, divided the empire into the Kingdom of Hungary and the lands of "Cisleithania," or non-Hungarian territories such as Lower Austria across the river Leitha from Hungary. The ruler of Austria-Hungary, as the empire was now known, would serve as emperor of Austria and king of Hungary as the two halves of the empire maintained their own legislative and legal sovereignty while sharing common ministries for foreign affairs, finances, and the military.

Although the Czech nationalists split into Old Czech and Young Czech factions, both were united in opposition to the December Constitution because of its failure to address the historic state rights of Bohemia or to grant special privileges to the most developed and industrialized part of the empire. In response to the constitution, the Czechs boycotted the Reichrat and the diets as Palacký, Rieger, and other leaders pursued outside assistance from France or Russia. However, a visit to St. Petersburg by Palacký and Rieger in May 1867 failed to generate any commitment on the part of Alexander II, and a memorandum sent to Napoleon III on behalf of the Slavs of the empire in 1869 inspired little French interest. France's defeat in the Franco-Prussian War of 1870–1871 provided the opportunity for Bismarck's proclamation of a unified German Reich in January 1871.

TOWARD A MODERN CZECH NATION, 1880–1914

After negotiations with the minister-president Count Eduard Taafe, Czech delegates returned to the imperial Reichsrat and pursued a policy of cooperation in return for reforms such as the language ordinances of 1880, which confirmed German as the internal language of administration in Bohemia and Moravia, but allowed for the use of Czech in external contact with the population. Additional new measures divided the university in Prague into separate Czech and German institutions and increased the number of Czech-speaking voters by reducing the tax requirement for suffrage in towns and rural areas. After 1882, many of the leading Czech intellectuals and national leaders emerged from the Czech section of the university. In spite of the reforms, however, some of the Young Czechs broke with the Czech Club

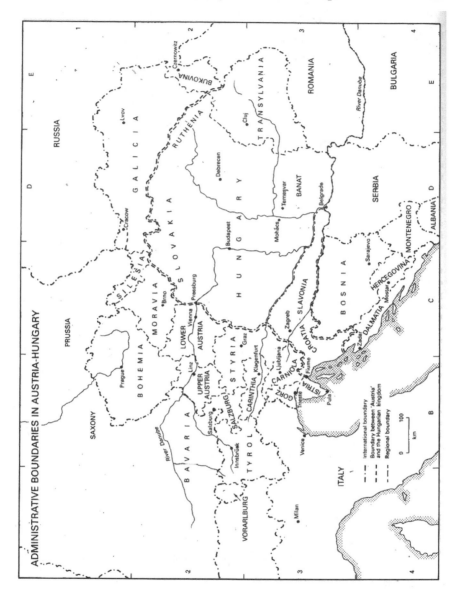

Austria-Hungary administrative map. (*An Atlas of Eastern Europe in the Twentieth Century,* by Richard Crampton and Ben Crampton, 1997. Reproduced by permission of Taylor & Francis Books UK.)

in the Reichrat during the 1880s and abandoned cooperation in favor of opposition to imperial policies.

Bohemian Germans who were already disturbed over concessions to the Czechs initiated their own boycott of the Bohemian Diet in 1887, two years after reorganization created a Czech majority in that body. In order to return the Germans to the diet, Taafe opened negotiations with the Old Czechs and the Germans in January 1890. The result of the deliberations was the effective division of Bohemia into Czech and German regions with judicial institutions, school boards, and business and economic organizations constituted along national lines. Reiger's defense of the agreement failed to prevent the demise of the Old Czechs as a political force as the 1891 Reichsrat elections sent 37 Young Czechs and only 2 Old Czechs to Vienna.

In 1897, the Young Czechs ended their opposition when the Badeni laws placed the Czech language on an equal footing with German in Bohemia. Count Kasimir Badeni, appointed minister-president of Austria in 1895, introduced new ordinances that determined that cases be administered in the language in which they were submitted and required officials and employers in the Czech lands to become bilingual. Fearing an end to Austrian cultural dominance and the primacy of the German language in imperial affairs, German liberals and nationalists agitated in the Reichsrat as demonstrations began in Vienna and elsewhere. After widespread opposition drove Badeni from office, the ordinances were repealed in 1899, and the Czechs in the Reichsrat engaged in opposition tactics of their own. In 1906, however, the introduction of universal manhood suffrage in the Austrian half of the empire allowed for a more representative Czech presence in the imperial parliament.

The decades after the midcentury revolutions witnessed continued population growth and expansion of the industrial sector in the Czech lands. From approximately 6.74 million inhabitants in 1850, the population increased to 10.15 million in 1910, encompassing some 6.4 million Czechs and 3.5 million Germans. Industrialization continued from 1848 to 1873 and then recovered after a period of depression to undergo another strong period of growth from 1880 to 1914. Iron and steel, chemicals, textiles, coal and paper joined engineering, food processing, and brewing as productive areas of the Czech economy.

The opening of the Burgher Brewery in Plzeň, or Pilsen, in 1842 introduced the world to a new type of bottom-fermented beer, which bore the name of its Bohemian city of origin as "pilsener." In 1869, Plzeň became the birthplace of a well-known industrial concern after the engineer and entrepreneur Emil Škoda purchased the machine plant in which he was employed and expanded it into an extensive and widely respected enterprise, the Škoda Works. In an economic context, the Czech lands became vitally important to the Austrian half of the empire by the early 1900s because Bohemia, Moravia, and

Silesia produced two-thirds of the industrial output of the non-Hungarian territories of Austria-Hungary.

By 1914, economic progress and modernization had created a more modern, educated, and urban society in the Czech lands, one in which the traditional nobility had lost its economic advantage and the rising middle classes embraced Czech nationalism and sought to extend their political influence. With the continued influx of Czech speakers from rural areas, the cities grew increasingly Czech, and the tensions between the Czech and German national communities increased.

The evolution of a Czech national community during the 19th century coincided with the emergence of a national identity among the Germans of the Czech lands. The two national communities responded to each other's activities and provocations, shared tactics, and often clashed with each other in ways that traversed the boundaries of faith, social class, and local and regional traditions and institutions. Although urban areas occasionally witnessed physical clashes in the streets, it was the public spaces and public life that became the cultural battleground for the Czech and German nations seeking to gain an edge by politicizing historical figures and events. Buildings, monuments, holidays, public celebrations, and cultural events assumed symbolic overtones of national pride and identity, with the Czechs slowly gaining the advantage in Prague.

In 1848, the large square that had been known as Horse Market since the 14th century was renamed Václavské námĕsti (Wenceslas Square) after Bohemia's patron, St. Václav. The stone bridge across the Vltava became Charles Bridge in 1870, and by the mid-1890s, streets and squares in Prague bore the names of Hus, Žižka, Jiři z Podĕbrad, and Palacký. Street signs that once displayed German names above their Czech designations had the order reversed in 1861 as Czech became the language of administration for Prague officials. In the 1890s, German names disappeared from the signs altogether, and the red and white colors of the Czechs replaced the traditional imperial colors of black and yellow.

Founded in 1862, the *Sokol* ("Falcon") movement supported the national cause by promoting Czech patriotism and the development of the body and mind through gymnastics, physical activities, and the arts. Composers such as Antonín Dvořák, Leos Janacek, and Bedřich Smetana composed music celebrating national ideals, historical figures, and the natural beauty of the Czech lands, as in Smetana's *Ma Vlast* (My Country).

The opening of Prague's National Theater (Národní Divadlo) in 1881 represented an important moment in the cultural lives of Czechs living in a city long dominated by German theaters. Funded through the donations of numerous Czechs living in the towns and countryside, the theater rested on a foundation of stones gathered from historically significant locations across the land. Palacký, the "Father of the Nation," and Smetana set the first stones in 1868. Intentionally designed to be larger than two nearby German theaters, the National Theater was damaged by fire shortly after opening, but was rebuilt and began hosting performances again in 1883. During the 1890s, Prague also became home to the Czech Academy of Arts and Sciences and the Czech Philharmonic.

Czech political life also changed during the last decades of the 19th century as modern political parties arose to represent class and confessional interests in place of the liberal and nationalist movements of recent decades. In 1893, an independent Social Democratic Party was founded in the Czech lands to represent the interests of the working class as electoral reforms continued to extend the franchise. Established in 1898, the Czech National Socialist Party spoke for workers, artisans, and shopkeepers opposed to the national agenda of the Bohemian Germans and the political programs of the Young Czechs and Social Democrats. The Young Czechs dominated Czech politics from 1891 to 1906 as the Old Czechs slowly faded as a political entity. By 1911, however, the Social Democrats emerged as the largest of the Czech political parties.

In 1899, the founding of the Agrarian Party offered the rural population a political alternative to socialism or the confessional agendas of the traditionalist Catholic parties. By 1914, František Udržal, an Agrarian deputy in the Bohemian Diet and imperial Reichrat, assumed leadership of the party and would later become an influential political figure in the Czechoslovak government after World War I.

The most significant figure to emerge in Czech politics at the end of the century was Tomáš Garrigue Masaryk, born in Moravia to a Slovak father and a German-speaking Moravian mother in 1850. Masaryk rose from working-class origins to become a professor of philosophy at the Prague university during the 1880s, and it was in his journal *Atheneum* that the so-called RMZ medieval manuscripts were exposed as fabrications in 1886. Liberal and democratic in his political views, Masaryk initially believed that Austria-Hungary could be reformed and reorganized into a democratic federal state with full rights for all nationalities. He also espoused the rights of women, taking his wife Charlotte's family name as his own middle name and advocating the moral and political equality of the sexes. Possessing a strong and independent religious spirit, Masaryk drifted away from his Catholic roots and long opposed the influence of the clergy in political matters.

From 1891 to 1893, Masaryk represented the Young Czechs in the Bohemian Diet and the Reichrat before resigning his duties during the imposition of martial law after demonstrations in Prague in 1893. Although the battle over the RMZ manuscripts gained Masaryk some measure of notoriety, his involvement in the Hilsner trial of 1899 made him a focal point for controversy. In September 1899, a Jewish vagrant named Leopold Hilsner was put on trial for the murder of a young Catholic woman named Anežka Hrůzová. The bloody nature of the murder convinced many that the killing had been ritual in nature. As the nationalist press worked to stir up anti-Semitic passions, Masaryk chose to publish a defense of Hilsner as a matter of his own personal principles. Although the emperor Francis Joseph commuted the death sentence to life imprisonment, Masaryk's defense of Hilsner drew a strong reaction from many nationalists in spite of his claim that ethics applied to nationalism as well as to personal behavior.

After growing critical of both the Old Czechs and the Young Czechs, Masaryk collaborated with Karel Kramář and others in founding the Czech Realist Party, which merged with some members of the Radical Progressive Party in 1900 to form what became known as the Czech Progressive Party in 1905, although its members were still popularly known as the Realists. Masaryk returned to the Reichsrat as a Realist deputy from 1907 to 1914.

HUNGARY AND THE SLOVAK NATION, 1849–1914

For the Slovaks, the period after the midcentury revolutions initially involved efforts by imperial authorities to manage Slovak affairs after the events of 1849. Kollár took up residence in Vienna as an advisor to the government on Slovak issues, although Štúr and Hurban became targets of police monitoring after turning down government appointments. Štúr remained active in linguistic work, however, and at a conference in Bratislava in October 1851, participants reached an agreement on a new Slovak orthography based on the Czech model. Štúr also promoted Pan-Slavism as a solution to Slovak problems in Hungary, as argued in his 1853 manifesto, *Slavdom and the World of the Future*.

On June 6, 1861, Slovak nationalists gathered in Trcanský Sväty Martin to delineate their demands in a "Memorandum of the Slovak Nation" with the goal of presenting the proposals to the Hungarian authorities in Budapest. In this critical document, influenced by Štefan Marko Daxner's "Voice from Slovakia," the authors argued that although the concept of historic state rights did not apply to a people without a state, the Slovaks deserved political autonomy based on their natural rights as a distinct nation. Slovak leaders called for federalization of Hungary through the creation of an autonomous Slovak district in North Hungary with clearly defined borders and the right of Slovaks to use their own language in education and administrative business. The memorandum also demanded civic equality with Magyars, equal rights and freedoms, and the establishment of a Slovak institution of legal studies and a chair of Slavonic literature at the university in Pest. A delegation presented the document to the Hungarian Diet, which discussed the issue of rights while dismissing the proposal for federalization.

Inspired by the Czech *Matice čĕská* and a similar Serbian institution, Slovak nationalists chose Trcanský Svätý Martin as a home for the cultural organization *Matica Slovenská* after the town offered the use of land without charge. Founded in 1863, *Matica Slovenská* became instrumental in promoting Slovak literature and culture through the central organ in Trcanský Svätý Martin and branches across Slovakia.

A year after the *Ausgleich* established the Dual Monarchy and granted the Kingdom of Hungary autonomous status within the empire, the Nationalities Law of December 1, 1868, undermined the positions of the non-Magyar nations by relegating them to the status of ethnic groups within the indivisible Hungarian political nation. The Slovaks would be allowed to maintain cultural and other organizations as well as to use the Slovak language in elementary schools and lower-tier administrative offices, but Magyar remained the language of governance and higher education. Other concessions would be linked to individual freedoms and not to the recognition of distinct nationalities or national rights and identities in a corporate context. With Hungary free of direct interference from Vienna, the process of Magyarization could now continue, with the Slovaks directly under Magyar authority and subject to Hungarian laws.

In response to the actions of the Hungarian Diet, Slovak nationalists led by Viliam Pauliny-Tóth and others mobilized in defense of the 1861 Memorandum. Pauliny-Tóth, a Slovak deputy in the Diet and vice president of *Matica Slovenská*, became cofounder and leader of a new Slovak National Party established in Trcanský Svätý Martin in 1871. With nationalists split into "Old School" and "New School" factions, Pauliny-Tóth led the former in supporting the program of 1861 from its base in Trcanský Svätý Martin. The New School, centered in Pest, promoted a more liberal agenda and abandoned the idea of an autonomous Slovakia in favor of cooperation and negotiations with the Magyars, especially after the Slovak National Party proved unsuccessful in efforts to elect representatives to the Diet in 1872. The Old School denounced the New School's acceptance of the *Ausgleich* and National-ities Law, while the Slovak National Party chose to follow the path of political non-cooperation.

In April 1875, the Hungarian prime minister Kálmán Tisza ordered the closing of *Matica Slovenská* and the seizure of its property on the basis of there being no legal Slovak nation to justify a center for Slovak culture. The government closed the remaining state secondary schools for Slovaks by 1877 and decreased the number of religious schools allowed to teach children the Slovak language. In 1883 Magyar became the compulsory language of education, and in 1907, authorities imposed a loyalty oath on teachers and threatened dismissal if educa-tors failed to instruct their students in Magyar at a satisfactory level. For Slovak students seeking a university education, studying at foreign universities became an important option as the Elizabeth University in Bratislava remained accessible only to Hungarians and Magyarized Slovaks.

During the 1880s, a new generation of Slovak leaders included the poet Pavol Országh-Hviezdoslav; the new head of the SNP, Pavol Mudruň; and Hurban's son, the writer Svetozár Hurban Vajanský. As Magyarization proceeded in the Slovak lands, the Slovak National Party maintained a policy of abstention in regard to the Diet to the end of the century. For Slovak nationalists, however, the restrictions on educational institutions and national organizations and the failure of the Hungarians to fulfill promises of extended suffrage hampered political activity and a revival of national culture on a par with devel-opments in the Czech lands by 1914.

After 1890, some interest in "Czechoslovak" cooperation arose among Czech intellectuals, especially in the writings of the philosopher and politician Tomáš Garrigue Masaryk. Influenced by Masaryk, Vavro Šrobár and Pavel Blaho founded the monthly journal *Hlas* (*The Voice*, 1898–1904), which advocated cooperation between Czechs and Slovaks. Along with the journalist Milan Hodža, Šrobár and Blaho represented the rising young generation of leaders at the beginning of a new century. Hodža's newspaper *Slovenský týždennik* (*Slovak Weekly*) first appeared in 1903 and reflected his democratic ideals and his belief that education would help peasants to create better lives from themselves.

In the elections of February 1905, Hodža was one of only two Slovaks elected to the Diet along with František Skyčak of the Slovak People's Party, announced in 1905 after a clerical defection of the populist priest Fr. Andrej Hlinka and others from the Hungarian People's Party, but not formally established until 1913. Hodža belonged to the Slovak National Party, which had returned to participation in the electoral

process in 1901 and restructured itself as a coalition of Slovak national-
ists, including agrarians like Hodža as well as liberal Hlasists like
Šrobár and Blaho. In June 1905, nationalist workers formed the Slovak
Social Democratic Party after receiving assistance from the Czech Social
Democrats in publishing a newspaper for workers.

The elections of May 1906 brought seven Slovaks to the Diet, including Hodža and Blaho, although the year also proved significant for the
arrest in December of Hlinka. Suspended by his bishop in June for his
political activities, Hlinka was later charged with anti-Magyar agitation
and sentenced to two years' imprisonment and a fine in December. On
October 27, 1907, villagers in Hlinka's birthplace of Černová requested
Hlinka's release so that he could attend the dedication of a local church.
The authorities denied the request, and when villagers reacted against
the arrival of the Bishop of Spis's representatives, the Hungarian
gendarmes opened fire on the crowd, causing 15 fatalities in what
became known as the "Černová massacre." Once released from incarceration, Hlinka continued his political work and, in July 1913, was
chosen to serve as president of the Slovak People's Party.

For the Czechs and Slovaks, the years after the *Ausgleich* of 1867
brought the continued evolution of national culture and identity
under very different circumstances within the Dual Monarchy. However, by 1914, the dualist system was already undergoing irreversible
erosion from within and would not survive the world war that devastated Europe from 1914 to 1918. In spite of their unique historical paths
of development, the disintegration of the Austro-Hungarian Empire
would bring the Czechs and Slovaks together into a common state
after proponents of a "Czechoslovak" solution lobbied successfully
during the war years to make the proposal a reality in the fall of 1918.

NOTES

1. See Peter Brock, *The Slovak National Awakening: An Essay in the Intellectual
History of East Central Europe* (Toronto: University of Toronto Press, 1976).

2. For further reading on modern Czech women's history and portraits of
significant individuals, see Wilma A. Iggers, *Women of Prague* (Providence, RI:
Berghahn Books, 1995).

3. See Derek Sayer, *The Coasts of Bohemia* (Princeton, NJ: Princeton University
Press, 1998), and Peter Brock and H. Gordon Skilling, eds., *The Czech Renascence
of the Nineteenth Century* (Toronto: University of Toronto Press, 1970).

6

World War I and the First Czechoslovak Republic (1914–1938)

T. G. MASARYK AND THE CZECH NATION

As a leading figure in prewar Czech political life, Tomáš Garrigue Masaryk, parliamentarian and philosophy professor at Charles University, has been characterized as a "non-conformist" and "an unrelenting critic of conventional wisdom, established institutions, customary practices and habits in Bohemia and in Austria-Hungary as a whole."[1] Concerned over the growing political uncertainty of the 1880s and 1890s and the future of the Czechs in the Austro-Hungarian Empire, Masaryk addressed the political and historical status of the Czech Lands in his work, *The Czech Question*, in the mid-1890s. Although events would soon erode Masaryk's support for the Habsburg administration, he argued at the time that it was in the best interest of the Czechs to develop a positive program and national identity in regard to the Austrian state and the continued existence of the Czechs within the empire.

Masaryk challenged František Palacký's earlier claims that the cultural struggle against German influences represented the defining element of Czech history, claiming that although the conflict was an important factor in the historical development of the Czechs, the Czech national identity should not be defined primarily in terms of that struggle. Masaryk also questioned the pan-Slavic and Slavophile traditions that led many of his predecessors and colleagues to view czarist Russia as a desirable alternative to the Germans and Austrians. It was Masaryk's belief that in a very realistic sense, Czech links to the Russians and other Slavonic peoples were far less substantial than those to the peoples of the West, especially the French and the Germans, from whom the Czechs had learned so much over the centuries.

Efforts to link practical Christian ethics to modern social and political realities reflected Masaryk's convictions that the true meaning of Czech history lay in the concept of "Czech humanism," as embodied in the teachings of the Hussite movement and the Czech Brethren of the Czech Reformation. The historical evolution of the Czech lands therefore possessed an inherent religiosity even as Enlightenment rationalism and national revival led to the revolutionary activities of 1848, the modernization of Czech society, and the development of a Czech national identity.

Masaryk also recognized that the legacy of the Hussites created a potential paradox for the Czechs because it included both pacifism (Hus, and later Comenius) and violent action (Žižka) in the name of a cause. Although Masaryk had long opposed violent solutions in the pursuit of national goals, the Russian Revolution of 1905 and the growing possibility of war convinced Masaryk that the failure of the imperial government to address Czech concerns might well justify revolution or hopes of military defeat as a means of achieving greater autonomy or perhaps even national liberation.

In the years leading up to World War I, Masaryk's belief in the continued existence of the Austrian state turned to rejection of that state and the dynasty that ruled it. Masaryk would later write that, "especially after 1907, the better I got to know Austria and the Habsburg Dynasty, the more I was driven into opposition. This Dynasty which . . . seemed so powerful, was morally and physically degenerate. Thus Austria became for me both a moral and a political problem."[2] For most Czechs, however, an independent Czech state seemed an impossible dream, especially given the assumption on the part of many that the collapse of the Austro-Hungarian Empire would result in the incorporation of the Czech lands into the German Reich.

As a result, the best course of action for the Czechs prior to 1914 seemed to be continued pressure for greater autonomy within a federalized empire.

ON THE EVE OF WAR

As a Czech Realist deputy in the Reichsrat in 1909, Masaryk delivered speeches in which he criticized the legal proceedings initiated against 53 members of a Serbo-Croat coalition on charges that they were in the pay of Serbia, legal actions that resulted in the Zagreb treason trial of 1909 and a subsequent libel case filed by the defendants. Masaryk helped to generate public support for the South Slavs by exposing as forgeries important documents provided by the Austro-Hungarian Foreign Ministry as evidence against the accused.

The Bosnian Crisis of 1908 and the Balkan Wars of 1912–1913 increased tensions in that region in part by creating a larger Serbia suspicious over Austria-Hungary's interference in the region. The conflicts also increased Russia's interest in the Balkans, although many European leaders came to believe that containment of the conflicts to the Balkan Peninsula served as evidence that local wars would not necessarily lead to conflict between major powers or between the Triple Alliance (Germany, Austria-Hungary, Italy) and the Triple Entente (Great Britain, France, Russia). By 1914, however, friction between Austria-Hungary and Serbia on one hand and Russia and Austria-Hungary on the other established a context whereupon, under the right conditions, a local conflict could develop into a large-scale military confrontation involving at least two of Europe's major powers.

On June 28, 1914, a Bosnian Serb nationalist student, Gavrilo Princip, assassinated the Archduke Franz Ferdinand, the Habsburg heir, and his wife Sophie while they were engaged in an official state visit to Sarajevo in Bosnia. The Austro-Hungarian declaration of war against Serbia on July 28 precipitated the outbreak of World War I as Russia's military intervention on behalf of Serbia preceded German declarations of war against Russia and France, Germany's invasion of neutral Belgium, and Britain's declaration of war on Germany on August 4. Hopes that the conflict between Serbia and Austria-Hungary would remain confined to the Balkans proved empty as the breakdown of the international system escalated into hostilities involving the Entente, or Allies, and the Central Powers, Austria-Hungary and Germany.

THE CZECHS AND THE OUTBREAK OF WAR

As Austria-Hungary mobilized for war, the nationalities of the empire responded to the military conflict in different ways. Whereas Magyars and Croats tended toward enthusiasm and support for the war effort, Serbs in the empire had little reason to support an invasion of neighboring Serbia. The Ruthenes, Czechs, and Slovaks, meanwhile, generally performed their military obligations with little patriotic fervor. In fact, many Czechs and Slovaks resented having to fight their fellow Slavs, the Serbs and later the Russians. Opportunities for expressing opposition to the war diminished rapidly, however, as the emergence of a military-influenced wartime regime brought censorship, suppression, and eventually the banning of political parties and the suspension of the Reichsrat and Land Diets.

Some Czechs acted upon their opposition to the war by avoiding military service or deserting their units, a problem that gradually expanded from individuals to entire units as the war progressed. In April 1915, the 28th Prague Infantry Regiment, the so-called "children of Prague," went over to the Russian side *en masse* at Dukla on the Carpathian front and was relocated to Kiev in Ukraine.

For the German-speaking inhabitants of the Czech lands, the war offered an opportunity for patriotic activities and enthusiastic participation in Austrian military units on behalf of the Central Powers. Radical German nationalists viewed the Czechs as the least trustworthy of the nationalities under the Habsburg monarchy, and some held out hope that the war would lead to the consolidation of Central Europe under German leadership.

The circumstances of the war helped to sever the emotional connection that many Czechs had to the Habsburg monarchy and the empire in a manner similar to Masaryk's own transformation a few years earlier. Leading Czech politicians had already begun looking to Russia by the beginning of 1914, and the war intensified the desire of the Russophiles and Pan-Slavs to cast the lot of the Czechs with their Slavic brethren to the east. In January 1914, Václav Klofáč, the head of the National Socialists, had traveled to St. Petersburg to meet with Russia's foreign minister Sergei Sazanov in regard to internal Czech resistance to the Austro-Hungarian empire. In May, and in anticipation of a possible war, Karel Kramář offered a proposal for a confederation of Slavs that would be ruled by the Russian czar. Klofáč and Kramář became so convinced of a Russian advance on Prague that they remained in the city early in the war to greet Russian forces upon their arrival. In consequence of their actions, both were arrested and granted the death sentence, only to benefit later from a declaration of amnesty in July 1917.

For Masaryk, the Russian connection proved problematic due to his lack of trust in the czarist regime, the Russian military, and the Russian government's understanding of the Czechs and their culture. Masaryk and Kramář agreed that the defeat of Austria-Hungary was essential to the future of the Czech nation, but Masaryk wanted an independent Czech state and not a Russian-ruled Slavic empire.

When Czar Nicholas II issued an edict on August 2 ordering the expulsion of enemy nationals from the Russian empire, the majority of Czechs living in Russia immediately sought Russian citizenship or attempted to volunteer for service in the Russian military. The czar agreed to meet with Czech representatives, and the consultations generated general promises of freedom to the nationalities of Austria-Hungary and the Russian ruler's sudden interest in Slovak territories and grievances, as well as the Czech proposal for the affiliation of a free Crown of St. Václav with the Russian crown of the Romanovs.

In August, the Czechs in Russia received permission to establish their own military regiment, and by the end of October, the Czech legion, or *Družina*, could count on roughly 800 volunteers ready to enter combat against the Central Powers. Czech leaders hoped to use the legionnaires in developing a future Czech army and to recruit Czech prisoners of war to the cause, but the Russians proved more interested in using the *Družina* for propaganda purposes than as an actual fighting force.

During the early months of the war, Masaryk was encouraged by Austrian setbacks in Serbia and by the Russian advance to Cracow and the Carpathian Mountain passes leading into Slovakia. However, this enthusiasm was tempered by the devastating defeats suffered by the Russians at Tannenburg and Masurian Lakes in East Prussia in late August and mid-September as the Germans halted the Russian offensive on that front.

Feeling isolated at home, Masaryk, now 64, departed Austria-Hungary in October under a Serbian passport in order to assess the international situation and to promote Czech interests elsewhere. His travels took him first to the neutral nations of Switzerland and Italy before he eventually arrived in London and received an appointment as professor of Slavonic studies at King's College London in 1915. Masaryk believed that the Entente powers could assist in the complete transformation of Central Europe, and that it was therefore essential for the Czechs to determine their own future by participating in the military defeat of Austria-Hungary. His longtime association with the

Slovaks persuaded Masaryk to propose that the liberation of the Czechs would lead not to an independent land of the Czechs alone, but rather to a larger Czecho-Slovak state. By the beginning of 1915 then, Masaryk and his colleagues had shifted the focus of their political program toward an independent state shared by Czechs and Slovaks.

THE SLOVAK RESPONSE TO WAR

For the Slovaks, the early stages of the war were marked by Magyar patriotic fervor and little Slovak enthusiasm. Slovak nationalists and opponents of the war faced censorship, arrest, and occasional physical attacks in public as the wartime authorities cracked down quickly on internal opposition. National leader and poet Pavol Országh Hviezdoslav expressed his antiwar sentiments in the poetry cycle, *Bloody Sonnets*, written in August 1914 but unpublished until 1919 due to wartime conditions.

The actions of the Slovak League of America, an umbrella organization founded in Cleveland in 1907, offered a reminder of the lobbying power and organizational resources offered by Slovak and Czech communities in Europe and North America. From 1860 to 1900, some 276,000 Slovaks left their homeland to settle in the United States and other countries, and over the following 18 years, another 695,000 emigrated abroad. In the initial months of the conflict, the secretary of the Slovak League of America was Ivan Daxner, son of Štefan Marko Daxner, whose "Voice from Slovakia" had earlier inspired the "Memorandum of the Slovak Nation" in 1861. Although initially supportive of Slovak autonomy within the Kingdom of Hungary, the war brought about a change in strategy for the Slovak League, as reflected in an October 1914 article written by the league chairman calling for the union of Bohemia, Moravia, and Slovakia as the best available option for Slovaks.

As the early Russian offensive shifted the front closer to Slovakia, the Russian occupation of Slovak lands and an advance on Budapest seemed quite plausible over the coming months. In this context, Slovak political leaders began to consider the ramifications of a military defeat for the Central Powers in terms of options ranging from autonomy within the Kingdom of Hungary to connections with Russia or possibly confederation with the Poles. The option that slowly gathered support at home and abroad, however, was a Czecho-Slovak one, predicated upon the belief that cooperation with the Czechs offered the best hope for Slovak self-determination in the wake of the empire's defeat and likely disintegration.

By the middle of November, Russian units entered eastern Slovakia through the Carpathian passes and occupied the towns of Humenné and Bardejov before being driven out by Austro-Hungarian counterattacks. Fighting continued in the region's mountainous terrain until May 1915, when a German offensive originating in the Gorlice-Tarnów area near Cracow led to the total collapse of Russian lines on the Galician front and the retreat of Russian forces into Ukraine and Byelorussia. For those Slovaks and Czechs hoping for liberation by the Russians, the disastrous battlefield results of 1914–1915 offered little justification for continued enthusiasm.

TOWARD A CZECHOSLOVAK FUTURE

In February 1915, Masaryk hoped to return to Prague, but warnings of possible arrest for treason forced him to reconsider and to meet instead with his Czech colleague Edvard Beneš in Geneva. Beneš conferred with Masaryk and then returned to Prague to deliver Masaryk's plans to Czech politicians with whom Masaryk maintained close relations. During the early days of March and under direction from Masaryk, Beneš assisted in the establishment of a secret resistance committee at home in order to further Czech goals through a working collaboration with Masaryk and Czech organizations abroad. The *Mafie*, as the committee came to be known, included Beneš, Karel Kramář and Alois Rašín of the Young Czechs, *Sokol* chief Josef Scheiner, and the lawyer Přemysl Šámal, whom Masaryk had placed in charge of his own Realist Party in December.

On July 6, 1915, Masaryk marked the 400th anniversary of the martyrdom of Jan Hus with a speech in Geneva in which he praised the spirit of the Hussites as a means of rallying support for the Czech and Slovak cause. Masaryk offered his first public declaration of the fight against Austria-Hungary, calling for an end to the empire and the creation of an independent Czech state at the close of the war. Meanwhile, in Prague's Old Town Square, the monument to Jan Hus, commissioned in 1900, received an unofficial unveiling that same day after authorities refused to sanction an official ceremony. Czechs responded by covering the monument with flowers in honor of their national hero.

In September, Beneš successfully avoided the authorities in departing Prague for Paris, where he arrived with information and documents that he passed on to the French Ministry of War. In Paris, Beneš and Masaryk collaborated with Milan Rastislav Štefánik, a Slovak nationalist who left his homeland in 1904 and eventually gained employment as an astronomer at the Meudon Observatory in Paris. At the start of the war, Štefánik volunteered for service in the French air force, rising to the rank of general and taking French citizenship. After being wounded on the Serbian front in late 1915, Štefánik returned to Paris, where he joined Masaryk and Beneš in lobbying for a Czecho-Slovak state and facilitated communication with the French government. Among the trio's key goals was the coordination of activities among the Czech and Slovak committees located in North America, France, Great Britain, and Russia.

In the United States, Czech organizations such as the Czecho-American Committee for Independence and Support of the Czech Nation and the Czech National Alliance had been formed in the early months of the war to further the Czech agenda abroad, while the Slovak League lobbied on behalf of the Slovaks. On October 22, 1915, members of the Slovak League and Czech organizations in the United States signed the Cleveland Agreement in support of the establishment of a federal state comprising Bohemia, Moravia, Czech Silesia, and Slovakia, with universal and direct suffrage and officially recognized independent territories for Czechs and Slovaks. As a concession to Slovak demands, Slovaks gained the promise of their own Diet and a separate administration with Slovak as the official language.

On November 14, Masaryk announced the founding of the Czech Committee Abroad in Paris in order to conduct negotiations with the government of the Allied nations. Leaders of the committee, renamed the Czechoslovak National Council in February 1916, included Masaryk, Štefánik, Beneš, and the Agrarian Party representative Josef Dürich. Dürich, however, disagreed with Masaryk over Russia's role and, in January 1917, assumed leadership of the rival Czechoslovak National Council in Petrograd (St. Petersburg), shortly before the March Revolution rendered the czarist-leaning organization ineffectual. With the departure of Nicholas II, Russia's new Provisional Government displayed little interest in Dürich and his fellow Russophiles on the council.

WARTIME NEGOTIATIONS

In February 1916, Masaryk grew worried over the possibility that Austria-Hungary would seek a separate peace in order to avoid disintegration or division. Meeting with the French prime minister, Aristide Briand, Masaryk proposed dividing Austria-Hungary along national lines, and his words received some measure of coverage in French and British newspapers as an assertion of the rights of nationalities in the empire. Beneš also argued in favor of the dissolution of Austria-Hungary in a pamphlet entitled "Destroy Austria-Hungary!" which was written in French in an attempt to win French support for creation of a Czecho-Slovak state, an autonomous Poland, and a Serb-led union of the South Slavs as a means of guarding against future German and Austrian aggression.

An increase in political activism on the home front led most of the Czech political parties to establish a National Committee in November as a means of pursuing a common agenda against the Habsburg monarchy and the German nationalists in the Czech lands through a central organization in Prague. When the emperor Franz Joseph passed away at age 86 on November 21, the dedication to a common cause by Czech politicians appeared to be an important step forward in the wake of events that weakened the wartime imperial administration of Franz Joseph's nephew and successor, Karl I.

In late December 1916, American president Woodrow Wilson requested a statement of war aims from the major combatants, several months before the United States declared war on Germany and entered the conflict on the side of the Entente in April 1917, although the American declaration of war on Austria-Hungary would be delayed until December 7 of that year. The Allied response to Wilson's request came on January 10 and included a specific reference to the liberation of the nationalities—Slavs, Italians, Rumanians, and Czecho-Slovaks—from imperial control, although without firm support for the dismantling of Austria-Hungary after the war.

Karl I's new foreign minister, Count Ottokar Čzernín, sought to counter the Allied response by having all political parties declare their loyalty to the Austro-Hungarian Empire. In a major setback for Masaryk and his colleagues, the Union of Czech Deputies, established two months earlier by the Czech representatives in the final prewar Reichsrat, wrote to Čzernín on January 31, that the Czechs would continue to improve the Czech position from within the empire and under the authority of the Habsburgs.

Early in 1917, Čzernín composed a secret communication advising Emperor Karl to seek peace with the Allies by the end of the summer in order to avoid military disaster and the possible destruction of the empire. When increasing shortages triggered strikes in the spring, the imperial administration responded with force. Twenty-three protesting workers were shot and killed in Prostějov in April, and another 13 workers died in Moravská Ostrava in August. As opposition to the imperial government intensified and grew more organized, Karl announced that the Reichsrat, dormant for three years, would convene on May 30 in order to provide the nationalities of Austria-Hungary with political representation based on the results of the last prewar election in 1911.

On May 17, and in advance of the opening session of the Reichsrat, a group of nearly two dozen Czech writers and intellectuals issued a manifesto critical of the Union of Czech Deputies for its profession of loyalty to the empire. The authors of the document called for the creation of a democratic Europe composed of free peoples and autonomous states, while reminding the Czech deputies in the Reichsrat of their responsibilities to the Czech nation and challenging them either to promote Czech rights or forfeit their seats in the parliament. The deputies chose the former course of action, and at the inaugural session of the Reichsrat, František Staněk read a statement in the name of the Czech Union in which he called for the creation of a democratic state shared by Czechs and Slovaks based on the fundamental right of self-determination and, additionally for the Czechs, on the basis of the historic rights of the Czech lands.

For Masaryk, Beneš, and other Czech and Slovak representatives abroad, the consequences of the March Revolution and the end of the czarist regime in Russia in 1917 required direct negotiations with the new Provisional Government and an assessment of the Czech and Slovak cause in light of the changes in Russian leadership. To that end, and traveling under a British passport as Thomas George Marsden, Masaryk arrived in Petrograd on May 15.

Once in Russia, Masaryk joined Štefánik in lobbying Prime Minister Georgy Lvov and Minister of War Alexander Kerensky for the creation of a legitimate Czechoslovak army, as opposed to relying on a force that the Russians viewed as an instrument of propaganda. During the Kerensky Offensive against combined Austro-Hungarian and German forces, all the Czechoslovak units fought together for the first time at Zborov in Ukraine and contributed to the only significant victory in an offensive marked by early advances and eventual defeat, retreat, and desertions. With Masaryk in Petrograd, the success of the Czechoslovak units at Zborov on July 2 allowed for the participation of Czech and Slovak prisoners of war in the legions and the expansion of the *Družina* by another 21,760 recruits by September. After Zborov, Kerensky and the Russian High Command recognized the authority of Masaryk's Czechoslovak National Council over Czech and Slovak military forces in Russia, and when Masaryk visited legionnaire units and POWs, he received a welcome befitting a national leader.

When the November Revolution brought V. I. Lenin and the Bolsheviks to power, Masaryk opened negotiations with the Bolshevik military command and, in February 1918, gained the legionnaires the status of armed neutrals who would not be used by either side in the emerging civil war, but with the right to fight in their own defense if attacked. The *Družina* would be transported from Ukraine to the port of Vladivostok in the east by means of the Trans-Siberian railroad before being shipped to Western Europe, where the Czechoslovak legions would join the French army and participate in the fighting in the trenches of northern France.

During the six months that Masaryk spent in Russia after the Bolshevik rising, he witnessed firsthand the consequences of Bolshevism in Petrograd and Moscow and found little in Bolshevik policies to warrant his support. Upon his departure from western Russia, Masaryk reached Vladivostok well before the legionnaires and traveled to the United States, where he met with Czech and Slovak organizations, as well as American leaders in Washington. For the legionnaires, the departure from Russia grew more complicated after the signing of the Treaty of Brest-Litovsk on March 3, 1918, because the agreement ended the fighting between Russia and the Central Powers and prevented the Russians from allowing activities hostile to Austria-Hungary on Russian soil.

During their "Anabasis," the legionnaires came under attack by both the Bolshevik Red Army and the anti-Bolshevik White forces as they became strung out along the railway line across Siberia. The first engagement of consequence occurred in mid-May near Chelyabinsk as a minor rock-throwing incident involving a train loaded with German and Hungarian POWs resulted in the arrest of 10 legionnaires for killing the prisoner suspected of the offense. This incident eventually led to the occupation of parts of the town by legionnaires in pitched battle with the local governing soviet. As a result of fighting elsewhere along the railroad line, the Czech and Slovak legions eventually gained control of long stretches of the Trans-Siberian Railway as they moved eastward toward Vladivostok. Ultimately, the evacuation of the legions stretched from January 1919 to November 30, 1920, as an estimated 56,451 troops and over 10,000 Czechoslovak civilians departed Russia for home.

Elsewhere, efforts by Masaryk, Beneš, and Štefánik to expand the military role of Czechs and Slovaks garnered official French recognition of the Czechoslovak army under the political leadership of the Czechoslovak National Council in December 1917. At the beginning of 1918, French prime minister Georges Clemenceau cosigned an agreement with Beneš guaranteeing Czechoslovak representation at the postwar peace conference. With Štefánik overseeing recruitment efforts across the Atlantic, some 3,000 Americans of Czech and Slovak descent volunteered to serve in Czechoslovak units in France, Russia, and Italy prior to U.S. entry into the war. After the United States joined the conflict and began sending troops to Europe the number of American Czechs and Slovaks serving in U.S. forces rose to approximately 40,000.

In the wake of the military disaster at Caporetto in the autumn of 1917, Italian authorities reversed their position on allowing Czech and Slovak POWs to serve in active military units, and in mid-April 1918, Štefánik signed an agreement with Prime Minister Vittorio Orlando establishing an independent Czechoslovak army on Italian soil. The Italians also abandoned opposition to an independent Czech and Slovak state, which had arisen due to Italy's own aims in regard to the lands of the South Slavs and consequent aversion to talk of independence.

THE END OF THE WAR AND THE BIRTH
OF THE REPUBLIC

On January 6, 1918, Czech Reichsrat deputies and politicians from Bohemia, Moravia, and Czech Silesia gathered in Prague during the holy day of the Epiphany and issued a manifesto inspired by growing support for the self-determination of nations in the Allied capitals and postrevolutionary Russia. The Epiphany Declaration called for the creation of an independent state for Czechs and Slovaks, inclusive of the traditional territories of Slovakia and the Kingdom of Bohemia, as well as proper representation for Czechs and Slovaks at the future peace conference.

However, two days later, on January 8, Woodrow Wilson delivered his Fourteen Points speech to the U.S. Congress, in which he would go no further than to speak of American support for the peoples of Austria-Hungary in their pursuit of autonomy within the empire. British prime minister David Lloyd George followed a similar course in informing Austria-Hungary that Great Britain's war aims did not include dismemberment of the empire

Internally and militarily, though, all was not well for Austria-Hungary at the beginning of the final year of the war. At the end of January 1918, a wave of strikes spread into the Czech lands from Lower Austria as Czech workers engaged in a general strike in support of their fellow workers in Austria. On February 1, Czech and South Slav sailors participated in a mutiny at Kotor Bay on the Adriatic, raising a red flag of revolution and demanding an end to the war and the implementation of the right of self-determination of nations. The mutineers called upon comrades in the Austro-Hungarian navy to join the cause, but the authorities ended the insurrection after three weeks, only to have discontent spread to the army. In February, defections occurred among some Czech units of the Austro-Hungarian army in Italy, followed by similar actions by soldiers at Mostar in Herzegovina. Slovak soldiers, who to this point in the war had not engaged in mass desertions, became more willing to engage in acts of rebellion by 1918. In June of that year, 44 Slovak soldiers faced execution after participating in a mutiny at Kragujevac in Serbia.

As Foreign Minister Czernín continued to criticize Masaryk and the efforts to create an independent state, representatives of the Czechs, Slovaks, and South Slavs attended a Congress of Oppressed Nationalities in Rome on April 10 and argued in favor of self-determination. Slovak political leader Vavro Šrobár used the occasion of a May Day gathering of the Social Democrats at Liptovský Sväty Mikuláš to declare support for the self-determination of the nationalities of the Austro-Hungarian Empire and to call for the creation of a Czecho-Slovak state that would unite two branches of the same Slavic family. Šrobár's actions convinced many Slovaks abroad that Masaryk's plan for a new state had received the blessing of Slovaks within the empire, although issues arose regarding the Slovak leadership due to Šrobár's arrest by Hungarian authorities and Štefánik's possession of French citizenship.

On May 24, the Slovak National Party convened for a secret session in Turciansky Sväty Martin and heard Andrej Hlinka declare an end to the failed 1,000-year relationship between Slovaks and Hungarians. Like Šrobár, Hlinka encouraged Slovaks to embrace the concept of Czecho-Slovak cooperation in building a new state, a sentiment shared by the leaders of all the major Slovak political parties. On May 30, members of Czech and Slovak organizations in the United States joined Masaryk in signing the Pittsburgh Agreement, drafted by Masaryk as a means of providing joint endorsement of a common and independent state comprising the lands of the Czechs and Slovaks. By agreement, the Slovaks would possess linguistic rights as well as their own autonomous administration, assembly, and judicial system within the common state.

Masaryk met with Woodrow Wilson on June 19, and shortly thereafter, France recognized the Czechoslovak National Council in Paris as the precursors to the government of a new state. The United States offered its own recognition of the CNC's status on July 2, and Great Britain confirmed the same on August 9. In Prague, a revitalized National

Committee appeared on July 3 under the leadership of Kramař, Švehla, and Klofáč and in spite of opposition by Austro-Hungarian authorities.

Concerned over what he perceived to be uncertain policies of the Entente governments toward Austria-Hungary, Beneš announced on October 14 that the Czechoslovak National Council in Paris had become the provisional government of Czechoslovakia, a proclamation that prompted formal declarations of support from the Allies. Masaryk assumed the position of president in the new government, with Beneš serving as foreign minister and minister of the interior, and Štefanik as minister of national defense.

On October 16, Emperor Karl made a belated attempt to preserve Austria-Hungary by offering to federalize the Austrian half of the empire, a plan that would not have bettered the lot of the Slovaks under the Hungarian administration. Karl also appealed to Wilson and the Allies to agree to peace negotiations on the basis of the American president's Fourteen Points, leaving Austria-Hungary intact as an empire. The emperor's offer convinced Masaryk to alter his timing and issue the "Washington Declaration," a declaration of independence for the Czechoslovak nation, in Washington, D.C., on October 18.

The public revelation of the Austro-Hungarian government's willingness to accept Wilson's terms for negotiating a cease-fire led to a declaration of independence in Prague on October 28. Kramař, Klofáč, Švehla, Rašín, the Slovak representative Šrobár, and other members of the National Committee, some having only just returned from a meeting with Beneš in Geneva two days earlier, interpreted the news to mean that the defeat and surrender of the monarchy was nigh. As a result, they seized the opportunity to declare independence for Czechs and Slovaks and the birth of a new Czechoslovak state out of what would essentially become a bloodless revolution. The signing of the declaration occurred at the municipal house prior to the public proclamation at the monument to St. Václav on Wenceslas Square as celebrations began in the streets of Prague. During the negotiations with Beneš and as a result of Masaryk's "Washington Declaration," agreement had been reached that the new government would be a republic.

For the German population of the newly declared Czechoslovak state, the agreements between Czech and Slovak politicians ran counter to their own interests, which involved maintaining links to Austria and planning for the creation of several autonomous German provinces. On October 29, German deputies from the Czech lands announced in the Reichsrat that the territories of *Deutschböhmen* (German Bohemia) would become a province of Austria. One day later, deputies from Moravia and Silesia called for similar status for the German-populated Sudetenland. Many of these decisions were made under the assumption that Austria would be allowed to undergo an *Anschluss*, or merger, with its Central Powers ally in the name of a Greater Germany. Although the Reichsrat voted in favor of Austria's annexation by Germany on November 12, the Allies prevented the *Anschluss* in great part because the restructuring of Central Europe would have rewarded a defeated Germany with major territorial gains. The British and Americans also supported the French request that any decisions regarding revisions to the historic Czech lands be made at the upcoming peace conference. On March 4, 1919, the newly elected Austrian National Assembly met for the first time, as many Germans in the Czech lands, denied the right to participate in the Austrian electoral process, engaged in angry demonstrations. The harsh response by the Czech military and gendarmerie left 52 Germans dead and another 84 wounded.

With the war drawing to a disastrous close, Hungarian authorities sought to convince the Slovaks to maintain their political and territorial connections to Hungary. To this end, the government allowed the Slovak National Party to schedule a public gathering at Turciansky Sväty Martin on October 30, during which participants instead declared their support for the new Czechoslovak state, although they were unaware of the events in Prague two days earlier due to the absence of relevant news in the Hungarian press. Delegates elected a Slovak National Council to represent the Slovaks in negotiating rights as part of an independent Czechoslovakia.

On November 1, disturbances broke out in Slovakia as the Hungarians declared their independence from Austria-Hungary, leaving the Slovaks uncertain as to Hungarian intentions. Šrobár arrived from Prague in the company of a Slovak provisional government and an armed contingent with the intention of establishing order. Incursions by the Hungarian military pushed Šrobár's force back to the Moravian border as Beneš conferred with the French in an effort to have the Allies clarify the status of Slovakia in regard to armistice terms with a now-independent Hungary. Hodža undertook his own negotiations with Hungarian authorities in order to convince the Hungarians to withdraw their forces and delineate a territorial boundary line in advance of the peace conference. However, the provisional government in Prague repudiated Hodža's negotiations and gained a more favorable line of demarcation as a result of Beneš's discussions with the French, who demanded the withdrawal of Hungarian forces from Slovakia on December 19. Within weeks, former legionnaires, now serving as the nascent army of the new Czechoslovak republic, occupied Slovak territory in order to protect the new state.

On November 5, two days after Austria-Hungary signed an armistice with the Allies, Beneš and other leaders of the Czech foreign mission returned to Prague on the same day that Kramař announced the birth of an independent and democratic republic. Just over a week later, on November 13, the National Committee ratified a provisional constitution establishing a Revolutionary National Council, with Masaryk serving as president and elected by a unicameral assembly, which also bore responsibility for drafting a permanent constitution. The 268 seats in the national assembly were apportioned on the basis of electoral results from the 1911 Reichsrat elections, although the national minorities of the Czech lands and Slovakia lacked representation entirely. The following day, the revolution entered the final stage as the new national assembly announced the end of Habsburg rule in the Czech lands, formally elected Masaryk president, and accepted the ministerial appointments of Kramař as prime minister and Beneš as foreign minister. Masaryk departed New York on November 18 and, after official state visits to Britain, France, and Italy, returned home to Prague on December 21 to assume his duties as provisional president of the Czechoslovak republic.

Prior to the opening of the Paris Peace Conference on January 18, 1919, a secondary territorial dispute arose over the Duchy of Těšín, or Cieszyn to the Poles who claimed this Silesian territory on the basis of historic rights and a heavily Polish population. As a minority in the region, the Czechs claimed the territory based primarily on the historic rights argument, but also because Těšín's coal resources, prosperity, and railway link to Slovakia offered significant economic benefits. The Czechs occupied Těšín in January, although after the Poles appealed to the peace conference for assistance, the Czechs received orders to withdraw their troops from the area. On January 28, 1920, the Council of Ambassadors determined that Czechoslovakia would be granted possession of the coal resources and railroad, but since neither side was satisfied with the decision, Těšín would remain a point of contention between the neighboring nations.

The Paris Peace Conference formally opened on January 18 and continued with sessions and negotiations until June. Most major issues regarding Czechoslovakia were discussed and acted upon by the middle of April, although the formal treaties with Germany (Versailles), Austria (St. Germain), and Hungary (Trianon) would come later. Led by Kramař and Beneš, the Czechoslovak contingent gained confirmation of territorial claims that included the historic

Czech lands, Slovakia, Lusatia, Těšín, and Sub-Carpathian Ruthenia in the east. When the Hungarians countered the historic rights claim to Slovakia with one of their own, Beneš successfully argued for the strategic and economic necessity of including the Slovak lands. However, negotiations excluded Beneš's proposal for a corridor across Hungary linking Czechoslovakia to the lands of the South Slavs. As part of the negotiated settlements, Czechoslovakia signed a minorities treaty guaranteeing protection for national minorities and accepted the requirement of liberation payments, which was also imposed upon Poland, Rumania, and Yugoslavia as independent former territories of Austria-Hungary.

In late March 1919, the Bolshevik journalist Bela Kun gained power as the leader of a radical Hungarian Soviet Republic, which attempted to regain Slovakia through a military incursion by the Hungarian Red Army at the beginning of May. The Hungarians occupied two-thirds of Slovakia and instituted local soviets in some areas of Slovakia and Ruthenia. A Slovak Soviet Republic appeared in Prešov on June 16 with its leaders declaring their support for the Soviet Republics in Hungary and Russia. By mid-July, however, the threat of military action by the major powers forced the Hungarians to abandon Slovak territory, leading to the collapse of the Slovak Soviet Republic as Czechoslovak forces regained Slovakia.

Although most Slovaks chose to support Czechoslovak-oriented political parties in pursuit of Slovak goals, demands for Slovak autonomy within the new state inspired the resurrection of the Slovak People's Party, founded in 1913 but with political activities suspended during the war years. Party cofounder Msgr. Andrej Hlinka served as a member of the Slovak National Council in 1918 and had joined other leading Slovak political figures at Turciansky Sväty Martin in signing the declaration of support of a Czechoslovak state. After the reappearance of the Slovak People's Party in December 1919, though, Hlinka and some of the l'udáci (Ludaks, or populists) grew resentful over the anticlericalism of the Czechs and the perception that Lutherans were being shown favoritism over Catholics in the selection process for key political offices.

With little hope that the pro-Czechoslovak deputies of the Slovak Club in the national assembly would press for Slovak autonomy, Hlinka accepted the advice of a pro-autonomy deputy, Dr. František Jehlička, and departed for Paris at the end of August with the goal of bringing the issue of autonomy to the Paris Peace Conference. Hlinka and Jehlička delivered a memorandum to the Allied delegations, but the conference had already begun to wind down and there was little hope for changes in the treaty and agreements. When informed of the activities of Hlinka and Jehlička, the Slovak Club in Prague denounced their proposal and stripped the pair of their standing with the assembly. Jehlička departed for Budapest, where he attached himself to Hungarian revisionists seeking to regain Slovakia. Hlinka underwent arrest and temporary incarceration, but gained status as a political martyr after the government failed to build a case for treasonous activity.

THE FIRST CZECHOSLOVAK REPUBLIC

The Czechoslovak state that emerged from World War I did so as a consequence of the military conflict, the international environment, the defeat and disintegration of Austria-Hungary, and the efforts of Czechs and Slovaks at home and abroad to achieve independence from the empire. This new nation-state of Czechs and Slovaks included one-quarter of the population of the former Austro-Hungarian Empire, as well as one-fifth the territory and two-thirds of the industrial base. Wealthier in the west and poorer in the east, Czechoslovakia included approximately 7 million Czechs, 2 million Slovaks, over 3 million Germans, some 750,000 Hungarians, 500,000 Ruthenians, and 80,000 Poles for an estimated population of 13,374,364 in 1921. According to data from that year, 49 percent of the population of Czechoslovakia resided in Bohemia, 22 percent in Slovakia, 19.6 percent in Moravia, and the remainder in Silesia and Ruthenia. Approximately 76 percent of the citizens belonged to the Roman Catholic Church, with the Lutheran, Greek Catholic (Uniate), and Czechoslovak National faiths accounting for 4 percent each. By 1930, the Jewish population stood at approximately 1 percent in Bohemia and Moravia, 4.1 percent in Slovakia, and 14.2 percent in Ruthenia.

On February 29, 1920, the provisional national assembly in Prague formally ratified the democratic constitution of the First Czechoslovak Republic as a nation of Czechs and Slovaks. The bicameral National Assembly included a Senate with 150 deputies elected for eight-year terms and a Chamber of Deputies with 300 members serving for six years. Universal suffrage and proportional representation determined the composition of the National Assembly, which elected the president for a term of seven years and approved the ministerial appointments of the prime minister. The constitution did not include autonomy for the Slovaks, although the designation of "Czechoslovak" as the official language was meant to reflect the equality of Czechs and Slovaks in the republic.

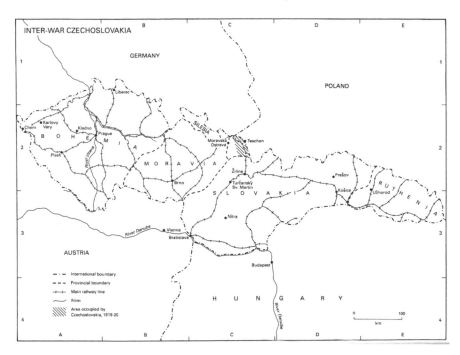

Interwar Czechoslovakia. (*An Atlas of Eastern Europe in the Twentieth Century*, by Richard Crampton and Ben Crampton, 1997. Reproduced by permission of Taylor & Francis Books UK.)

The constitution offered strong protection for minority rights and included in Article 106 the declaration that there would be no discrimination based upon sex, occupation, or birth. As Masaryk had promised in the Washington Declaration in 1918, women shared legal equality with men, as well as equal status in the political, social, and cultural spheres. Women now gained seats in the assembly, entered administrative positions at all levels, and, after 1930, received appointments as judges. However, feminists expressed concerns over Article 126, which placed marriage, motherhood, and the family under legal protection, and therefore seemed to uphold traditional gender roles by defining citizens on the basis of gender. In 1923, the founding of the Women's National Council by Františka Plamínková provided women's groups with a common organization to protect legal equality and to lobby on behalf of women's rights and issues such as divorce and the right to work.

In the republic's first parliamentary elections in May 1920, the Czechoslovak Social Democrats received 26 percent of the total vote nationally, which allowed party leader Vlastimil Tusar to continue as prime minister in a "Red-Green" coalition with the Agrarians. Among the other leading parties, the German Social Democrats tallied 11 percent to slightly less than 10 percent for the Agrarian Party. In Slovakia, the Czechoslovak Social Democrats earned 38 percent, the Slovak National and Agrarian Party 18 percent, and the Czechoslovak People's Party 17.55 percent. The victory for left-leaning parties in Slovakia tended to reflect concern over economic conditions after the war, as well as the consequences of the earlier occupation by the Hungarian Soviet Republic.

On May 27, the National Assembly elected Tomáš Garrigue Masaryk president, a post he would hold until 1935 as a result of subsequent reelections by the assembly. Masaryk's personality and leadership would help to provide stability to a political system marked by 17 cabinets during the period from 1918 to 1939. During that period, the changes in cabinets generally occurred by political arrangement, as no governing coalition ever dissolved except as a result of electoral maneuvering by leaders of the coalition parties, and no government fell as a result of a vote of no confidence. The only major victim of a political assassination was Alois Rašín, murdered by a deranged former Communist in 1923.

The traditional image of the First Czechoslovak Republic as a peaceful, moderate, and stable democracy guided by a philosopher-president is a powerful and attractive one, although the political system contained some undemocratic elements that, while not corrosive of democracy, tarnish somewhat the idealized vision of the interwar era. The centralized nature of the new state led to resentment on the part of the national minorities and the Slovaks and Ruthenes who believed they had been promised autonomy in the wartime agreements. A large and diverse roster of political parties competed in national elections from across the political spectrum, but as the system evolved, five of those parties came to dominate policy making in the government.

As president, Masaryk served the nation as a highly respected leader of great moral stature, although one willing to use his influence to shape government policies and diplomacy directly and indirectly. In addition to the extensive powers of the presidency, which included the right to dissolve and appoint governments, Masaryk held the constitutional right to institute direct presidential rule during a period of national crisis. From his office in Prague Castle, Masaryk presided over an informal and influential coterie of politicians and intellectuals known as the *Hrad* (Castle), which became the target of much criticism from the political right due to the group's influence on policy.

The right-centrist Agrarians emerged as the largest party after internal frictions left the Social Democrats divided and weakened. In September 1920, the radical Marxist left of the Social Democrats broke away from the party and departed the governing coalition. After the subsequent resignation of Tusar's ministry, Masaryk appointed a non-party government of experts under Jan Černý, who served as prime minister until he was replaced by Edvard Beneš in late September 1921. The five leading parties then agreed to cooperate in directing the Černý government's policies through the legislative process, thereby introducing the concept of an unofficial, unconstitutional, yet stable "*Pětka*" (Five) into Czechoslovak politics. Led by Švehla and the Agrarians, the *Pětka* included the Social Democrats, the Czechoslovak Socialists (known as the National Socialists until 1918), National Democrats (formerly the Young Czechs), and the Catholic and populist Czechoslovak People's Party under Msgr. Jan Šrámek. The leaders of the five participating parties staffed the government with party members and required their members in the National Assembly and government positions to implement common *Pětku* policies.

The Agrarians developed a strong relationship with the Czechoslovak People's Party within the government coalition, which gained the support of the National Democrats, a party representing industrial and financial interests and hoping to exercise influence over economic policies. The Czechoslovak Tradesmen-Business Professional Party joined the coalition with a political orientation similar to that of the Agrarians on many issues. The Socialists, who were growing more centrist, could claim Beneš as a member, although his links to the party were more the result of Masaryk's request that he identify with a party than any strong ideological affinity.

In May 1921, the breakaway members of the Social Democratic Party established the Communist Party of Czechoslovakia under their founder, Bohumír Šmeral. The Communists developed links with the Soviet Union and the Communist International (Comintern), eventually coming under pro-Bolshevik influence when Klement Gottwald assumed party leadership in 1927 as the personal choice of Soviet leader Joseph Stalin. The Communists opposed the Czechoslovak state, but were not deemed enough of a threat to warrant government measures rendering the party illegal, as would be the case for other communist parties in the region. As a result of the defection, electoral support for the Social Democrats dropped from 38.1 percent in 1920 to no more than 11 percent in future elections.

Masaryk had counted on German participation in the government, but the German parties opposed the new state and initially refused to cooperate with the government in Prague. Although the German National Socialist Party and right-wing German National Party consistently maintained an oppositional and anti-state stance, others like the German Agrarian Party, the German Social Democrats, the German Christian–Social People's Party, and the Communists eventually made connections with Czechoslovak parties pursuing similar political goals. Racist, anti-Semitic, pan-German, and virulently opposed to Czechoslovak democracy, the German National Socialist Party modeled itself after Adolf Hitler's National Socialists in Germany and had nothing in common with Beneš's Czechoslovak National Socialists, who assumed that party title in 1926 in recognition of their earlier history.

Hungarian parties followed a course similar to that of the German parties in terms of initial opposition to the Czechoslovak state as a result of the reactionary and irredentist policies of the Horthy government in Budapest. Eventually, some of the parties of the Hungarian minority accepted the political status quo and initiated contact with similar Czechoslovak parties.

For Slovaks and Ruthenes, whose acceptance of the Czechoslovak state rested on expectations of autonomy, the creation of a centralized state administered from Prague brought disappointment in spite of the general support shown for the new political arrangement. Resentment grew as Czech efforts to modernize regions that had remained underdeveloped as a result of Magyarization often displayed little understanding of national traditions that had developed in Slovakia and Ruthenia. Many Czechs spoke of Czechoslovakia and common Czechoslovak citizenship, but their cultural and political identification remained firmly Czech. As a result, the majority of Czechs failed to understand the importance of autonomy to Slovaks because they did not identify the Slovaks as a nation separate from themselves. Even Masaryk had declared in 1921, "There is no Slovak nation; that's an invention of Hungarian propaganda."[3]

A lack of political experience hindered the Slovaks, although events may have played out differently had Milan Rastislav Štefánik not perished in an airplane crash near Bratislava as he was returning to his homeland on May 4, 1919. His military career and activities on behalf of the founding of Czechoslovakia made him a highly respected Slovak leader who might have provided a critical unifying force among Slovaks.

At the end of 1918, Vavro Šrobár's arrival in Slovakia on behalf of the Czechoslovak government had brought an end to the Slovak National Committee and marked the beginning of the transition from the administrative institutions of the Hungarians to the apparatus of the new state. As a supporter of Masaryk and a leading figure in the Hlasist faction, Šrobár promoted the Czechoslovak agenda but succeeded in driving many Slovaks toward autonomism when he appeared politically biased toward Protestants at the expense of the majority Catholics. Šrobár's political demise came in the wake of difficulties caused by the economic reorientation away from Hungary and after police shot and killed striking agricultural workers in Rumanová in March 1920. Poor results for the Slovak Agrarian Party in the 1920 elections led to Šrobár's ouster as party leader and his replacement with Milan Hodža.

Given the distribution of seats in the National Assembly, the Slovaks found it difficult to exert influence over political affairs and government policies at the start of the republic. Holding 31 of 150 seats in the Senate and 63 of 300 in the House of Deputies in 1920, the Slovaks sought the creation of a Slovak diet and regional government, but made little progress with the request even after the submission of a formal proposal in 1922.

The results of the 1925 elections indicated the changes that had occurred in Czechoslovak politics since the first parliamentary elections five years earlier. The Czechoslovak Social Democrats declined from 25.65 percent of the vote in 1920 to 8.88 percent in 1925, while the Communist Party of Czechoslovakia recorded 12.86 percent in earning political capital from discontent over economic difficulties. The Agrarians emerged with increased electoral support, as did the populist parties. The Slovak People's Party, which renamed itself Hlinka's Slovak People's Party (HSĽS) in 1925, polled 6.88 percent of the vote across Czechoslovakia, but earned a major victory among the Slovak electorate with a 34.3 percent showing to 17.4 for the Czechoslovak Agrarians and 13.9 for the Communists.

On March 18, 1926, health issues led the Agrarian leader Švehla to resign as prime minister, a position he had held since October 1922. Masaryk chose to replace Švehla's ministry with a second nonparty government under Jan Černý, which lasted until October 1926, when Švehla returned to resume the premiership. Švehla's new center-right coalition included the Czechoslovak People's Party, the Tradesmen's Party, and significantly the German Agrarians and German Christian Social People's Party, leading to the appointment of two German ministers.

The inclusion of the National Democrats led to period of the "Gentlemen's" or "Green-Black" governing coalition from 1927 to February 1929. During that time, the National Assembly reelected Masaryk as president, and the government instituted agricultural tariffs and clerical salaries to satisfy different constituencies. On July 1, 1928, Public Law No. 125 replaced the existing administrative system with institutions designed to extend policy-making authority to the four new Lands of Bohemia, Moravia-Silesia, Slovakia, and Carpatho-Ruthenia. Each province would come under the authority of a provincial president and possess a Land assembly with limited powers, although the Prague government held responsibility for final decisions.

Since the institution of the provincial system was interpreted as a step toward autonomy for Slovakia, Hlinka's Slovak People's Party entered Švehla's "Gentlemen's Coalition" as Ján Drobný of the HSĽS became Slovakia's first provincial president. In elections to the Slovak Land Diet on December 2, 1928, Hlinka's party gained 15 seats to 16 for the Agrarians and 5 for the Communists, with 18 divided among other parties.

In early 1928, the HSĽS newspaper *Slovák* had published an article entitled "Ten Years after the Martin Declaration," in which Vojtech Tuka argued that failure to grant Slovakia full autonomy by the end of the year would lead to the negation of Czechoslovak laws, as supported by secret conditions set out in the Martin Declaration of 1918. Tuka, who clandestinely served as an agent of Hungarian irredentists after the war, became the leader of the radical wing of the HSĽS, having drafted a proposal for Slovak autonomy in 1921 and then serving as editor-in-chief of *Slovák* at Hlinka's invitation in 1922. A year later, Tuka founded the paramilitary organization, the *Rodobrana*, a body of HSĽS extremists that shared his negative views toward Czechs, Protestants, and Jews. By 1925, Tuka reached the upper ranks of the HSĽS leadership and served the party in the Czechoslovak parliament from 1925 to 1929.

When Tuka's article appeared in 1928, Slovak leaders of the pro-Czechoslovak political parties began an investigation into his earlier activities on behalf of Hungary and in opposition to the Czechoslovak state, leading to charges of treason and conspiracy against the republic. Once stripped of parliamentary immunity, Tuka became the focal point of the most noteworthy political trial of the First Republic, and one that resulted in a 15-year prison sentence for Tuka in October 1929. As a result of the Tuka affair, the HSĽS abandoned the government coalition and then suffered a decrease in electoral support in the national parliamentary elections of October 1929, slipping to 28.3 percent of the vote in Slovakia and 5.8 percent nationally. The Czechoslovak Agrarians polled 19.5 percent in Slovakia, the Hungarian Regional Christian-Socialists 15.9, and the Czechoslovak Communists 10.7, although the HSĽS remained the dominant party.

On a national level, the Agrarian Party remained strong, and with Švehla stepping down due to continued poor health in February 1929, František Udřzal assumed leadership of the Agrarians and served as prime minister in a governing coalition of eight parties until late October 1934. However, the coalition had little time to set a political course before economic crisis struck Czechoslovakia and the world immediately after the election.

CZECHOSLOVAK FOREIGN POLICY IN THE 1920S

In the wake of the Paris Peace Conference, the fledgling Czechoslovak state entered the European community of nations as a small country in a vulnerable geographical position, but without a powerful enemy among the major powers. The new democratic Germany that arose out of the military defeat did not provide an immediate threat, especially in light of the reduction of German military power mandated by the Treaty of Versailles. Austria and Hungary remained unsatisfied with territorial adjustments and the terms of the peace treaties, but both had been weakened by the disintegration of Austria-Hungary and the consequences of the war. Furthermore, the Allied powers encouraged the development of a democratic Czechoslovakia in a region where the collapse of empires had led to the birth or rebirth of nations and the potential for instability.

In spite of the activities and persistence of the wartime Czech and Slovak exiles in garnering support from the Allied powers, Beneš and others believed that the creation of an independent Czechoslovak republic and the very successful negotiations at the Paris Peace Conference were largely the result of decisions made by the Allied governments and less so the rewards of efforts made by the Czechs and Slovaks themselves. As a result, Beneš and the framers of interwar foreign policy in Czechoslovakia tended to approach foreign relations with a sense of dependency and without full confidence in Czechoslovakia's ability to act without the support of patron nations like Great Britain and France. As the United States withdrew from European affairs and Bolshevik Russia remained a pariah in the eyes of Allied governments, leadership fell to Great Britain and France, with the former moving slowly toward disengagement during the 1920s. France, meanwhile, proved increasingly less willing to act without the support of Great Britain.

As Masaryk's choice to head the Ministry of Foreign Affairs, Beneš dominated diplomatic affairs during the interwar period and displayed personal and policy characteristics that made him very unlike the philosopher-president in a number of key ways. Beneš, who completed an abbreviated term as prime minister in 1921–1922, approached foreign affairs as a field in which emotion was to be subordinated to rational analysis and an almost scientific approach to policy making. In Beneš's view, Czechoslovakia would benefit most from a preservation of negotiated borders and the conditions set down in the Treaty of Versailles and by avoiding diplomatic or military relations that would expose the republic to dangerous risks or rivalries. Security lay in flexibility and in equilibrium, which in turn would stem from collective security in Europe, a strong League of Nations, and continued cooperation between Great Britain and France. Like Masaryk, Beneš believed that there was little to be gained from isolating the Soviet Union from European affairs, and in this regard wanted Czechoslovakia to assume the role of bridge between east and west that had traditionally belonged to the lands of the Bohemian crown. Beneš worked tirelessly on behalf of this strategy, making numerous trips abroad during the 1920s and promoting support for the League while serving as chair of the League Council six times and once as chair of the Assembly.

Relations between Czechoslovakia and Austria began to improve after the Allied governments blocked efforts at an *Anschluss* that would have united Austrian territory with Germany. In December 1921, Austria and Czechoslovakia signed the Treaty of Lány, a pact of friendship that opened the way for improved diplomatic and economic relations and mutual agreement toward maintaining stability in the region. In November 1925, a commercial treaty followed the easing of tensions, although the political victory of Benito Mussolini and the Fascists in Italy gave cause for concern due to Mussolini's plans for extending Italian influence into Austria, Hungary, and the Balkans.

Efforts to improve relations with Hungary proved difficult after the war as the regent Admiral Miklós Horthy and the Hungarian government adopted an irredentist approach to the Treaty of Trianon and the loss of what many Hungarians believed to be historic Magyar territories in Slovakia, Transylvania, and the Balkans. Beneš failed to achieve rapprochement with a revisionist Hungary, but Hungarian policies drove Rumania closer to Czechoslovakia and proved instrumental in the creation in 1920–1921 of the Little Entente, an alliance of Czechoslovakia, Rumania, and Yugoslavia, primarily directed toward mutual defense against Hungarian ambitions. Beneš hoped to use the alliance as a counterweight to Germany, especially when supported by military alliances with France, but Germany proved to be of much more concern to Czechoslovakia than to the other members of the Little Entente.

During the crisis year of 1923, the runaway inflation and the occupation of the Ruhr in Germany created difficulties for Masaryk and Beneš as a result of France's continued hard-line policies toward the Germans. Beneš believed that cooperation between France and Germany was essential to maintaining long-term stability in Europe, but his attempts to mediate a solution failed to prevent the occupation of the Ruhr industrial region by French and Belgian troops.

On January 25, 1924, agreement on a French-Czechoslovak alliance brought cooperation on maintaining existing military links, preserving the status quo, and blocking the restoration of the old ruling dynasties in Austria and Germany. Czechoslovakia also concluded friendship treaties with Italy in July 1924 and Poland in April 1925, although Beneš viewed a potential alliance with the Poles as much too risky because of the recently restored Poland's vulnerable position between Germany and the Soviet Union. Poland was an ally of France, but Poland also enjoyed good relations with Hungary, whose irredentist tendencies remained a source of great concern to the Czechoslovak foreign ministry.

Beneš's faith in arbitration as a means of addressing grievances seemed to be well placed as he chaired the committee responsible for drafting the Geneva Protocol in 1924. Supporters of the protocol hoped to increase the role of the League of Nations and to replace traditional diplomatic practices with a system that provided for arbitration of international disputes. Czechoslovakia ratified the protocol, but Great Britain and France refused to do so and chose instead to negotiate new agreements at a conference in Locarno, Switzerland, in October 1925. Beneš and his Polish colleague, Alexander Skrzyński, received little attention at the conference as diplomats from Great Britain, France, Belgium, Germany, and Italy drew up the Locarno agreements. The negotiations ushered in a new spirit of conciliation toward Germany as France and Germany agreed to maintain their territorial frontier as defined in the Treaty of Versailles, with Great Britain and Italy ready to intervene if either nation violated the border through military action. The agreements did not, however, guarantee Germany's eastern frontier in the same fashion, although Germany signed arbitration treaties with Poland and Czechoslovakia, and in a 1925 agreement, France strengthened military commitments to Czechoslovakia in the event of a German military threat. Germany's entry into the League of Nations and an improvement in relations with Czechoslovakia offered hope that the extension of collective security might offset the failure to guarantee the permanence of that nation's eastern borders.

At the midpoint of the decade, Beneš's faith in democracy and the pursuit of collective security seemed to offer hope for peace and stability in the future. In 1929, however, European affairs began to change dramatically as a global economic crisis and the growing threat of political extremism threatened the Versailles System and placed the democracies on the defensive. With the death of Germany's foreign minister, Gustav Stresemann, in 1929, the spirit of cooperation stemming from the Locarno conference had seemingly run its course as Europe entered a decade of crisis.

THE GREAT DEPRESSION AND THE 1930S

By the mid-1920s, the economy of Czechoslovakia had overcome the loss of traditional markets and economic relationships from the days of the Austro-Hungarian Empire as the nation reoriented trade toward the rest of Europe and the world. Czechoslovakia weathered a continent-wide economic downturn from 1921 to 1923, and although severe deflationary policies enacted by Alois Rašín as finance minister in 1922 probably lessened the impact of the hyperinflation plaguing Germany and Austria in 1923, they did not save Rašín from becoming a scapegoat for the economic crisis. The shooting of Rašín by a mentally disturbed young radical on January 5, 1923, came amid growing unpopularity and constant attacks in the press by critics on the left.

With the process of creating a unified internal market completed, the economy exceeded prewar levels in agricultural and industrial production, which by the end of the decade allowed the nation to enjoy a good measure of economic stability and prosperity. Legislation introduced the eight-hour workday in December 1918 and child labor laws two years later, with sickness and accident protection enacted in 1924 and old-age pensions for workers in white-collar positions in 1926.

By 1928, conditions began to deteriorate, first with a downturn in international trade and then in 1929 with a serious decline in prices for agricultural products. On October 24, 1929, the New York stock market crash precipitated a global economic crisis, which struck Czechoslovakia the following year. Industrial production went into immediate decline, with light industry being hit particularly hard, especially in border regions with a German-speaking population. By 1932, the production of industrial concerns barely reached 60 percent of pre-1929 levels, and the nation's foreign trade had declined dramatically and to near-critical levels. Unemployment numbers, which had reached postwar lows in 1929, rose to close to one million without jobs in 1933, according to official government reports. In Slovakia and

Ruthenia, the crisis became even more acute as high unemployment combined with government cutbacks in social benefits to leave large numbers of people without any means of support.

The worsening crisis and the slow reactions of the government triggered public demonstrations and strikes, often with the support of the nation's intelligentsia and cultural leaders. Unprepared to respond quickly to deteriorating economic conditions, the government coalition reacted with moderation in coping with wages, prices, and currency, while responding with force to public expressions of discontent. Over the years between 1930 and 1933, the police and gendarmes were responsible for 29 deaths and over 100 injuries in confrontations with demonstrators and striking workers. The growing radicalization of political life brought increased support for the Communists on the left and the fascists and extremists on the right.

The appointment of a new government under František Udržal's successor, the Agrarian Jan Malypetr, on October 29, 1932, led first to legal limits regarding public protests and then, in June 1933, to a parliamentary special powers law, which granted the government the authority to intervene in economic matters and to set policies by decree. By 1934, production began a slow rebound, although the economy moved into a stage of depression as credit crises and the poor state of agriculture prevented a return to economic health. During that year, the government worked to stabilize grain prices, lower interest rates, increase foreign trade, and devalue the Czechoslovak currency, the koruna, or crown. In 1935–1936 production continued to rise as a result of increased investment, especially in the armament sector.

THE 1935 ELECTION AND THE POLITICS OF NATIONALISM

A year after Masaryk's reelection as president, the results of the April 1935 parliamentary election confirmed that the economic crises of the 1930s had intensified nationality issues and increased dissatisfaction with the government in Prague. Social problems stemming from the decline in industrial production in the German-speaking areas and the deterioration of the agrarian sector in Slovakia caused many to question the effectiveness of Czechoslovak democracy and to support autonomist or nationalist parties as an alternative to centralist, Czechoslovak parties.

The Agrarians emerged from the election with 14.3 percent of the vote, as the left-wing Czechoslovak Social Democrats polled 12.6 percent and the Communists 10.3 percent. Among the antidemocratic parties, the National Fascist League under Gen. Radola Gajda earned only 2 percent of the vote, but in a shocking surprise, the opposition Sudeten German Party (SdP) emerged with 15.2 percent of the overall vote and two-thirds of the votes cast by ethnic Germans. The German Social Democrats forfeited over half of their seats, while the other German parties also lost ground to a party of radical German nationalism, founded by Konrad Henlein in 1935 out of his Sudetenland Homeland Front (SdP) and the banned Nazi and extremist German organizations in Czechoslovakia. The victory of Henlein's SdP led to the withdrawal of Germans from the government in Prague and the establishment of closer ties between the SdP and Hitler's Germany.

At the beginning of November, Masaryk, now 85, appointed Milan Hodža the country's first Slovak prime minister before resigning the presidency on November 21 as a result of medical problems stemming from a stroke he had suffered in May 1934. Upon his retirement, the "President Liberator" requested that Beneš be allowed to succeed him as president and after the HSĽS joined Hodža's Agrarians in supporting Beneš's candidacy, he was elected as the second president of Czechoslovakia on December 15, 1935. The death of Masaryk on September 14, 1937, completed the transition to a new, albeit short-lived, phase of the First Republic.

In Slovakia, support for autonomy increased among Slovak populists in the 1930s as a consequence of Depression-era economic conditions and the emergence of new leaders like Karol Sidor and Jozef Tiso from among the younger members of the HSĽS and the *Nástup* (Step Forward) circle. In late June 1932, representatives of the rising generation of Slovak intellectuals held a Congress of the Young Slovak Generation in the town of Trečianske Treplice. The gathering quickly evolved into a rally in support of Slovak autonomy as many delegates denounced the centralist Czechoslovak state, the Slovak political leaders, and the capitalist system, which they held responsible for the poor state of the Slovak economy. Press coverage of the congress increased public interest in the autonomist agenda of Hlinka's party, which had not even participated in the planning of the congress.

At the end of December 1932, Hlinka delivered a keynote speech at a congress in Trenčín in which he reiterated his position that in defending Slovak interests, the HSĽS would not willingly forfeit the "right of national sovereignty *even at the price of the Czechoslovak Republic.*"[4] In Bratislava on June 5, 1938, Hlinka chose the 20th anniversary of the Pittsburgh Agreement to announce the third proposal for Slovak autonomy for submission to the government in Prague. The proposal included demands for a separate Slovak government and diet, with joint Czech and Slovak responsibility for defense, foreign policy, and finances and the right of Slovak representatives to veto measures introduced by the Czechoslovak assembly and government. Beneš, who was occupied with issues involving the Sudeten Germans and threat of German intervention, gave his approval to decentralization within Czechoslovakia. On August 16, 1938, weakness and ill health claimed Hlinka, and the party subsequently elected Tiso to serve as leader of the HSĽS.

DEPRESSION-ERA FOREIGN POLICY

With the onset of the economic crisis, friction arose between Czechoslovakia and the nation's allies in the Little Entente as the importation of agricultural products from Yugoslavia and Rumania generated opposition from domestic producers. Czechoslovak policies eventually allowed Germany to move into those markets as a supplier of industrial goods in return for agricultural products. Efforts to establish an Austro-German Customs Union offered cause for alarm in 1931 as a potential step toward *Anschluss*, but opposition by Czechoslovakia, France, and Italy blocked the union on the grounds that it violated earlier treaties.

During the era of the Weimar Republic, and in spite of Stresemann's desire to revise the Versailles treaty, fear of German aggression had subsided as Germany entered the League of Nations in 1926 and remained on stable terms with Czechoslovakia. With the appointment of Adolf Hitler as Chancellor in January 1933, however, Germany embarked upon a course that challenged the European democracies and threatened revisions of the eastern borders with Poland and Czechoslovakia. In 1933, Hitler's initial foreign policy maneuvers included withdrawal from the League and departure from an international disarmament conference for which Beneš was serving as secretary-general.

Aware that the Těšín settlement remained a source of friction with the Poles, Beneš attempted to negotiate with his Polish counterpart, Col. Josef Beck, but suffered a major setback when Poland concluded a nonaggression treaty with Nazi Germany in 1934. Beneš later denounced Poland's decision as an "ill-considered, arrogant mark of defiance" that strained Poland's relations with France, Czechoslovakia, and the Soviet Union at a time when France's interest in Central European affairs had already begun to wane.[5]

During the early months of 1933, the Soviet Union had made overtures to France and to the Little Entente, and so in 1934, French foreign minister Louis Barthou responded to the Polish-German agreement with an eastern strategy linking Czechoslovakia and the Soviet Union with France. Beneš and Masaryk desired a stronger role for the Soviet Union as a counterweight to Germany, but the Soviets did not take concrete action until the following year, when they entered the League of Nations and began promoting collective security in the face of the threats posed by Fascist Italy and Nazi Germany.

Barthou's assassination in 1934 led to a redirection of French policy under Pierre Laval, who supported two separate treaties of mutual assistance, Franco-Soviet and Soviet-Czechoslovak, in place of Barthou's plans for three-way cooperation. Signed during the year of Germany's announced plans for rearmament and preceded by formal diplomatic recognition, the Soviet-Czechoslovak treaty of May 1935 guaranteed Soviet assistance in the event of a direct military threat to Czechoslovakia, although only after the French had honored their own treaty commitments from 1925 first.

When Beneš assumed the presidency after Masaryk's departure, he was replaced by Milan Hodža before eventually selecting the historian and diplomat Kamil Krofta to serve as minister of foreign affairs in February 1936. The following month, German troops reoccupied the Rhineland in defiance of the Versailles treaty, and Beneš joined Poland and the Soviet Union in offering support to the French, who chose instead to look to the British for assistance. The lack of a strong response concerned Beneš enough to raise the previously unthinkable option of a nonaggression treaty with Nazi Germany. France approached Beneš about Czechoslovakia's willingness to assist in the defense of Poland, but in spite of Beneš's positive response, the Poles refused to reciprocate in defense of Czechoslovakia. When Beneš proposed through French intermediaries in August 1936 that Czechoslovakia and Poland undertake joint military preparations against Germany, the Poles again refused to cooperate. Beneš and Krofta engaged in secret conversations with German diplomats during November and December, but disagreement over the status of the Sudeten Germans and opposition by Hitler and his foreign minister, Konstantin von Neurath, to Beneš's interpretation of the terms eliminated any possibility of a final agreement.

Hitler despised Czechoslovakia as an artificial nation containing an ethnic German population destined to become part of a Greater German Reich. Konrad Henlein and his Sudeten German Party, already funded in great part by the Reich government, offered Hitler the mechanism by which the Reich would gain possession of the German-speaking territories of the Sudetenland. With Czechoslovakia's position growing ever more precarious in regard to Nazi Germany and the Sudeten

Germans, the Munich Agreement of September 1938 would allow Hitler to achieve his goal of acquiring the Sudetenland as Great Britain and France chose to abandon Czechoslovakia rather than risk the outbreak of another major European war.

NOTES

1. H. G. Skilling, *T. G. Masaryk: Against the Current, 1882–1914* (University Park: Pennsylvania State University Press, 1994), xii.

2. Dr. Thomas Garrigue Masaryk, *The Making of a State: Memoirs and Observations 1914–1918* (London: George Allen and Unwin, Ltd., 1927), 47.

3. Cited in R. J. W. Evans, "Hungarians, Czechs, and Slovaks: Some Mutual Perceptions, 1900–1950," in *Czechoslovakia in a National and Fascist Europe 1918–1948*, ed. Mark Cornwall and R. J. W. Evans (Oxford: Oxford University Press, 2007), 114.

4. James Ramon Felak, *"At the Price of the Republic": Hlinka's Slovak People's Party, 1929–1938* (Pittsburgh, PA: University of Pittsburgh Press, 1994), 96.

5. Edvard Benes, *Memoirs of Dr. Eduard Benes: From Munich to New War and New Victory* (Westport, CT: Greenwood Press, 1978), 10.

7

The Munich Agreement and World War II (1938–1945)

KONRAD HENLEIN AND THE SUDETEN GERMANS

By 1936, the Prague government faced growing threats not only from an aggressive Nazi Germany, but also from an internal German population that was becoming more radicalized and willing to turn to Hitler's regime for support. The worsening economic crisis in the German-speaking borderlands of Bohemia and Moravia-Silesia generated high unemployment and social dislocations stemming from shuttered enterprises and lost wages. Out of this crisis arose Konrad Henlein and the Sudeten German Party as the self-proclaimed defenders of the rights of the German national minority in Czechoslovakia.

In early October 1933, Henlein, the head of a gymnastics organization in Czechoslovakia, established the Sudeten German Patriotic Front, which quickly gained recruits from the banned German National Socialists and German National Party before transforming itself into the Sudeten German Party (SdP) prior to the elections of

April 1935. Henlein hoped to capitalize on the discontent of all the German inhabitants of Czechoslovakia, later gaining an ally in the Carpatho-German Party (KpD) of Franz Karmasin, which claimed to speak for the majority of Germans living in Slovakia.

Henlein's party offered Hitler an organization useful in the pursuit of Germany's expansionist and pan-German goals leading to the creation of a Greater German Reich in Central Europe. Henlein's party received funding from Nazi Germany during the 1935 elections, and in November 1937, Henlein expressed his willingness to reorient the SdP to assist Hitler in his efforts to seize Czech territory. Henlein's letter to Hitler overstated the problems of the Sudeten Germans in regard to the Czechs and the Prague government, while also inviting the Germans to acquire the border territories in fulfillment of what Henlein claimed to be a major goal of the Sudeten German Party. Shortly after Hitler's remilitarization of the Rhineland in 1936, the Czechoslovak National Assembly responded to the SdP's activities and friction over the frontier territories by passing a law granting the military broad authority within a zone stretching just over 15.5 miles from the border and including a high percentage of Bohemia's German population. Germany greatly increased the flow of funds to the SdP in hopes of exploiting the growing anger and radicalization of the party's followers.

Prime Minister Milan Hodža believed that his Slovak background would allow him to negotiate with the Germans without the obstacles faced by his Czech colleagues. In February 1937, the Hodža government responded to discontent among the nationalities by offering proposals for addressing the economic, social, and cultural concerns of the minorities and for filling positions in the civil service in a fairer and more proportional manner. However, Hodža's efforts to negotiate with Henlein in the fall of that year failed completely, and in early 1938, Agrarian leader Rudolf Beran's calls for accommodations that would bring the SdP into the government were met with angry opposition from the Czechoslovak public.

In June 1937, German military planners developed a secret plan called "Operation Green," which called for the rapid seizure of Bohemia and Moravia and the institution of military governments to administer the occupied regions. The plan included neither the occupation of Slovakia, nor the incorporation of ethnic Czechs into the citizenry of the Greater German Reich. When combined with an *Anschluss* with Austria, the Reich stood to gain 5–6 million people, new resources for the production of armaments, and improved borders for defensive purposes. Hitler had also come to believe that if Germany moved against Czechoslovakia,

Poland would not respond to military activities on its border, while Great Britain and France were unlikely to commit to the defense of Czechoslovakia if it meant escalating a regional problem into a much larger war. The Sudeten Germans, therefore, became the focal point of German preparations for the planned actions against Czechoslovakia.

When Nazi Germany completed the successful incorporation of Austria into the Greater German Reich with the *Anschluss* of March 12, 1938, Hitler's planners delivered a revised version of "Operation Green," which assumed action against Czechoslovakia in the near future, in spite of the opposition voiced by Hitler's top military commanders. On March 28, Henlein visited Hitler and received the Führer's assurances that his leadership of the SdP remained secure and that the party should continue to appear willing to negotiate with the Czechoslovak government, while at the same time escalating demands to impossible levels. A month later, on April 24, Henlein delivered a speech before the SdP congress at Karlovy Vary in which he demanded full equality between the Sudeten Germans and the Czechs. Additionally, Henlein demanded German-run local administrations in clearly defined German territories and under the authority of the Sudeten German Party, along with the right of the Germans to subscribe to racial and political views, which were effectively Nazi in orientation.

As Henlein's followers prepared for municipal elections through intimidation and violence against antifascists and supporters of the republic in the border territories, the government in Prague lifted the post-*Anschluss* ban on public gatherings so that pro-democratic parties could offer a show of solidarity in defense of the republic on May Day. On May 20, rumors of German troop movements near the border led to a "May Crisis" involving the partial mobilization of Czechoslovak military forces as a sign that Czechoslovakia would defend its home soil against a German incursion.

THE ROAD TO MUNICH

As the Sudeten Crisis worsened, Beneš and the Prague government came to believe that postwar treaties and agreements would not, in fact, bring Czechoslovakia the expected level of foreign support against Germany. Stalin's show trials and purges in the Soviet Union led to reservations about the ability of the Soviets to contribute militarily to Czechoslovakia's defense. Under Conservative prime minister Neville Chamberlain and the foreign secretary, Lord Halifax, Great Britain embraced a policy of appeasement in hopes of avoiding war through negotiated settlements, which meant that Czechoslovakia's treaties with the Soviet Union and France created complications that in the latter case could draw Great Britain into war with Germany. Chamberlain had dispatched Lord Halifax to Germany to assure German leaders that the British government would consider revisions to Germany's eastern borders if carried out through peaceful negotiations. In Chamberlain's view, Czechoslovakia's location made defense of that country by the British, French, and Soviets virtually impossible. As a result, Czechoslovakia had little choice but to negotiate with Germany and the SdP. Henlein exploited British uncertainty through a propaganda campaign designed to convince the British that the source of the problem remained a Czechoslovak government unwilling to confront the concerns of the German minority.

The French, who had signed a treaty with Czechoslovakia in 1925, found themselves under pressure from the British to back away from direct support for Czechoslovakia or risk weakening Anglo-French co-operation. The British hoped to convince the Prague government to negotiate a long-term agreement with the German minority that would ease tensions and thereby allow France to escape dangerous entanglements in Czechoslovak-German affairs. Beneš and Hodža, however, expressed concerns that granting concessions to the Sudeten Germans would lead to demands by the other minorities and to the eventual destabilization of the country. The response by the British and the French was to demand that the Czechoslovak government accept an outside mediator to oversee negotiations with Henlein and the SdP.

The mediator dispatched to Czechoslovakia was Sir Walter Runciman, a British shipping tycoon with no real qualifications for his assignment. Runciman remained in Czechoslovakia from August 3 to September 16, but the Runciman Mission achieved little amid the staged demonstrations, social occasions, and inundation of reports and memoranda. Runciman and his wife were entertained by members of the ethnic German nobility and heard countless tales of mistreatment by the Czechs and by the Prague government, but efforts by leaders of the democratic German parties to consult with Runciman met with failure.

Beneš participated in negotiations with the SdP, which on September 7 led to acceptance of terms set out by Henlein in April as the Karlovy Vary, or Karlsbad, program. Surprised by the concessions, Henlein ceased communication until after Hitler's speech at a rally in Nuremberg on September 12, in which the German leader enthusiastically emphasized German support for the Sudeten Germans. By the following morning, violent demonstrations broke out in the Sudetenland and other frontier regions, leading to the deaths of several Czech police officers and the vandalism of shops owned by Czechs, Jews, and democratic Germans. The authorities imposed a state of emergency in the frontier districts on September 13–14, granting emergency power to the police and courts, and issuing orders to police, military, and security forces not to fire unless under attack. By September 15, the situation stabilized somewhat as the government declared the SdP an illegal organization and issued a warrant for the arrest of Henlein, who avoided capture by crossing the border into Germany.

After requesting a meeting with Hitler several days earlier, Chamberlain landed in Munich on September 15 and traveled to Hitler's mountaintop residence at Berchtesgaden by train. From his compartment windows, Chamberlain could observe the movement of German military forces by rail toward the border with Czechoslovakia. At the meeting, Hitler fulminated against the alleged atrocities committed against the Sudeten Germans and demanded that the British and French governments allow Germany to take possession of the Sudetenland, a concession that Chamberlain had already assumed was a necessary step in avoiding war, even though it went well beyond Henlein's calls for greater autonomy.

At 2:00 a.m. on September 21, Great Britain and France delivered Beneš and his government an ultimatum stating that if Czechoslovakia chose to defy Hitler in his demands, the country would be left on its own to suffer the consequences of its actions. The governing parties split over the official response, with the National Democrats and the People's Party calling for resistance and the other parties reluctantly advising acceptance. Beneš held out until 5:00 p.m., when the Czechoslovak government announced acceptance of the Berchtesgaden demands. In Prague, the streets filled with demonstrators demanding Hodža's ouster as the Committee for the Defense of the Republic urged public defiance of the ultimatum.

The following day, as Chamberlain met with Hitler at Godesberg, General Jan Syrový assumed the duties of prime minister and informed the public that the nation would defend itself if called upon to do so. At Godesberg, however, Hitler added new demands, which would require immediate Czechoslovak withdrawal from the frontier territories as well as acceptance of the territorial claims made by Poland and Hungary the previous day. As Premier Èdouard Daladier and the French expressed opposition to Hitler's new conditions, the British ambassador in Berlin informed Hitler of Chamberlain's acceptance of the terms. On September 23, Beneš received word from the British and

French that they no longer opposed the mobilization of Czechoslovak military forces, and on the following day, the Czechoslovak army, now numbering 1.5 million men, moved into fortifications and defensive positions along the border.

In the wake of Hitler's speech in Berlin on September 26, in which he denounced Beneš personally for his role in the alleged atrocities perpetrated against the Sudeten Germans, Chamberlain once again attempted to dissuade Hitler from engaging in actions that could lead to war. As a result, Hitler eventually agreed to a meeting in Munich on September 29. Hitler's ally Mussolini would be present at the session, as would Chamberlain and French premier Édouard Daladier, but not representatives of the Soviet Union or of the Czechoslovak government out of fear that they might obstruct the negotiations.

At the Munich Conference, the four leaders agreed to a draft written by the German foreign minister Joachim von Ribbentrop and presented for discussion by Mussolini. This Munich Agreement sanctioned the German occupation of the Sudetenland with the resulting loss of some 2,825,000 Germans, nearly 800,000 Czechs, and 11,000 miles of Czechoslovak territory that had never been a part of the modern German state. The territories acquired in the *Anschluss* included 80 percent of Czechoslovakia's textile, glass, and chemical concerns, as well as over 70 percent of iron and steel production and vast reserves of lignite and black coal. All territories with a majority German population would be transferred immediately, while those with a German minority would hold plebiscites, which would, in fact, never be held. In return, Hitler agreed to respect the sovereignty of the remaining Czechoslovak state.

During the early hours of the following day, Chamberlain called in the Czechoslovak representatives and informed them that the fate of the Sudetenland had already been determined and that any response on their part would be without merit. Believing that they had successfully avoided war as a result of the Munich agreement, Chamberlain and Daladier then returned to their homelands to great public acclaim, although the settlement would ultimately fail to prevent either the dismemberment of Czechoslovakia or the outbreak of war.

THE SECOND REPUBLIC (OCTOBER 1938–MARCH 1939)

Two days after leading generals threatened to remove him from the presidency if he did not willingly resign, Beneš abdicated his office on October 5 as Germany pushed for more compliant leadership in carrying out the terms of the Munich Agreement. Beneš departed Czechoslovakia on October 22, stopping in London before continuing on to North

America. Beneš quickly established contact with the American government and emigré organizations such as the Slovak National Alliance and the Czech National Alliance.

In Prague, Czechoslovakia's former ambassador to Italy, František Chvalkovský, replaced Krofta as foreign minister and cooperated in the implementation of conditions required by the international agreements. Opposing the policy of acceptance, the Czechoslovak Communist Party urged workers to unite in support of resistance to Germany's actions, but party leaders such as Bohumir Šmeral, Klement Gottwald, and Rudolf Slánský eventually departed for the Soviet Union, especially after the government placed a ban on the Communist Party at the end of December.

After earlier negotiations with Henlein and the SdP reached an unfruitful end, Beneš and Hodža had opened talks with Tiso and the HSĽS in an effort to rally Slovaks to the defense of the republic. Beneš offered his support for a Slovak parliament and new language laws, but although autonomists generally did not abandon the republic in the pre-Munich days, many in the HSĽS then came to reject the existing Czechoslovak state in favor of promoting Slovak autonomy. On October 6, the day after Beneš's resignation, discussions at Zilina involving autonomists and centralist parties like the Social Democrats and Communists produced an HSĽS-sponsored declaration of Slovak autonomy, which led the Czcechoslovak prime minister Syrový to grant full autonomy to the Slovaks and appoint Msgr. Jozef Tiso as Slovak premier.

With the creation of the Tiso government, the HSĽS became the sole legal party in Slovakia as political organizations that had supported the former centralist state fell victim to the new political conditions. When the elections were held for the first Slovak parliament on December 18, the only available list of candidates included members of the HSĽS-dominated coalition.

Czechoslovakia suffered further territorial losses as the result of the First Vienna Award when the foreign ministers of Germany and Italy met on November 2 and agreed to requests to alter the borders of Slovakia, granting Hungary sections of Ruthenia and stretches of southern and eastern Slovakia in which a Hungarian majority resided. Poland, which had already sent troops into the disputed region of Těšín in early October, received designated areas in Silesia and Slovakia.

By mid-November, Czech political parties merged into coalitions, with the parties of the right and the majority of the National Socialists forming the Party of National Unity, and the Social Democrats and left-leaning National Socialists joining the opposition National Party of Labor. On November 19, the National Assembly in Prague passed Constitutional Law No. 299, formalizing Slovak autonomy and changing the country's name to "Czecho-Slovakia." A second measure provided a legal foundation for Ruthenian autonomy, with only the Communists opposing the two laws. The assembly then chose Emil Hácha as president on November 30. Hácha, an elderly lawyer and president of the Supreme Administrative Court, was a respected legal expert but otherwise a man completely lacking in political experience. Rudolf Beran of the Agrarians was appointed prime minister, with Karol Sidor chosen to serve as vice premier and minister of Slovak affairs.

During the months following the Munich Conference, Hitler became convinced that a Slovak declaration of independence and the resulting collapse of Czechoslovakia would allow Germany to seize Bohemia and Moravia without drawing Great Britain and France into a military conflict over the Czech lands. Since the terms of the Munich Agreement would no longer apply to a defunct Czechoslovak state, the British and French would be free of the guarantees of Czechoslovak territory and therefore unlikely to oppose the German occupation of Czech lands.

In late February, Beran's concern over Slovak intentions led to the demand that the Slovaks renounce the idea of an independent state and instead offer a declaration of loyalty to Czecho-Slovakia. Frustrated by the Slovak response, Beran and Hácha sent police and army units into Slovakia and ousted Tiso as prime minister under the claim that Tiso and the fascist Hlinka Guards were orchestrating a move toward independence. When Karol Sidor began forming a new Slovak government on March 11, Tiso became more receptive to communication from Hitler, for whom the armed response by the Prague government proved beneficial at a time when his representatives had failed to convince Tiso and Sidor to declare independence. After being summoned by Hitler, Tiso arrived in Berlin and was informed that failure to move toward independence would result in Slovakia being left vulnerable to Hungarian expansionism. After meeting with Hitler and Ribbentrop, Tiso contacted Hácha from Berlin and requested a meeting of the Slovak parliament for March 14. At that session, the Land Diet followed Tiso's advice and enacted a law establishing an independent Slovak state under Tiso's leadership.

With the Czecho-Slovak republic disintegrating, Hácha requested his own meeting with Hitler, who received the president and his foreign minister Chalkovský on the night of March 14–15. Subjected to three hours of threats and intimidation, culminating in a physical breakdown or possible heart attack, Hácha succumbed to the intense pressure and signed a request for German military protection of Bohemia and Moravia. In the meantime, however, the German invasion of Czecho-Slovakia had already begun.

As the German military advanced into Bohemia and Moravia from Austria and the north, Hitler's propaganda minister Joseph Goebbels delivered a radio address in the early morning hours of March 15 in which he claimed Bohemia and Moravia as historic German lands and blamed the collapse of Czecho-Slovakia on Slovak independence and the mistreatment of national minorities by the Czechs. During the morning and into the afternoon, the Luftwaffe took control of Ruzyně airfield in Prague as four German military columns surged across the country, meeting only scattered resistance and advancing as far as the Váh River in Slovakia. Ruthenia's leaders declared independence and requested German assistance in an attempt to avoid occupation, but the independence lasted only a single day before the Hungarians occupied Ruthenian territory and a small part of Slovakia on the basis of an agreement with Germany.

On March 16, a victorious Adolf Hitler arrived in Prague and issued a decree from Prague Castle establishing the Protectorate of Bohemia and Moravia under the authority of a Reich Protector, Baron Konstantin von Neurath. Neurath would assume his duties a month later in collaboration with State Secretary Karl Hermann Frank, a Sudeten German who was rabidly anti-Czech. Under the Protectorate, citizenship in the German Reich was extended to all Germans living in Bohemia and Moravia, while Czechs would be treated as citizens of the Protectorate. Five days after the proclamation of the Protectorate, President Hácha dissolved the National Assembly, eliminated existing political parties, and banned social, cultural, educational, and athletic organizations such as *Sokol* and the Boy Scouts.

On the day of the German invasion, Beneš contacted the leaders of Great Britain, France, the Soviet Union, and the United States via telegram to protest Germany's actions and to inform these governments of his intention to resume a role in political affairs in order to restore the Czechoslovak state. Beneš declared both the German occupation and the Slovak declaration of independence to be illegal, claiming that Germany's violation of Czechoslovak territory invalidated the Munich Agreement and therefore required the restoration of the country's pre-Munich borders, as well as the government of the First Republic. That same day, Neville Chamberlain informed Parliament that since the collapse of Czechoslovakia was due to internal problems, Great Britain's responsibility for guaranteeing the country's frontiers had come to an end.

For the Slovaks, the occupation of Bohemia and Moravia meant the signing of a treaty on March 23 that granted Slovakia the status of a protected state with a Slovak-run administration and German authority over foreign policy and military matters. Tiso would head the new Slovak government as prime minister, with Sidor as minister of the interior, Ferdinand Ďurčanský in charge of foreign affairs, and Vojtech Tuka, released from prison in 1938, serving as vice prime minister. Germany would also be allowed to maintain a military presence in Slovakia and to have access to Slovak resources in a manner that proved very favorable to the Germans. On July 21, the new constitution came into effect, and on October 26, elections were held for the Slovak Parliament with Tiso assuming the presidency of the Slovak republic.

By mid-April, Czech and Slovak organizations in the United States declared their support for Beneš as leader of Czechoslovaks living outside the Protectorate and Slovakia. Efforts to create a government-in-exile brought Roosevelt's supposed promise of recognition by neutral America during talks with Beneš in May, two months before Beneš returned to Great Britain and took up residence in London with no official standing. Although the British government requested that Beneš abstain from overt political engagement, Beneš remained the primary representative of Czechoslovak interests abroad.[1]

LIFE IN THE PROTECTORATE

During the initial phase of the Protectorate from March until the autumn of 1939, the Czechs and the Germans maintained an uneasy relationship in adapting to the new system. With Hácha as president and Gen. Alois Eliáš heading the government as prime minister, the Czechs maintained their own administration, police, and small, largely token army. Foreign affairs, defense, and other responsibilities fell to the Germans and the Reich Protector, who could overrule any government actions deemed detrimental to Reich policies. President Hácha, although far from a strong or charismatic figure, gained some measure of sympathetic public support due to the precarious position of the Protectorate government and an understanding that with the exception of enthusiastic collaborators, members of the Czech government continued to place the good of the nation above cooperation with the Germans.

Economic life in the Protectorate changed as a consequence of Germany's needs and the outbreak of World War II in September 1939.

Decisions regarding the price of goods came from experts working under the Reich Protector, while the Czech government of the Protectorate instituted rationing of food, clothing, and other items early in the conflict. In October 1940, the Protectorate joined the Reich's Customs Union and sent just over 70 percent of Czech exports to the Reich, while receiving 80 percent of imports in return. The population of the Protectorate also offered the Reich an important source of labor, primarily in terms of the war effort and the requirements of an expanding German empire.

During the first months of the Protectorate, the Czech public turned to passive resistance and small acts of protest to express discontent over the loss of independence. Many Czechs chose cultural venues to express their patriotic feelings as performances of national compositions like Smetana's "*Má Vlast*" drew enthusiastic audiences and often inspired spontaneous renditions of the national anthem. The increasing displays of nationalism eventually drew the ire of Nazi officials, who instituted a ban on singing patriotic songs in restaurants, theaters, and other public spaces.

In June 1939, the murder of a German policeman in the industrial town of Kladno led to the execution of over 200 people as a prelude to more brutal policies introduced at the outbreak of the war. As German forces invaded Poland on September 1, German authorities transported thousands of Czech citizens to concentration camps such as Dachau in an effort to prevent disturbances or open opposition. On October 28, police fired on crowds engaged in demonstrations on the anniversary of Czechoslovakia's independence. Medical student Jan Opletal later died of wounds inflicted by the police, and his funeral on November 15 offered an occasion for further demonstrations against the occupation. Under orders from State Secretary Frank, security forces staged a raid on student residences in Prague on the night of November 16–17, arresting over 1,800 students and sending another 1,000 or more to the camp at Oranienburg. The Nazis resorted to the closing of all colleges and universities and the suppression of intellectual and cultural life as a means of stifling opposition and criticism among the Czech intelligentsia.

For the Jewish population of the Protectorate, the Nazi program of Aryanization brought the extension of Germany's Nuremburg Laws of 1935 to the Protectorate in June 1939. The new measures instituted eliminated legal protections for Jews and placed restrictions on travel, education, cultural affairs, and professional and commercial activities. The decrees also required Jews to wear the yellow Star of David and reduced access to rationed foodstuffs.

BENEŠ AND THE CZECHOSLOVAKS ABROAD

In the fall of 1939, Beneš's efforts to create a national committee in Paris initially met with resistance from the French, who had little interest in cooperating with the former Czechoslovak president after the events of the previous year. However, Beneš succeeded in gaining French and British recognition for a Czechoslovak National Committee, although not for a government-in-exile.

As they had done under the leadership of Masaryk in World War I, Czechs and Slovaks abroad began organizing military units in the days prior to the assault on Poland in September. When the Polish government hesitated in granting permission for a Czechoslovak legion, many of the volunteers departed for France, and it was not until two days after German forces rolled across the border that a Czechoslovak legion under Col. Ludvík Svoboda appeared in Poland before most of the legionnaires fell into Soviet hands and were held as prisoners.

In June, the Protectorate prime minister, Gen. Eliáš, had dispatched a representative of the Czech resistance to communicate with the French government and to organize Czechoslovak military units there. Beneš convinced first the French and later the British to recognize the authority of the CNC in Paris over Czechoslovak armed forces during the last months of 1939. Two army regiments joined Czechoslovak pilots and other personnel in the French air force in the defense of France when German forces invaded France and the Low Countries in May 1940. Approximately 4,000 Czechoslovak soldiers were evacuated to Great Britain as the French defeat unfolded, and in September 1943, the relocated infantry formed the Czechoslovak Independent Armored Brigade, which returned to Continental soil in the fall of 1944. An estimated 110 Czechoslovak airmen served in British and Polish squadrons during the Battle of Britain, which began in midsummer 1940 with Luftwaffe attacks on military targets and then cities.

During the first year of the war, two different organizations claimed to represent the Czechoslovak cause in exile, with Beneš and his colleagues headquartered in Paris and then London, and a Communist-dominated contingent operating in cooperation with the Soviet leadership in Moscow. On September 8, 1939, Jan Masaryk sent out his first radio broadcast from London on behalf of the Czechoslovak committee in exile, accepting an offer by the BBC to make weekly broadcasts into Europe. After the defeat of France and the transfer of the CNC to London, Britain offered to recognize Beneš's committee as a government-in-exile, although on a provisional basis. This provisional government included Beneš as president, Msgr. Šrámek of the former People's Party as head, and a range of party representatives and independent figures such as Masaryk, Gen. Sergěj Ingr, Gen. Rudolf Viest, the former Slovak parliamentarian Juraj Slavík, and others.

As the leading political figure in the London group, Beneš played a major role in promoting the vision of a Czechoslovak state restored to pre-Munich borders and with a revived republic altered in form and practice to conform to the social, economic, and political changes brought about by the war. Beneš also blamed the Munich debacle on the failure to involve the Soviet Union in European affairs as a means of maintaining diplomatic stability. As a result, he envisioned a postwar order based on cooperation between east and west in the name of collective security. A restored Czechoslovakia would need to develop positive relations with the Soviet Union, while at the same time maintaining constructive diplomatic links with the Western nations.

Gottwald and the Moscow contingent also believed in the restoration of the republic, but with major transformations of social and economic conditions and a shift in power from the ruling elites to the working class. The security of the Czechoslovak state would not be the product of a balance of power, but rather of protection provided by the Soviet Union. Until 1940, Czechoslovak Communists refused to cooperate with the London committee as some members of the Moscow group called for uprisings against the imperialist governments of Europe and advised Beneš to travel to the Soviet capital to negotiate plans for liberation with Stalin's government.

Two major wartime developments aided Beneš in his efforts to have the Munich Agreement abrogated and his provisional government recognized as a legitimate successor to the pre-Munich republic. The first arose from the resignations of Daladier as French premier in March 1940 and Chamberlain as Britain's prime minister in favor of Winston Churchill two months later. The second occurred when Hitler's invasion of the Soviet Union in June 1941 brought the Soviets into the war and allowed Beneš to pursue a treaty, signed on July 18, which granted recognition to the Beneš government and promised mutual cooperation against Germany. On that same day, Great Britain eliminated the provisional status of the Czechoslovak government-in-exile and accepted Beneš's organization as a legitimate government with direct ties to the Allied powers. However, not until July 1942 did the British government prove willing to repudiate the Munich Agreement and thereby accept Beneš's argument that he represented a direct and legal link to the First Republic.

RACIAL POLICIES AND THE FINAL SOLUTION

Under the Protectorate, German authorities attempted to institute racial policies that would Germanize the Czech lands and institute a new racial hierarchy in line with the Nazi ideology and goals. Those individuals deemed worthy would undergo Germanization, and those determined to be racially inferior would face relocation to the east or imprisonment in camps. In March 1942, the Nazis required all residents of the Protectorate born in designated years to submit to questioning regarding race and politics. During the following month, schoolchildren became subject to testing by x-ray machine under the guise of tuberculosis protection for the young.

For the Jewish population of the Protectorate, whose numbers represented 1 percent of the prewar citizenry of the Czech lands, the situation became dire as the Nazis began transporting Jews to extermination camps in October 1941. Stripped of legal protection and isolated from other citizens, the approximately 118,300 Jews of the Protectorate fell victim to mass deportations and then to the genocidal policies of the Final Solution, instituted after Adolf Eichmann and Reinhard Heydrich, an SS officer and head of Reich Security, met with security officials, bureaucrats, and Nazi Party functionaries involved with the "Jewish question" at the Wannsee Conference on January 20, 1942. Housing shortages and other concerns in Germany and the Protectorate contributed to the targeting of Jews in those territories with the intention of evacuating all Jews to extermination camps such as Auschwitz-Birkenau in Poland and other camps in the east.

Prior to the decision to pursue a "final solution" to the "Jewish problem," German authorities and Czech gendarmes began transporting Jews from Prague, Brno, and other Czech cities to the Bohemian fortress town of Terezín (Theresienstadt) in November 1941, as a ghetto was established there to serve as a transit camp for Jews from the Protectorate and to a lesser extent from Austria and Germany. Heydrich created the camp at Terezín after he was appointed deputy Reich Protector that fall. By the end of 1942, the Germans transported nearly 50,000 Jews from Bohemia and Moravia to Terezín as another 20,000 were moved directly to other camps. As thousands of Jews continued to arrive, the confining walls of the 18th-century fortress produced severe overcrowding in a town that had previously been home to 7,000 residents. Hitler intended Terezín to serve as an ideal and "independent" Jewish community with a thriving cultural and social life that would impress visitors like the representatives of the Red Cross who visited the town in 1944. The inhabitants of the ghetto organized and attended concerts, lectures, poetry readings, cabaret, and representative Czech, German, and Jewish plays, but Terezín remained a temporary residence for Jews awaiting transportation to the extermination camps. When Soviet troops arrived to liberate the ghetto in May 1945, they discovered that only about 8,000 of the Jews from the Protectorate remained alive.

By the end of the war, some 75,000 Jews of the Protectorate had perished in the Holocaust. The vast majority died in concentration camps, although others were killed in the fighting or simply murdered under other circumstances. The genocidal policies of the Final Solution had proven devastating to the Jews of Bohemia and Moravia.[2]

The Gypsy, or Roma, population of the Protectorate also suffered as a result of German policies, since they stood somewhere between the Slavs and the Jews in the Nazi racial hierarchy. Under the First Czechoslovak Republic, legislation passed in 1927 required that every "wandering Gypsy" older than 14 apply for proper identification and contact local officials when arriving in a town or district. Such records would later make the identification of Gypsies a simpler process for authorities.

In May 1939 the Nazis undertook their first major action against the Gypsy population of the Protectorate by prohibiting large groups from traveling together in the Czech lands. During 1940, police in the Protectorate began arresting individuals lacking a permanent residence and shipping them off to labor camps such as Lety and Hodonín, where many "wandering Gypsies" and itinerants met their end. By the spring of 1942, identification documents bore a "Z," representing the German word for Gypsy, as the Nazis proceeded with racial categorization and deportations to the extermination camps. At Auschwitz-Birkenau, where over several thousand Gypsies perished, the wearing of a black triangle marked the community as one apart from the other inhabitants of the camps. In Slovakia, the Tiso regime set up special labor camps for the Roma, and after the German occupation in 1944, there were mass killings of Gypsies on Slovak soil.

RESISTANCE ACTIVITIES IN THE PROTECTORATE

Czech resistance organizations began forming even before the onset of war in 1939, but it was not until the early months of 1940 that the Central Committee of Home Resistance (ÚVOD) coalition emerged as the central resistance body recognized by Beneš's committee abroad. As prime minister of the Protectorate government, Gen. Eliáš cooperated with the resistance underground from the start, although after the Germans entered Paris in May 1940 they uncovered damaging evidence of Eliáš's activities on behalf of the resistance from his office in Prague. However, whereas Eliáš proved more than willing to risk his life in working with the opposition, President Hácha became progressively more compliant in regard to the Nazis as age and cerebral sclerosis adversely affected his mental state. In the spring of 1940, Hácha reversed his earlier resistance and signed an oath of allegiance to Hitler after K. H. Frank threatened to kill 2,000 Czech students already consigned to concentration camps.

The Communist Party (KSČ) developed an underground organization fairly early on, although the Slovak Communists separated from the Czech organization after the division of Czechoslovakia and declaration of Slovak independence. The KSČ maintained direct links to the Soviet regime through Klement Gottwald, who had taken up residence in Moscow, while many Slovak Communists hoped for Slovak integration into the Soviet Union. After the invasion of the USSR, however, the Czech and Slovak communist organizations resumed cooperation against common enemies. During the summer of 1941, the KSČ and ÚVOD agreed to coordinate their resistance activities under the leadership of a Central National Revolutionary Committee (ÚNRV).

By September 1941, Hitler had already lost faith in Neurath's policies of moderation in the Protectorate and granted the Reich Protector a leave of absence, rather than accept Neurath's resignation. Reinhard Heydrich assumed the duties of deputy Reich Protector on September 27, but with orders to take a much harder line toward the Czech government, public opposition, and the resistance. Upon arriving in Prague, Heydrich instituted a martial-law crackdown, arresting Eliáš and then delaying his execution for a later time. Others, however, paid a more immediate price for their activities and by the time Heydrich ended the period of martial law on December 1, some 400 people had been executed.

The Protectorate government fell victim to Heydrich's policies as parliamentary institutions lost power and the removal of Eliáš allowed for the replacement of all but three of his ministers with individuals willing to collaborate with the Germans. Heydrich planned to keep the Czech labor force working productively by offering higher wages and greater access to rationed goods as a counterbalance to the tactics of fear and brutality, but the Beneš government determined that assassinating Heydrich was preferable to risking too much public cooperation with the Nazis.

On December 28, 1941, a British Halifax bomber conveyed Czechoslovak resistance fighters from Great Britain to the Protectorate, air-dropping them onto Czech soil outside of Prague. The parachutists had been trained by Great Britain's Special Operations Executive (SOE) to engage in anti-German activities and to carry out the assassination of either Heydrich or Emanuel Moravec, a former Beneš colleague who had fully embraced the Nazi agenda for the Czechs and now served as collaborationist minister for the Office of Public Enlightenment.

After making their way to Prague in January 1942, the Czech Jan Kubiš and the Slovak Jozej Gabčik prepared to undertake a special mission, code-named "Operation Anthropoid," which involved the assassination of Heydrich, the "Hangman of Prague." On the morning of May 24, Kubiš and Gabčik awaited the arrival of Heydrich's car in the suburb of Holešovice, taking up positions at a spot where a curve in the road would reduce the speed of the car and leave Heydrich vulnerable. When a tram brought Heydrich's vehicle to a halt, Gabčik attempted to open fire with a Sten gun, but the weapon jammed, allowing Heydrich to target Gabčik with his own pistol, which also misfired. Given an opportunity to attack from the other side of the car, Kubiš threw a grenade that hit the right rear fender and exploded through the bodywork, wounding Heydrich with shrapnel. Heydrich attempted to pursue Gabčik, but collapsed and was taken to Bulovka Hospital in a delivery van. On June 4, Heydrich died of his wounds as the doctors failed to prevent the spread of septicaemia.[3]

The Nazi response to the assassination of the deputy Reich Protector proved immediate and violent. The Protectorate returned to a state of martial law as security forces began arresting anyone connected with or in possession of knowledge about the attack. On orders from Hitler and Frank, the entire village of Lidice was obliterated on June 10 out of the belief that Gabčik and Kubiš had spent time there. The Wehrmacht field police and SD security forces murdered the 173 male inhabitants and some of the women during the course of the day before sending the surviving women and the children to concentration camps in Germany and Poland. The Germans razed and bulldozed the village to cover the evidence. Two weeks after the massacre at Lidice, the Germans arrived in the tiny village of Ležáky and beheaded all adult men and women at Pardubice Castle before transporting the children elsewhere.

In Prague, the assassins and their allies were betrayed to the Germans, who assaulted the Orthodox Church of Sts. Cyril and Methodius where Gabčik, Kubiš, and members of the resistance were in hiding. After a fierce exchange of gunfire, all of the defenders had died or chosen to take their own lives rather than face capture and interrogation. The Germans then executed Bishop Gorazd and all of the clergy who had given aid to the resistance. By the time the terror drew to a close, the response to Heydrich's murder claimed over 1,000 lives and seriously incapacitated the ÚNRV, which abandoned tactics that might draw a similar response from the Germans. As part of the reprisals, the authorities carried out the execution of Gen. Alois Eliáš on June 19.

After Heydrich's death, authority passed to State Secretary Frank, who came under pressure from Hitler's government to step up production in support of the German war effort, especially with the onset of Allied bombing raids on urban and industrial targets inside Germany. Since the Protectorate remained free of large-scale raids until late 1944, the Czech lands became important for the production of armaments as well as a relatively safe location for industrial works transferred there from Germany. To this end, the Škoda works in Plzeň produced tanks and airplane engines for the Reich, while other major industrial concerns played their own assigned economic roles in the Protectorate. The Reich government relied on Frank to manage the Czech economic contributions to the war and to mobilize the growing labor force needed to meet German demands for industrial output. Many Czech workers were forcibly sent to work in factories in Germany, and by the fall of 1943, their numbers had reached 30,000, with more to come as the Luftwaffe's requirements for aircraft production brought in another 10,000 workers in the spring of 1944.

THE CZECHOSLOVAK GOVERNMENT-IN-EXILE

For Beneš and the Czechoslovak government-in-exile, changing military conditions generated greater support from both Allied combatants and the Communists, who declared their recognition of the Beneš government and then agreed to allow several party members to join the state council in London. In June 1942, the Soviet foreign minister Vyacheslav Molotov informed Beneš that his government was willing to dismiss as illegitimate all political and territorial changes that occurred as a result of the Munich Agreement.

The entry of the United States into the war in December 1941 led to increased efforts to convince the Americans to accept the legitimacy of the Beneš government as more than a provisional organization. Meeting with Roosevelt, Jan Masaryk requested the elimination of provisional status with the observation that the many downed Czech pilots in Europe were more than provisionally dead. Roosevelt then dispatched a telegram to Beneš on October 28, 1942, Czechoslovakia's independence day, in which he addressed Beneš as the "President of the Republic of Czechoslovakia" and announced that references to a provisional government would cease. The following year, Beneš traveled to the United States and gained the impression that the United States was also willing to disregard the Munich Agreement and accept the continuity between his government and the pre-Munich republic.

In December 1943, Beneš arrived in Moscow to negotiate a formal agreement of mutual assistance against the German Reich and was received as Czechoslovak head of state in discussions with Stalin and other Soviet officials. The signing of the Treaty of Friendship, Mutual Assistance, and Postwar Cooperation marked an important step in Beneš's diplomatic plans to involve both the east and west in Czechoslovakia's restoration and postwar security, but in a more immediate sense, the pact seemed to provide critical guarantees of national independence and the prevention of another Munich betrayal.

As Soviet forces continued a westward advance that began with a post-Stalingrad breakthrough in July 1943, the need to plan for the liberation of Czechoslovakia and the end of the war became acute. In May 1944, Beneš's Czechoslovak government signed an agreement with the Soviet Union guaranteeing that authority over territories deemed free of military action would be transferred from the Red Army to the Czechoslovak government and that representatives of that government would be assigned to cooperate with Soviet officers in areas that remained contested.

THE SLOVAK REPUBLIC, 1939–1942

At the end of July 1939, the new constitution of an independent Slovak republic established a one-party state with authoritarian characteristics similar to the governments of Italy and Austria and with special privileges for the German minority in the country. Facing no opposition in the October election, Jozef Tiso became president of the republic, in addition to serving as commander-in-chief of the country's armed forces and head of the HSĽS, the lone legitimate political party. At the beginning of December, Tiso overcame a key political obstacle when he received the formal recognition of the Vatican, which had initially expressed reservations about having a member of the clergy serving as Slovak head of state.

From the start, however, the HSĽS did not present a united front as the dominant political organization. Tiso could count on the support of the conservative faction in the party as well as on the Germans, but party radicals under Karol Sidor, Alexander "Sano" Mach, Ferdinand Ďurčanský, and Vojtech Tuka proved more than willing to challenge Tiso's policies and authority. Radicals such as Mach and Tuka possessed strong sympathies for Hitler's policies and, with the support of the Hlinka Guards, sought to mobilize anti-Semitic and anti-Czech forces in Slovakia. Durčanský was a leader of the *Nástup* group in the HSĽS, which although ultranationalist and ideologically of the extreme right, stood against the Hlinka Guards and opposed following the German lead at the expense of what was best for Slovakia.

Founded in 1938 out of sports organizations, the boy scouts, and nationalist groups, the Hlinka Guards counted a quarter of a million members at the beginning of 1939 under the leadership of Sidor and then Mach as Supreme Commander. However, Sidor paid the political price for his refusal to declare Slovak independence and received a posting to the Vatican as Slovakia's ambassador. Similar in many ways to other radical nationalist or fascist organizations, such as the Ustasha movement in Croatia and the Arrow Cross in Hungary, the Hlinka Guards wore black military-style uniforms and tassel-bedecked hats with gold trim. Members greeted each other with *"Na straz!"* (On Guard!). When in September 1939, the government instituted an order requiring that all males aged 16–60 enter the military or join radical nationalist organizations like the Hlinka Guards, membership in the Guards and the Hlinka Youth increased. Germany's Waffen SS also engaged in a recruiting offensive in Slovakia, although only about 6,000 members of the German minority had volunteered by the end of 1941. Beginning in November 1942, changes in policy allowed Slovak males to fulfill the requirements of military service by serving in the Waffen SS without forfeiting their Slovak citizenship.

For the Tiso regime, though, independence proved more elusive than expected as German authorities continued to extend their influence into virtually every area of governance in their efforts to bring the Slovak government into line with German policies. In order to avoid the complete Nazification of Slovakia, Tiso and his ministers attempted to compromise with Hitler's Reich in a manner that pushed them ever closer to the status of a puppet regime.

Slovakia participated in the German invasion of Poland in September 1939, but Foreign Minister Ďurčanský otherwise attempted to pursue a diplomatic course that was beneficial to Slovakia rather than compliant with German demands. In July 1940, Hitler summoned Tiso to a meeting in Salzburg, where Ribbentrop confronted the Slovak leader with a request to replace certain people in the government and HSĽS. Hitler then followed with a demand that Ďurčanský be removed in favor of the more radical and pro-German Tuka. The Germans reminded Tiso that there were limits to Slovakia's independent course and dispatched

German advisors to Slovakia with the intention of installing them in important government positions in Bratislava.

As a result of the meeting in Salzburg, the radicals Tuka and Mach took over from Ďurčanský in Foreign Affairs and Interior, respectively. Tiso responded to the radical threat by blocking proposed revisions to the constitutions of the government and HSĽS, which were designed to increase Tuka's authority and benefit the party's extremists. Fear of Nazification brought public support for Tiso, and on August 6, 1940, the presidium of the HSĽS voted to endorse Tiso as party leader and to accept his leading role in mediating internal disputes.

As a result of signing the Tripartite Pact in November 1940, Slovakia became part of the Axis and therefore more directly linked to the military and diplomatic plans of the German Reich. This led the Slovak government to declare war on the Soviet Union in June 1941 and to commit some 50,000 members of Slovakia's armed forces to Operation Barbarossa, although desertions drastically reduced that number as German-led forces drove into the Soviet Union. On December 12, 1941, Slovakia declared war on the United States and Great Britain, five days after the Japanese attack on Pearl Harbor and one day after Germany's own declaration of war on the Americans. In spite of a general lack of enthusiasm for the campaign, Slovak troops advanced as far as the Caucasus in 1942, but in the early months of 1944, the division was relocated to Transylvania and to Italy, where security units were later assigned to construction details.

RACIAL POLICIES AND THE HOLOCAUST IN SLOVAKIA

Although the Jewish population of Slovakia in 1940 numbered only 89,000, or 2 percent of the population, the HSĽS began instituting measures against the Jews fairly early in the republic. The removal of Jews from positions in the government, schools, and officer corps of the armed forces preceded the restrictions placed upon the rights of Jewish citizens in April 1939, when Tiso and Tuka initiated policies designed to identify the Jews and isolate them from public and professional life.

In September 1941, a Jewish Codex, produced by Interior Minister Sano Mach in collaboration with the SS, introduced racial categorization along Nazi lines and opened the way to deportation of Slovak Jews to concentration camps after the signing of an agreement between Germany and Slovakia in March 1942. From March to October, Slovak gendarmes, military personnel, and members of the Hlinka Guards and Volunteer SS transported nearly 60,000 Jews to the Reich and to

German-controlled territory in Poland, where all but a few hundred died in the camps. The deportations occurred in spite of the open opposition of the Vatican and Slovak bishops, the latter expressing their opposition to the ill treatment of fellow citizens in a pastoral letter read from the pulpits in Slovakia on April 12, 1942. On May 15, new legislation stripped Slovakia's Jews of their citizenship and provided a basis for further deportations, while also allowing for presidential pardons under certain circumstances.

By the fall of 1942, Tiso received reports of Slovak Jews being killed at Auschwitz, Sobibor, and other camps in Poland and, as a result, the Slovak president refused to deport the 24,000 Jews who remained in Slovakia. Jews would now be held in labor camps in Slovakia, usually under the supervision of the Hlinka Guards, who found ways to profit from their responsibilities at the expense of their prisoners. Hitler, however, remained unsatisfied at the Tiso government's refusal to institute harsher measures against the Jews of Slovakia.

In the spring of 1943, Hitler met with Tiso in Salzburg and demanded a more drastic solution to the "Jewish problem," but the transportations did not resume in earnest until German troops moved into Slovakia in 1944 and nearly 13,000 more Jews were deported in the final months of the year. Some 6,000 Jews managed to escape to Hungary, but several thousand were killed on Slovak soil while in hiding or engaged in partisan activities. By the end of the war, the camps and the genocidal violence during the war years had claimed the lives of more than 60,000 Jews who had been living in Slovakia.

SLOVAKIA, 1943–1945

Since the beginning of the war, many Slovaks chose to fight openly or as members of the resistance in opposition to Tiso's HSL'S-dominated regime. Some Slovaks departed their homeland and joined the First Czechoslovak Army Corps under Gen. Ludvík Svoboda to fight alongside the Soviet Red Army, while others joined the Czechoslovak units under Gen. Rudolf Viest in France or flew for the Royal Air Force in Great Britain.

Slovak Communists created the first resistance organization after June 1941, as Hitler's forces drove into the Soviet Union with Slovak participation. The Communists also proposed and attempted to generate support for the "Soviet Slovakia" plan, which would lead to the incorporation of Slovakia into the Soviet Union.

In spite of the government's extensive use of police power and informers, the unpopularity of Slovakia's involvement in the invasion of the Soviet Union and the government's racial policies and deportations of Jews increased public opposition to the regime and encouraged the expansion of resistance activities. In London, Beneš hoped to mobilize resistance to the Tiso government and to encourage support among Slovaks for the restoration of the Czechoslovak republic after the war. To this end, Beneš and his British colleagues used radio broadcasts and other means to inspire discontent among Slovaks and to portray Slovak independence as the work of traitors and criminals who had little interest in what was best for the Slovak people.

By the early months of 1943, the German defeat at Stalingrad and the onset of economic problems that limited access to many basic necessities weakened support for the HSĽS government and increased the popularity of Beneš with his calls for resistance and the restoration of Czechoslovakia. More Slovaks proved willing to accept the legitimacy of Beneš's government-in-exile, especially after the signing of the mutual assistance treaty brought recognition by the Soviet Union and the Slovak Communists, who ceased to promote the annexation of Slovakia by the Soviets. In December 1943, Gustáv Husák, Karol Smidke, and the Slovak Communists joined representatives of the democratic Citizens Bloc, including Jozef Lettrich and Ján Ursíny, in signing the Christmas Agreement, establishing the Slovak National Council (SNR) as the central body for the coordination of resistance activities in Slovakia. The signatories also agreed to cooperate in the planning of an uprising designed to remove Tiso and the HSĽS regime from power.

As the Red Army continued to advance westward, the front lines drew closer to Slovakia and partisan activities increased in frequency and intensity, with members of the Hlinka Guards often being targeted by their rivals and enemies. On August 27, 1944, a German military mission returning by train from Rumania fell into the hands of a Slovak resistance garrison in Turciansky Sväty Martin. Ignoring the orders of Lt. Col. Ján Golian to transport the prisoners to Banská Bystrica for questioning, a lieutenant at the scene instead carried out the directive of the local partisan commander to have the German officers and their families shot the next morning. Severe reprisals instituted against civilians and military personnel by the government forced resistance and partisan leaders to move up the date of the uprising and to give the signal earlier than planned.

Golian and the SNR had planned the uprising to coincide with the arrival in Slovakia of the Red Army from Poland and the Soviet Union, but serious complications arose in coordinating timing and plans with the Soviets, who moved partisan fighters into Slovakia from Ukraine without consulting with the SNR. As the partisans struck at the infra-structure and attacked military and security targets, they drew the attention of the Tiso government and the Germans, who gained Tiso's acceptance of military assistance and began moving troops into posi-tion in Slovakia. Critically, the Germans also disarmed the two Slovak divisions with responsibility for securing Dukla Pass and other moun-tain passes during the uprising in order to facilitate the arrival of Soviet troops.

Shortly after the government's defense ministry announced the German occupation of Slovakia on August 29, Golian issued the code words "Begin the Evacuation," thereby setting the Slovak National Uprising (SNP) in motion and opening the way to the first engage-ments between the resistance and the Germans towards evening. The following day, Free Slovak Radio offered patriotic broadcasts in sup-port of the uprising as Slovaks were called upon to assist the resistance in overthrowing the HSĽS dictatorship and liberating the country from the Germans. Meeting in Banská Bystrica, the Slovak National Council announced to the nation their goals of reestablishing the Czechoslovak state and of joining the Allied nations in liberating Europe from the Nazis and their allies.

During the early days of the struggle, the Slovak resistance could claim only 18,000 soldiers and officers in the field against the 85,000 under the authority of the Tiso regime, although new mobilizations on September 5 and 26 increased the size of the resistance forces to 60,000, divided into six tactical units and a single air group. The nearly 8,000 partisans participating in the uprising received their orders from Kiev, which added to the difficulties faced in coordinating the upris-ing. Additionally, the military units of the resistance lacked antitank weapons and heavy armor, with only a half-dozen tanks to send against advancing German forces. The Slovak Insurgent Air Force possessed only a small number of mostly outdated aircraft. In mid-September, the Germans battled the resistance with some 48,000 soldiers, representing four Waffen-SS divisions, two other German divisions, and one allied Slovak military group. However, the promise of assistance that Beneš had received from Stalin and Molotov in December 1943 remained unfulfilled. Soviet troops and the First Czechoslovak Army Group suffered heavy losses and failed to drive through the Dukla Pass on the Polish border from September 8 to the end of October.

On September 5, Ján Golian received a promotion to general and was granted authority over all Slovak forces participating in the uprising. That same day, the president of the Supreme Court, Štefan Tiso, replaced Tuka as prime minister and also assumed control of the foreign and justice ministries. The German occupation had effectively eliminated the relative autonomy of the Slovak government and left little more than a puppet regime in place.

With the Soviet Union and the Western Allies arguing over providing assistance to the Slovak resistance and the Soviets warning against Allied interference in the Soviet sphere of influence, the uprising suffered a serious setback in terms of supplies and other forms of aid. Weapons, ammunition, and medical necessities arrived from Allied-controlled southern Italy in mid-September and mid-October, although Allied leaders quickly ordered an end to the supply missions after protests by their Soviet allies.

With Gen. Golian unable to end the squabbling between the resistance, the partisans, and the Beneš government, Gen. Rudolf Viest flew to Slovakia from London and arrived on October 7 with orders to take control of the resistance forces from Golian. On October 16, the Germans launched a decisive offensive against the rebels after moving 35,000 troops and heavy armor north from Hungary and demanding that the Slovak forces offer their unconditional surrender. Under orders from Stalin, the Red Army moved out of eastern Slovakia and refocused its efforts on driving the Germans out of Hungary and Poland.

After German-led forces had regained much of the territory that had fallen into the hands of the opposition, resistance units under Generals Viest and Golian abandoned Banská Bystrica on October 27, hoping to find safety in the mountainous terrain around Donovaly to the north. With his forces harassed from the air by the Luftwaffe and rapidly falling into disorganization and confusion, Viest ordered the remaining insurrectionist units to engage in partisan-style guerilla warfare and then sent a message to the Allies that organized resistance had reached an end. Viest and Golian moved east through the Hron Valley to the village of Pohronský Bukovec, where they were captured by German special forces on November 3. The two commanders were then transported to Germany as POWs and later executed at the Flossenbürg concentration camp in 1945.

In retaliation for the uprising and the continued attacks by partisans and the surviving units of the Czechoslovak resistance, German *Einsatzgruppen* launched a campaign of terror, executing many civilians and suspected supporters of the rebellion, in addition to destroying nearly 100 villages considered sympathetic to the cause. The killings that occurred during the reprisals added over 5,000 more victims to the approximately 5,000 who died fighting during the uprising itself. For the German minority community in Slovakia, the uprising and its aftermath brought attacks and executions at the hands of partisans and commandos, especially in towns of the Špiš area and the region of central Slovakia. A large number of ethnic Germans fled north to Poland or accepted transportation to Bohemia and Moravia as mandated by the Reich government in mid-November 1944.

German success in crushing the Slovak National Uprising ultimately failed to preserve the government in Bratislava or the German occupation of Slovakia. At the end of December, the advancing Soviet and Rumanian armies liberated southern Slovakia from Nazi control, and in January 1945 the Soviet Red Army moved into key eastern Slovak cities like Prešov, Košice, and Bardejov. On March 25, Soviets forces took Banská Bystrica, and on April 4, the Red Army reached Bratislava and entered the capital. Tiso and his ministers departed for Kremsmünster in Upper Austria and, on May 8, formally surrendered to the American representative of the Allies, Gen. W. A. Collier, on the same day that Germany surrendered to the Soviet Union and one day after Germany's capitulation to the western Allies. After the surrender, Tiso became a prisoner of the Americans before being returned to the restored Czechoslovakia in October 1945.

THE PRAGUE UPRISING AND THE END OF THE WAR

For Beneš, who had successfully achieved the support of the Allies and the Soviets for the restoration of an independent Czechoslovakia, the final stages of the war brought greater Soviet influence and military presence than he had hoped. As head of the Czechoslovak government in London, Beneš believed that his role would prove critical in assuring a stable transition to a postwar republic, but the KSČ was relying on Soviet backing to ensure a greater voice than previously expected in postwar political life. Additionally, Stalin and the Soviets had agreed to restore the pre-Munich borders of Czechoslovakia, which would have required the inclusion of Sub-Carpathian Ruthenia. When the Red Army moved into Ruthenia in October 1944, the Soviet authorities installed local soviets to promote Soviet interests, especially in regard to the fate of Ruthenian territory after the war. Stalin then delivered a radio address on November 7 in which he declared that it was the long-held dream of the Ruthenians to be united with the neighboring Ukraine, which would mean the incorporation of Ruthenia into the USSR and therefore violation of the agreement with Beneš, who ultimately accepted the loss of Ruthenia as a reality born of changing wartime conditions.

Beneš traveled to Moscow in March 1945 to discuss the creation of the National Front government that would assume power in Prague at the end of the war. Since the London government had provided no plan of its own, the proposal came from Gottwald and the Communists, who held discussions with representatives of the Social Democratic, National Socialist, and People's parties. By agreement, each party would be allowed three representatives in the government, but with the Czechoslovak Communist Party and the Slovak Communist Party standing as separate organizations and holding three positions each. Zdeněk Fierlinger of the Social Democrats became prime minister, primarily due to his willingness to cooperate with Moscow. The Communists would hold the two vice-premierships, assigned to Klement Gottwald of the KSČ and Viliam Široký of the KSS, as well as the portfolios of Interior, Agriculture, Labor, Social Affairs, and Information. Gen. Ludvík Svoboda, who fought alongside the Red Army in the war as commander of the First Czechoslovak Army Group, would serve as defense minister.

During the negotiations of March 22–29, the delegation representing the Slovak National Council (SNR) received little recognition and found itself excluded from the new government and from participating in any major discussions other than those regarding relations between Czechs and Slovaks in the restored Czechoslovakia. The SNR delegation, which argued in favor of a federal system as a means of guaranteeing equality between Czechs and Slovaks, included the democrat Vavro Šrobár, the agrarian Ján Ursíny, and members of the KSS such as Gustáv Husák and Laco Novemesky. However, the opposition of the KSČ to the idea of a federal state and the promise of equal status convinced the SNR delegates to abandon their proposal in hopes that the issue could be raised again after the liberation of Czech and Slovak soil was completed. Participants accepted the validity of the Czechoslovak treaty with the Soviet Union as the basis for future relations and agreed to assume mass guilt on the part of the German and Hungarian minorities in revoking citizenship and carrying out postwar legal proceedings against collaborators and traitors. Only those who had been victimized during the war or could claim antifascist activities would remain safe from policies of retribution.

On March 31, the Czech and Slovak delegates departed Moscow and arrived in the liberated city of Košice in eastern Slovakia, where on April 5, Beneš announced the existence of the National Front government. By the end of the month, the Red Army had liberated Slovakia and much of Moravia, interfering in Slovak affairs and arresting Czechoslovak citizens for deportation to labor camps on Soviet soil. In the west, the U.S. Third Army under Gen. George S. Patton moved into Bohemia and advanced as far as Karlovy Vary before receiving orders to halt, leaving the liberation of Prague to the Red Army.

The town of Přerov, near Olomouc, witnessed a spontaneous uprising on May 1 that set off similar disturbances across the Czech lands. Four days later, the Prague Uprising began with a signal-phrase broadcast by radio in the capital as Czech police moved to seize the radio station from resistance fighters who occupied the building on Vinohradská. Calls for assistance went out over the radio all day as demonstrators took to the streets in defiance of the Germans and the Czech government of the Protectorate. Czechoslovak flags appeared on buildings across Prague as Czech representatives met with K. H. Frank and German police and security organizations. Declaring that it was acting in the name of Beneš and the National Front government in Košice, the Czech National Council (ČNR) took over responsibility for coordinating the uprising, although the ČNR did not participate in the initial sessions with Frank.

On the night of May 5 and into the following day, the fighting in the streets of the capital intensified as countless barricades were erected to slow the movement of German troops and security units. Radio broadcasts called upon the British and Americans to battle the Luftwaffe and to bomb the main access roads into the city as the Wehrmacht and SS advanced toward the city center from outside of Prague. By morning, the Luftwaffe engaged in bombing raids on central Prague as fighting spread into outlying areas and Frank and his staff continued to communicate with the ČNR. The Germans failed to capture the radio station, and many German units became surrounded as the resistance took control of nearly half of the city.

During the daylight hours of May 6, the U.S. Army moved into Plzeň, roughly 50 miles from the capital, and fielded requests for assistance from the insurgents in Prague. However, the Americans could not move forward without orders, which were not forthcoming due to agreements made with the Soviets, who themselves failed to respond to the appeals of the Czechs. The rebels in Prague did receive assistance from a completely unexpected source when Gen. Andrej Vlasov's Russian Liberation Army joined the struggle against the Germans. Vlasov's anti-Communist troops had been allied with the Wehrmacht and engaged in attacking Jews and Communist partisans in Moravia before moving westward in the face of the Soviet advance. Their hope was to surrender to the Americans and face imprisonment in the West, rather than fall into Soviet hands, although they intended to participate in the uprising for only a short time.

During the several days of the Prague Uprising, the Czechs sent approximately 30,000 armed insurgents, men and women, against the nearly 40,000 German troops stationed in and around the capital. As the brutal street fighting intensified, the SS resorted to using civilians as human shields for their tanks, while the Czechs began seizing German officials and civilians in retaliation. Both sides carried out frequent spontaneous executions of known or suspected enemies.

The Germans continued to move troops and armor into Prague on May 7 as major fighting raged around the railway station and radio broadcast center. During the following day, Vlasov's forces departed toward American lines as the Germans drove toward the center of the city, taking the Old Town Square as bombing and firefights set buildings in the historic heart of Prague ablaze.

On May 8, the ČNR reached an agreement with the Germans when it became apparent that assistance from the Allies and the Soviets would not arrive and that the city itself faced destruction if the fighting continued. According to the terms of the agreement, the Germans would spare the city if the resistance ceased fighting and allowed German military units and civilians to depart or to move through the city without incident. Although most of the Germans left the city immediately, some SS units continued rearguard actions until armored units of the First Ukrainian Front of the Red Army reached the capital on May 9 to a warm welcome by the Czech citizens of Prague.[4] Frank and other members of the Protectorate government fled in an attempt to surrender to the Americans at Plzeň, but extradition later delivered them into the hands of Czechoslovak authorities to face legal proceedings.

With the departure of the Germans and the surrender of the Reich government to the Western Allies and the Soviets on May 7–8, World War II reached an end for the Czechs as the German defeat brought liberation and hopes for a Czechoslovakia reborn. On May 8, Beneš departed Košice with plans to travel to Prague by car and by train, so as to appear in as many Slovak and Czech communities as time would allow. Enthusiastic crowds greeted Beneš and his companions in cities such as Banská Bystrica, Bratislava, and Brno before he reached Prague on May 10. With the return of Beneš and his fellow exiles, the Czech National Council was disbanded and the National Front government installed as the first government of postwar Czechoslovakia.

NOTES

1. For Edvard Beneš's observations on the Munich Agreement and wartime diplomacy, see Edvard Beneš, *Memoirs of Dr. Eduard Beneš: From Munich to New War and New Victory* (Westport, CT: Greenwood Press, 1978). For an American perspective on the Munich Agreement and its consequences, see George F. Kennan, *From Prague after Munich: Diplomatic Papers 1938–1940* (Princeton, NJ: Princeton University Press, 1968). For a fine analysis of Beneš's policies and diplomatic activities within the context of Czechoslovak and European affairs during the 1930's, consult Igor Lukes, *Czechoslovakia Between Stalin and Hitler: The Diplomacy of Edvard Beneš in the 1930's* (New York: Oxford University Press, 1996).

2. For the fate of the Jewish population of the Protectorate of Bohemia and Moravia during the Holocaust, see Livia Rothkirchen, *The Jews of Bohemia and Moravia: Facing the Holocaust* (Lincoln: University of Nebraska Press, 2005).

3. See Callum MacDonald, *The Killing of SS Obergruppenführer Reinhard Heydrich* (New York: Free Press, 1989).

4. Life in Prague under the Protectorate is the subject of two recent works: Chad Bryant, *Prague in Black: Nazi Rule and Czech Nationalism* (Cambridge, MA: Harvard University Press, 2007), and Peter Demetz, *Prague in Danger: The Years of German Occupation, 1939–1945: Memories and History, Terror and Resistance, Theatre and Jazz, Film and Poetry, Politics and War* (New York: Farrar, Straus and Giroux, 2008).

8

The Postwar Era and the Communist Regime (1945–1989)

As the war drew to a close and Beneš returned to Prague as president of a restored Czechoslovakia, the consequences of post-Munich events became evident in the loss of territory and population, as well as in the damaged economy and the changes in the political landscape. The loss of some 400,000 lives, overwhelmingly civilian, represented a reduction by 2.7 percent of Czechoslovakia's prewar population. The transfer of Ruthenia to the Soviet Union decreased the size of the country, although Czechoslovakia acquired a small amount of Hungarian territory outside Bratislava and south of the Danube.

TERRITORIAL CHANGES AND POPULATION TRANSFERS

To add to the already chaotic conditions in 1945, the postwar period opened with the so-called "wild transfer," the often violent expulsion of ethnic Germans from the Czech lands after the defeat of the Reich.

In May 1945, a presidential decree provided the basis for the large-scale seizure of property belonging to collaborators and to the German and Magyar national minorities. This sorting out of nationalities coincided with the "wild transfer" of May–August 1945 in which Germans and collaborators became targets of both spontaneous and organized acts of violence in Prague and across Bohemia, Moravia, and the former Sudetenland. Soviet soldiers reportedly engaged in raping German women and looting properties on a large scale and were sometimes joined in the brutality by Czech soldiers. German military personnel and SS officials underwent torture and execution by the local population, especially in areas where they had victimized citizens of the Protectorate in a similar manner.

In May, some 20,000 people set out from Brno accompanied by local workers, soldiers, and others who intended to expel them from Czechoslovakia at the Austrian border. Some 8,000 more ethnic Germans were forced to join the march before Austrian authorities blocked their progress and turned them back. In consequence, thousands were placed in internment camps, and possible close to 2,000 perished from the march or from acts of violence along the way. On July 31, a massacre of resident Germans occurred at Ústi nad Labem in northern Bohemia after an unexplained explosion at an ammunition dump killed over two dozen people. Although local citizens attempted to help the victims, a group of primarily Czech and Soviet soldiers drowned, shot, and beat to death some 2,000 to 3,000 Germans.

Although Beneš had initially favored transferring the Sudeten Germans through a combination of voluntary departures and forced expulsions, he did little to condemn or contain the violence of the "wild transfer," having already spoken of the need to "liquidate" the German and Magyar national minorities "in the interest of the united national state of Czechs and Slovaks."[1] His government also failed to take action beyond some ineffectual protests, while Foreign Minister Jan Masaryk declared that the time had now passed for Czechs and Germans to be able to coexist in Czechoslovakia. Across Bohemia, the expulsion of the Germans left political affairs firmly in the hands of the Czechs as even place names lost their German designations.

On June 29 and October 27, 1945, Beneš signed retribution decrees to revoke the citizenship of Germans and Hungarians and to establish extraordinary courts for the punishment of traitors, collaborators, and others linked to the Nazi administration under the Protectorate. Further presidential decrees shuttered the German university in the capital, eliminated German associations, and sanctioned the seizure of property belonging to Germans, Magyars, and those who had collaborated with the Nazi authorities. New regulations required Germans to register with the police and to wear a patch with a large "N" (for *němec*, or German) on their clothing.

At the Potsdam Conference, held outside of Berlin from July 7 to August 2, the Allied governments granted approval for the humane "organized transfer" of the German population from Czechoslovakia, although a similar transfer of Magyars would require negotiations between the governments of Hungary and Czechoslovakia. However, the violence of the radical "wild transfer" continued until more organized methods of expelling the Germans could be implemented. In January 1946, the "organized transfer" resumed as railways were utilized for the relocation of the German population to the Allied- and Soviet-controlled military zones in Germany.

By the time the transfer drew to a close, an estimated 600,000–900,000 Germans had been expelled from Czechoslovakia or had chosen to leave without any distinctions having been drawn between Sudeten Germans, Carpathian Germans, and Germans from the Reich proper or elsewhere. During the months immediately following liberation and the end of the war, 19,000–30,000 Germans perished, at least 6,000 as victims of violence or as internees in camps at Terezin and elsewhere in Czechoslovakia. According to census data in 1950, only 165,000 Germans remained in Czechoslovakia as a consequence of the expulsions and settling of accounts at the end of the war.

For the Magyars of Czechoslovakia, the Košice Agreement approved the revocation of citizenship, as well as resettlement or assignment to forced-labor projects. In early 1946, negotiations between Prague and Budapest resulted in an agreement leading to the transfer of 74,000 Magyars from Slovakia to Hungary and nearly as many Slovaks from Hungarian territory to Slovakia. The exchanges, which began in April 1947, resulted in 44,000 Magyars shifting from Slovakia to the Sudetenland.

The departure of many Magyars and the expulsion of nearly all the Germans from the Czech lands and Slovakia added to the population loss caused by the death of so many Czechoslovak citizens during the war. The dynamic society of the Masaryk era, with its Czechs, Slovaks, Germans, Magyars, Jews, and Roma, had not survived the relatively brief, yet extremely destructive period of conflict, Nazi racial policies, and postwar population transfers.

For some of the individual figures associated with the Nazi administration and the Protectorate government, the immediate postwar years brought justice, retribution, or self-inflicted demise. Konrad

Henlein took his own life while a captive of the Americans in May 1945, while Emanuel Moravec, the "Czech Quisling," committed suicide rather than face a trial and execution for treason. After the Americans extradited Karl Hermann Frank to Czechoslovakia, he was tried during the spring of 1946 and executed by hanging in late May of that year. The Reich Protector, Konstantine von Neurath, appeared before the International Military Tribunal at Nuremberg in 1946 and was found guilty on four counts before being sentenced to 15 years' imprisonment. He remained in Spandau Prison in Berlin until 1954, when he was released due to deteriorating health. Former president Emil Hácha died in a prison hospital on June 26, 1945, while awaiting legal prosecution.

PRECONDITIONS FOR A SEIZURE OF POWER

In the political sphere, the Košice program of April 1945 determined the composition of the National Front government installed in Prague at the end of the war. With parties of the right prohibited from participating in the political process, the primary voices in the government belonged to the National Socialists, People's Party (led by Msgr. Šrámek), Slovak Democrats (under Jozef Lettrich), Social Democrats, and the Communist Party's two wings, the Communist Party of Czechoslovakia and the Communist Party of Slovakia. The Communists represented the strongest political organization, with the National Socialists as their chief rival and the Social Democrats as a potential ally, although the latter party succumbed to in-fighting between the party faithful and the pro-Soviet and pro-Communist prime minister, Zdeněk Fierlinger. The Czech and Slovak resistance organizations were effectively ignored, although the Slovak National Council (SNR) continued to exist and argued without success for the establishment of a federal system. Slovakia instead received its own parliament and Board of Commissioners as part of an asymmetrical system that granted the Slovaks some measure of influence over their affairs, but without a federal state.

Beneš and the National Front governed Czechoslovakia from May 8 until October 28 without an elected parliament, setting policies and constructing the foundation of the postwar government by means of presidential decrees. The newly instituted government gained public support from the start, with the Communists benefiting from the positive feelings toward the Soviet Union in the wake of national liberation. The Communists took pains to avoid activities that would make them appear radical to a population that greatly desired the stability that had eluded the country at the time of the Munich Agreement.

That the Czechoslovak Communists and the Soviet Union had refused to accept the Munich betrayal also worked to the benefit of both. The withdrawal of Soviet and American troops from Czechoslovakia in October and November offered hope for stability and a swift return to normal political life.

Social and economic restructuring began in earnest with Beneš's decree of October 14, 1945, that allowed for the nationalization of financial establishments, industrial concerns, and agriculture, ultimately placing nearly two-thirds of Czechoslovakia's industrial sector under state supervision. Less than two weeks later, the provisional assembly instituted an economic recovery plan designed to exceed prewar levels of industrial production and to expand investments in Slovak industry with the goal of improving Slovakia's economic status relative to that of the Czechs.

Soviet actions at the end of the war created immediate problems for reconstruction efforts as Soviet military commanders in Slovakia ordered the seizure of livestock, mills, breweries, and warehouses geared toward the production and storage of agricultural products. In October 1945, a secret treaty relinquished control over the strategically important uranium mines at Jáchymov to Soviet authorities, who proceeded to seal off the area and transport in Soviet and East German mining experts and researchers.

On May 26, 1945, voters participated in a free and fairly contested election for the Constituent National Assembly with the Communist Party of Czechoslovakia (KSČ) emerging with 38.12 percent of the vote nationally and just over 40 percent in the Czech lands as their allies the Slovak Communist Party (KSS) tallied 30.3 percent in Slovakia. The National Socialists (ČSNS) gained 18.37 percent nationally and 23.6 percent among Czech voters, while the People's Party (ČSL) polled 15.71 percent overall and the Social Democrats (ČSD) 15.51 percent. The Slovak Democrats, although earning only 13.13 percent of the vote across Czechoslovakia, outpolled the Communists in Slovakia with 62 percent of the Slovak vote, in a result that greatly angered the Communist leadership. The electoral results allowed the Communists to hold nine positions in the newly formed National Front government under Communist leader Klement Gottwald, with the Social Democrats holding three and the ČSNS, ČSL, and ČSD four positions each. Two nonparty figures, Ludvík Svoboda and Jan Masaryk, were chosen to serve as minister of defense and minister of foreign affairs, respectively.

The Communists responded to their electoral showing among Slovaks by convincing National Front coalition partners to cooperate in restricting Slovak autonomy and extending the control of the

Prague government over Slovak affairs. The strong expression of Slovak nationalism in support of the Slovak Democrats moved the Communists to try Msgr. Jozef Tiso before a Slovak court on counts of treason against Czechoslovakia and the Slovak National Uprising, as well as for collaboration with Nazi Germany. The National Court found Tiso guilty in spite of pleas for leniency, and after Beneš refused to intervene on his behalf, the nationalist priest was hanged in his clerical attire on April 18, 1947. Controversy over Tiso's wartime leadership and policies would continue for decades.

Under Interior Minister Václav Nosek, the security forces, the National Security Corps (SNB) and State Security (StB), became weapons that the Communists could use against their political enemies. Plans by Communist leaders to undermine the credibility of the Slovak Democrats by fabricating evidence of treasonous activities failed as Minister of Justice Prokop Drtina exposed the conspiracy before further action could be taken. However, the policies of Nosek and the police led to the arrest of some 400 people in October as the Communists moved to extend their authority over the Board of Commissioners in Slovakia.

During 1947, the Communists suffered an erosion of public support as they bore much of the blame for economic problems and setbacks on the international front. The less-than-dynamic performance of the nationalized economy combined with poor harvests, food shortages, inept distribution, and a growing black market to undermine faith in the Communists who controlled the ministries responsible for the poor economic performance. The Communists responded by promoting populist measures such as additional nationalization and land redistribution, the restructuring of financial institutions, and the so-called "millionaire's tax" on the wealthy. Already wary of Communist economic and social policies, as well as their use of the Ministry of Information for purposes of censorship and cultural interference, the National Socialists, People's Party, and Slovak Democrats cooperated in blocking Communist proposals and initially proved successful in their efforts to stop the new Communist offensive.

In international affairs, Beneš's plan for Czechoslovakia to serve as a bridge between East and West in an environment of collective security proved too idealistic as the wartime alliance of the Western democracies and the Soviet Union gave way to the Cold War. Masaryk found himself in a personally untenable position as Czechoslovakia continued to support the Soviet Union in diplomatic matters, even as the Soviet Union grew more aggressive in relations with the British and the Americans. The institution of the Marshall Plan recovery program in June 1947 initially drew the interest of the Czechoslovak government, which sent representatives to the conference in Paris. However, Czechoslovakia withdrew from consideration for American funds after Masaryk and Gottwald traveled to Moscow to meet with Stalin and the Soviets, who had denounced the Marshall Plan as a conspiracy to place the nations of Europe under American influence. In September 1947, Czechoslovakia instead turned eastward, joining the Cominform (Communist Information Bureau), the Soviet-dominated successor to the prewar Comintern as an organization of Communist parties.

That same month, ministers Drtina, Masaryk, and Zenkl received parcels that contained explosive devices disguised as bottles of perfume, and although no one was hurt in the crude plot, Drtina claimed that evidence seemed to point to members of the Communist Party based in Olomouc. Two months later, Social Democratic party members removed Fierlinger from his leadership position, but the appointment of Bohumíl Lausman eased the concerns of the Communists and the Soviet government when Lausman proved willing to cooperate with them.

The slow ebb of public faith in the Communists resulted in the mobilization of labor as a means of influencing the National Assembly with negotiations on the new constitution effectively stalled and Drtina's Ministry of Justice continuing to block Communist efforts to use the Interior Ministry and the security services to target political enemies in the other parties. In January 1948, Drtina's ministry linked Communist leaders and parliamentarians to two more cases at a time when declining public support seemed to guarantee electoral backsliding for the Communists in the upcoming spring elections. As a result, on January 20, the Presidium of the KSČ's Central Committee committed the Communists to a seizure of power in Czechoslovakia as soon as conditions would allow.

THE FEBRUARY CRISIS OF 1948

On February 13, Drtina reported to the Cabinet that the commander of the National Security Corps in Bohemia had ordered the remaining eight noncommunist district police chiefs transferred out of Prague, with the support of Interior Minister Nosek. Noncommunist members of the Cabinet agreed to order Nosek, who was not present at the meeting, to reverse his position and prevent the transfers.

Four days later, on February 17, ministers representing the National Socialist, People's, and Democratic parties agreed that if Nosek refused to cooperate, the noncommunist ministers, with the hoped-for participation of the Social Democrats, would submit their resignations and bring down the government. President Beneš would then either appoint a short-term government and schedule new elections or refuse to accept the resignations and force the Communists either to negotiate with the other coalition parties or accept responsibility for the government's dissolution. When the 12 ministers tendered their resignations three days later, the desired show of unity failed to materialize. The Social Democratic ministers refused to resign, as did Masaryk and Svoboda, with the latter clear in his support of the Communists.

On February 21, a quarter of a million people gathered in Prague's Old Town Square at the behest of the Communists, who continued to look to the trade unions and mass organizations for political support and possible mobilization as a militia. Prime minister and KSČ leader Gottwald called upon Beneš to accept the resignations and allow Gottwald to form a new government that would include Masaryk, but otherwise reflect stronger Communist influence. Beneš chose not to react hastily to the crisis, but the pressure increased over the next two days as a consequence of the mass meetings of peasants and workers and the assurance by Minister of Defense Svoboda that the Czechoslovak army stood with the crowds.

At noon on February 24, two and a half million people participated in a one-hour general strike in support of the Communists. Beneš consulted with Lettrich, the party chief of the Slovak Democrats, before announcing that he would be willing to accept the resignations as long as there was agreement among the parties involved. This would be the president's last communication with the democratic parties before a Communist delegation visited him on the morning of February 25 to recommend immediate acceptance of the resignations and the restructuring of the government according to Gottwald's proposal. Exhausted, in poor health, and believing he was without any viable options, Beneš conceded to the Communists and allowed Gottwald to appoint a National Front Cabinet of Communists, Social Democrats, and left-wing allies from other coalition parties. Gottwald chose to announce the formation of the new government from a balcony on Wenceslas Square, where he appeared before the public intoxicated and in a celebratory mood.

In the aftermath of the Communist coup and his ouster as minister of justice, Prokop Drtina allegedly chose to end his own life by throwing himself from a third-story window on February 26. In the early morning hours of March 10, Jan Masaryk became another victim of defenestration as his body was discovered dressed in pajamas below the window of his apartment at Černín Palace, the home of the

Ministry of Foreign Affairs. The Communists quickly announced to the nation that Masaryk's death had come at his own hand, but friends and colleagues responded by accusing the Communists of covering up a murder. Masaryk's death would remain a source of controversy long after 1948, with an investigation in the early 1990s pointing to suicide and forensic research by the police in Prague in 2004 supporting the accusation of murder.

On June 7, 1948, Edvard Beneš resigned as president of Czechoslovakia, and on September 3, he died a defeated man at his villa in Sezimovo Ústí. Gottwald assumed the presidency upon approval by the National Assembly as fellow Communist Antonín Zapotocký replaced Gottwald as prime minister.

THE COMMUNIST CONSOLIDATION OF POWER

The Communist consolidation of power began shortly after the coup as noncommunist parties effectively ceased operations and the KSČ ordered the arrest of party leaders and the purge of the democratic politicians from the National Assembly and government institutions. In May the reconstituted National Assembly approved the new constitution, and the following month, the Social Democrats united their party with the Communists as the National Front coalition became little more than a Communist instrument of power. Election returns on May 30 showed the National Front with 89.2 percent of the vote, although voters were provided with only two options, to cast their ballots for a list of National Front candidates or submit a blank, white ballot in rejection of the official list. With the National Assembly now entirely in Communist hands, the Central Committee of the KSČ assumed responsibility for policy making and directing national affairs. Purges carried out in the schools, the legal system, and other areas of national life allowed the Communists to reorient Czechoslovakia according to their own vision.

In Slovakia, the asymmetrical system established at the close of the war ended as the Communist Party of Slovakia (KSS) took control of the state offices, the Slovak National Council, and other governmental institutions in the name of the Czechoslovak Communist Party. Under Karol Smidke, chairman of the Slovak National Council, the KSS removed all political opponents from that body as the Slovak Democrats were brought to heel as the Revival Party, part of the KSS-dominated National Front in Slovakia.

The transformation of the Czechoslovak economy began immediately and according to the Soviet model for centralized planning. Rapid and extensive nationalization brought state ownership of all enterprises with over 50 employees, and by the end of the decade, state management extended to over 95 percent of those employed in the industrial sphere. The new Central Planning Commission borrowed from the Soviet Five-Year Plans in setting production quotas and mobilizing resources according to a timetable established by economists and government experts. The First Five-Year Plan (1948–1953) targeted growth of 57 percent in industrial production and moderate-to-extensive growth in areas such as metallurgy, chemicals, coal mining, and power production.

The collectivization of agriculture began in 1949 with the replacement of privately owned farms with Unified Agricultural Cooperatives (JZDs) in 80 percent of the nation's villages. Initial calls for voluntary collectivization failed to generate the desired response, so coercion and then the threat of incarceration in forced-labor camps as class enemies became the government's policies of choice. Those designated as class enemies in Czechoslovakia also risked retribution against their children in the form of limited options for employment or lost opportunities for higher education.

With the creation of Comecon (Council for Mutual Economic Assistance) in January 1949, Czechoslovakia's economy became more closely linked to those of the other nations of the Soviet bloc in Eastern Europe. As a Soviet-dominated response to the Marshall Plan, Comecon provided a common economic framework primarily to the benefit of the Soviet Union. With every member assigned an individual and specific role, expectations for Czechoslovakia required an emphasis on heavy industry and the production of machinery for the bloc. Czechoslovakia now found trade redirected toward the Soviet Union and the less developed countries in the region. Stalin's demands for military development skewed the economy by granting the army priority status in terms of industrial support and raw materials. From 1950 to 1953, the Czechoslovak military increased to over twice the former size and shifted industrial production and mining away from activities that would have proven more beneficial to trade and the standard of living. In 1955, Czechoslovakia joined the Soviet-led Warsaw Pact military coalition established in the Polish capital with the signing of the Treaty of Friendship, Cooperation and Mutual Assistance, an agreement on mutual defense and the coordination of military command structures.

The suppression of internal opposition and the institution of terror as a weapon of political control began shortly after the February coup as Gottwald and the first secretary of the KSČ, Rudolf Slánský, took a hard line against criticism. In June, a new measure ostensibly for the defense of the "people's democracy" provided legal justification for large-scale arrests and the elimination of parties and organizations in opposition to the Communist regime. With the Action B program of October 1949, the regime promoted class warfare against the Czechoslovak bourgeoisie and engaged in mass arrests and transportation to forced-labor camps, including the horrific uranium mines at Jáchymov and Pribam in Bohemia. Targeted members of the bourgeoisie underwent relocation from urban areas and faced restrictions on employment, especially in their former occupations. Further legislation in June 1950 provided for the extension of forced labor camps, to which several hundred thousand people would be sentenced or assigned.

The regime moved against the military in June 1949, by targeting Gen. Heliodor Píka, former head of the wartime Czechoslovak Military Mission in Moscow and a man who had proven loyal to Beneš both during and after the war. Beneš had promoted Píka to deputy chief of the general staff, but in May 1948, he was arrested on the charge of spying for Great Britain and then later executed for treason. After Píka's demise, some 5,000 Czechoslovak military officers faced trials and purges for representing bourgeois class enemies of the "people's democracy."

Efforts to silence the Catholic Church in Czechoslovakia and to sever diplomatic connections with the Vatican led to the imprisonment of priests and nuns, the elimination of religious orders, the closing of monasteries and convents, the subordination of clergy to state authority, and the institution of legal proceedings against bishops and Church leaders. In July 1949, the Vatican had ordered the excommunication of Communists and the Catholics who supported them, while the archbishop of Prague, Josef Beran, coordinated the country's high clergy in their denunciation of Communist policies and prevented the clergy from swearing the oath of loyalty imposed by the Communists. In response, the regime placed him under house arrest before incarcerating him in various locations until he was allowed to travel to receive his appointment as cardinal at the Vatican in 1965 on the condition that he not return.

In Slovakia, the authorities moved against the religious orders and placed Catholic bishops Ján Vojtassák and Michal Buzalka on trial, along with Pavol Peter Gojdič, bishop of the Greek Catholic Church in Prešov. The imprisonment of Gojdič seriously weakened the Greek Catholic Church in Slovakia, and Gojdič himself died in a prison hospital on his birthday in 1960. Beatified by the Vatican in 2001, Bishop Gojdič received recognition by the Vad Yashem Holocaust Memorial in Jerusalem in 2008 as one of the "Righteous Among the Nations" for his efforts on behalf of the Jewish people during the Holocaust.

As Yugoslavia pursued its own national path to socialism under Josip Broz Tito, the Stalin regime and the various governments of the Soviet bloc countered the "heresy" of "national communism" by instituting purges of party officials who diverged from the orthodox Soviet line. The political purges, which borrowed from the Stalinist purges of the 1930s, served as a cover for eliminating political rivals, leaders of the former democratic parties, or those who had drawn the wrong kind of attention to themselves for one reason or another. As political theater, the show trials and their predetermined verdicts were designed for maximum shock value in regard to crimes and punishment on both the national and international levels.

In late June 1950, Milada Horáková, the leader of the National Socialists, was sentenced to execution by hanging on the charges of treason and conspiracy at the conclusion of a show trial in which she defended her position in spite of the scripted legal proceedings. The show trials continued as members of the government, security offices, and eventually even the general secretary of the Communist Party, Rudolf Slánský, fell victim to the purges. Believing that they needed a more highly visible and powerful scapegoat to increase the political and psychological impact of the purges, Gottwald and other party leaders had Slánský arrested in November 1951 and, after a year of physical torture and psychological abuse, placed him on trial along with 13 codefendants on November 20, 1952. Ironically, Slánský had sanctioned the purge trials in Czechoslovakia and even drafted the letter requesting that Stalin send Soviet experts, who now acted against him.

Slánský's codefendants, most of them Jewish, faced charges of treason and espionage with the expectation that they would play their roles and confess to the relevant crimes. Stalin's interest in providing proof of a global conspiracy against the Communist nations influenced the trial, as did the Soviet leader's growing anti-Semitism and fear of Zionist plots. In the end, Slánský confessed to being a Trotskyite and a Titoist in league with Zionists and "working for the aims of the Anglo-U.S. imperialists ... these aims being the restoration of capitalism and the preparation of a new war."[2] In spite of his work with the wartime resistance, Slánský confessed to having collaborated with the Nazis against his own people. Slánský and 11 of the other defendants received death sentences and were hanged at Prague's Pankrác Prison on December 3, 1952. The other defendants received life sentences.

In Slovakia, Jan Ursiný and other leaders of the now-banned Slovak Democrats received long prison terms in April 1948 on the basis of false evidence provided by the security services. Officials in the Slovak government and the Slovak Communist Party also fell afoul of the KSČ, which feared that Slovak nationalism promoted Slovak separatism. As a result, the so-called Slovak "bourgeois nationalists" were arrested in 1950–1951 and then brought to trial in April 1954. The former Czechoslovak foreign minister Vladimír Clementis had already been executed as a member of the alleged Trotskyite-Titoist-Zionist conspiracy at the conclusion of the Slánský trial, so the defendants in the 1954 trial of the "bourgeois nationalists" included, among others, Gustáv Husák, the president of the Slovak Council, and Ladislav Novomeský, a poet and former Slovak education minister. Husák and Novomeský confessed, receiving a life sentence in Husak's case and ten years' imprisonment in Novomeský's.

AFTER STALIN, AFTER GOTTWALD

A new era dawned with the death of Joseph Stalin on March 5, 1953, and the passing of Klement Gottwald nine days later, shortly after he attended Stalin's funeral in Moscow. In keeping with the Soviet strategy of "collective leadership" after Stalin, the Czechoslovak Communists chose Antonín Zápotocký to replace Gottwald as president, Viliam Široký to serve as prime minister, and Antonín Novotný as first secretary of the party's Central Committee.

In Moscow, the Soviet leadership embarked upon a "New Course" designed to alter or curb some of the harsher aspects of the Stalinist system and to improve the standard of living through the increased production of consumer goods. Restrictions placed upon the police and security organs helped to usher in a post-Stalinist "Thaw" and a turn away from the purges and policies of terror. For the Communist leaders who had presided over the purges in Czechoslovakia, the shift in attitude by the Soviet regime represented a threat to their own status and influence. New policies on currency and savings implemented in May 1953 further undermined the hard-liners as citizens lost their savings and took to the streets in widespread demonstrations and urban riots. Strikes occurred at over 100 enterprises, including the V. I. Lenin Works where the police and People's Militia confronted approximately 20,000 strikers bearing portraits of Masaryk and Beneš at the former Škoda concern in Plzeň.

The Czechoslovak Communists continued to resist the pressure for change until Zápotocký met with Soviet officials in Moscow in July and received strong criticism for effectively maintaining the emphasis on heavy industry over consumer goods that the Soviets had required under Stalin. In September, Zápotocký and the KSČ finally introduced a "New Course" of their own, signaling an increased emphasis on consumer-oriented production and greater productivity in agriculture through a more moderate approach to collectivization. However, although the new policies improved the standard of living and brought the political purges to a close in 1954, they did not alter the fundamental structure of the economy with its centralized planning and focus on heavy industry and the production of machinery. The leadership's refusal to leave the Stalinist era behind was reflected in the official unveiling of a large statue of Stalin in Prague in May 1955 and the appointment of a committee to look into the purge trials, but with the intention of preventing any serious challenge to the cases against the defendants.

On February 25, 1956, Party Secretary Nikita Khrushchev delivered his "secret speech" before a closed session of the Twentieth Congress of the Communist Party of the Soviet Union. In his address, Khrushchev advanced the cause of "de-stalinization" by criticizing the activities of the secret police and exposing the extent and inhumanity of the Stalinist purges, which took the lives of countless innocent citizens. Citing Lenin's political testament of 1922–1923 as a warning against Stalin's dictatorial tendencies, Khrushchev criticized Stalin for encouraging a self-serving "cult of personality" as leader and for leaving the Soviet Union unprepared and vulnerable prior to the Nazi invasion in 1941.

After Khruschev's denunciation of Stalin became public, the hard-liners of the KSČ could not prevent word of the Soviet leader's actions from spreading across Czechoslovakia. The institution of heavy censorship and an official Press Section immediately after the 1948 coup significantly limited internal newspaper and radio sources in disseminating information, but foreign broadcasts into Czechoslovakia by the BBC, Voice of America, and Radio Free Europe allowed for radio contact with Western news sources and clandestine access to information.

For the KSČ, the Soviet "Thaw" and the process of de-stalinization represented a threat to party leaders directly connected to the purges, regardless of the official commission's decision in 1957 to uphold the sentences imposed at the show trials. The emergence of more reform-minded Communists such as Władysław Gomułka in neighboring Poland provided an additional threat to the hard-liners as those promoting less rigid policies seemed to reflect the limited but prevailing spirit of de-stalinization. Because of the purges, no native reformer like Gomułka had arisen in Czechoslovakia, and so the hard-liners hoped to stifle discussion of Khrushchev's revelations and wait out what they assumed would be a temporary political storm. Public disturbances brought

Gomułka to power with Soviet support in October 1956, but when the reformer Imre Nagy attempted to restore a multiparty political system during the Hungarian uprising later that same month, First Secretary Novotný and KSČ leaders called for Soviet intervention with the assistance of Czechoslovak military forces. On November 4, the Soviet Union launched an invasion of Hungary and brought the rebellion to a quick and bloody end as tanks rolled through the streets of Budapest.

When Zápotocký died on November 13, the election of Novotný as president allowed for the extension of the personal authority he continued to maintain as first secretary. However, ongoing problems with the economy necessitated vital reforms in the centralized system in order to increase productivity. In June 1958, the Eleventh Party Congress deliberated proposals to decentralize decision making by allowing managers of enterprises to determine production beyond necessary quotas. Backed by renewed state investment in the enterprises, the limited reforms initially proved successful, but by 1962, they had been undermined by opponents of reforms pushing for a return to fully centralized planning.

By the end of the 1950s, the standard of living improved with the introduction of universal health care and the greater availability of food and many consumer goods, although certain goods remained scarce for those without access to special stores that stocked Western products available only to the well placed. Women benefited from the official policy of gender equality and access to employment, although the equality failed to extend to wages and positions of real authority in the government and economy. Women were well represented in the labor force in terms of numbers, but held additional responsibilities as wives and mothers at home.

The approval of a new constitution in 1960 allowed Novotný and the hard-liners to proclaim the party's leadership of the nation successful in all areas of Czechoslovak life. Based on Stalin's Soviet constitution of 1936, the document declared that the nation had reached the stage of socialism and would thereafter officially be recognized as the Czechoslovak Socialist Republic (ČSSR). For the Slovaks, the constitution offered a major reversal in that it eliminated the Board of Commissioners and other institutions of self-government in favor of more direct control from Prague. As a gesture of conciliation, the regime declared amnesty for surviving victims of the purge trials, as with the "bourgeois nationalist" Gustáv Husák, although no effort was made to alter the verdicts or rehabilitate the defendants.

After Khrushchev renewed his criticism of Stalin at the Twenty-Second Congress of the CPSU in October 1961, the KSČ leadership combined stalling on de-stalinization with cosmetic changes seemingly in keeping with Khrushchev's policies. In 1962, authorities destroyed the enormous granite Stalin Monument in Prague's Letna Park and removed the former Soviet leader's name from street and place names, as well as from industrial enterprises that had been named in his honor. Gottwald's body, which had been placed in a dedicated mausoleum in the Žižkov district of Prague, was removed and cremated during the same year.

After numerous alterations, the commission's final report on the purge trials appeared in 1963 and led to changes in the party leadership as Novotný proved willing to secure his own authority by allowing others associated with the purges to bear responsibility for the abuses described in the report. In Slovakia, Alexander Dubček, a popular and loyal Communist, became first secretary of the Slovak Communist Party and served as a reminder that the new, emerging generation of leaders and officials lacked the direct connection to the purges that had linked Novotný and the old guard to the Stalinist past. The generational split contributed to the growing divisions within the party over economic reforms and the need to confront real and existing problems in Czechoslovakia.

Within two years after the implementation of the Third Five-Year Plan (1961–1965), it became clear that both the plan and the economic changes instituted in 1958 had failed to prevent a downturn, which Novotný blamed on the decentralization of the decision-making process. Novotný responded to the crisis by demanding a reversal of decentralization and by citing external factors, such as disruptions of trade caused by the friction between China and the Soviet Union and the Cold War consequences of the Berlin Wall and Cuban Missile Crisis.

The party turned to Ota Šik, a critic of centralized planning, to lead a committee in drafting a program of economic reforms, later approved by the Central Committee of the KSČ as the New System of Economic Management in 1965. The plan called for the introduction of market-oriented elements that would generate competition among enterprises based upon factors such as demand and expenses, rather than strict adherence to a plan. Although the work of Šik's commission represented an important attempt to integrate market dynamics into a planned economic system, failure to implement the full range of reforms after some initial progress in industry and wholesale prices undermined the proposals and led to poor results by 1967. For the true proponents of economic reform, the pressure to restore strict control of the economy simply intensified the desire to alter the system and created deeper divisions within the party. The push for true liberalization would begin in earnest in 1967–1968.

In Slovakia, the opening of large industrial enterprises, primarily in the east, had already initiated changes in Slovak society by creating new employment opportunities and by shifting large numbers of people away from agriculture and into the cities. In the late 1940s, roughly half the population of Slovakia worked in the agricultural sector, but by the end of the 1980s, the percentage had dropped to 13 percent. In the 1960s, state support for agricultural cooperatives provided new housing for rural workers, whose standard of living improved greatly with the modernization of village life through rural electrification and an improved infrastructure.

The national economic problems of the 1960s contributed to growing discontent among Slovaks, who resented Novotný's negative attitude toward Slovakia and the earlier persecution of the Slovak "bourgeois nationalists." As new and younger Slovak leaders like Dubček gained influence, Slovak issues and political demands again came to the fore as a source of division within the Communist Party. Support for the restoration of Slovak political institutions came not only from the Slovak public, but also from officials in the Slovak Communist Party. Novotný did little to defuse tensions when he seemingly went out of his way to offend Slovaks during his travels there in the summer of 1967.

CULTURAL RENEWAL AND LIBERALIZATION

As pressure for reform grew in the 1960s, new cultural currents allowed for publication of literary works critical of the misplaced idealism of the early communist years and the social and artistic consequences of the regime's policies. In 1963, Prof. Eduard Goldstücker hosted a conference on the writer Franz Kafka at Liblice Castle, which led to the rehabilitation of a key early-20th-century literary figure held in low regard by Communist critics. Bookstores featured books by foreign authors whose works had been unavailable for many years or by important writers like Russia's Alexander Solzhenitsyn, whose 1962 novel *One Day in the Life of Ivan Denisovich* helped to expose the cruelties associated with life in Stalin's labor camps. In 1965, the Academy Award for Best Foreign Film went to the first Czechoslovak film to earn that honor, *The Shop on Main Street*. Set during the Nazi occupation and the implementation of Aryanization policies, the film was shot entirely in Slovakia and produced at the Barrandov Film Studio in Prague.

In 1966, two novels critical of the recent Communist past cleared the censors and found extensive readership at home and abroad, primarily because their emphasis on the errors of the recent Communist past paralleled the official reexamination of that past. Ludvík Vaculík's *The Axe* described a rural community in which traditions had been undermined by an ideology that eroded the long-standing sense of community without offering anything positive in its place. In the novel, a journalist returns to his village in Moravia and is forced to confront his relationship with a deceased father who had once idealistically espoused the goals of a Communist ideology that now seemed disconnected from the realities of the 1960s.

Milan Kundera's novel, *The Joke*, focused on the theme of lost idealism on the part of a generation conscious of the disparity between utopian dreams and the rigidity of a regime that would allow a simple joke scrawled on a postcard to alter the life of a young and dedicated Communist, Ludvík, and, through his efforts at revenge, the lives of some of his former comrades. Kundera himself had undergone a transformation from idealistic supporter of the Communist cause to disenchanted critic of the regime, as had many of the leading figures of the cultural reawakening of the 1960s.

In the mid-1960s, plays by Václav Havel like *The Garden Party* and *The Memorandum* offered absurdist commentaries on the dehumanizing effects of bureaucracy, authority, and the hierarchies of power. In *The Memorandum*, the introduction of an artificial language, Ptydepe, is meant to facilitate communication in an organization, but efforts to establish bureaucratic order by means of a language in which the largest word is the one for "wombat" run afoul of human nature and the mundane pursuit of food.

When the Czechoslovak Writer's Union held the organization's Fourth Congress at the end of June 1967, attendees denounced the regime's restrictions on cultural activities and called for an end to censorship and policies that stifled creative expression. Vaculík, Kundera, and Havel contributed to the debates and to the reports, as did other leading writers like Pavel Kohout and Ivan Klíma. The public reading of a letter from Alexander Solzhenitsyn led to the exodus of party officials, which preceded official actions against some of the writers and attendees.

By the end of October 1967, Alexander Dubček and other party leaders used sessions of the Central Committee to challenge the efforts of Novotný and his colleagues to return to centralized planning and to avoid much-needed reforms. With many writers, artists, and intellectuals already in the reformist camp, university students, representing a generation removed from the events of 1948, became active on behalf of both curricular reforms and broader national issues. Students in Prague offered a public demonstration of discontent on October 30, 1967, after a series of power outages in the recently constructed residences on Strahov Hill. Students moved through the streets holding candles as they descended the hill into Prague, where they were attacked and arrested by the police. Students elsewhere held meetings and debated the possibility of a general strike, but eventually abandoned the idea. Media coverage intensified criticism of Novotný's regime, but the divisions within the party and the need to secure Soviet support limited Novotný's options in responding to the growing challenge to his leadership. For many party members, it was becoming apparent that Novotný stood little chance of weathering the storm with his authority intact. The situation drew the attention of the Soviet Union, as well, when Leonid Brezhnev, general secretary of the CPSU, visited Prague on December 8–9 and realized that fractures within the KSČ were too severe for Novotný to continue.

On January 5, 1968, the Central Committee of the KSČ elected Dubček to replace Novotný as first secretary. Although his dedication to the Communist vision had deep roots, Dubček came to believe that the key to revitalizing socialism in Czechoslovakia lay in constructive reforms. Dubček's personality and sincerity made him a popular figure and certainly a very different leader from Novotný, which, in turn, led Dubček to consult with Brezhnev and the leaders of other Warsaw Pact nations in order to convince them that reforms would not threaten the leading role of the Communist Party in Czechoslovakia. Convinced that Dubček and the reformers had no intention of undermining the party's leading role in Czechoslovakia or that country's diplomatic and military links to the Soviet Union, Brezhnev offered Dubček his support.

For Dubček and his political allies, the successful evolution of true socialism required the reintroduction of democratic elements that had been missing in Czechoslovakia since 1948. One of Dubček's colleagues, the reform communist Zdeněk Mlynář, argued that apathy and alienation from the socialist system could best be countered by incorporating elements of liberal democracy, including political pluralism, into that system. In order to restore public confidence in socialism, Dubček was willing to allow broader participation by both communist and noncommunist organizations, liberated from the restrictions of heavy censorship and police surveillance.

THE PRAGUE SPRING

At the beginning of March 1968, Dubček and party leaders agreed to an easing of censorship, which removed authority over the media from the administrative office of press censorship and shifted responsibility to the editors themselves. This critical step brought the gradual elimination of censorship by early June and the exposure of the public to issues and information that had long been banned and that were now open to public discussion. The Prague Spring had begun.

On March 14, the Presidium of the party's Central Committee adopted a policy of rehabilitation in regard to those who had been unfairly victimized by the political trials of the 1950s. A commission of the Central Committee then recommended the total rehabilitation of former party leader Rudolf Slánský and other members of the KSČ targeted by the purge trials. The living members on the list of the rehabilitated included one of Dubček's fellow reformers, Jozef Smrkovský, soon to be elected chairman of the National Assembly in mid-April.

Encouraged by the direction of events, the Slovak National Council proposed in mid-March a constitutional law that would grant the SNC full legislative authority in what they hoped would be a Slovak government in a federal state. Several weeks later, the Slovak Communist Party decided to support efforts to create a federal system for Czechoslovakia. Gustáv Husák, soon to be named deputy premier of Czechoslovakia, called for the establishment of the federation first, with democratic reforms to follow, although many Slovaks declared that democratic reforms needed to precede federalization for the reconfigured state to succeed.

Growing public demands for Novotný's resignation as president were satisfied on March 22 as Novotný stepped down in the wake of a scandal involving a personal friend, Gen. Jan Šejna. Accused of using state property for personal profit, Šejna hastily departed Czechoslovakia, but not until he had photographed secret military documents that ended up in American hands after Šejna's defection. Ludvík Svoboda, who had suffered a career reversal as a result of the purges, replaced Novotný as president by a vote of 282–6 in the National Assembly, and in late May, Novotný was expelled from the KSČ.

At the beginning of April, the Central Committee approved the reformist "Action Program," which received the support of the National Assembly a month later. Authored in part by Mlynář, now a member of the party's Central Committee and Secretariat, the "Action Program" sought to define a "Czechoslovak way to socialism." Politically, the program called for renewal of a National Front coalition whose four smaller parties and various associated organizations had long been dominated by the KSČ. The "Action Program" promised political pluralism, judicial independence, protection of civil liberties, and a new constitution by the end of the decade, although the Communist Party retained its leading role as the dominant force in national life. For the Slovaks, the program proposed a federal system in which the Czech and Slovak nations possessed legal equality in the Czechoslovak socialist state.

The economic reforms proposed in the "Action Program" included decentralization of decision making in favor of individual enterprises, fewer restrictions on international trade, a currency convertible on world markets, and protection of the rights of workers and consumers. Although citizens would be allowed to own enterprises on a small scale as a concession to market forces, the state would continue to own and manage all large-scale operations. With the economic reformer Oldřich Černík replacing Jozef Lenárt as prime minister and the ministries of defense and interior in the hands of reformist allies, the KSČ moved forward with the plans to alter the status quo.

The Prague Spring of 1968 represented an attempt by the Czechoslovak Communist Party to institute extensive political and economic reforms with the support of reformist leaders and intellectuals increasingly at odds with the old system. With the easing of censorship and growing public support for Dubček and his fellow reformers, old organizations like *Sokol* and the Scouts reappeared, trade unions and the noncommunist parties regained their voices, and new, unaffiliated groups arose in support of cultural renewal and further democratization. When the government ceased jamming radio broadcasts, young Czechs and Slovaks enjoyed greater access to Western rock music and youth culture, with many choosing to emulate the hippie lifestyle of the era. Civil society reemerged as the public abandoned apathy and passivity in favor of genuine interest in national affairs, cultural activities, newspapers and other media, as well as foreign travel. Taking advantage of the new openness, visitors and journalists arrived from the West to observe firsthand the implementation of "socialism with a human face," as Dubček described the political experiments of the Prague Spring.

By the beginning of May, developments in Czechoslovakia inspired new warnings from Brezhnev, as well as from the some of the more rigid and right-wing members of the KSČ, including Vasil Biľak, Dubček's replacement as first secretary of the Slovak Communist Party. On May 4–5, Dubček joined Biľak, Černík, and Smrkovský in Moscow for new talks with the Soviet leadership. The Czechoslovak delegation assured Brezhnev and Kosygin that the KSČ remained in firm control of events and that the country would not undergo a counterrevolution, a restoration of capitalism, or a return to pre-1948 conditions. However, Dubček and his colleagues agreed to host joint military exercises on Czechoslovak soil in June. From May 17 to May 22, Kosygin visited Karlovy Vary in Czechoslovakia, allegedly for health treatments in the spa town, although the Soviet premier also met with Czechoslovak officials and pronounced himself satisfied with current conditions in the country.

At the end of June, the National Assembly accepted a plan to create a federal state with two national republics, the Czech Socialist Republic and the Slovak Socialist Republic, maintaining separate governments and assemblies while sharing a federal administration and new bicameral Federal Assembly. The distribution of seats in the House of the People and the House of Nations favored the Slovaks in terms of passing constitutional legislation and other bills, although the policy-making authority of the KSČ's Presidium limited the power of the assembly.

However, it was the publication of Ludvík Vaculík's "Two Thousand Words" manifesto in *Literární noviny* and newspapers that represented a likely tilting point for the Soviet leadership's toleration of the Prague Spring. Vaculík blamed the Communists for the political and economic conditions that created the need for reform, but also gave credit to those within the party who recognized that essential changes were necessary. The manifesto called upon the public to engage in demonstrations and political activities on behalf of democratization and to be willing to defend the reforms, with arms if necessary, against interference by outside forces. The 70 signatories of the manifesto included not only writers and intellectuals, but also athletes, scientists, and people from a wide range of backgrounds. The "Two Thousand Words" document generated strong criticism from the KSČ, which began to move against those who had signed the manifesto. For Brezhnev and the Soviets, the manifesto seemed to offer proof of what they already suspected, that Dubček and the reformers had allowed the situation in Czechoslovakia to slip beyond their control.

On June 19, the summer military exercises, codenamed "Šumava," opened in Czechoslovakia, with the armed forces of the host country participating alongside some 27,000 Soviet troops and smaller units from Poland, Hungary, and East Germany. Although the exercise concluded during the first half of July, Soviet troop withdrawals continued into August as Czechoslovakia and its Warsaw Pact allies debated the threat of counterrevolution. With the United States unwilling to enflame Cold War tensions by intervening in the affairs of Soviet Bloc nations and West Germany also refusing to interfere in the growing crisis, the fate of the Prague Spring lay in Czechoslovakia's continuing talks with the Soviet Union and fellow members of the Warsaw Pact.

When Rumania chose not to participate and Czechoslovakia lobbied for bilateral talks over group negotiations, the five remaining Warsaw Pact allies gathered in Warsaw on July 14–15 and agreed to deliver a letter to Dubček expressing general support for the concerns expressed by the Soviet leadership. Several days later, the letter from "the Five" appeared in the Czechoslovak press, along with the Czechoslovak refutation of the claims that the country had passed into a state of counterrevolution. Dubček appeared on television to speak out against the accusations of "the Five," but the media in the other Warsaw Pact countries covered only the initial letter to Czechoslovakia and not the refutations that followed. As tensions increased, Czechoslovak military commanders informed the Warsaw Pact countries and Yugoslavia of the army's unconditional support for Dubček as head of the KSČ.

After the Presidium of the KSČ agreed to a Soviet request for a meeting, Dubček and his delegation arrived in Čierna nad Tisou, a Slovak town on the border of Soviet Ukraine, to participate in four days of talks beginning on July 29. Held in the town's train station, the sessions went so poorly that the brutal criticisms of Ukrainian Communist Party chief Pyotr Shelest reduced Dubček to tears.

All of the Warsaw Pact countries gathered in Bratislava on August 3 and agreed to a joint statement, the Bratislava Declaration, which supported individual national paths to socialism, but with the warning that challenges to the socialist order in one state would be considered a threat to all socialist states. Unbeknownst to the Czechoslovak representatives, Brezhnev added a passage to the document stating that the entire Warsaw Pact held responsibility for responding to threats to socialism in any one country, a policy that would become known as the Brezhnev Doctrine. Before the meeting drew to a close, an aide to KSČ hard-liner Drahomír Holder passed along to Shelest a secret "letter of invitation" in which Biľak, Holder, Alois Indra, and two other party conservatives asked the Soviet Union to respond to the current counterrevolutionary situation in Czechoslovakia by any means necessary.

Brezhnev and the Soviets decided to act before the opening of the Fourteenth Congress of the KSČ and the even earlier gathering of the Slovak Communist Party on August 26. After the Soviet leaders informed Dubček of their dissatisfaction with the Czechoslovak response to recent agreements, the Central Committee of the CPSU met in Moscow on August 15–17 and decided to take direct military action with the cooperation of Biľak and the antireform group, whose members would assume control of the media, the Czechoslovak military, and the Ministry of the Interior.

INVASION

When the Presidium of the KSČ convened on August 20, Biľak and the hard-liners attempted to hold a vote of no confidence to undermine Dubček and have him replaced with an emergency government amenable to the Soviets. However, Dubček successfully tabled Biľak's motion by continuing with party business as set out in the agenda for the session. As debate continued late into the night, members of the Presidium received word that the Warsaw Pact had launched an invasion of Czechoslovakia without informing Dubček or leading government officials. The Presidium issued a condemnation of the military intervention as a violation of the independence of a fellow socialist state and called upon the public to remain calm and avoid any direct provocation or armed response. The army and air force received orders not to undertake armed resistance in the nation's defense and as a result did not move against the advancing Warsaw Pact forces.

Code-named "Operation Danube," the invasion of Czechoslovakia included military units from the Soviet Union, Poland, Hungary, East Germany, and Bulgaria, with 165,000 Soviet troops and 4,600 tanks in the vanguard. The Warsaw Pact forces drove into Czechoslovakia on the night of August 20 and during the following day, crossing the border from Hungary, East Germany, and Poland. Soviet military personnel secured Prague's Ruzyně Airport for the landing of 120 AN-12 aircraft during the first day. By the end of the first week, the number of foreign troops in Czechoslovakia had risen to half a million, with more than 6,000 tanks providing support. The Prague Spring was coming to an end, along with Dubček's experiment in "socialism with a human face." Dubček would later write that the invasion had come as a complete surprise to him: "My problem was not having a crystal ball to foresee the Russian invasion. At no point between January and August 20, in fact, did I believe that it would happen."[3]

On August 21, the National Assembly joined labor organizations, journalists, scientists, broadcast media, and party and government officials in condemning the invasion. In response, the Soviets broadcast a statement claiming that Czechoslovakia's Warsaw Pact allies had been invited by individuals in the KSČ and government to provide assistance in ending the threat of counterrevolution. The Soviets effectively kidnapped Dubček, Černík, Smrkovský, František Kriegel (chairman of the Central Committee of the National Front), and two others, removing them under KGB supervision to Warsaw, Ukraine, and then Moscow.

With the public out in the streets in great numbers and engaging in angry demonstrations, a general strike, and nonviolent acts of obstruction, the hard-liners failed to move quickly in organizing a new, pro-Soviet government, in part because the Biľak group lacked the kind of leader needed to fill the vacuum caused by Dubček's removal. Meanwhile, citizens took down street names, signs, and house numbers to create confusion as many confronted tank crews and attempted to convince the foreign conscripts that the invasion was a tragic mistake and that the Warsaw Pact troops should go home. Petitions circulated in Prague demanding withdrawal of the troops and the release of Czechoslovak leaders who had been taken into custody. Critically, the public avoided the kind of acts of resistance that had caused major bloodshed during the crushing of the Hungarian Uprising in 1956. Citizens were encouraged to follow "The Ten Commandments" of resistance as published in *Večerni Praha*: "1. don't know 2. don't care 3. don't tell 4. don't have 5. don't know how to 6. don't give 7. don't go 8. don't sell 9. don't show 10. do nothing"[4]

On August 22, over 1,200 KSČ delegates defied the Soviets and KSČ collaborators by attending an Extraordinary Fourteenth Party Congress at the ČKD factory in the Prague district of Vysočany. Those present at the congress were overwhelmingly Czech due to the immediacy of the planning, but the delegates decided that quick action was necessary in repudiating the "invitation" that allegedly preceded the invasion. The congress called for a one-hour work stoppage, expressed strong support for Dubček as party leader, and installed a new, pro-reform Central Committee.

The following day, Dubček and his group arrived in Moscow after Svoboda and his associates had already reached the Soviet capital. Dubček refused to cooperate with Brezhnev and Kosygin in agreeing to accept the military intervention as legitimate, although Svoboda was able to convince the Soviets to return Dubček and the others to Czechoslovakia. The Soviets also demanded that the Czechoslovak leaders disavow the Fourteenth Party Congress and its activities. On August 26, the Soviets met with Svoboda, Dubček's group, and the hard-liners, with the Soviets and the Czechoslovak contingent agreeing to the Moscow Protocol, a 15-point document that negated the decisions and declarations of the recent party congress and called for the defense of socialism in Czechoslovakia, the denunciation of the Fourteenth Party Congress, the restoration of censorship, and the removal of pro-reform officials from key party and government positions. Dubček and his colleagues retained their positions, but in spite of the absence of references to the post-January policies as counter-revolutionary, the protocol otherwise mandated a reversal of the reforms of the Prague Spring and left Dubček and the reformers vulnerable to future actions.

Meeting in Bratislava on August 26–29, delegates to the Extraordinary Fourteenth Congress of the KSS listened to Gustáv Husák report on the Moscow sessions and then elected Husák to replace Biľak as first secretary of the Slovak Communist Party. The Slovak congress had initially declared support for the KSČ congress held at Vysočany, but upon his arrival, Husák questioned the validity of the Prague meeting due to the absence of adequate Slovak representation.

On August 27, the Czechoslovak representatives returned to Prague with Dubček and Svoboda later delivering a radio broadcast to inform the public in general terms of the consequences of the discussions held in Moscow. That same day, Soviet troops began withdrawing from the city center and the area around Prague Castle. A report issued in September would claim that the occupation of Prague had resulted in 2 deaths and 431 cases of serious injury, along with physical damage to many buildings in the city.

AFTERMATH AND "NORMALIZATION"

During the final days of August and into September, Kriegel, Šik, Foreign Minister Jiří Hájek, Minister of the Interior Josef Pavel, and leading reformers in the government either resigned or were replaced. Efforts by Dubček to elect reformers to the Presidium of the KSČ met with criticism from Brezhnev, who supported Biľak and the conservatives. On January 7, Smrkovský failed to gain enough support to retain his position as chair of the National Assembly, and the reformers lost yet another key position. Husák, who had been supportive of the Prague Spring, was now proving to be an opportunist looking to take advantage of the end of reform and the changes in the political climate.

Dubček, Černík, and Husák met with Brezhnev and other Soviet leaders in Moscow on October 3–4 to discuss the "normalization" of Czechoslovak affairs and the continued presence of Soviet troops in that country. Following further negotiations, the Czechoslovak representatives were pressured into signing a treaty that allowed for the "temporary" stationing of approximately 80,000 Soviet troops on Czechoslovak soil. The National Assembly voted 228–4 to ratify the treaty, although some 50 deputies chose not to attend the session. At the end of the month, as Czechoslovakia celebrated the 50th anniversary of independence on October 28, the plan for federalization that had been proposed during the summer passed into constitutional law as signed by President Svoboda at Bratislava Castle two days later.

On January 16, 1969, a Charles University student named Jan Palach chose a spot in front of the National Museum at the top of Wenceslas Square in Prague, removed his coat, and after dousing himself with flammable liquid, attempted an act of self-immolation as the designated "Torch Number One." A note pinned to Palach's coat explained that he had been chosen by lot to make this sacrifice in defiance of the Soviet-led invasion of his homeland and the return to policies of repression. After being taken to the hospital with serious burns over 85 percent of his body, Palach died three days later, and a nation mourned his passing with a procession in Prague and a funeral ceremony on January 25 that became the last major pro-democracy demonstration before the onset of full "normalization." From January 20 to 25, 19 students at Comenius University in Bratislava engaged in a hunger strike in solidarity with Palach's act of defiance.

In late March 1969, the ice hockey World Championships in Stockholm provided the citizens of Czechoslovakia with good reason to celebrate as their national team defeated the Soviet squad both times they met. The victories over the Soviets inspired some 500,000 people to attend nationwide demonstrations after the second game, while in Prague, a crowd of several thousand assaulted the offices of the Soviet state airline, Aeroflot. In the midst of the outpouring of patriotic feeling and anger, Dubček's critics chose to move against him as the Soviets dispatched a delegation to Prague with demands that the disturbances be brought under control and that Dubček be relieved of his duties. Lurking behind the Soviet response was the threat of further military action against Czechoslovakia as 8,000 Soviet troops relocated from East Germany to bases in Czechoslovakia.

During a meeting of the KSČ's Central Committee on April 17, Dubček stepped down as first secretary of the party and successfully proposed Husák as his replacement, although Dubček continued to serve on the Presidium. Faith in Husák to preserve some of the reforms of the Prague Spring was very much misplaced, as the turn to normalization brought repression and a rollback of reforms instead. The reintroduction of censorship brought tight state control of the press, radio, and television, as well as an end to publications sponsored by reformers.

The public, however, was not quite ready to forget the events of August 1968, and on the first anniversary of the Soviet-led invasion, on August 19–21, 1969, demonstrators appeared in the streets of Prague, Brno, and other Czechoslovak cities. Efforts by the army and the national militia to restore order left 5 dead, over 30 injured, and nearly 300 under arrest. Writers and intellectuals such as Havel, Vaculík, and Kohout chose the first anniversary of the invasion to issue a "Ten Points Manifesto" condemning the return to repression and the policies of normalization. The government's response to the criticism was to institute legislation designed to maintain order and facilitate legal action against critics and those engaged in unsanctioned public gatherings.

During the autumn months of 1969, the purge of reformers continued as Dubček and Smrkovský lost their positions in the National Assembly and the KSČ began a full-party weeding out of pro-reform members and technocrats in favor of restoring its working-class base. President Svoboda later outlined the primary goals of normalization in his address to the nation on New Year's 1970, stressing both the leading role of the KSČ in Czechoslovak affairs and the importance of the nation's diplomatic and military links to the Soviet Union. That same month, further purges of the party and government led to Dubček's resignation from the Central Committee and appointment as Czechoslovakia's ambassador to Turkey. Černík was removed from the Presidium and replaced as prime minister with the deputy premier, Lubomír Štrougal, who would hold that position until October 1988.

In May 1970, the government recalled Dubček from Turkey and the KSČ expelled him from party ranks, an action also taken against a number of others deemed unworthy of membership in the KSČ. Zdeněk Mlynář, the key contributor to the reformist Action Plan, underwent expulsion from the party and lost his position at the Czechoslovak Academy of Sciences, spending the next seven years employed in the etymology department of the National Museum. By the end of the year, Husák and KSČ officials reported that only 78 percent of the party members screened had been allowed to remain in the party. Meeting in May 1971, the officially sanctioned Fourteenth Congress of the KSČ openly repudiated the actions of the Extraordinary Fourteenth Party Congress in Vysočany in August 1968.

As part of the purge of party and society, unsanctioned student groups and organizations such as *Sokol* and the Scouts once again became proscribed. Thousands of educators, scholars, scientists, journalists, members of the broadcast media, and others found their employment at an end as artists and writers faced bans on exhibitions, performances, and publication. Many who had once supported the reforms of 1968 now found themselves victims of retribution by those seeking to eliminate all traces of the Prague Spring in reactionary defense of the old status quo. Others chose to depart the country, and by the final days of 1971, some 130,000 to 140,000 Czechs and Slovaks departed for new homes elsewhere.

In the economic sphere, normalization meant a return to centralized planning and the reintroduction of compulsory quotas and strict price controls. Šik's earlier changes to the system and the better-than-expected performance of the agricultural sector allowed the economy to move forward in some areas during the 1970s, although productivity, wages, and consumption failed to reach the desired levels in spite of strong government investment in many enterprises. Growing problems with the quality of goods also undermined the sale of Czechoslovak products on a global scale. Regardless, the regime celebrated the equalization of income and an improved standard of living as evidence of the successful evolution of "real existing socialism" by the mid-1970s.

By the end of the decade, however, problems began to mount due to a severe shortage of housing and the inability to meet demand with the construction of drab and crowded prefabricated concrete apartment blocks, or *paneláks*, in urban areas. When the OPEC oil crisis in 1974 generated drastic price increases around the world, the rising cost of Soviet oil doubled what Czechoslovakia had been paying within a year and then continued to increase into the early 1980s. As the cost of other raw materials also began to rise, the sale of Czechoslovak-manufactured goods could not keep pace with the increases, and the economy responded accordingly.

The reliance on large industrial and armaments enterprises in Slovakia left the Slovaks vulnerable to declining markets, increasingly outdated technology, and the military requirements of the Warsaw Pact. The authorities could boast full employment in Slovakia due to the continued trade with the Soviet Union and Eastern Europe, but in many areas, production far outstripped demand. Additionally, the negative environmental impact of large-scale metallurgical, chemical, and electrical production could be seen in the polluted air and waterways, as well as in the seriously damaged woodlands.

On May 5–6, 1970, negotiations between Czechoslovakia and the Soviet Union produced a treaty of friendship and mutual cooperation reflecting Soviet support for the Husák regime and the normalization of life in Czechoslovakia. The adoption of the "Lessons from the Crisis Development of the Party and Society after the Thirteenth Congress of the KSČ" by the Central Committee in December 1970 gave Soviet leaders further cause for satisfaction. Neo-Stalinist in tone and content, the "Lessons" returned Czechoslovakia to a course favored by the Soviet Union by rejecting the reforms of the Action Program and the events of 1968 as counterrevolutionary. The KSČ substituted instead an ideological primer for national distribution and required study by workers in positions of authority and individuals involved in education, science, and cultural affairs. By linking its leading role to the principles and doctrines contained in the "Lessons," the KSČ assumed a rigid stance that precluded concessions to the public, should conditions arise that called for flexibility of policies over repression. In 1975, Husák extended his personal authority over Czechoslovakia by assuming the presidency after a struggle to convince the now-senile Svoboda to step down.

DISSIDENTS AND HUMAN RIGHTS

As the decade of the 1970s progressed, the normalizers failed to produce the kind of leaders or ideological fervor necessary to generate widespread public acceptance of the system defined by the "Lessons." Conformity, obedience, and repression led not to a dynamic system that could erase memories of 1968, but rather to widespread public apathy in the face of bureaucratization and long-term stagnation. Little had survived of the Prague Spring, but normalization seemingly had little to offer in place of the lost reforms.

For some, the hope that normalization would eventually give way to a more humane system led to acts of opposition likely to result in arrests and legal persecution by authorities content with a cowed public and unwilling to consider changes to the system. Writers and intellectuals maintained connections in unofficial and informal ways, turning to underground *samizdat* (from the Russian in reference to "unofficial publishing" or "self-publishing") practices to avoid the censors and circulate banned documents, journals, and books. Writers such as Ludvík Vaculík, Václav Havel, Pavel Kohout, and Ivan Klíma formed small circles and exchanged clandestine copies of their typewritten works. Other writers, like Milan Kundera, became emigrés and chose to live outside of Czechoslovakia on a long-term or permanent basis. Kundera relocated to Paris in 1975, later taking French citizenship and developing an international reputation for novels such as *The Unbearable Lightness of Being* and *The Book of Laughter and Forgetting*.

To facilitate the exchange of ideas and to assist Czech and Slovak writers in circulating their works outside official channels, Vaculík established his *Edice Petlice* (Padlock Editions) in 1972 and published nearly 400 banned works by the end of the 1980s. Between the years 1975 and 1981, Havel published 122 volumes of writings by Czech dissidents as part of his *Edice Expedice* (Expedition Editions), and when he later served time in prison for his dissident activities, his wife Ogla and brother Ivan M. Havel continued his work. The writer Josef Škvorecký joined his wife, writer and actress Zdena Salivarová, in departing Czechoslovakia for Canada, where they established Sixty-Eight Publishers in Toronto in 1971 in order to publish works by Czech and Slovak emigré authors and writers whose works could not be published in Czechoslovakia.

Havel chose a more direct approach to criticizing the policies of normalization when he sent an open letter to Gustáv Husák in April 1975. In the document, Havel discussed the moral crisis and general apathy that had descended upon Czechoslovakia as a result of the loss of hope and the environment of fear created by the ubiquitous secret police and the superficial consensus of a "normalized" society. Havel claimed that rather than leading to any true form of normalcy, normalization had created a society in which "Despair leads to apathy, apathy to conformity, conformity to routine performance—which is then quoted as evidence of 'mass political involvement.'"[5] Although it is not known whether Husák actually read Havel's letter, the playwright had the letter returned with a warning from Husák's office claiming that by providing the foreign media with copies of the letter, he had identified himself as an enemy of the Czechoslovak people. In Czechoslovakia, access to the missive remained limited and private, but the media abroad reported on Havel's challenge to the regime as translated versions became available in the West.

Several months later, on August 1, 1975, the government of the Czechoslovak Socialist Republic joined the Soviet Union, members of the Warsaw Pact, the United States, Canada, and nearly all the other states of Europe in signing the Final Act of the Conference on Security and Cooperation in Europe (CSCE) in Helsinki, Finland. The signers of the Helsinki Accords, as they were also known, agreed to guarantee human rights and the fundamental liberties of their citizens. One year later, Czechoslovakia participated in the ratification of two United Nations conventions on human rights, which allowed references to the protection of such rights to become part of the country's legal code.

The hypocrisy of the regime's stance on human rights was not lost on the country's dissidents or on the musicians arrested in 1976 for performing music without official approval. Shortly after the invasion in 1968, Milan Hlavsa recruited fellow musicians to form the counterculture band the Plastic People of the Universe, which covered songs by non-mainstream American musicians like the Velvet Underground, the Fugs, Captain Beefheart, and Frank Zappa and the Mothers of Invention. The band took its name from Zappa's song, "Plastic People," and developed close ties to another group, DG 307, named after the mental diagnosis for schizophrenia and founded in 1973 by bassist Hlavsa and the poet Pavel Zajíček. With concerts that included theatrical sets and costumes, as well as light shows and the trappings of psychedelia, the Plastic People eventually provoked a response from the authorities, who declared the musicians to be nonconformists, stripped them of their professional status, and took away their license to perform public concerts.

The turning point for the band came on February 21, 1976, when the wedding of manager and artistic director Ivan Jirous in Bojanovice provided the setting for the Second Festival of the Second Culture. On March 17, the authorities arrested over 20 people for participating in the event, including Jirous, all members of the Plastic People, and Zajíček. After legal proceedings, which Havel described as Kafkaesque due the predetermined verdicts and treatment of the defendants as criminals rather than critics of the regime, most of the people involved were released. However, Jirous received a prison sentence of 18 months, Zajíček a year, and saxophonist Vratislav Brabanec 8 months. Brabenec eventually succumbed to forced exile and departed for Canada in the early 1980s, while Zajíček relocated to Sweden and then New York.

The trials brought Havel together with other writers and intellectuals in opposition to the regime's proceedings against the musicians. In early January 1977, Havel and his colleagues introduced the Charter 77 initiative with a document, or charter, demanding that the Husák regime uphold human rights as defined by the country's laws and constitution, as well as by the Helsinki Accords and other international agreements to which Czechoslovakia had been a signatory. On January 6, Havel joined Vaculík and actor-playwright Pavel Landovský in attempting to deliver copies of the Charter to the government, parliament, and journalists at the official ČTK agency, in addition to mailing copies of the manifesto to those whose signatures it bore. However, security police prevented the trio from completing their tasks when they stopped the car and took all three into custody prior to engaging in interrogations, house searches, and other forms of harassment directed against a number of the cosigners. Havel remained in detention from mid-January until late May before being charged with subversion based upon his earlier open letter to Husák. Zdeněk Mlynář lost his position at the

National Museum in Prague for signing the Charter and left for Vienna and exile during the summer.

The first three spokespersons for Charter 77 included Havel, the philosopher Jan Patočka, and the historian and political scientist Jiří Hájek. After an ongoing series of interrogations, Patočka suffered a fatal brain hemorrhage while in the hands of the police on March 13. The authorities placed Havel and three other Chartists on trial in October 1977, with Havel receiving a suspended 14-month sentence. In late January 1978, Havel again faced arrest on the charge of "disturbing the peace" and was held until the middle of March before being released.

The leaders of Charter 77 hoped for a restoration of civil society and chose to engage in "antipolitics" and moral opposition to Husák and the politics of normalization, rather than undertaking political activities against the state. In his 1984 book *Antipolitics*, Hungarian writer George Konrad described "antipolitics" in terms of operating outside of a political system that, because it is political, is essentially corrupt. For Charter 77, taking the moral path necessitated remaining apart from the corruption, but extremely limited access to political institutions left the dissidents with few options in that regard. Charter 77 operated primarily in Bohemia and Moravia in the early years, although a small group of Slovak intellectuals, including the philosopher and educator Miroslav Kusý and the philosopher and writer Milan Šimecka, worked toward common cause with their Czech colleagues.

In April 1978, members of Charter 77 established a separate organization with the mission of monitoring police harassment of citizens and the denial and abuses of legal rights. VONS, or the Committee for the Defense of the Unjustly Prosecuted, collected evidence and investigated charges of abuses in regard to trials and judicial decisions, police actions, environmental concerns, and issues related to minorities. The intellectuals and workers who carried out the work of VONS underwent the same type of official persecution as the signatories of Charter 77, from police surveillance to the loss of jobs and professional careers leading to limited opportunities and often menial employment.

In 1978, Havel produced another far-reaching challenge to the system with an essay, "The Power of the Powerless," which he dedicated to the late Jan Patočka. In the essay, Havel described the actions of a greengrocer called upon to post the slogan, "Workers of the World Unite!" in his shop window. Havel claimed that rather than displaying loyalty to the regime or to its ideology, the greengrocer placed the note in the window without enthusiasm and in keeping with the expected norms of ritual and obedience. Normalization had so demoralized individual citizens that they had become alienated from themselves and therefore willing to live a lie. For Havel, the alternative was for citizens from all walks of life to begin "living in truth" by undertaking small acts of self-liberation as simple as writing poetry or refusing to behave in an expected manner. On a larger scale, citizens' initiatives and opposition groups could generate a second, or parallel, culture in opposition to official organizations and culture. This parallel culture would assist in the restoration of civil society in Czechoslovakia.

In May 1979, the authorities arrested 15 members of VONS and Charter 77 on charges of criminal subversion in cooperation with foreign agents. Six defendants were brought to trial in October and sentenced to incarceration, including Havel, who received a sentence of four and a half years but gained his release in March 1983 due to poor health brought on by a long period of hard labor.

By the late 1970s, the Jazz Section of the Union of Musicians had taken up the cause of musicians seeking to tread artistic paths deemed nonconformist and unacceptable by the authorities. With a membership of over 7,000, the Jazz Section assisted young musicians by promoting public performances and publishing music representing jazz and other genres. Declaring the Jazz Section to be engaged in counterrevolutionary endeavors, the authorities eventually banned the organization in March 1985 and arrested leading members the following year.

CZECHOSLOVAKIA IN THE 1980S

When strikes and demonstrations in 1980 led to the Polish regime's acceptance of the Gdańsk Agreements and the recognition of the independent trade union Solidarity, public opposition to the Communist government represented the first such large-scale action since the Prague Spring. Hopes for extensive reforms ended in December 1981, however, when the new prime minister, Gen. Wojciech Jaruzelski, declared martial law and arrested Lech Wałęsa and other Solidarity leaders as part of a nationwide crackdown.

In Czechoslovakia, the events of 1980 gave the Husák regime reason for concern after a long period of stagnation and repression. The Czechoslovak government tried to convince Brezhnev and the Soviet leadership to take direct action against counterrevolutionary activity in Poland, but the imposition of martial law rendered such action unnecessary. With the crisis in Poland under control, Husák and the KSČ continued to avoid reform and to preserve the post-1968 status quo. When Brezhnev's death in 1982 resulted in the brief terms of Yuri

Andropov and Konstantin Chernenko as general secretary of the CPSU, little changed before the two leaders passed away in 1984 and 1985, respectively. The Brezhnev Doctrine provided Husák with a sense of security as he held to the "Lessons" and, backed by hard-liners such as Bil'ak, refused to consider fundamental changes to the system.

Without structural reforms and some degree of market incentives, the system slowly succumbed to various problems by the mid-1980s, from technological obsolescence and deteriorating machinery to the wasteful use of raw materials and resources, growing environmental damage and pollution, and an overreliance on oil and natural gas provided by the Soviet Union. Attempts to solve the latter problem through investment in nuclear energy and domestic supplies of brown coal led to an increase in air pollution as the burning of coal generated greater amounts of unhealthy smog in cities like Prague.

The government responded to discontent over economic conditions by tolerating an unofficial "grey" economy, in which citizens could practice entrepreneurship on a limited scale. By turning a blind eye to practices it could not openly condone, the government defused some of the social tension and political criticism, but at the cost of corruption, bribery, theft, cynicism, and what Havel and the dissidents referred to as the country's ongoing moral crisis.

In the Soviet Union, the Politburo's election of Mikhail Gorbachev to replace the deceased Chernenko as general secretary in March 1985 opened the way to true reform in that country and eventually in other countries of the Soviet bloc. Gorbachev believed that something similar to the Prague Spring could occur in Moscow under the right conditions and without jeopardizing the leading role of the Communist Party. To that end, Gorbachev introduced the policy of *glasnost*, or openness, as a means of generating discussion of the country's problems by government officials and the public through a loosening of censorship and the opportunity to participate in the revitalization of communism. According to Gorbachev, not until the last vestiges of Stalinism disappeared would communism reach its potential in the Soviet Union. By 1988, Gorbachev's political reforms would allow for the election of critics within the CPSU and even noncommunist politicians to the Congress of People's Deputies, in what became a key step toward political pluralism.

Gorbachev's policy of *perestroika*, or restructuring, addressed the shortcomings of the Soviet economy in an attempt to increase efficiency and improve the lives of Soviet citizens. Gorbachev believed that a reduction of centralized planning and the introduction of market forces and controlled privatization would save the Soviet economy from decades of mismanagement. Chronic problems with agricultural production could be overcome through reduced centralization and greater emphasis on market factors and local decision making. The effects of *perestroika* were felt not only in the Soviet Union, but also across Eastern Europe as a result of Comecon and the economic links among the participating countries.

In Czechoslovakia, Gorbachev's reforms ran counter to the ideological principles of the "Lessons," but since the Soviet leader hoped to decrease the Soviet Union's military presence in the region, he wanted the countries of the bloc to adopt reforms similar to his own in order to ensure stability and progress. The implementation of limited reforms eventually moved forward in January 1987, when the KSČ introduced some market elements into the economy and attempted to decentralize the decision-making process. However, the problem for KSČ leaders looking to limit the scope of reforms remained the same as it had been in 1967–1968 in terms of pursuing constructive changes to the economy while preventing reforms to the political system.

When Gorbachev visited Prague in 1987, crowds serenaded him with cries of "Gorby, Gorby" in support of his reformist policies at home and in hopes that similar reforms would be implemented in Czechoslovakia. Many also believed that Gorbachev's willingness to allow some measure of diversity among the communist regimes in the region meant the abandonment of the Brezhnev Doctrine. Gorbachev chose not to speak to the Brezhnev Doctrine directly, but while visiting Prague, he commented that responsibility for assessing the events of 1968 fell to the people of Czechoslovakia themselves. For the top officials of the Husák regime, legitimacy rested upon acceptance of the August 1968 invasion as a justifiable military intervention. Reassessment of the invasion threatened to undermine the policies of Husák and the KSČ since that time.

As the influence of Gorbachev continued to spread, and younger members of the KSČ like Miloš Jakeš and Ladislav Adamec lobbied for a greater role in party leadership, Husák announced his resignation as general secretary in December 1987. Although he would continue to serve as the country's president, Husák was replaced as party chief by Jakeš, who spoke of instituting *přestavha*, or the Czechoslovak version of *perestroika*, but in fact showed little inclination to undertake major reforms. In 1988, however, events in Hungary and Poland combined with growing discontent at home to move Czechoslovakia toward the endgame that would lead to the conclusion of four decades of Communist rule during the autumn of 1989.

NOTES

1. Quoted in Chad Bryant, *Prague in Black: Nazi Rule and Czech Nationalism* (Cambridge, MA: Harvard University Press, 2007), 239. For further information on postwar retribution against war criminals and collaborators, see Benjamin Frommer, *National Cleansing: Retribution against Nazi Collaborators in Postwar Czechoslovakia* (Cambridge: Cambridge University Press, 2005).

2. From the transcript of Rudolf Slánský's trial, as cited in Alfred French, *Czech Writers and Politics 1945–1969* (New York: Columbia University Press, 1982), 80.

3. Alexander Dubcek, *Hope Dies Last: The Autobiography of the Leader of the Prague Spring* (New York: Kodansha International, 1993), 128.

4. Cited in Ivan Sviták, *The Czechoslovak Experiment 1968–1969* (New York: Columbia University Press, 1971), 161.

5. Václav Havel, "Letter to Dr. Gustáv Husák," in *Living in Truth*, ed. Jan Vladislav (London: Faber and Faber, 1990), 11.

9

The Velvet Revolution, the "Velvet Divorce," and the Two Republics (1989–2009)

In January 1988, an interview with Alexander Dubček appeared in *L'Unitá*, the newspaper of the Italian Communist Party. After years living in relative obscurity in Bratislava and under surveillance as a clerk with the Forestry Service in Slovakia, Dubček returned to the public eye as a result of a loosening of restrictions coinciding with Gorbachev's visit to Czechoslovakia in 1987. In his interview with the Italian publication, Dubček expressed his support for the Soviet leader's policy of *glasnost* based on his long-held belief that reform communism remained both possible and essential. Dubček also stressed the similarities between the Prague Spring and Gorbachev's reforms, claiming that had someone like Gorbachev been in power in the Soviet Union in 1968, events would have played out very differently and military intervention could have been avoided.

During the 1980s, the Czechoslovak public began to display a willingness to express limited, but open, discontent toward some of the policies of the existing regime. At the same time, intellectuals, artists, and writers turned from "antipolitics" to direct and active opposition to the government and KSČ. An increasing number of independent groups emerged and established connections with Charter 77 and the other opposition organizations, which, in turn, were increasing their activities on behalf of reform and a civil society.

Leading religious figures also became more active in national affairs after the mid-1980s. František Cardinal Tomášek, the elderly archbishop of Prague, had earlier supported the reforms of 1968, but had never been very outspoken in his criticism of the KSČ regime during the period of normalization. After the election of an anticommunist pope, John Paul II, in 1978, Tomášek became an advocate for Charter 77 and human rights organizations. With Tomášek's encouragement in 1988, nearly 600,000 Roman Catholics signed a petition, "Suggestions of Catholics for the Solution of the Position of the Faithful," calling on the government to allow greater religious freedom.

In Slovakia, Roman Catholics angry over the suppression of religious freedom joined clergy banned from performing their religious duties in establishing a clandestine church organization linked to Bishop Ján Chryzostom Korec, a Jesuit and dissident who had served time in prison from 1960 to 1968 and then turned to *samizdat* publishing to circulate his writings. On March 25, 1988, a peaceful demonstration in Bratislava by primarily elderly Catholic women resulted in forceful action by the police in breaking up the gathering. The involvement of students reflected the growing willingness of a new generation to engage in public acts of opposition to the government.

By 1988, a rising generation of young Czechs and Slovaks with no direct personal connection to the events of the Prague Spring brought new energy to national life in the era of Gorbachev. The participation of student organizations in street demonstrations commemorating significant historical milestones would prove crucial in the events leading to the fall of communism in the autumn of 1989. When the authorities reacted with armored vehicles, water cannons, and attack dogs against young people, the credibility of the regime eroded even further and the number of demonstrations began to increase by the middle of 1988.

On August 21, 1988, a crowd of more than 10,000 people and composed primarily of students took to the streets of Prague to commemorate the 20th anniversary of the Warsaw Pact invasion and to express their desire for reforms similar to those instituted by Gorbachev in the

Soviet Union. Student leaders read a petition calling for democratization and an end to repression before the procession moved through central Prague toward Old Town Square. As the demonstration neared an end, police used tear gas and batons to disperse the remaining thousand or so marchers, although the authorities were surprised to discover the absence of leading members of Charter 77 and other organizations, who had earlier departed the city in order to avoid arrest.

By the end of 1988, deteriorating economic conditions placed the Husák-Jakeš regime in a vulnerable position in regard to reform. The Czechoslovak Institute for Economic Forecasting issued a report predicting continued economic decline and growing social problems for a country that slipped to 70th place among the world's industrialized nations by the 1980s. Prime Minister Lubomír Štrougal embraced the institute's recommendations on necessary economic and political reforms, but in mid-October, KSČ chief Jakeš and his conservative colleagues moved against Štrougal and others who seemed sympathetic to changes in the system. Ladislav Adamec, a longtime KSČ apparatchik and recent Czech prime minister, replaced Štrougal as prime minister of Czechoslovakia after Štrougal had served in that post for 18 years.

During the 70th anniversary of the founding of Czechoslovakia on October 28, 10,000 people gathered on Wenceslas Square in an unofficial demonstration held in spite of open warnings by the government, which had finally reinstated the anniversary as a public holiday. In anticipation of the demonstration, the authorities detained well-known members of Charter 77 and the student-run Independent Peace Association, after the latter had played a very visible role in the August demonstration. During the October gathering, members of the crowd chanted Masaryk's name and "Freedom! Freedom!" before the police moved in with tear gas, water cannons, and clubs, taking into custody a number of demonstrators and bystanders.

The final major demonstration of 1988 occurred on December 10, as a crowd of 5,000 gathered in Prague to celebrate Human Rights Day. A state visit by French president François Mitterand may have inspired the government to grant official permission for the gathering, but tensions escalated due to the participation of Charter 77 and VONS, the appearance of Václav Havel on the podium, and the circulation of leaflets and a petition calling for freedom for political prisoners of the regime. Under orders from Prague's KSČ chief, Miroslav Štěpán, the police once again responded with force, spraying the crowd with water cannons in spite of the cold winter weather.

ENDGAME, 1989

With resistance to reforms obstructing efforts to revive the economy, conditions continued to worsen. By August 1989, the state planning office increased the official number of unprofitable enterprises to 30 percent of the country's total as unofficial environmental groups continued to warn of the ecological damage caused by industrial and power-generating operations, especially in the pollution-ridden areas of northern Bohemia where declining life expectancy and high rates of infant mortality had reached crisis levels.

As the 20th anniversary of Jan Palach's self-immolation approached in mid-January, 1989, the government issued a ban on all demonstrations in an attempt to dissuade students and others from engaging in opposition political activities during Palach Week under the guise of commemorating the student leader's sacrifice. On January 15, organized demonstrations occurred around Prague as opposition leaders chose to take to the streets the day before the actual anniversary in order to draw attention to Czechoslovakia's participation in the signing of a document on human rights at the CSCE conference in Vienna that very day. In their now-customary response, the police attacked the demonstrators and arrested leading activists in an attempted crackdown on dissenters. As a result of his participation in these activities, Havel received a nine-month prison sentence, although poor health would lead to his early release in May.

Developments in neighboring Poland and Hungary served as both a warning to the Husák-Jakeš regime and a source of encouragement for the growing opposition in Czechoslovakia. In Hungary, the removal of János Kádár as party head in May 1988 served as a prelude to the transition to a market economy and the introduction of legislation in January 1989 to allow for pluralism in Hungarian politics. When elections concluded in August, the Hungarian Democratic Forum emerged victorious and participated in the dismantling of the Communist regime in that country.

Nationwide strikes in Poland during August 1988 forced the government to hold the "Roundtable Talks" with Lech Wałęsa and other Solidarity representatives beginning in February 1989. The negotiations resulted in constitutional changes to establish both a presidency and a Senate, with the former weakening the authority of the Communist Party's general secretary. The results of the June 1989 elections gave Solidarity 99 percent of the seats in the new Senate, and although 35 percent of the seats in the lower house, or Sejm, had been guaranteed to the Communists, they received little electoral support as some Communist candidates running unopposed suffered defeat at the hands of write-in Solidarity candidates. The Communists installed Gen. Wojciech Jaruzelski as president of the new government, but in August, a stalemate led Jaruzelski to appoint Solidarity's Tadeusz Mazowiecki to serve as the first noncommunist prime minister in four decades.

During the opening days of June 1989, the Chinese government used extensive military force to crush the student-led pro-reform demonstrations in Beijing's Tiananmen Square, an act of suppression to which KSČ chief Husák gave his open and public support. That same month, Havel and other opposition leaders circulated the "Just a Few Sentences" manifesto, which denounced the Czechoslovak government's heavy-handed and often violent tactics in dealing with dissent at a time when the regime offered only hypocritical and empty support for human rights and Gorbachev-style reforms. The document, which gained 40,000 signatures over the next three months, demanded immediate steps toward democratization; the release of political prisoners; the elimination of censorship and restrictions on freedom of expression, assembly, and religion; reassessment of the Prague Spring; and greater attention to environmental problems. Noting that "civil society is shaking itself out of its lethargy," the manifesto warned that the movement toward greater public activism "is coming onto a progressively more dangerous collision course with the inertia of power; social tension is growing and has threatened to start an open crisis, which none of us wants."[1]

Czechoslovak dissidents received encouragement from a Polish Solidarity delegation in July, when members of Parliament and former dissidents Adam Michnik, Jacek Kuroń, and Zbigniew Bujak arrived in Prague and met with Havel and other leaders of the opposition. The secret police filmed the sessions, but otherwise took no action as the official press complained about the presence of the Solidarity delegation. On August 11, the Polish Senate repudiated the Warsaw Pact invasion of August 1968 and apologized to the citizens of Czechoslovakia for the participation of Polish military forces in the intervention.

When the anniversary of the invasion arrived on August 20, the Czechoslovak government deployed some 13,000 troops and 155 tanks alongside riot police in an effort to contain and control any possible demonstrations. After demonstrations were underway in Prague and other cities, the regime responded with the usual force and repressive measures. In Bratislava, Charter 77 members Ján Čarnogurský, Miroslav Kusý, and fellow dissidents attempted to lay flowers in remembrance of a teenaged girl killed by Soviet troops during the invasion in 1968, but arrests ensued as the government moved against the protesters.

By September and into October, events elsewhere contributed to the pressure building against the Husák-Jakeš regime to move forward with reforms in line with Gorbachev's *glasnost* and *perestoika*. With Erich Honecker and other leaders of the German Democratic Republic also opposed to altering the existing communist system and warning of a Tiananmen-style solution, large numbers of East German citizens began leaving for neighboring Czechoslovakia and Hungary. Those who exited their homeland by car or by train claimed to be going on vacation, but the true goal was asylum in Austria or democratic West Germany. The Hungarian government, which had already begun dismantling the barbed wire and fortifications at the frontier in the spring, formally announced the opening of the border with Austria on September 10. Over the next several days, some 10,000 East Germans chose to follow the 50,000 fellow citizens who had already departed in a legal emigration. The flood of refugees continued through October as East Germans abandoned Trabants and other vehicles in the streets of Prague, and more than 11,000 camped out on the grounds of the West German embassy awaiting the official granting of asylum.

As a result of the demonstrations and growing discontent, Gorbachev warned the East German leadership that failure to address public concerns could very well jeopardize the continued existence of the regime. On October 18, the Socialist Unity Party (SED) pressured Honecker into resigning as general secretary and replaced him with Egon Krenz. When the East German government announced an opening of the border with West Germany and West Berlin on November 9, a misunderstanding in a press briefing allowed over four million East German citizens to cross into West Germany over the next two days. With the Berlin Wall now irrelevant, authorities stood by as citizens of both East and West Berlin danced atop the Wall and tore down sections of the structure over the next several weeks. In December, the SED forfeited its leading role in politics and society, leading to the dismantling of the police state and a transition to democracy as an essential step toward the reunification of the Two Germanies in October 1990.

With communist regimes falling in Poland, Hungary, and East Germany, the KSČ regime in Czechoslovakia found itself increasingly isolated in the region and facing growing opposition from students, intellectuals, and various unofficial organizations calling for democratization, the protection of human rights, and greater attention to environmental issues. In mid-October, Democratic Initiative applied for official status as the first independent party in Czechoslovakia since the communist coup in February 1948. Later in the month, on October 25, Václav

Neumann and the Czech Philharmonic Orchestra joined journalists in boycotting state-run television in retaliation for the ongoing harassment of those who had signed the "A Few Sentences" petition since June. Three days later, crowds again gathered in celebration of the country's independence, although the public demonstrations seemed less urgent than the previous year as a result of the hope inspired by the progress of reform elsewhere.

THE VELVET REVOLUTION

The event that triggered Czechoslovakia's Velvet Revolution occurred in Prague on Friday, November 17, 1989, as students assembled in the streets of the capital to commemorate the 50th anniversary of Jan Opletal's funeral and the closing of Czech universities by the Nazis. Organized by a partnership of official and independent student organizations, the memorial march drew a much larger crowd than expected as 15,000 arrived at the start of the event, which opened with speakers calling for the implementation of reforms. The marchers then proceeded from the student residences to Vyšehrad for a ceremony at the grave of 19th-century poet Karel Hynek Mácha before moving on toward Wenceslas Square. Students carried banners as well as flowers and candles, with many shaking their keys at the police who had imprisoned so many fellow students and dissidents.

By the time the procession reached Národni třída (National Avenue) and turned toward Wenceslas Square, the number of marchers swelled to some 55,000 people singing the Czech national anthem and demanding democratic reforms. A young member of the state security office (StB) posing as a student leader, "Ruzicka," helped to divert the front ranks of the remaining 5,000 marchers into what turned out to be an ambush by police and units of the antiterrorist "Red Beret" group. After a tense and lengthy delay in which demonstrators were prevented from either moving forward or returning to the Vltava embankment, the security forces attacked the students, beating hundreds and arresting many of the marchers, in spite of the students displaying their empty hands in a gesture of nonviolence. "Ruzicka" apparently pretended to be a victim of the violence, and the StB spread rumors that a student, "Martin Šmíd," had died in an effort to blame the demonstrators for the consequences of their actions.

The assault by security forces on a peaceful student demonstration set off a wave of public anger directed at the government as opposition leaders held meetings and talk of nationwide strikes spread rapidly. On November 18, students engaged in their own strike, seizing university buildings and calling upon the citizens of Czechoslovakia to participate in a general strike on November 27. The theater community in Prague refused to stage performances, instead opening theaters to students and collaborating in discussions and planning sessions as other actors began arriving from outside of Prague. In Slovakia, students expressed their solidarity with their Czech comrades by occupying universities and making similar demands.

The government responded by attempting to portray the students as irresponsible and indolent, but public support for the students continued to grow as parents began to question how the authorities could use brute force against the young. With Soviet leaders opposed to Tiananmen-style tactics of violence, the Husák-Jakeš regime determined that accepting the offer of top military officials to engage the armed forces against the opposition did not represent a viable solution in light of the bloodshed and casualties such action would cause.

Meeting at the Činoherní Klub (Drama Club) on November 19, representatives of Charter 77, VONS, and Democratic Initiative gathered with intellectuals, artists, writers, former KSČ members of the *Obroda* (Revival) pro-reform group, independent members of the Socialist and People's parties, leaders of the Independent Students' Union, and various others to found Civic Forum (*Obcanské Fórum*), a broad coalition of opposition groups and organizations calling for the removal of Husák, Jakeš, Štěpán, and others responsible for the attack on the students two days earlier. Present at the meeting were Václav Havel, Jiří Dienstbier, Václav Klaus, and fellow dissidents destined to play significant roles as events unfolded in Czechoslovakia. After the initial sessions, Civic Forum set up a base of operations at *Laterna magica*, the Magic Lantern Theatre, in central Prague.[2] One day after the founding of Civic Forum, actor Milan Kňažko, dissident Ján Budaj, sociologist Fedor Gál, and a similar collection of opposition figures met in an art gallery in Bratislava to establish the Public Against Violence (VPN) group as a Slovak ally of Civic Forum in defense of civil society.

In Prague, a crowd of 20,000 assembled on November 19 to call for the resignation of Jakeš as head of the KSČ, but without any direct response by the security forces. The following day the number of demonstrators on Wenceslas Square swelled to 200,000, including many university and high school students, as demands for resignations, political pluralism, and an end to censorship grew in intensity. Similar demonstrations occurred in Bratislava, Brno, and other cities, while representatives of Civic Forum and Public Against Violence visited schools, factories, and a range of institutions in order to garner support for a nationwide strike. Students contributed to the efforts nationwide by spreading videotaped footage of the attack on fellow students by the security forces on November 17.

On Tuesday, November 21, Civic Forum and Public Against Violence opened direct communication in order to coordinate activities across the country. On Wenceslas Square, 200,000 people listened to Václav Havel speak from the balcony of the Melantrich building, which housed the Socialist Party newspaper *Svobodné Slovo* (Word of Freedom). Havel warned the regime that a general strike loomed on November 27 unless officials opened an investigation of the events of November 17 and met demands for the release of political prisoners and the institution of civil liberties such as freedom of the press. During the demonstration, chants of "Dubček to the Castle!" rose from the crowd in recognition of the leader who had sought to develop "socialism with a human face" during the Prague Spring. However, the crowds also displayed great respect for Havel, who had emerged as a modest and sympathetic national figure as a result of his activities on behalf of human rights and the periods of imprisonment stemming from those actions.

In April, Dubček had participated in a long interview with journalist András Sugár for Hungarian television in which he defended the reformist policies of the Prague Spring and condemned the military intervention by Czechoslovakia's Warsaw Pact allies. On November 22, Dubček spoke to a public gathering for the first time since 1969 when he addressed a very receptive crowd of nearly 100,000 in Bratislava. Afterwards, Dubček departed for Prague by bus to speak with Havel and the other leaders of Civic Forum.

As the opposition leaders gathered, students traveled to factories to engage workers in support of the planned strike on November 27, offering to take their places so that the workers could join in the massive work stoppage. The following day, 10,000 workers from the ČKD enterprise in Prague participated in another large demonstration as one of their number, Petr Miller, accepted an invitation to serve as a workers' representative among the leaders of Civic Forum. A demonstration in Bratislava that day drew tens of thousands in protest against government policies.

Dubček and Havel appeared together on the balcony on Wenceslas Square on November 24 and were greeted with tremendous enthusiasm by the 200,000 present as Dubček made his first public address in Prague since his departure from politics two decades earlier. Prior to the speeches, music provided a bridge across those 20 years as Marta Kubišová, a member of Charter 77 and very popular singer who had been banned from public performances since 1970, sang Bob Dylan's "The Times They Are A–Changin.' "

On the night of the November 24, the Central Committee of the Communist Party of Czechoslovakia decided to replace Miloš Jakeš as general secretary and to appoint the hard-liner Karel Urbánek in his place. This led to the mass resignation of Jakeš and the entire party presidium on November 25 as the younger Urbánek, long a supporter of "normalization," assumed leadership of the KSČ. However, the shuffling of personnel in the highest ranks of the party did not deceive the public into believing that reforms were forthcoming. Instead, tens of thousands of people from across the country attended František Cardinal Tomášek's televised mass in celebration of the canonization of Blessed Agnes of Bohemia. Later in the day, some three-quarters of a million people gathered on Letna Plain in Prague to hear speeches by Dubček and Havel calling for genuine changes in leadership. In Bratislava, half a million people assembled for a protest demonstration at the Square of the Slovak National Uprising. By the end of the day, Urbánek proclaimed the government's willingness to open negotiations as Prague party chief Miroslav Štěpán and some of the remaining hard-liners submitted their resignations.

Civic Forum decided to begin discussions with the federal government, rather than the KSČ, so Havel and representatives of Civic Forum met with Prime Minister Adamec in Prague's City Hall on the November 26. After both sides agreed to further negotiations, Adamec addressed the crowd of half a million massed on Letná Plain and promised that the government would respond to public demands to the best of its ability. In Bratislava, Public Against Violence rallied the support of large crowds for the next day's planned general strike and for the list of demands the group had compiled. In Prague, Civic Forum produced its own agenda for negotiations under the title, "What We Want." In addition to political pluralism, civil liberties, social justice, sound environmental policies, and an independent judiciary, Civic Forum called for the introduction of a market-oriented economy and a reorientation of the country's foreign policy away from the Warsaw Pact and Comecon so that Czechoslovakia could rejoin the community of European nations.

At noon on November 27, the two-hour general strike brought the entire country to a standstill in a display of public solidarity that convinced the government that the only option remaining was to agree to the demands submitted by the opposition. Officials estimated that nearly 80 percent of the population participated in the strike, which contributed to the major fissures in the party and government as the party's newspaper, *Rudé Právo*, criticized the pace of reforms and some of the younger proponents of change within the party distanced themselves from the KSČ by forming their own organization, the Democratic Forum of Communists.

Adamec met with Civic Forum on November 28 and offered to have a commission to look into the events of November 17, but the opposition had little faith in the prime minister's promise to eliminate the KSČ's leading role in government and society by the following day and to appoint a new coalition government by December 3. Urbánek then informed the KSČ's Central Committee that the party's monopoly on political life had become untenable and, in consequence, the Federal Assembly took action on the November 29 to eliminate the constitutional guarantee of the leading role of the Communists, thereby opening the way to a pluralist political system.

On November 30, Civic Forum held the first direct negotiations with representatives of the KSČ's Central Committee under Vasil Mohorita as the government announced plans to eliminate the fence separating Czechoslovakia from neighboring Austria. Simultaneously, in Bratislava, Public Against Violence engaged in discussions with the government of the Slovak republic in an effort to force resignations and reforms similar to those occurring on the federal level.

On the first day of December, Mohorita and the Central Committee declared the Warsaw Pact invasion of August 1968 to be a mistake, a stance supported by Gorbachev's declaration that the Prague Spring represented the desire of the people of Czechoslovakia for a more democratic system. Three days later, the Soviet Union and other members of the Warsaw Pact chose a conference attended by Adamec and Urbánek to offer a joint denunciation of the invasion as an illegal act.

The announcement of Adamec's new provisional government on December 3 met with criticism from Civic Forum and Public Against Violence due to the appointment of communists to 15 of the 20 ministerial posts in the Cabinet and the refusal of Husák to resign from the presidency. The opposition leaders called for further public demonstrations and threatened another general strike on December 11. The following day, hundreds of thousands staged antigovernment protests in Wenceslas Square as Civic Forum demanded the scheduling of open elections for June and the immediate establishment of a government with greater representation for the opposition.

After two days of negotiations with Civic Forum, Public Against Violence, *Obroda*, and representatives of the noncommunist parties, Adamec and his ministers chose to resign on December 7, rather than accept the changes demanded by the opposition. When the commission investigating the events of November 17 recommended that Jakeš and Štěpán be removed from the Federal Assembly, the KSČ moved against the pair by expelling them for errors in political judgment and in light of their remaining a serious liability. Deputy prime minister Marián Čalfa replaced Adamec as prime minister and then met with the opposition the next day to discuss constitutional procedures for creating a new federal government.

The celebration of International Human Rights Day on December 10 coincided with the resignation of Husák and the installation of a new "Government of National Understanding," in which the communists, with 10 of 21 posts, held minority status for the first time since 1948. With responsibility for governing Czechoslovakia until the elections, the provisional government included two ministers each from the Socialist Party and the People's Party and seven from Civic Forum, but none from Public Against Violence.

During the negotiations, both sides had agreed to the election of a new and noncommunist president by the end of January, although Čalfa would occupy that position until the elections. Leading candidates included Adamec and Dubček, and although Havel expressed reservations about succeeding Husák, the chants of "Havel to the Castle!" at public rallies served as evidence of his extensive and growing popularity. In order to avoid creating friction between Czechs and Slovaks, Dubček and Havel agreed that Havel would serve as the primary candidate of the opposition, with Dubček offering support and cooperation as a political ally.

Speaking before the Federal Assembly on December 19, Prime Minister Čalfa declared that efforts to reform the ailing command economy would cease and that the government would instead begin the transition to a market-oriented economy. Čalfa also announced plans to disband the StB and promoted Havel's candidacy for president as the most sensible option for the future.

On December 20, the Communist Party of Czechoslovakia held a congress at which the party announced support for a multiparty political system and apologized for its role in the events that occurred after the crushing of the Prague Spring. The KSČ proposed the democratization of party organs and the elimination of the position of general secretary in favor of the new positions of party chairman, to be held by Adamec, and first secretary, with Mohorita chosen to fill that post.

By agreement, deputies targeted by the opposition submitted their resignations on December 28, allowing for a reconstituted Federal Assembly that included deputies from the opposition groups. The new assembly chose Alexander Dubček as chairman and, on the following day, elected Václav Havel president of the Czechoslovak republic by the unanimous vote of 323 parliamentary deputies.

František Cardinal Tomášek marked the occasion with a special mass as crowds celebrated outside Prague Castle. The new government included dissidents and reformers in leading positions with Havel as president, Dubček as parliamentary chair, and Václav Klaus as finance minister. In January, Prime Minister Čalfa left the Communist Party and aligned himself with Public Against Violence in Slovakia.

The nonviolent Velvet Revolution began with outrage over the beating of students on November and concluded with the collapse of the communist regime during the holiday season at the end of the following month. The term "Velvet Revolution" apparently originated with Western journalists covering events on Czechoslovakia before it was adopted by Havel and his fellow opposition leaders. However, whereas four decades of communist control ended with a negotiated transition in Hungary and Poland, the emergence of democracy occurred quickly in Czechoslovakia and required that leaders of Civic Forum, Public Against Violence and other opposition groups begin managing the country's affairs immediately.[3] To do so, the new government would need to confront the consequences of the Soviet-inspired KSČ regime, which Václav Havel defined in a speech to the U.S. Congress in February 1990 as "a legacy of countless dead, an infinite spectrum of human suffering, profound economic decline, and above all human humiliation."[4]

THE POSTCOMMUNIST ERA, 1990–1992

In his New Year's presidential address to the nation, Havel spoke of the difficult task that lay ahead in rebuilding democracy in a Czechoslovakia where four decades of communism had allowed corruption, apathy, and cynicism to poison society and undermine morality and trust. Havel invoked the name of the country's founder, Tomáš Garrigue Masaryk, and praised his expectations of high moral standards in politics. Charismatic and highly respected himself, Havel valued idealism, morality, and democracy in much the same way as Masaryk, and he consciously chose to emulate Masaryk as leader of the nation. However, Havel also had his creative and unorthodox side as president and could occasionally be found negotiating the hallways of Prague Castle dressed in jeans and a sweater and riding a scooter. In an effort to make Prague Castle less intimidating, Havel selected Theodor Pistek, the costume designer for the film *Amadeus*, to replace the old khaki military-style attire of the Castle Guards with blue, white, and red uniforms with tassels.[5]

The transition to a democratic system proceeded during January 1990 as legislation enacted by the Federal Assembly on January 23 established a free, pluralist political system allowing full participation by the KSČ and former partners in the National Front. A week later, the political composition of the parliament changed as 122 of the 242 communist deputies resigned or were replaced by independents or members of Civic Forum and Public Against Violence. Further parliamentary legislation restored civil liberties and eliminated censorship, limits on travel abroad, and the death penalty,

In collaboration with Foreign Minister Jiří Dienstbier, Havel sought to restore Czechoslovakia to the community of European nations in a manner similar to Beneš's efforts to have the country serve as a bridge between East and West. Havel wanted to reestablish positive connections with the rest of the world, and to that end he traveled to Poland, Hungary, and the two Germanies in January before visiting Washington, D.C., and Moscow the following month. On February 26, Czechoslovakia and the Soviet Union signed an agreement on the withdrawal of the Soviet military from Czechoslovakia, initiating a process that would continue until June 27, 1991. In June 1990, members of the Warsaw Pact agreed at a meeting in Moscow that the military alliance no longer served a common purpose and would therefore be dissolved with collective security becoming the responsibility of the Organization of Security and Cooperation in Europe (OSCE).

Czechoslovakia welcomed noteworthy foreign visitors in 1990 as the Dalai Lama, Tenzin Gyatso, arrived at the beginning of February, and Pope John Paul II toured the lands of the Czech republic in late April. In mid-November, George H. W. Bush arrived in Prague as the first American president to visit the city. Writers and actors such as Harold Pinter, Philip Roth, and Jane Fonda were among the many foreign celebrities who visited and contributed to Prague's emerging reputation as a cultural wonderland and a new mecca for tourists. When musician Lou Reed of the Velvet Underground arrived to interview Havel for a music magazine, Havel showed him formerly banned copies of Reed's lyrics in Czech and invited him to join the Plastic People of the Universe in playing songs by the Velvets that they had performed during the repressive years of the 1970s and 1980s.[6]

On the darker side, the collapse of communism brought a rise in the crime rate, which many blamed on Havel after his declaration of amnesty for 2,500 prisoners regardless of whether or not their crimes had been political in nature. Since the communists had done little to integrate the Roma into national life, they frequently took the blame for increased criminal activity and became the victims of racism and violence, especially as skinheads and racist groups took advantage of the new freedom to espouse extremist views and to attack students and workers from the Asian and African communities.

In April, Prague state prosecutor Tomáš Sokol attempted to take legal action against the KSČ in an effort to have the party banned and therefore removed from the political landscape. Many citizens supported official action against the Communist Party, and those participating in a strike on April 11 demanded that property belonging to the KSČ be seized by the new government. Controversy grew as former opposition figures counseled against retaliation by arguing, like Havel and Jan Urban, that all citizens had collaborated with the former regime in some fashion. Interior Minister Richard Sacher chose to allow members of the former StB to retain their positions in the security apparatus and then caused a further outcry when he announced that over 10,000 confidential secret police dossiers had either been destroyed or had gone missing during the revolution. For those who had demanded exposure of state security officials and informants prior to the June elections, the loss of the files proved a major setback.

Approximately 96 percent of eligible voters participated in the elections of June 1990, in which Civic Forum and Public Against Violence earned 47 percent of the vote and 170 of the 300 seats in the Federal Assembly. Civic Forum registered 53.2 percent of the vote in the Czech republic and Public Against Violence 32.5 percent in Slovakia as the latter could count recognized opposition figures such as Dubček, Budaj, Kňažko, Kusý, and Šimecka in its ranks. Election results allowed Public Against Violence to choose Vladimír Mečiar as prime minister of the Slovak republic.

Led by Vasil Mohorita, the Communist Party retained a voice in political affairs at the federal level, earning 47 seats in an electoral showing stronger than many expected. The Christian Democrats (a coalition of the People's Party, Christian Democratic Party, and Slovak Christian Democratic Movement) earned 40 seats, and a regional party representing the interests of Moravia and Silesia registered a modest showing with 7.89 percent of the vote in the Czech republic.

In July, the Federal Assembly reelected Václav Havel president with Marián Čalfa, now of Public Against Violence, continuing as federal prime minister in opposition to the wishes of Civic Forum. Vladimír Mečiar presided over the Slovak government and former dissident Petr Pithart the Czech cabinet.

Relations between Czechs and Slovaks began to deteriorate in 1990, and the friction continued to build over the following two years. Slovaks once again voiced claims of exploitation by the Czechs and a general lack of concern for social and economic conditions in Slovakia. As evidence, they pointed to Foreign Minister Dienstbier's declaration in January that Czechoslovakia would no longer act as an arms dealer to the world. Given the importance of armaments production to the Slovak economy, the consequences of such a policy would have a negative impact on Slovak productivity and employment.

Over the early months of 1990, proposals to return the country's name to the "Czechoslovak Republic" drew the ire of Slovak nationalists, who criticized Havel, Civic Forum, and Public Against Violence for once again placing Slovaks in a secondary position. To avoid an escalation of tensions and to prevent an increase in calls for Slovak independence, the federal government altered the name to "Czechoslovak Federal Republic" to reflect the existence of the two republics within the country's borders. When this failed to placate Slovak critics demanding the use of the hyphenated term "Czecho-Slovak," authorities attempted to end the "hyphen war" by adopting the name, "Czech and Slovak Federative Republic," on April 19 and shifting greater authority and decision-making responsibilities to the governments of the two republics.

By December, the country drifted toward a constitutional crisis as disagreements over sections of the planned constitution drove some Slovak parliamentarians to threaten the application of Slovak laws in place of federal statutes. Havel denounced the negative consequences of nationalist agendas and requested that the Federal Assembly establish a constitutional court and grant the president expanded powers to cope with the destabilizing crisis.

During the fall of 1990, Czech and Slovak political parties and organizations began to change in response to the new political environment or as a result of internal frictions or diverging agendas. In November, the Communist Party of Czechoslovakia became the Communist Party of Bohemia and Moravia in the Czech Republic and the Party of the Democratic Left in Slovakia, with the latter developing along the lines of left-wing parties found elsewhere in Europe.

For Civic Form and Public Against Violence, however, the coalition nature of the organizations and the lack of political experience led to divisions and the emergence of new political parties reflecting the different political programs of coalition members. At the congress of Civic Forum in October, members elected Finance Minister Václav Klaus party chairman. Klaus, whose views as an economist reflected the free-market influence of Friedrich von Hayek, called for the creation of an organized party structure and an active pursuit of political goals, but concerns over a possible turn to the right by the party led some left-leaning party members to begin drifting away.

By February 1991, Civic Forum had split into two factions, the Klaus-led Civic Democrats (ODS) and the Civic Movement (OH) under Deputy Prime Minister Jiří Dienstbier. Most of the government ministers aligned themselves with the left-of-center Civic Movement. A third group, the Civic Democratic Alliance (ODA), arose over differences with the OH, although all three organizations continued to work together in the government until 1992.

The transformation of the communist-era economy also proceeded during 1990 as the government moved to dismantle the old centralized command system in favor of a full market-oriented economy. The process began with drastic reductions in state support and the devaluation of the koruna in January. Then in November, the Federal Assembly provided for the widespread privatization of state enterprises as well as new systems of taxation and organized capital. While many warned that too rapid a transition to a market economy could lead to serious economic disruptions, lost savings, and extensive social dislocation, Klaus favored an expeditious series of changes that would create hardships in the short term but lead to stability much sooner than a cautious approach that simply spread out the hardships over a longer period of time. One of the earliest major shocks came with the liberalization of prices on January 1, 1991, and the consequences of rapid price increases that drastically outpaced any changes in wages.

Restitution of property seized from private owners after February 1948 represented one approach to denationalizing property held by the state. Previous owners or their heirs submitted requests for restitution of farmland, apartments, and other property, which then became subject to negotiated settlements. However, as the large-scale transfer of property to private hands moved forward, authorities received criticism at home and abroad for choosing 1948 as the target date, thereby excluding Jewish property seized by the Germans or German property lost during the postwar expulsions.

The government's plan for privatizing small-scale and larger state-owned enterprises involved consecutive phases with restaurants, shops, and other small businesses to be transferred to private ownership in the first phase beginning in January 1991, and larger enterprises made available to citizen shareholders in later waves. By the time the auctioning of shops and restaurants drew to a close at the end of 1993, over 22,000 new businesses had been established in the country. The government also looked to foreign investors to purchase formerly state-held industrial enterprises, as when Volkswagen purchased Škoda Auto in 1991.

The mechanism by which private interests could buy shares in the larger enterprises was the voucher, which citizens could register for a fee of 1,035 korunas, an amount equal to just under half the average worker's monthly salary. The voucher could be used to purchase shares in enterprises when they came up for auction, or they could be used in consultation with investment experts or funds. The initial registration period for vouchers began on November 1, 1991, with 6.5 million Czechs and 2.5 million Slovaks participating. At the beginning of May 1992, those who possessed vouchers became eligible to invest in available enterprises or to negotiate with investment funds. The process of voucher privatization required five rounds and several years before nearly 2,500 enterprises became available to the public, although many citizens became victims of unreasonable expectations of immediate wealth or of unscrupulous investors and others who purchased the vouchers from their owners at an unfair price. The liquidation of inefficient enterprises led to an immediate 35 percent drop in Czechoslovak industrial production as a consequence of the privatization process. In the midst of the economic transition, Czechoslovakia also ended participation in Comecon and decided to rejoin the International Monetary Fund and the World Bank, from which the communist regime had withdrawn the country in 1954.

As Czechoslovakia embarked upon the new postcommunist course, Havel, Dienstbier, and other leaders continued to reevaluate and redirect the country's relations with Europe and the world. On a regional level, Havel took the first steps toward reconciliation with the Germans on Christmas 1989 when he addressed a letter to President Richard von Weizsäcker of West Germany apologizing for the postwar expulsion of the Germans. Although Havel's action generated a negative response among the citizens of Czechoslovakia, Weizsäcker responded with a similar gesture when he visited Prague in March 1990, 51 years after Nazi Germany occupied Czechoslovakia. After a long period of negotiations, the neighboring countries agreed to a treaty of friendship and cooperation signed by Havel and Chancellor Helmut Kohl of a reunified Germany on February 27, 1992.

On February 12, 1991, Havel met with President Lech Wałęsa of Poland and Prime Minister Jozef Antall of Hungary in the Hungarian town of Visegrád to discuss matters of common regional interest. Key to the agenda of the "Visegrád Troika" was a signed agreement on cooperation in eliminating the Warsaw Pact and facilitating membership in an expanded European Union. The latter represented a priority for Havel because of his desire to return Czechoslovakia to the European fold as quickly as possible. To that end, Czechoslovakia became a member of the Council of Europe in February 1991 and then signed a declaration of cooperation with the Organization for Economic Co-operation and Development (OECD) in June and an association agreement with the European Union in December.

Havel altered his initial thinking on collective security in favor of pursuing Czechoslovakia's participation in the NATO alliance. On March 21, 1991, the president delivered an address before the NATO Council of Ministers in Brussels in which he spoke of the need for security and the benefits of associate membership as Europe proceeded down the complicated path toward becoming a stable community of independent, democratic, and peaceful nations. The country's membership in the Warsaw Pact drew to a close in 1991 after Czechoslovakia joined Poland and Hungary in announcing in January that their support for the military alliance would end on July 1, as it did with the formal dismantling of the alliance during a meeting in Prague on that date.

By the end of June 1991, the Soviet Union barely met the agreed-upon deadline for the withdrawal of Soviet troops from Czechoslovakia. In an environment of restored freedoms, Czech artist David Černý stirred up controversy by celebrating the Soviet withdrawal with a coat of pink paint applied to a tank serving as a war memorial to Soviet troops who lost their lives in the liberation of Prague at the end of World War II. Černý, who would go on to design controversial sculptures at home and abroad, claimed that the "pink tank" in Prague's Kinský Square represented a statement of protest against the Soviet-style dictatorship that arose after the war.

Another confrontation with the recent past occurred in October 1991 when the Federal Assembly passed a controversial decommunization measure, the Lustration Law, banning former officials of the Communist Party, members of the People's Militia, members of the state security agency, and suspected collaborators from performing a wide range of government, military, economic, academic, and media functions for a period of five years ending on January 30, 1996. In spite of Havel's opposition to the law, the Assembly later extended the ban to the year 2000. The law, which allowed for the use of files assembled by the former secret police, the StB, eventually targeted tens of thousands of Czech and Slovak citizens in a process opposed by many foreign and domestic critics as a violation of human rights and an application of the principle of guilt by association. However, since the law allowed for legal appeal, many of those who fell victim to the ban were eventually able to clear their names or to sue the Ministry of the Interior for slander.

In terms of relations between the Czechs and Slovaks, internal politics contributed to growing tensions during 1991 and 1992. As Slovaks increasingly embraced the idea of confederation, Czechs continued to believe that federation, even with greater authority for the republics, remained the country's best option for the future. Havel attempted to preserve the federal system by holding talks with representatives of the federal government and the two republics in early 1991, but the negotiations generated few tangible results.

Slovak prime minister Vladimír Mečiar parted ways with Public Against Violence in early March over disagreements with party leaders regarding Mečiar's political agenda and allegedly dictatorial tactics. On April 23, the Presidium of the Slovak National Council then removed Mečiar as prime minister and replaced him with Ján Čarnogurský of the Christian Democratic Movement on the basis of allegations of political improprieties. Within several days, Public Against Violence fragmented into two parties, which later developed into Mečiar's Movement for a Democratic Slovakia (HZDS) and the Civic Democratic Union–Public Against Violence (ODÚ-VPN), as the party was christened in October before eventually dropping the Public Against Violence name and shifting to the political right. As the latter party's fortunes fell, however, Mečiar and his nationalist-populist approach continued to develop a strong public following as shown by the large demonstration of support held in Bratislava on April 26.

On July 8, the Federal Assembly passed legislation allowing the dissolution of the federal system in Czechoslovakia only on condition of a referendum in which the majority of the citizens in the two republics voted to eliminate the common state. When Havel paid an official visit to Bratislava on the October 28 anniversary of the founding of Czechoslovakia, pro-independence Slovak nationalists responded to his presence by throwing eggs and shouting political slogans at the president. The majority of Slovak politicians denounced the actions of the nationalists, but the failure of the post-1989 federal government to grant top priority to relations between the Czech and Slovak republics proved a critical factor in the breakdown of those relations. Part of the problem was the delay in drafting the constitution, which led to an agreement to postpone the process until after the scheduled elections in 1992. With pressure building, Havel announced in a televised speech on November 11 that in order to prevent a national crisis, he would request legal and constitutional changes to his presidential powers that would allow him to schedule a referendum without the consent of the Federal Assembly and to govern by decree in the case of a national emergency.

TOWARD A "VELVET DIVORCE"

With national elections scheduled for the beginning of June 1992, Slovak politicians capitalized on nationalist sentiments and the growing frustration over economic conditions and an 11 percent unemployment rate well above the Czech rate of 4 percent. Although only the right-wing Slovak Nationalist Party openly demanded independence, Mečiar and the HZDS sought to mobilize discontent in pursuit of electoral victory with a combination of nationalist rhetoric, calls for confederation, populist appeals, and left-wing opposition to Klaus's economic reforms and rapid privatization. The result was a victory for the HZDS, with 37 percent of the vote in Slovakia and the appointment of Mečiar as Slovak prime minister.

In the Czech lands, the center-right coalition of Civic Democrats and Christian Democrats emerged with 30 percent of the vote and with Václav Klaus of the Civic Democrats the primary candidate to serve as prime minister of Czechoslovakia. As architect of the country's economic transformation, Klaus believed strongly in the preservation of a federal state, preferring the creation of two independent countries to any agreement on confederation. For Klaus, Slovakia represented a drain on the economy due to the old reliance on now-inefficient heavy industry and the traditional allocation of social welfare funds. As a result, the loss of Slovakia would provide a major boost to the Czech economy, already abetted by foreign investments channeled through Prague.

On June 7, Havel named Klaus as the federal prime minister and asked him to form a government based on the results of the election. Klaus turned down the offer in order to serve as prime minister of the Czech republic instead. As head of the Czech government, Klaus opened negotiations with Mečiar on the future of the country as the two leaders met in Bratislava to discuss options for the future. Neither leader initially sought to dissolve the common state, but when Mečiar began to press for greater autonomy for Slovakia, he was unprepared for Klaus's willingness to divide the country rather than accept Slovak demands. As a result of the conflicting viewpoints, the decisions made on June 20 only resulted in agreement on a reduced federal government, shortly thereafter to be led by Jan Stráský of the Civic Democrats.

When Václav Havel stood for reelection as president on July 3, Slovak deputies in the Federal Assembly blocked efforts to return Havel once his term ended at the close of the year. Havel was resolved to finish his term as president, although he was aware that his efforts to preserve the common state of Czechs and Slovaks were being under-mined elsewhere. Within hours after the Slovak National Council passed a declaration of sovereignty on July 17 by a vote of 113–24, Havel reversed his decision and resigned as president rather than serve as caretaker for a disintegrating federation. One of Havel's final acts before departing was to request that Mečiar and Klaus negotiate the establish-ment of a new federal system.

Six days after the Slovak parliament's declaration of independence, however, Mečiar and Klaus agreed in Bratislava to divide the country and to allow the parliaments of the republics to negotiate the details of the breakup. The lack of common ground in the discussions led to a stalemate and the decision to divide Czechoslovakia without resort-ing to the constitutional requirement of a referendum on the issue. Had that referendum been held, it is likely that voters would have handily rejected the dissolution of Czechoslovakia, given the results of polls taken among Czech and Slovak citizens. A poll taken in 1991 showed that only 9 percent of Czechs and 15 percent of Slovaks favored a division into two separate and independent countries, although the percentage had risen in Slovakia by the summer of 1992.

Meeting in Brno on August 26, representatives of the two govern-ments settled upon December 31 as the date on which the division of the country would take place. Negotiations on a constitutional distri-bution of federal property continued for several weeks, with the Czechs receiving an agreed-upon two-thirds share. On September 1, the Slovak National Council adopted a new constitution, signed two days later in Bratislava Castle. When the Federal Assembly met on November 25 to vote on the dissolution, ratification of the measure succeeded by a vote of 183–117, or only three votes over the required three-fifths majority. The new Czech constitution then made an appearance on November 10 and was adopted on December 16, the day before the Federal Assembly held its final session.

As the Czechs and Slovaks moved toward their parting of the ways, Czechoslovakia lost a respected elder statesman when Alexander Dubček died on November 7 at age 70 as a result of injuries suffered in what many deemed a suspicious automobile accident on the D1 highway two months earlier. In 2000, Slovak police investigators closed the case, ruling that the accident was truly an accident.

On January 1, 1993, the "Velvet Divorce" became a reality as the Czech and Slovak Federative Republic came to an end and the new era of the independent Czech and Slovak republics began. As the Velvet Revolution had ended four decades of communist rule through peaceful public protest, so too had the Velvet Divorce been orchestrated through peaceful and legislative means.[7]

THE CZECH REPUBLIC AFTER 1992

As the Czechs moved forward into a new stage in their history, they did so without their long-term coresidents of the Czech lands, the Germans and the Jews, and their more recent partners, the Slovaks, Hungarians, and Ruthenians. The population of the Czech Republic was now overwhelmingly Czech.

The election of Václav Havel as Czech president on January 26, 1993, restored the playwright and former dissident to a position of leadership, while the center-right coalition of Václav Klaus and the Civic Democrats provided continuity in government for the independent Czech Republic from July 1992 and the final months of the Czechoslovak state through December 1997.

One holdover political organization that failed to survive intact was the Czech Communist Party, which suffered a defection of revisionists in June 1993. The old party retained both the official name and a resistance to abandoning its ideological or historical foundation. In order to appeal to the electorate, the Communist Party of Bohemia and Moravia adopted a program that promoted chauvinistic nationalism and attacked the neoliberal economic policies of the Klaus government. This approach allowed the Communists to attract a steady 10–18 percent of the voters in elections after 1992, although the party's legacy prevented the Communists from serving as a partner in any governing coalition.

As Czech prime minister, Klaus maintained the economic strategy introduced after the Velvet Revolution and based upon the neoliberal, free-market principles he had long embraced in keeping with his stated admiration for the social and economic policies of Margaret Thatcher's Great Britain in the 1980s. Consequently, a second wave of voucher privatization occurred in 1993–1994, involving six million Czech citizens and an available 676 state-owned enterprises. As a result of the voucher initiatives and other measures, the new private sector was producing some 80 percent of the country's GNP by the final months of 1994.

Critics, however, claimed that the focus on economic growth through privatization, investment, and attracting foreign capital created major social problems and ignored the need for reforms establishing and protecting the rule of law. Failure to establish proper rules for financial activities and relationships or to institute government regulation in key areas of the economy contributed to corruption in state banking and accusations of "cowboy capitalism" and exploitation in regard to the voucher program. Government neglect of education, health, and serious environmental issues combined with the failure to address housing shortages in fueling the growing discontent. Klaus responded by preserving much of the social safety net in an apparent contradiction to neoliberal principles and at the expense of long-overdue structural changes to state-owned enterprises. The government could point to low unemployment figures, but the numbers were based less on successful economic strategies than on the delayed consequences of government policies.

The Czech Social Democratic Party (ČSSD) capitalized on the mood of the electorate in the months prior to the scheduled parliamentary elections on May 31–June 1, 1996, which also allowed voters to choose representatives for the new Senate created over Klaus's objections in the fall of 1995. The Social Democrats emerged from the elections as the nation's second-largest party, with 26.4 percent of the vote behind the Civic Democrats with 29.6 percent. The governing coalition's loss of 13 seats in the Chamber of Deputies meant the loss of a majority by two seats and therefore the necessity of bringing another party into the coalition in order to form a new government. With neither the Communists nor the far-right Republicans a viable option, Klaus negotiated with the Social Democrats in order to gain their support for a minority government led by the Civic Democrats. In return, the Social Democrats gained ministerial positions in the government, and the Chamber of Deputies selected ČSSD party leader Miloš Zeman as chairman.

After the elections, the Social Democrats continued to build on their popularity as the Klaus government fell victim to a series of charges and scandals over the following year. The Klaus government introduced new economic reform measures in April and May 1997, but the failure to fix critical flaws in earlier policies led to serious problems and corruption in the management and distribution of capital and in enterprises where structural problems remained unresolved. Because Klaus so openly opposed government regulation of businesses and financial institutions, the Czech Republic lacked bankruptcy laws, rules for the financial sector, or the agencies needed to enforce the rules and take legal action against corruption in the system.

In the political realm, the Klaus government hindered the development of a dynamic party system in an effort to forestall electoral challenges, although the Civic Democrats fell victim to a major scandal brought on by accusations of fraudulent practices related to campaign funding. The Civic Democrats and their political allies faced charges of filling party coffers through questionable loan agreements and privatization deals involving donations by nonexistent foreign interests. Rumors spread that the Civic Democrats maintained a secret bank account in Switzerland and Jaroslav Lizner, the head of the Coupon Privatization Center, was arrested and charged with accepting over eight million korunas from a businessman seeking to buy a dairy. Lizner received a prison sentence and was also fined for accepting bribes. The scandals and media exposure finally led to Klaus's resignation as prime minister in December 1997 after the Civic Democratic Alliance and Christian Democratic Union–Czechoslovak People's Party (KDU-ČSL) abandoned the governing coalition at the end of the previous month.

As Klaus's replacement, President Havel chose Josef Tošovský, head of the Czech National Bank, to run the government until the next election in June 1998. Havel also chose to put aside his usual reluctance to address party-related matters by speaking critically of Klaus and his policies as prime minister. Opposition to Klaus within his own party drove some members of the Civic Democrats to break away and form the Freedom Union (US) under Ján Ruml.

The elections of June 19–20, 1998 resulted in a victory for the Social Democrats, whose 32 percent of the vote bested the 28 percent gained by the Civic Democrats. The Communist Party placed third with 11 percent, followed by the Christian Democratic Union–Czechoslovak People's Party with 9 percent and the new Freedom Union fifth with 8.6 percent. When negotiations with the KDU-ČSL failed to gain the Social Democrats an alliance partner, the Civic Democrats returned the favor of the previous election and accepted an Opposition Agreement, allowing a minority left-wing ČSSD government under Miloš Zeman in return for ODS leadership of both parliamentary houses and a number of major committees.

The racist and xenophobic Republican Party fell short of the 5 percent of the vote required to earn parliamentary representation, a result representing a 3 percent decline since 1996 and the loss of a parliamentary presence begun in 1992. Led by Miroslav Sládek, the Republicans primarily targeted Roma and ethnic Germans and had opposed the dissolution of Czechoslovakia in light of their belief in a "Greater Czechoslovakia" that would include the Ruthenian territories lost to the Soviet Union. The party openly called for the expulsion of the 200,000–250,000 Roma living on Czech soil.

For the Roma, conditions in the Czech Republic continued to create problems in terms of citizenship and standard of living. The law on citizenship requiring individuals to produce evidence of a clean police record for a period of five years drew international criticism and convinced the government of the Czech Republic to reduce the term to two years in 1996. The lack of skills needed in the work force caused high unemployment among Roma and brought an increase in criminal activities and prostitution as government funding for education and social programs declined due to general economic conditions. Anti-Roma sentiment increased in cities and towns like Ústi nad Labem, where authorities unsuccessfully attempted to construct a wall dividing Roma apartment buildings from neighboring areas. Violence against Roma was also on the rise as skinheads and members of far-right, racist groups singled out the Roma community as a target for their anger.

In January 1998, Václav Havel was reelected to the presidency by the first-ever joint vote of the two parliamentary chambers, although Havel's victory came by one vote in the second round. As 1998 progressed, the Czech Republic entered a period of recession as unemployment rose to 6 percent, with women representing 60 percent of the jobless rate and one-third of those without work under the age of 25. With unemployment figures continuing to rise, the Zeman government sought to counter the recession by courting foreign investment and delaying the privatization of the nation's banks. The government then continued to work toward creating an attractive environment for foreign investment into the first years of the new millennium.

The parliamentary elections of June 2002 benefitted the Social Democrats with 30.2 percent of the vote to 24.5 percent for the Civic Democrats and 18.5 percent for the Communists, who recorded their strongest showing since 1989. After developing a formerly weak Social Democratic Party into a leading political organization, Miloš Zeman retired as party leader before the elections and selected Vladimír Špidla as his replacement. Špidla assumed the premiership on July 12 at the head of a coalition that included the centrist Christian Democrats and Freedom Union, and he led the government until July 19, 2004, when Stanislav Gross of the ČSSD took his place. After Gross chose to resign following allegations regarding personal financial improprieties, party colleague Jiří Paroubek replaced him on April 25, 2005, and served as Czech prime minister until August 16, 2006.

Zeman's candidacy to succeed Havel as president failed in February 2003 as Vaclav Klaus earned that honor by virtue of his election by the two houses of the parliament with a majority of 142 votes out of 281. Disagreements that had already arisen between Zeman and the leadership of the ČSSD worsened under Chairman Jiří Paroubek and led to Zeman's departure from the party in March 2007.

The Czech Republic's international relations gained a new dimension when the country was invited to participate in negotiations on membership in NATO and the European Union in the summer of 1997. On March 12, 1999, the Czech Republic formally entered the NATO alliance alongside Poland and Hungary, but not Slovakia due to that country's failure to meet the stated requirements for membership. The Czech Republic had already assumed Czechoslovakia's membership in the United Nations and the Council of Europe, adding participation in the Organization for Co-operation and Security in Europe (OSCE) in 1995.

After signing an association agreement with the European Union in 1994, the Czech Republic formally applied for membership in 1996 and gained "fast track" status a year later. When the Czechs brought the controversial Temelín nuclear power station online in October 2000, strong opposition by the Austrian government threatened to block Czech entry into the European Union, but negotiated agreements over safety standards in November 2001 eased tensions between the two governments and removed a potentially serious obstacle to Czech membership in the EU. After winning the 2002 parliamentary election, the Social Democrats made progress in instituting the reforms required for membership, and on May 1, 2004, the Czech Republic officially entered the European Union as a full member. The Czech Republic would later hold the presidency of the Council of the European Union from January 1 to June 30, 2009.

National elections in June 2006 failed to allow for the immediate creation of a governing coalition after the 200 seats in the Chamber of Deputies were equally split between politicians of the right and the left. When the stalemate stretched into September, President Klaus stepped in and appointed a center-right government under Mirek Topolánek, who succeeded Klaus as leader of the Civic Democrats in November 2002. After the Topolánek government lost a parliamentary vote of no confidence the following month, Klaus reappointed Topolánek as prime minister in November as talks began on the formation of a grand coalition with the Green Party and the Christian Democratic Union–Czechoslovak People's Party. In January 2007, Klaus granted presidential approval for a three-party governing coalition.

On February 8–9, 2008, the Czech Parliament once again convened to elect a president as Václav Klaus's five-year term came to an end. Klaus earned reelection by barely defeating the University of Michigan professor and Havel advisor, Jan Švejnar, in a third round of voting on February 15 after the earlier rounds failed to produce a clear winner. Švejnar, who had been nominated by the Green Party, was a pro-EU candidate who gained the backing of Havel, the Social Democrats, and other political organizations against the Euro-skeptic Klaus, who believed that membership in the European Union represented a reduction of sovereignty for the Czech Republic.

Another parliamentary vote of no confidence toppled Topolánek's second government in March 2009 as a result of the government's handling of the country's economic crisis. The procedure had been engineered in the lower house by the Social Democrats and the Communists and resulted in a 101–96 vote against the three-party coalition. The economist Jan Fischer was invited to head the government until early elections could be held in November, although the Parliament later voted against early elections and decided to move forward with regularly scheduled elections in June 2010.

THE SLOVAK REPUBLIC AFTER 1992

At midnight on December 31, 1992, crowds gathered in Bratislava's Square of the Slovak National Uprising and celebrated independence as flags waved and a band played the Slovak national anthem. The city had once again become the capital of an independent Slovak state, although a state that needed to be constructed out of new administrative, political, and diplomatic materials after the federal administrative offices lost their function.

Under Prime Minister Vladimír Mečiar of the Movement for a Democratic Slovakia (HZDS) and the new National Council of the Slovak Republic, formerly the Slovak National Council, Slovakia entered the new era as a multinational state of 5.4 million residents. Mečiar also served as acting president until Michal Kováč of the HZDS, elected by the Parliament in February 1993, could assume the post on March 2. Like Mečiar, Kováč was a nationalist and former Communist who underwent some degree of persecution by the party during the period of normalization. Kováč served as Slovakia's finance minister from 1989 to 1991.

With the departure of Finance Minister Ľudovít Černák from the government in March 1993 and the resignation of eight HZDS deputies from the National Council over Mečiar's heavy-handed leadership, the Slovak government became a one-party minority administration under the HZDS by June. Mečiar's dictatorial tendencies became major cause for concern and soon led President Kováč to criticize the prime minister for his tactics and for the government's inability to improve Slovakia's economic fortunes.

The transition from a heavy reliance on arms production to the production of consumer goods decreased armaments as a percentage of industrial output from over 6.3 percent in 1988 to 0.9 percent in 1992. Additionally, the process of privatization begun prior to the Velvet Divorce had transferred only 30 percent of eligible property to private hands by the time the division occurred at the end of 1992. From the beginning of 1993 onward, the HZDS faced criticism for a lack of preparation that left the new Slovak Republic with a weak currency, declining profits from trade, taxation and insurance systems in need of reorganization, and a state budget inadequate to cover existing expenses.

Mečiar's response to the criticism and to challenges to his leadership was to exert greater control over the party and the HZDS ministers, replacing Foreign Minister Milan Kňažko with Jozef Moravčík in part because Kňažko was promoting closer ties to the West at a time when Mečiar preferred looking east to Russia and Ukraine. Relations with the Czech Republic had not warmed since the breakup of the federal state and Slovak anger over the unilateral decision by the Czechs to adopt the old Czechoslovak flag as their own. Mečiar had turned down an opportunity for Slovakia to join the Czech Republic, Hungary, and Poland in the Visegrád group in the belief that economic and diplomatic relations with Slovakia's eastern neighbors were in the country's best interests. However, Mečiar soon reversed his position and joined Kováč in lobbying for Slovakia's entry into NATO and the European Union. Slovakia also became a member of the Visegrád Four after the dissolution of Czechoslovakia at the beginning of 1993.

Frictions arose in the Slovak Republic over the status of the national minorities as a result of issues held over from the Czechoslovak era. According to the 1991 census, the population of Slovakia remained overwhelmingly Slovak at 85.7 percent, but with Hungarians representing 11 percent of the people and mostly opposed to the division of Czechoslovakia. Slovakia also contained much smaller numbers of Roma, Czechs, Germans, Ruthenian-Ukrainians, Poles, Croats, and Jews. As a result, the declaration of the republic as a Slovak nation as included in the preamble of the new constitution generated controversy among the other nationalities.

When Hungarians took the lead in seeking guaranteed minority rights and a greater measure of autonomy, they met opposition from the governing Movement for a Democratic Slovakia, which argued that extensive minority rights already existed and did not require expansion. Residing primarily in the southern part of Slovakia, the Hungarians faced not only long-held animosity, but also a scarcity of Hungarian-language schools and educators, since training of those teachers had effectively ceased after 1968. A battle over languages had commenced in the fall of 1990, when *Matica Slovenska* sought legislation limiting the use of languages other than Slovak.

Conditions in Slovakia also proved difficult for the Roma, second in number to the Hungarians as a national minority. Residing primarily in rural eastern Slovakia, the Roma faced unemployment, poverty, and limited educational opportunities. Reports of attacks by skinheads and far-right nationalists failed to generate a strong response by the government and led to comments by well-known nationalist politicians apparently supporting racist actions against the Roma community. By 1997–1998, many Roma chose to leave Slovakia in search of asylum elsewhere.

In Slovakia's political affairs, the early months of 1994 produced a shifting of the tides against Mečiar, as evidenced by President Kováč's state of the nation address to the Parliament in March in which he criticized the negative aspects of the current state of government leadership. The National Council removed Mečiar as prime minister and invited Jozef Moravčík of the Democratic Union to form a new government, which included the Christian Democratic Movement and the Party of the Democratic Left in addition to Moravčík's own party. However, the opportunity for opposition parties to make their mark on government policies proved short-lived as the scheduled elections in October resulted in a victory for Mečiar's coalition of the HZDS and the Farmer's Party of Slovakia (RSS). The 35 percent of the vote the coalition received proved 10 percent higher than expected and distanced the HZDS from the left-leaning Common Choice coalition, which finished in second place with 10.41 percent, and the Hungarian coalition with 10.18 percent of the vote. In order to form a government, Mečiar chose to ally the HZDS with the radical Association of Workers of Slovakia (ZRS) and the nationalist Slovak National Party (SNS).

At the beginning of November, the new governing coalition moved to strengthen control over the National Council and parliamentary committees in order to guarantee authority over legislation. Promoting a populist, nationalist agenda with too little regard for the democratic process, the coalition appointed party members to government boards overseeing the media and targeted Kováč as a political enemy, revoking the president's membership in the HZDS in 1995.

On August 31, 1995, a political scandal broke as the president's son, Michal Kováč Jr., was abducted in Bratislava and transported to Hainburg, Austria, for extradition to Germany, where authorities had indicted him for financial crimes in connection with the so-called Technopol case. Assuming the involvement of the Slovak Information Service, an organ of state security, the Austrians issued a strong protest and sent the younger Kováč home. The president and his supporters blamed the Mečiar government for the kidnapping, which also led to a worsening of diplomatic relations with Austria.

Relations with Hungary had already deteriorated as a result of quarrels over the Gabčíkovo-Nagymaros dams project, which stemmed from a bilateral treaty with Slovakia in 1977. Hungary abandoned its role in the project in 1989 with the announcement that construction of the power plant on the Danube at Nagymaros in Hungary would cease and that the bilateral treaty of 1977 was no longer valid. The subsequent Slovak decision to continue with its own part of the Gabčíkovo-Nagymaros project, which involved diverting the Danube at Gabčíkovo, drew both Hungarian opposition and international criticism over the potential impact on the environment.

In spite of growing tensions with neighboring Austria and Hungary, the Slovak Republic made progress in improving the country's international status since becoming the 180th member of the United Nations in January 1993. With Slovakia struggling to meet the political and economic requirements for membership in the European Union, the country was the only one of 10 eligible states denied an invitation to discuss conditions of membership in the EU and NATO in the summer of 1997. Of primary concern to the two organizations was the state of Slovakia's progress toward full democratization.

Economic problems continued to plague Slovakia as well. In 1997, the Mečiar government introduced a budget allowing for large deficits, in spite of warnings by the International Monetary Fund that Slovakia needed to institute tighter controls over fiscal policies and expenditures. Old practices of cronyism and corruption had not been eliminated, and the country's trade deficit continued to grow.

When Michal Kováč completed his term as president in March 1998, the failure of the National Council to elect a replacement allowed Prime Minister Mečiar to appoint himself president as the constitution allowed and to exercise presidential powers until October of that year. As president, Mečiar then granted amnesty to some of those implicated in the abduction of Michal Kováč Jr. in 1995.

The elections of September 1998 brought another HZDS victory, but by a very slight margin, 27 percent to 26.33 percent, over the Slovak

Democratic Coalition. With only the Slovak National Party interested in becoming a coalition partner, Mečiar failed to form a government and was forced to allow the four opposition parties to take the initiative. A tearful Mečiar then made a televised appearance to announce that he would be stepping down as prime minister on October 29. Mikulaš Dzurinda of the Slovak Democratic and Christian Union-Democratic Party replaced Mečiar as prime minister and governed as the head of a five-party coalition with the HZDS and SNS in opposition.

Dzurinda immediately set out to reverse Mečiar's authoritarianism and economic policies, as well as to improve relations with the national minorities and international organizations like the European Union. Along with opening the way to much-needed economic reforms and modernization, Dzurinda eliminated the amnesties Mečiar had granted in March and worked to restore democracy to state institutions previously dominated by Mečiar and his allies. The Dzurinda government also drafted a proposal for the direct election of the president, a measure approved by the National Council in January 1999.

With presidential elections scheduled for mid-May, Kováč and six other candidates became eligible by petition, while the Parliament nominated Rudolf Schuster and Ján Slota (SNS) before surprising the other candidates by including Mečiar at the last moment. Efforts to form a coalition against Mečiar failed, although Kováč withdrew his name and called for the election of Schuster, who received 47.3 percent of the votes to 37.2 percent for Mečiar, although Schuster fell short of the required 50 percent mark. In a second round of voting, Schuster defeated Mečiar by a margin of 57.18 percent to 42.8 percent.

Victory in the September 2002 general elections allowed Dzurinda to retain his position as prime minister after his right-of-center Slovak Democratic and Christian Union, founded in 2000, overcame a second-place finish (15.05 percent) to Mečiar's HZDS (19.5 percent) by virtue of the support of three other center-right parties, including the Hungarian Coalition Party. In April 2004, Ivan Gašparovic of the Movement for Democracy defeated Mečiar in the second round of the presidential elections to earn the position by an electoral margin of 59.9 percent to 40.1 percent.

In spite of problems with unemployment and increases in the cost of living, the Dzurinda government continued to pursue policies designed to modernize the economy and allow Slovakia to compete in global markets. During Dzurinda's second term (2002–2006), the Slovak Republic enjoyed an economic growth rate of 8.3 percent, the highest among OECD members. By 2007, the growth rate had increased to

10.4 percent as consumer price inflation continued to decrease. As conditions improved, Slovakia overcame earlier obstacles and gained membership in NATO on March 29, 2004, followed by entry into the European Union on May 1 of that year. On January 1, 2009, Slovakia joined the Euro zone by adopting the currency of the European Union in place of the Slovak koruna.

The parliamentary elections of June 2006 produced an electoral victory for Robert Fico's leftist-populist Direction–Social Democracy (Smer-SD), which formed a coalition government with the Slovak National Party and Mečiar's renamed People's Party–Movement for a Democratic Slovakia. Ivan Gašparovic gained reelection as president of the Slovak Republic in April 2009 with the support of Smer-SD and the Slovak National Party, defeating Iveta Radičová of the Slovak Democratic and Christian Union 55.5 percent to 45.5 percent in the second round of the election. In early July 2010, Gašparovic appointed Radičová to be Slovakia's first female prime minister as head of a four-party, center-right coalition, after Fico and Smer-SD failed to capitalize on a first-place finish and form a governing coalition of their own.

Under the strong influence of nationalist politicians, relations with both Hungary and the Hungarian national minority continued to deteriorate by the end of 2009 due to controversy over language laws. The passage of a state language law in 1995 provided punishments for failure to use Slovak in official communication, although the Constitutional Court struck down the most controversial elements of the law. In 1999, the European Union required that as a condition of membership, Slovakia would be required to allow the public use of minority languages in areas where the minority accounted for 20 percent of the population. A decade later, in 2009, the Slovak government decided to amend the 1995 legislation to require the use of spoken and written Slovak with only a few exemptions. Failure to adhere to the stated legal policies and to respond to written warnings would result in fines of 100 to 5,000 euros, depending upon the conditions of the offense. The measure drew very strong opposition from Slovakia's Hungarian minority, as well as from the government of Hungary.

Overall, however, Slovakia's economy and international status continued to improve in the new millennium, although the onset of global economic crisis at the end of the first decade adversely affected the Slovak Republic as it did other countries. Political problems arose during the Fico years, but Dzurinda's successful efforts to build a modern and democratic Slovakia had already overcome the slow and erratic progress of the Mečiar era.

NOTES

1. "Several Sentences," in Bernard Wheaton and Zdeněk Kavan, *The Velvet Revolution: Czechoslovakia, 1988–1991* (Boulder, CO: Westview Press, 1992), 196.

2. British historian and journalist Timothy Garton Ash offers an eyewitness account of Civic Forum and the Velvet Revolution in *The Magic Lantern: The Revolution of 1989 Witnessed in Warsaw, Budapest, Berlin and Prague* (New York: Random House, Inc., 1990).

3. See Tim D. Whipple, ed., *After the Velvet Revolution: Václav Havel and the New Leaders of Czechoslovakia Speak Out* (New York: Freedom House, 1991), for speeches, articles and interviews by Czech and Slovak leaders of the Velvet Revolution. For historical and political analyses of the Velvet Revolution and its aftermath, see Wheaton and Kavan, *The Velvet Revolution*, and Robin H. E. Shepherd, *Czechoslovakia, The Velvet Revolution and Beyond* (New York: St. Martin's Press, 2000).

4. Václav Havel, "Address to a Joint Session of the United States Congress," in Whipple, *After the Velvet Revolution*, 77.

5. For information about Havel's life and career, see Edá Kriseová, *Václav Havel: The Authorized Biography* (New York: St. Martin's Press, 1993), and John Keane, *Václav Havel: A Political Tragedy in Six Acts* (New York: Basic Books, 2000). Kriseová, a former journalist and dissident, was a friend of Havel and offers a hagiography from an insider's perspective.

6. British playwright Tom Stoppard examines the connection between rock music and democratic movements in his play, *Rock 'n' Roll* (New York: Grove Press, 2006), which moves from the Prague Spring of 1968 to the late 1980s. The play featured live music by members of the Plastic People of the Universe at the beginning and the end of the performance during its run at Prague's National Theatre beginning in early 2007.

7. For analyses of the causes of Czechoslovakia's dissolution, see Jiří Musil, ed., *The End of Czechoslovakia* (Budapest: Central European University Press, 1995).

Notable People in the History of the Czech Republic and Slovakia

Adalbert of Prague (Vojtěch, c. 956–997) Born into the Slavník family of the Czech nobility and later appointed Bishop of Prague. As a missionary, he spread Christianity in Hungary and Poland, but died a martyr's death at the hands of the Baltic Prussians and was later canonized as St. Adalbert.

Agnes of Prague (Anežka, 1211–1282) The youngest daughter of Bohemia's Přemysl Otakar I and sister of Václav I. As abbess of the Franciscan abbey of the Poor Clares in Prague, "Blessed Agnes" chose a life of poverty and charity over the wealth and privileges available to her. She was later canonized as St. Agnes in 1989.

Beneš, Edvard (1884–1948) A Czech politician and cofounder with Tomáš Garrigue Masaryk of the First Czechoslovak Republic. He served the republic as minister of foreign affairs from 1918 to 1935 and prime minister in 1921–1922, before succeeding Masaryk as president from 1935 to 1938. After resigning the latter post as a result of the Munich Agreement, Beneš served as head of the Czechoslovak government-in-exile in London during World War II and returned as president of a restored Czechoslovak republic from 1945 to 1948. After the Communists took power in the February Coup of 1948, Beneš resigned his position in June after refusing to accept the new constitution.

Bernolák, Anton (1762–1813) A Roman Catholic priest and linguist who codified a Slovak literary language as a first step toward establishing national language standards for Slovaks.

Borovský, Karel Havlícek (1821–1856) Journalist, writer, and Czech patriot who continued to criticize Austrian rule after the revolutionary year of 1848 and in spite of having to cease printing his newspaper and being forced to depart Prague for three years of exile in Brixen.

Bořivoj I (c. 852–889) The first duke of Bohemia and founder of the Přemyslid dynasty.

Čapek, Karel (1890–1938) A prolific and well-known Czech writer and humanist whose play, *R.U.R. (Rossum's Universal Robots)* introduced the term "robot" (from the Czech *robota*) to describe an artificial human. He also authored numerous short stories, plays, and novels, including *War With the Newts*, in addition to collaborating with his brother, the artist Josef Čapek.

Daxner, Štefan Marko (1822–1892) Lawyer and politician during and after the revolutionary events of 1848–1849, helping to draft the "Demands of the Slovak Nation" and, in 1861, writing the influential "Voice from Slovakia" in which he demanded recognition of Slovaks as a separate nation.

Dobrovský, Josef (1773–1829) Bohemian historian and philologist who became a leading figure in the Czech National Revival as a result of his historical studies and codification of the Czech language.

Dubček, Alexander (1921–1992) Slovak politician and first secretary of the Slovak Communist Party from 1963 to 1968 before becoming first secretary of the Czechoslovak Communist Party in January 1968. His support for reforms and the pursuit of "socialism with a human face" inspired the Prague Spring of that year before the Warsaw Pact invasion ended the experiment and eventually led to Dubček's replacement with Gustáv Husák. Dubček reemerged politically on the eve of the Velvet Revolution of 1989 and joined Václav Havel in addressing crowds of demonstrators in Prague. Dubček's death in an automobile accident in 1992 prevented him from playing an active role in the independent Slovak Republic established at the end of that year.

Gottwald, Klement (1896–1953) Moravian-born Communist politician who began his career as a journalist and party functionary in Slovakia before becoming leader of the Czechoslovak Communist Party in 1924. He later served as prime minister of Czechoslovakia (1946–1948) during the immediate postwar years before becoming president after the Communist coup in February 1948.

Havel, Václav (1936–) Playwright and dissident who cofounded Charter 77 in defense of human rights and was imprisoned by the government for his activities and for writing influential essays such as "The Power of the Powerless," which severely criticized "normalization" and the Communist regime. Havel later served as a leader of Civic Forum and as the public face of the pro-democracy movement during the Velvet Revolution of 1989. Havel was elected president of Czechoslovakia after the fall of the Communist regime and then president of the Czech Republic after the "Velvet Divorce."

Hlinka, Andrej (1864–1938) Catholic priest, political activist, and Slovak nationalist who founded the Slovak People's Party in 1913 and then chaired the party from its rebirth in 1918 until his death. In 1918, Hlinka joined the Slovak National Council and signed the Martin Declaration in support of a union of Czechs and Slovaks. His party was renamed the Hlinka Slovak People's Party in 1925 and, under Hlinka's guidance, turned to promoting Slovak autonomy as preferable to participation in the existing Czechoslovak state.

Hodža, Milan (1878–1944) Journalist, politician, and leader of the pre-1914 Slovak National Party. During World War I, Hodža helped generate support for a common state of Czechs and Slovaks, later serving as an Agrarian parliamentarian, prime minister (1935–1938), and in various ministerial positions under the First Czechoslovak Republic.

Horáková, Milada (1901–1950) Lawyer, feminist, and social democratic politician. Active in women's rights organizations and as a parliamentarian for the Czechoslovak National Socialist Party under the First Republic, Horáková joined the anti-Nazi resistance when the Germans invaded Czechoslovakia in 1939. Arrested by the Gestapo and held in Terezin and other camps and prisons, Horáková returned to the parliament after national liberation in 1945 and continued her political career until the Communist coup in 1948. In 1949, Horáková was arrested by the secret police and charged with treason and conspiracy as a result of her anticommunist activities, leading to a show trial and execution the following year.

Hus, Jan (c. 1369–1415) Priest, philosopher, and religious reformer influenced by the writings and sermons of the English theologian John Wyclif. Hus's own sermons in Prague's Bethlehem Chapel criticized the sale of indulgences and called for the supremacy of the Scriptures and the religious use of the vernacular. He was burned at the stake as a heretic after appearing before the Council of Constance and is memorialized in sculpture on Prague's Old Town Square.

Husák, Gustav (1913–1991) Slovak Communist politician and participant in the Slovak National Council and Slovak National Uprising of 1944. A victim of the purge of Slovak "bourgeois nationalists" by the Czechoslovak Communist Party in 1954, Husák later became first secretary of the Slovak Communist Party before attaining the same position in the Czechoslovak Communist Party after the crushing of the Prague Spring in 1968. Maintaining the oppressive policies of "normalization," Husák was elected president of Czechoslovakia (1975–1989) and continued as party head until he was replaced in 1987.

Hviezdoslav, Pavel Országh (1849–1921) Lawyer, poet, and Slovak nationalist who became a leading light of modern Slovak literature. Hriezdoslav was chosen as head of the Slovak cultural organization *Matica slovenská* when it was reestablished in 1919.

Jiři z Poděbrad (George of Poděbrady, 1420–1471) Utraquist, or moderate Hussite, leader elected king by the Bohemian estates as the first native Czech ruler since the end of the Přemyslid dynasty.

Jungmann, Josef (1773–1847) Bohemian poet and linguist who contributed to the Czech national renascence by promoting the use of Czech as a literary language and by publishing a Czech-German dictionary that helped define a modern Czech vocabulary.

Kafka, Franz (1883–1924) Born into a middle-class Jewish family in Prague, Kafka earned a degree in law and became one of the most unique and important writers of the 20th century through works such as "The Metamorphosis," *The Trial*, and *The Castle*. His themes of hope-lessness, alienation, and absurdity reflect a critical and existentialist perspective on the modern world.

Karel IV (Charles IV, 1316–1378) Holy Roman Emperor and second king of Bohemia from the Luxemburg dynasty. A patron of humanism and intellectual affairs, he made Prague the imperial capital and sponsored extensive building projects there in contributing to the golden age of Bohemia.

Klaus, Václav (1942–) Czech politician and economist. Klaus entered politics as Czechoslovak minister of finance and leader of Civic Forum and then the Civic Democratic Party after the Velvet Revolution. Named prime minister of the Czech republic after the June 1992 elections, Klaus negotiated the "Velvet Divorce" with Slovak prime minister Vladimír Mečiar. After serving as prime minister (1992–1997) of the independent Czech Republic, Klaus was elected president in 2003 and reelected in 2008.

Kollár, Ján (1793–1852) Slovak poet, scientist, politician and Lutheran pastor who promoted the development of a Czechoslovak language and achieved notoriety for his epic poem *"Slávy dcera"* ("Daughter of Slava").

Masaryk, Jan (1886–1948) Politician, diplomat, and son of Tomáš Garrigue Masaryk, founder of the Czechoslovak state, Jan Masaryk became minister of foreign affairs in the London-based Czechoslovak government-in-exile during World War II. Masaryk continued in that position until weeks after the Communist coup in February 1948, when he was later found dead under mysterious circumstances.

Masaryk, Tomáš Garrigue (1850–1937) Czech philosopher, sociologist, and politician who lobbied for the federalization of the Habsburg empire and served in the Austrian Parliament as a representative of the Young Czech Party and then the Realist Party until 1914. After Masaryk decided to pursue the creation of an independent state, his efforts on behalf of a union of Czechs and Slovaks during World War I led to the establishment of the First Czechoslovak Republic in October 1918. Respected as the founder of the Czechoslovak state, Masaryk served as president of the republic until his resignation due to poor health in 1935.

Mečiar, Vladimír (1942–) Member of Public Against Violence and prime minister of the Slovak republic in Czechoslovakia from 1990 to 1991. Mečiar then founded the party Movement for a Democratic Slovakia and, after his election as Slovak prime minister in June 1992, negotiated the dissolution of Czechoslovakia with Czech prime minister Václav Klaus. Mečiar served two terms as prime minister of an independent Slovakia and as acting president in 1998.

Mojmír I (?–846) Ruler of the Moravian principality who joined the Principalities of Moravia and Nitra together in 833 to form the Empire of Great Moravia.

Němcová, Božena (1820–1862) Writer and patriot, considered a founding mother of the Czech National Revival for her collections of folklore and for her much-loved novel *Babička* (The Grandmother).

Novotný, Antonín (1904–1975) Czech politician and first secretary of the Czechoslovak Communist Party from 1953 to 1968. Novotný also held the presidency of Czechoslovakia from 1957 to 1968.

Palach, Jan (1948–1969) A Czech university student who took his own life in protest against the Soviet-led invasion and crushing of the Prague Spring. His act of self-immolation on Wenceslas Square in Prague made him a national hero and his funeral developed into a major protest against the Warsaw Pact occupation.

Palacký, František (1798–1876) Historian and a leading figure in the Czech National Revival. Often called the "Father of the Czech Nation," Palacky served as a leader of the Prague Uprising against centralized Habsburg rule in 1848 and later completed a Czech-language history of the Czech people.

Přemysl Otakar II (c. 1233–1278) Known as the "King of Gold and Iron," Přemysl Otakar II dramatically expanded the borders and influence of the Bohemian kingdom before losing his life in a military defeat to Rudolf of Habsburg at Dürnkrut on the Marchfield.

Slánský, Rudolf (1901–1952) Czech communist politician who became first secretary of the Czechoslovak Communist Party in 1946. Arrested and charged with high treason during the political purges of 1951, Slánský underwent a show trial with 13 other defendants before being executed in 1952.

Samo (623–658) Frankish merchant who organized the Slavic tribes against attacks by the Avars and became first ruler of a "kingdom" or union of the tribes in what would later become Moravia, Slovakia, and Lower Austria.

Šafárik, Pavel Jozef (1791–1861) Poet, historian, and a major contributor to the Slovak national awakening. Because he wrote in Czech and supported the idea of a Czechoslovak language, he also contributed to the Czech national renascence.

Štefánik, Milan Rastislav (1880–1919) Slovak astronomer, politician, and general in the French army who helped found the First Czechoslovak Republic as a member of the Czecho-Slovak National Committee during World War I. He also organized the Czechoslovak Legion in Russia and became the new republic's minister of war, although he died in an air crash near Bratislava when he returned to Slovakia in 1919.

Štur, Ľudovít (1885–1856) Educator, Slovak political leader, and a leading figure of the Slovak national awakening. Štur's codification of the Slovak language allowed for the creation of a national literary language, and his efforts on behalf of the Slovak nation led him to participate in Slovakia's declaration of independence from Hungary during the revolutionary years of 1848–1849.

Tiso, Jozef (1887–1947) Catholic priest, politician, and member of the Hlinka Slovak People's Party who promoted Slovak autonomy prior to the German invasion in March 1939 and the subsequent establishment of a quasi-independent Slovak government. Having succeeded Hlinka as party leader, Tiso became a controversial figure as prime minister (1939) and then president (1939–1945) of what was effectively a puppet state of Nazi Germany until the Soviets liberated western Slovakia in April 1945. Tiso was later charged with treason and collaboration with the Nazis, leading to his execution by hanging in 1947.

Václav I (Wenceslas, c. 907–635) Duke of Bohemia, murdered by a group of nobles allied with his brother Boleslav. He was later canonized as St. Václav (St. Wenceslas), patron saint of the Czech state, and celebrated in the Christmas carol "Good King Wenceslas."

Wallenstein, Albrecht von (1583–1634) Bohemian nobleman and soldier who became a leading general for the Catholic forces of Holy

Roman Emperor Ferdinand II during the Thirty Years' War (1618–1648). Charged with treason for negotiating with Protestant Sweden and Saxony, he was assassinated by one of his own officers.

Žižka, Ján (c. 1360–1424) Follower of religious reformer Ján Hus and military leader of the Taborites during the Catholic crusades to eliminate the Hussite "heresy" in the Czech lands. Žižka's soldiers defeated the forces of King Sigismund on Vítkov Hill in Prague in 1420.

Bibliography

Agnew, Hugh. *The Czechs and the Lands of the Bohemian Crown.* Stanford, CA: Hoover Institution Press, 2004.

Beneš, Eduard. *Memoirs of Dr. Eduard Beneš: From Munich to New War and New Victory.* Westport, CT: Greenwood Press, 1978.

Beneš, Eduard. *My War Memoirs.* Translated by Paul Selver. Westport, CT: Greenwood Press, 1971.

Brock, Peter. *The Slovak National Awakening: An Essay in the Intellectual History of East Central Europe.* Toronto: University of Toronto Press, 1976.

Brock, Peter, and H. Gordon Skilling, eds. *The Czech Renascence of the Nineteenth Century.* Toronto: University of Toronto Press, 1970.

Bryant, Chad. *Prague in Black: Nazi Rule and Czech Nationalism.* Cambridge, MA: Harvard University Press, 2007.

Bugajski, Janusz. *Czechoslovakia: Charter 77's Decade of Dissent.* New York: Praeger, 1987.

Čapek, Karel. *Talks with T. G. Masaryk.* North Haven, CT: Catbird Press, 1995.

Cohen, Gary B. *The Politics of Ethnic Survival: Germans in Prague 1861–1914.* Princeton, NJ: Princeton University Press, 1981.

Cornwall, Mark, and R. J. W. Evans, eds. *Czechoslovakia in a Nationalist and Fascist Europe 1918–1948*. Oxford: Oxford University Press (The British Academy), 2007.

Cosmas of Prague. *The Chronicle of the Czechs*. Translated by Lisa Wolverton. Washington, DC: Catholic University of America Press, 2009.

Deák, István. *The Lawful Revolution: Louis Kossuth and the Hungarians, 1848–1849*. New York: Columbia University Press, 1979.

Demetz, Peter. *Prague in Black and Gold: Scenes from the Life of a European City*. New York: Hill and Wang, 1997.

Demetz, Peter. *Prague in Danger: The Years of German Occupation, 1939–1945: Memories and History, Terror and Resistance, Theatre and Jazz, Film and Poetry, Politics and War*. New York: Farrar, Strauss and Giroux, 2008.

Dowling, Maria. *Brief Histories: Czechoslovakia*. London: Hodder Arnold, 2002.

Dubček, Alexander. *Hope Dies Last: The Autobiography of the Leader of the Prague Spring*. Edited and translated by Jiri Hochman. New York: Kodasha America, 1993.

Dvornik, Francis. *The Slavs in European History and Civilization*. New Brunswick, NJ: Rutgers University Press, 1962.

Eubank, Keith. *Munich*. Norman: University of Oklahoma Press, 1963.

Evans, Robert J. W. *Rudolf II and His World: A Study in Intellectual History, 1576–1612*. Oxford: Clarendon Press, 1973.

Feinberg, Melissa. *Elusive Equality: Gender, Citizenship, and the Limits of Democracy in Czechoslovakia, 1918–1950*. Pittsburgh, PA: University of Pittsburgh Press, 2006.

Felak, James Ramon. *"At the Price of the Republic": Hlinka's Slovak People's Party, 1929–1938*. Pittsburgh, PA: University of Pittsburgh Press, 1994.

French, Alfred. *Czech Writers and Politics 1945–1969*. East European Monographs. New York: Columbia University Press, 1982.

Frommer, Benjamin. *National Cleansing: Retribution Against Nazi Collaborators in Postwar Czechoslovakia*. Cambridge: Cambridge University Press, 2005.

Garton Ash, Timothy. *The Magic Lantern: The Revolution of 1989 Witnessed in Warsaw, Budapest, Berlin and Prague*. New York: Vintage Books, 1990.

Goetz-Stankiewicz, Marketa, ed. *Good-bye Samizdat: Twenty Years of Czechoslovak Writing*. Evanston, IL: Northwestern University Press, 1992.

Golan, Galia. *Reform Rule in Czechoslovakia: The Dubček Era 1968–1969*. New York: Cambridge University Press, 1973.

Havel, Václav. *Disturbing the Peace: A Conversation with Karel Hvížďala*. New York: Random House, 1991.

Havel, Václav. *Living in Truth*. Edited by Jan Vladislav. London and New York: Faber and Faber, 1989.

Havel, Václav. *Open Letters: Selected Writings, 1965–1990*. New York: Vintage, 1992.

Holý, Ladislav. *The Little Czech and the Great Czech Nation: National Identity and the Post-Communist Social Transformation*. Cambridge: Cambridge University Press, 1996.

Iggers, Wilma A. *Women of Prague: Ethnic Diversity and Social Change from the Eighteenth Century to the Present*. Providence: Berghahn Books, 1995.

Ingrao, Charles. *The Habsburg Monarchy, 1618–1815*. Cambridge: Cambridge University Press, 1994.

Jelinek, Yeshayahu. *The Parish Republic: Hlinka's Slovak People's Party*. Boulder: East European Monographs, 1976.

Johnson, Lonnie R. *Central Europe: Enemies, Neighbors, Friends*. Oxford: Oxford University Press, 2002.

Kann, Robert A. and David V. Zdeněk. *The Peoples of the Eastern Habsburg Lands, 1526–1918*. Seattle: University of Washington Press, 1984.

Keane, John. *Václav Havel: A Political Tragedy in Six Acts*. New York: Basic Books, 2000.

Kennan, George F. *From Munich after Prague: Diplomatic Papers 1938–1940*. Princeton, NJ: Princeton University Press, 1968.

Kieval, Hillel. *Languages of Commnity: The Jewish Experience in the Czech Lands*. Berkeley: University of California Press, 2000.

King, Jeremy. *Budweisers into Czechs and Germans: A Local History of Bohemian Politics, 1848–1948*. Princeton, NJ: Princeton University Press, 2002.

Kirschbaum, Joseph M., ed. *Slovak Culture Through the Centuries*. Toronto: Slovak World Congress, 1978.

Kirschbaum, Joseph M., ed. *Slovakia in the Nineteenth and Twentieth Centuries*. Toronto: Slovak World Congress, 1973.

Kirschbaum, Stanislav J. *A History of Slovakia*. New York: St. Martin's Press, 1995.

Kirschbaum, Stanislav J., and Anne R. C. Roman, eds. *Reflections on Slovak History*. Toronto: Slovak World Congress, 1987.

Klassen, John M. *Warring Maidens, Captive Wives, and Hussite Queens: Women and Men at War and at Peace in Fifteenth Century Bohemia*. Boulder, CO: East European Monographs, 1999.

Klassen, John M., ed. *The Letters of the Rožmberk Sisters: Noblewomen in Fifteenth-Century Bohemia*. Rochester, New York: Boydell and Brewer, Inc., 2001.

Korbel, Josef. *The Communist Subversion of Czechoslovakia 1938–1948: The Failure of Coexistence*. Princeton, NJ: Princeton University Press, 1959.

Korbel, Josef. *Twentieth-Century Czechoslovakia: The Meanings of Its History*. New York: Columbia University Press, 1977.

Krejči, Jaroslav. *Czechoslovakia at the Crossroads of European History*. London: I. B. Tauris & Co. Ltd., 1990.

Kriseová, Edá. *Václav Havel: The Authorized Biography*. New York: St. Martin's Press, 1993.

Kusin, Vladimir V. *The Intellectual Origins of the Prague Spring: The Development of Reformist Ideas in Czechoslovakia 1956–1967*. Cambridge: Cambridge University Press, 1971.

Leff, Carol Skalnik. *National Conflict in Czechoslovakia: The Making and Remaking of a State, 1918–1987*. Princeton, NJ: Princeton University Press, 1988.

Lettrich, Jozef. *History of Modern Slovakia*. New York: Frederick A. Praeger, 1955.

Littell, Robert (ed.), *The Czech Black Book*. New York: Frederick A. Praeger, 1969.

Lukes, Igor. *Czechoslovakia between Stalin and Hitler: The Diplomacy of Edvard Beneš in the 1930s*. Oxford: Oxford University Press, 1996.

MacDonald, Callum. *The Killing of SS Obergruppenführer Reinhard Heydrich*. New York: Free Press, 1989.

Mamatey, Victor S., and Radomír Luža, eds. *A History of the Czechoslovak Republic 1918–1948*. Princeton: Princeton University Press, 1973.

Masaryk, Dr. Thomas Garrigue. *The Making of a State: Memoirs and Observations 1914–1918*. London: George Allen & Unwin Ltd., 1927.

Masaryk, Tomáš G. *The Meaning of Czech History*. Edited by René Welleck. Chapel Hill: University of North Carolina Press, 1974.

Mastny, Vojtech. *The Czechs under Nazi Rule: The Failure of National Resistance, 1939–1942*. New York: Colmbia University Press, 1971.

Mlynář, Zdeněk. *Nightfrost in Prague: The End of Humane Socialism*. New York: Karz Publishers, 1980.

Musil, Jiří, ed. *The End of Czechoslovakia*. Budapest: Central European University Press, 1995.

Navrátil, Jaromír, ed. *Prague Spring 1968: A National Security Archives Documents Reader*. Budapest and New York: Central European University Press, 2006.

Olivová, Věra. *The Doomed Democracy: Czechoslovakia in a Disrupted Europe 1914–38*. Montreal: McGill-Queens University Press, 1972.

Pánek, Jaroslav, and Oldřich Tůma, eds. *A History of the Czech Lands*. Prague: Karolinum Press, 2009.

Pelikán, Jiří, ed. *The Czechoslovak Political Trials, 1950–1954*. Stanford, CA: Stanford University Press, 1971.

Petro, Peter. *A History of Slovak Literature*. Montreal: McGill-Queens University Press, 1996.

Pynsent, Robert B. *Questions of Identity: Czech and Slovak Ideas of Nationality and Personality*. New York: Oxford University Press, 1994.

Rothkirchen, Livia. *The Jews of Bohemia and Moravia: Facing the Holocaust*. Lincoln: University of Nebraska Press, 2005.

Sayer, Derek. *The Coasts of Bohemia: A Czech History*. Princeton, NJ: Princeton University Press, 1998.

Seton-Watson, R. W. *A History of the Czechs and Slovaks*. Hamden, CT: Archon Books, 1965.

Shawcross, William. *Dubcek*. New York: Simon and Schuster Inc, 1990.

Shepherd, Robin H. E. *Czechoslovakia: The Velvet Revolution and Beyond*. New York: St. Martin's Press, 2000.

Šimecka, Milan. *The Restoration of Order: The Normalization of Czechoslovakia*. London: Verso Editions, 1984.

Skilling, H. Gordon. *Charter 77 and Human Rights in Czechoslovakia*. London and Boston: Allen & Unwin, 1981.

Skilling, H. Gordon. *Czechoslovakia's Interrupted Revolution*. Princeton, NJ: Princeton University Press, 1976.

Skilling, H. Gordon. *T. G. Masaryk: Against the Current, 1882–1914*. University Park: Pennsylvania State University Press, 1994.

Spector, Scott. *Prague Territories: National Conflict and Cultural Innovation in Franz Kafka's Fin de Siècle*. Berkeley: University of California Press, 2000.

Stein, Eric. *Czecho/Slovakia: Ethnic Conflict, Constitutional Fissure, Negotiated Breakup*. Ann Arbor: University of Michigan Press, 1997.

Sugar, Peter F., Péter Hanák, and Tibor Frank, eds. *A History of Hungary*. Bloomington: Indiana University Press, 1994.

Sviták, Ivan. *The Czechoslovak Experiment 1968–1969*. New York: Columbia University Press, 1971.

Teich, Mikulas, ed. *Bohemia in History*. Cambridge: Cambridge University Press, 1998.

Thomas, Alfred. *Anne's Bohemia: Czech Literature and Society, 1310–1420*. Minneapolis: University of Minnesota Press, 1998.

Toma, Peter A., and Dušan Kováč. *Slovakia: From Samo to Dzurinda.* Stanford, CA: Hoover Institution Press, 2001.

Wheaton, Bernard, and Zdeněk Kavan. *The Velvet Revolution: Czechoslovakia, 1988–1991.* Boulder, CO: Westview Press, 1992.

Whipple, Tim D., ed. *After the Velvet Revolution: Václav Havel and the New Leaders of Czechoslovakia Speak Out.* New York: Freedom House, 1991.

Williams, Kieran. *The Prague Spring and its Aftermath: Czechoslovak Politics 1968–1970.* Cambridge: Cambridge University Press, 1997.

Wingfield, Nancy M. *Flag Wars and Stone Saints: How the Bohemian Lands Became Czech.* Cambridge, MA: Harvard University Press, 2007.

Wiskemann, Elizabeth. *Czechs and Germans: A Study in the Historic Provinces of Bohemia and Moravia.* London and New York: Oxford University Press. 1938.

Wolchik, Sharon. *Czechoslovakia in Transition: Politics, Economics, and Society.* London: Pinter Publishers, 1991.

Wolverton, Lisa. *Hastening toward Prague: Power and Society in the Medieval Czech Lands.* Philadelphia: University of Pennsylvania Press, 2001.

Zeman, Zbyněk. *The Masaryks: The Making of Czechoslovakia.* London: Weidenfield and Nicolson, 1976.

Zeman, Zbyněk, with Antonín Klimek. *The Life of Edvard Beneš, 1884–1948: Czechoslovakia in War and Peace.* Oxford: Clarendon Press, 1997.

Index

"Action Program," 212–13,
220, 222
Adalbert (St. Vojtěch), 35,
39–40, 42, 265
Adamec, Ladislav, 228, 233,
240–42
Agnes of Prague (St. Agnes), 55,
240, 265
Albrecht of Habsburg, 71, 83
Andrew II, 58
Andrew III, 59
Anne of Bohemia, 66
Anschluss, 143, 154, 159,
164–65, 168
Árpád, xiv, 32
Ausgleich (1867), 119,
125, 127
Austrian Succession, War
of the, 94–95
Avars, xiii, 22–24

Bach, Alexander, 115, 117–18
Baroque style, 82
Bedřich, 44
Bela III, 58
Bela IV, 46, 58
Beneš, Edvard, xviii, 135–39,
142–45, 149, 153–54, 158–60,
166–69, 171, 174–75, 180–81,
185–86, 188–91, 193–95, 198,
200–201, 203, 205, 265;
decrees signed by, 194–95
Beran, Rudolf, 164, 170
bernoľacina, 51, 101, 103
Bernolák, Anton, xv, 101–2, 266
Bethlehem Chapel, 64–66, 268
Bethlen, Gabor, 88
bibličtina, 100–101, 103, 105
Biľak, Vasil, 213, 215–17
Blaho, Pavel, 126–27
Bocskay, Štefan, 87

Bohemus, 22, 30
Boii, xiii, 20
Boleslav I, 37–38
Bolesław I (Poland), 40–41
Boleslav II, 39–49
Boleslav III (Boleslav the Red), 41–42
Bonaparte, Napoleon, 103–4, 110
Bořivoj, xiv, 29–30, 36, 266
Borovský, Karel Havlíček, 111, 115, 266
Břetislav I, 40–42
Břetislav II, 43
Brezhnev, Leonid, 211, 213–14, 217–18, 226
Brezhnev Doctrine, 215, 227–28
Budaj, Ján, 238, 245

Cak, Matthew, xiv, 59–60
Čalfa, Marián, 242, 245
Calvinism, 75
Calvinists, 77, 97
Čapek, Karel, 266
Čarnogursky, Ján, 235, 250
Čech, 22
Celts, 19
Central Committee of Home Resistance (ÚVOD), 177–78
Central National Revolutionary Committee (ÚNRV), 178
Černík, Oldřich, 213, 216, 218, 220
Černín, Count Ottokar, 137, 141
Černova massacre, xvii, 127
Černy, David, 249
Černy, Jan, 149, 151
Chamberlain, Neville, 165–67, 171, 175
Charlemagne, 23–24
Charles IV (Karel), xiv, 49–55, 63–64, 269
Charles VI, 90–91

Charles Albert (Bavaria), 94–95
Charles Robert, 59–60
Charter 77, xix, 224–26, 232–33, 235, 237, 239, 267
Chelčický, Peter, 75
Chlumec, 43
Christian Democratic Party, 245, 251
Christian Democratic Union, 250
Chronica Boemorum, 22
Churchill, Winston, 75
Chvalkovský, František, 169–70
Civic Democratic Party (ODS), 247, 251, 253–55, 257, 269
Clemenceau, Georges, 139
Clementis, Vladimír, 205
Cleveland Agreement, xvii, 136
collectivization, 202
Comecon (Council for Mutual Economic Assistance), xviii, 202, 238, 240, 248
Comintern (Communist International), 149
Communist Party of Bohemia-Moravia (KSCM), 246, 253, 255, 258
Communist Party of Czechoslovakia (KSČ), xvii, xviii, 149, 151, 157, 169, 175, 178, 180, 188–89, 196–97, 199–202, 205–10, 212, 213, 215, 217–20, 222, 228, 232–33, 235, 237–38, 240–45, 266–68, 270
Communist Party of Slovakia (KSS), xviii, 184–85, 189, 196–97, 201, 205, 208–9, 213, 215, 218, 266
Compacts of Basel (Compactata), 71–73
Congress of Vienna, 104–5
Conrad Otto, 45
Corvinus, Matthias, xv, 72, 74, 84

Cosmas of Prague, 22, 29
Council of Constance, 67, 268
Cyril (Constantine), xiv, 26–27, 29, 87
Czech Agrarian Party, 123, 148–49, 151
Czech and Slovak Federative Republic, 246, 252
Czech Committee Abroad, 136
Czechoslovak Agrarian Party, 152–53, 157–58
Czechoslovak Legion (*Družina*), xviii, 133, 138–39, 271
Czechoslovak National Democratic Party, 149, 151, 167
Czechoslovak National Socialist Party, 132, 169, 197–98, 204, 267
Czechoslovak People's Party, 148–49, 167, 196–98, 242
Czechoslovak Social Democrats, 147–51, 157, 189, 196–97, 208
Czechoslovak Tradesmen-Business Professional Party, 149
Czech Realist Party, 124, 269
Czech Republic: economy of, 4–5; geography of, 2–3; government of, 6–9; population and demographics of, 3–4
Czech Social Democratic Party, 254–58

Daladier, Èdouard, 167–68
Daxner, Štefan Marko, 115, 124, 134, 266
Defenestration of Prague, xv, 78
"Demands of the Slovak Nation," 116, 266
Democratic Initiative, 236, 238
demographics. *See* population and demographics

DG 307, xix, 224
Dienstbier, Jiří, 238, 244, 246, 248
Direction–Social Democracy (Smer-SD), 263
Dobner, Gelasius, 106
Dobrovský, Josef, 106, 266
Domažlice, 70
Drahomíra, 36
Drtina, Prokop, 196, 200
Družina. See Czechoslovak Legion (*Družina*)
Dubček, Alexander, xviii, 208, 210–20, 231, 239, 242–43, 245, 252, 266
Ďurčanský, Ferdinand, 172, 181–83
Dürich, Josef, 136
Dürnkrut, xiv, 47, 270
Dvořak, Antonín, 122
Dzurinda, Mikuláš, xx, 262, 264

economy: of Czech Republic, 4–5; of Slovak Republic, 12–13
Edict of Toleration, 97–98
Eliáš, Gen. Alois, 172, 178, 180
Epiphany Declaration, 140
European Union, 248–49, 257, 259, 261, 263

February Crisis (1948), 199, 201–2, 265, 267–69
Ferdinand I (Austrian emperor), 110, 114–15
Ferdinand I (Habsburg king), xv, 74, 76, 85
Ferdinand II, 78–81, 88, 272
Ferdinand III, 88
Fico, Robert, 263–64
Fierlinger, Zdeněk, 189, 196
First Five-Year Plan (1945–1953), xviii, 202
Forchheim, Peace of, xiv, 28

Four Articles of Prague, 69
Francis II, 103–4
Francis Joseph I, xvi, 115, 118, 137
Frank, Karl Hermann, 171, 173,
    178, 188, 190, 196
Frederick I (Babenberg), 46
Frederick I Barbarossa, 44
Frederick II (Prussia), 94, 96
Frederick of the Palatinate
    ("Winter King"), 76
French-Czechoslovak alliance,
    155

Gabčík, Jozef, 179
Gabčíkovo-Nagymaros project,
    13–14, 262
Gajda, Gen. Radola, 157
Gál, Fedor, 238
Gejza, 34–35
geography: of Czech Republic,
    2–3; of Slovak Republic, 9–10
German Agrarian Party, 150
German Christian-Social Peo-
    ple's Party, 150
Germanic tribes, 20–21
German National Party, 150, 163
German National Socialist Party,
    150, 163
German Social Democrats, 148,
    150, 158
glasnost, xix, 227, 231, 36
Gojdič, Bishop Pavel Peter, 203–4
Golden Bull (Charles IV), 51, 89
Golden Bull (Hungary), 58
Golden Bull of Sicily, xiv, 45
Golian, Ján, 185–87
Gorazd, 29
Gorbachev, Mikhail, xx, 227–28,
    231–32, 235–36, 241
Gottwald, Klement, 149, 169, 175,
    178, 189, 197, 200, 202, 205,
    208, 267

government: of Czech Republic,
    6–9; of Slovak Republic, 14–17
"great guard," 37–38
Great Moravia, xiv, 23–35, 50,
    100, 270

Hácha, Emil, 170–73, 178, 196
Hájek, Jiří, 218, 225
Halifax, Lord, 165–66
Havel, Václav, xix, 210, 220,
    222–36, 233–35, 238–40,
    242–43, 246, 248–53, 255–56,
    258, 266–67
Helsinki Accords, 223
Henlein, Konrad, 158, 160,
    163–67, 169, 195–96
Heydrich, Reinhard, xviii,
    176, 178–80
Hilsener trial, 124
Hitler, Adolf, 150, 159–60,
    164–68, 170–71, 176, 178, 182
Hlas, 126
Hlasists, 127, 151
Hlinka, Andrej, xvii, 126–27, 141,
    145–46, 158–59, 267
Hlinka Guards, 170, 182, 184–85
Hlinka's Slovak People's Party
    (HSĽS), xviii, 151–52, 158–59,
    169, 181–85, 267, 271
Hodža, Milan, 116, 126–27, 143,
    155, 160, 164, 166–67, 267
Holder, Drahomír, 215
Holý, Prokop, 70–71
Horáková, Milada, 204, 267–68
HSĽS. See Hlinka's Slovak
    People's Party (HSĽS)
Hurban, Jozef, 115–16, 124
Hus, Jan, xv, 65–67, 72, 106, 109,
    130, 135, 268, 272
Husák, Gustáv, xviii, 185, 205,
    207, 212, 218–24, 226–36, 238,
    242, 266, 268

Hussites, 68–72, 75, 83, 86, 109, 130, 272
"hyphen war," 246

Indra, Alois, 215

Jakeš, Miloš, xix, 228, 233–34, 236, 238, 240–41
Jakoubek of Štribro, 67, 69
Janacek, Leos, 121
Jan Jindřich, 54–55
Jan Milíč of Kroměříž, 64
Janošík, Juro, 89–90
Jaromír, 41–42
Jehlička, Dr. František, 145–46
Jelačić, Baron Josip, 114, 116
Jeroným of Prague, 66
Jewish population, 4, 11, 38, 57, 70, 76, 97–98, 146, 173, 176–77
Jiři z Poděbrady, xv, 72–73, 122, 268
John of Luxemburg, 49–50
John of Nepomuk, (St. Jan Nepomuký) 57, 106
Joseph I, 89–90, 94
Joseph II, xv, 96–100, 105–6
Jungmann, Josef, 108–10, 268
"Just a Few Sentences," 235–37

Kafka, Franz, 210, 268
Karl I, 137, 142
Khrushchev, Nikita, 206
Klaus, Václav, xix, 238, 243, 246–47, 250, 254–58, 269–70
Klíma, Ivan, 210, 222
Klofáč, Václav, 132, 142
Kňažko, Milan, 238, 245, 259
Kohout, Pavel, 210, 220, 222
Kollár, Ján, 101–2, 108, 124, 269
Komensky, Jan Ámos (Comenius), 79, 109, 130

Košice Agreement, 195–96
Kossuth, Lajos, 111–12, 114, 116–17
Kosygin, Alexei, 213–14, 217
Kovač, Michal, xix, 258–61
Kralice Bible, 76, 86, 100
Kramář, Karel, 124, 132, 135, 142, 144
Krofta, Kamil, 160, 169
KSČ. *See* Communist Party of Czechoslovakia (KSČ)
KSCM. *See* Communist Party of Bohemia-Moravia (KSCM)
KSS. *See* Communist Party of Slovakia (KSS)
Kubiš, Jan, 179
Kundera, Milan, 210, 220
Kunigunde of Bohemia, 55
Kusý, Miroslav, 225, 235, 245

Ladislas I, 56
Ladislas V, 83
Landovský, Pavel, 229
language laws (Slovakia), 11–12, 260–63
League of Nations, 154–55, 159–60
Lechfeld, xiv, 33, 38
Lenárt, Jozef, 213
Leopold I, 82–83, 88
Leopold II, 98, 103, 105
"Lessons," 221–22, 227–28
Lettrich, Jozef, 185, 195, 200
Ležáky, xviii
Libuše, 30, 100
Lidice, xviii, 179
Lipany, xviii, 179
Little Entente, 155, 159
Lloyd George, David, 140
Locarno Agreements, 155
Louis II, xv, 84–85
Louis the German, 24–26, 27–28

Ludmila, 36–37
Ludvík I, 74
Lustration Law, 248
Luther, Martin, 75–86
Lutherans, 75, 77, 86–87, 90, 97

Mach, Alexander "Sano," 181–83
"Magyarization," xvi, 100, 118, 125–26, 150
Magyars, arrival of the, xiv, 32–34
Maiestas Carolina, 52, 57
Malypetr, Jan, 157
March Laws, 112, 115, 118
Marcomanni, xiii, 21
Marcus Aurelius. xiii, 21
Maria Theresa, xv, 90–91, 94–96, 99, 105
Marobuduus, 21
Masaryk, Jan, 174–75, 180, 194, 197, 200–201, 269
Masaryk, Tomáš Garrigue, xvii, 123, 126, 129, 132–33, 135–39, 141–42, 144, 147–51, 153–54, 157–60, 205, 233, 243, 265, 269
Matica česká, 109, 124
Matice Slovenská, xvi, 124–26, 260, 268
Maximilian II, 76, 85
"May Crisis" (1938), 165
Mečiar, Vladimir, xix, 245, 250–52, 258–63, 269–70
"Memorandum of the Slovak Nation," xvi, 124
Methodius, xiv, 26–30, 87
Metternich, Klemens von, 104, 110, 112
Mlynář, Zdeněk, 211, 220
Mohács, xv, 85
Mohorita, Vasil, 241–42, 245
Mojmír I, xiv, 25, 270

Mojmír II, 32–33
Mongols, 58–59
Moravčík, Jozef, 260
Moscow Protocol (1968), 217
Movement for a Democratic Slovakia, 250–51, 258–62
Munich Agreement, xvii, 161, 168, 170–71, 175, 180–81, 196–97, 264
Munich Conference, 168, 170
Mussolini, Benito, 168

NATO. *See* North Atlantic Treaty Organization (NATO)
National Fascist League, 158
National Front, xviii, 189–90, 196–97, 201, 213, 217, 244
National Socialist Party (Germany), 150
National Theatre, 122–23
Němcová, Božena, 109, 270
Neurath, Konstantin von, 160, 171, 178, 196
"normalization," xix, 218, 223, 226, 240, 267
North Atlantic Treaty Organization (NATO), xx, 8, 15, 249, 257, 259, 261, 263
Nosek, Václav, 198
Novomesky, Laco, 189, 205
Novotný, Antonín, xviii, 205, 207–12, 270

Obroda, 238, 241
ODS. *See* Civic Democratic Party (ODS)
Old Czechs, 121, 123–24
Oldřich, 41–42
"Operation Anthropoid," 179
"Operation Danube," 216
"Operation Green," 164–65
Opletal, Jan, 173, 217

Országh Hviezdoslav, Pavol,
126, 134, 268
Otto I, xiv, 37–39
Ottoman Turks, xv, 77,
83–84, 89

Palach, Jan,, 219, 234, 270
Palacký, František, 109–11, 113,
118–19, 122–23, 130
Paris Peace Conference, xvii,
144, 153
Party of the Democratic Left, 246
Patent of Tolerance, xv, 97
Patočka, Jan, 225
Pauliny-Toth, Viliam, 125
Peace of Westphalia, 81–82
perestroika, xix, 227–28, 236
"Pětka," 149
Piká, Gen. Heliodor, 203
Pittsburgh Agreement, xvii,
141, 158
Plamínková, Františka, 147
Plastic People of the Universe,
xix, 224, 244
political purges, xviii. 202–3, 270
population and demographics:
of Czech Republic, 3–4; of
Slovak Republic, 10–12
Pragmatic Sanction, xv, 90, 94
Prague Spring, xviii–xix, 212–19,
221–22, 232, 235, 239, 241–42,
266, 268, 270
Prague Uprising, xviii, 190–91
Přemysl, 30
Přemysl Otakar I, 45, 265
Přemysl Otakar II, xiv,
46–47, 270
Pribina, 28
privatization, 247–48, 253–54
Privilegium pro Slavis, xv, 60
Public Against Violence, xix, 238,
240–41, 243–46, 250, 270

Quadi, 21

racial policies and the Final
Solution, 176–77, 183–84
Rákócz, Ferenc, 89
Rákóczi, Gyorgy, 88
Rašín, Alois, 135, 142, 148, 156
Rastislav, 25–28
Re-Catholicization Patent, 79
Rejčka, Eliška, 56
Republican Party, 254–55
Ribbentrop, Joachim von, 168,
170, 182
Rieger, František Ladislav, 113,
115, 118–19
RMZ manuscripts, 107, 123–24
robota, 82, 97–98, 112
Rodobrana, 152
Rokycana, Jan, 69, 71–72
Roma, 4, 11, 177, 244–45,
255–56, 260
Roosevelt, Franklin Delano,
172, 180
Rudolf I, 48
Rudolf II, xv, 76–77, 87
Rudolf of Habsburg, 47
Runciman, Sir Walter, 166

Šafárik, Pavel Jozef, 101–2, 113
Samo, xiii, 23, 270
Scheiner, Josef, 135
Schwarzenberg, Prince Felix zu,
115, 117
Serfdom Patent of 1781, 98
Seven Years' War, 96–97
Sidor, Karol, 158, 170–72, 181–82
Sigismund of Luxemburg, 55, 57,
61, 67–69, 71, 83, 272
Šik, Ota, 208, 218
Šimečka, Milan, 225, 245
Široký, Viliam, 189, 205
Škoda, 121, 180, 247

Škvorecký, Josef, 223
Sládek, Miroslav, 255
Slánský, Rudolf, xviii. 169, 202, 204, 212, 270
Slav Congress, xvi, 113–14, 116
Slavs, arrival of the, 21–22
Slovak Agrarian Party, 148, 267
Slovak Christian Movement, 245, 250
Slovak Democratic and Christian Union, 262
Slovak Democratic Party, 196–98, 200, 204
Slovak League of America, xvii, 134
Slovak National Council, 143, 145
Slovak National Council (World War II), 185, 189, 196
Slovak National Party, xvi, 125, 141, 143, 251, 262–63, 267
Slovak National Uprising, xviii, 186–88, 198, 268
Slovak Peoples' Party, xvii, 127, 145, 151, 267
Slovak Republic: economy of, 12–13; geography of, 9–10; government of, 14–17; population and demographics of, 10–12
Slovak Soviet Republic, 145
Smeral, Bohumíl, xvii, 149, 169
Smer-SD. *See* Direction–Social Democracy (Smer-SD)
Smetana, Bedřich, 122–23
Smidke, Karol, 185, 201
Smrkovský, Jozef, 212–13, 216, 218, 220
Soběslav I, 43–44
"socialism with a human face," xviii, 216, 266
Sokol, xvi, 122, 135, 213, 220

Solidarity, 226, 234–35
Soviet-Czechoslovak Treaty, 160
Spytihněv I, 31
Šrámek, Msgr. Jan, 149, 175, 196
Šrobár, Vavro, 126, 141–44, 150–51, 189
Stadion Rudolf, 115, 117
Stalin, Joseph, 149, 175, 181, 188, 202, 204, 206–8
State Security (StB), 198, 238, 242, 245, 249
Štefánik, Milan Rastislav, 135–36, 138, 140–42, 150, 271
Štěpan, Miroslav, 233, 238, 240–41
Stephen I, xiv, 35, 40, 42, 58
Štrougal, Lubomír, 220, 233
Štúr, Ľudovit, xvi, 102, 111, 116, 124, 271
štúrovčina, 102–3
Sudeten German Party, 158, 160, 163, 165–67, 169
Svätopluk I, 27–30
Svätopluk II, 32
Svoboda, Gen. Ludvík, 174, 184, 189, 197, 200, 212, 217, 219–20, 222
Syrový, Gen. Jan, 167, 169

Taafe, Count Eduard, 119, 121
Táborites, 69
Temelín, 6, 257
"Ten Points Manifesto," 220
Terezín, 176–77, 195, 267
Těšín, 144, 159, 169
Thirty Years' War, xv, 80–82, 271
Thököly, Imre, 88
Tilly, Count Johann von, 78, 81
Tiso, Msgr. Jozef, xviii, 158–59, 169–70, 172, 177, 181, 183–86, 188, 198, 271
Tiso, Štefan, 187

Tomášek, František Cardinal, 240, 243
Tošovský, Josef, 232, 255
Treaty of Friendship, Nutual Assistance and Postwar Cooperation, 181, 202
Tuka, Vojtech, 152, 172, 181, 183, 187
Tusar, Vlastimil, 147, 149
"Two Thousand Words" 214
Tyl, Josef Kajetán, 109

Udržal, František, 123, 153, 157
Union of Brethren, 75, 83–84
ÚNRV. *See* Central National Revolutionary Committee (ÚNRV)
Urbanek, Karel, 240–41
Ursíny, Ján, 185, 189, 204
Utraquist, xv, 67, 70–72, 268
ÚVOD. *See* Central Committee of Home Resistance (ÚVOD)

Václav I (King of Bohemia), 45–46
Václav I (St. Wenceslas, Duke of Bohemia), xiv, 36–37, 143, 271
Václav II, 47
Václav III, xiv, 48, 59
Václav IV, 54–57, 65–68, 106
Vaculík, Ludvík, 210, 214, 220, 222–24
"Velvet Divorce," xix, 6, 252–53, 259, 267, 269
Velvet Revolution, xix, 237–43, 252–53, 266–67, 269
Versailles, Treaty of, 153–55, 159–60
Versailles System, 156
Viest, Gen. Rudolf, 175, 184, 187

"Visegrád Four," 259
"Visegrád Troika," 248, 259
Vladislas II, 84
Vladislav I, 43
Vladislav II, 44, 73–75
Vladivoj, 41
VONS, 225–26, 233, 238
Vrastislav I, 36
Vrastislav II, xiv, 42

Waldensians, 63
Waldhauser, Konrad, 64
Wałęsa, Lech, 226, 234, 248
Wallenstein, Albrecht von, 80–81, 271
Warsaw Pact, xix, 202, 215–16, 221, 232, 239–40
Warsaw Pact invasion (1968), 216–18, 241, 244, 248–49, 266
Washington Declaration (1918), 142, 147
"What We Want," 240
White Mountain, Battle of, xv, 78, 88, 97, 101, 105, 107, 110
Wiching, 29
Windischgrätz, Alfred von, 114–15
"wild transfer," xviii, 193–95
Wilson, Woodrow, 137, 140–41
Wyclif, John, 64–66, 268

Young Czechs, 119, 121, 123–24, 269

Zagreb treason trial, 131
Zapotocký, Antonín, 201, 205–7
Zborov, 138
Želivský, Jan, 68, 70
Zeman, Miloš, 254–57
Žižka z Trocnova, Jan, 69–70, 72, 122, 130, 272

About the Author

William M. Mahoney is an associate professor of history and coordinator of the Department of History and International Studies at West Virginia Wesleyan College in Buckhannon, WV. Dr. Mahoney teaches modern European history and serves as director of the international studies major.

Other Titles in the Greenwood Histories of the Modern Nations
Frank W. Thackeray and John E. Findling, Series Editors

The History of Afghanistan
Meredith L. Runion

The History of Argentina
Daniel K. Lewis

The History of Australia
Frank G. Clarke

The History of the Baltic States
Kevin O'Connor

The History of Brazil
Robert M. Levine

The History of Bulgaria
Frederick B. Chary

The History of Cambodia
Justin Corfield

The History of Canada
Scott W. See

The History of Central America
Thomas Pearcy

The History of the Central
Asian Republics
Peter L. Roudik

The History of Chile
John L. Rector

The History of China,
Second Edition
David Curtis Wright

The History of Congo
Didier Gondola

The History of Cuba
Clifford L. Staten

The History of the Czech
Republic and Slovakia
William M. Mahoney

The History of Egypt
Glenn E. Perry

The History of El Salvador
Christopher M. White

The History of Ethiopia
Saheed Adejumobi

The History of Finland
Jason Lavery

The History of France
W. Scott Haine

The History of Germany
Eleanor L. Turk

The History of Ghana
Roger S. Gocking

The History of Great Britain
Anne Baltz Rodrick

The History of Greece
Elaine Thomopoulos

The History of Haiti
Steeve Coupeau

The History of Holland
Mark T. Hooker

The History of India
John McLeod

The History of Indonesia
Steven Drakeley

The History of Iran
Elton L. Daniel

The History of Iraq
Courtney Hunt

The History of Ireland
Daniel Webster Hollis III

The History of Israel
Arnold Blumberg

The History of Italy
Charles L. Killinger

The History of Japan,
Second Edition
Louis G. Perez

The History of Korea
Djun Kil Kim

The History of Kuwait
Michael S. Casey

The History of Mexico,
Second Edition
Burton Kirkwood

The History of New Zealand
Tom Brooking

The History of Nicaragua
Clifford L. Staten

The History of Nigeria
Toyin Falola

The History of Pakistan
Iftikhar H. Malik

The History of Panama
Robert C. Harding

The History of Peru
Daniel Masterson

The History of the Philippines
Kathleen M. Nadeau

The History of Poland
M. B. Biskupski

The History of Portugal
James M. Anderson

The History of Puerto Rico
Lisa Pierce Flores

The History of Russia,
Second Edition
Charles E. Ziegler

The History of Saudi Arabia
Wayne H. Bowen

The History of Serbia
John K. Cox

The History of Singapore
Jean E. Abshire

The History of South Africa
Roger B. Beck

The History of Spain
Peter Pierson

The History of Sri Lanka
Patrick Peebles

The History of Sweden
Byron J. Nordstrom

The History of Thailand
Patit Paban Mishra

The History of Turkey
Douglas A. Howard

The History of Ukraine
Paul Kubicek

The History of Venezuela
H. Micheal Tarver and Julia C. Frederick

The History of Vietnam
Justin Corfield